IMPROVING
TOTAL PRODUCTIVITY

BOOKS BY PAUL MALI

Managing by Objectives
How to Manage by Objectives
Improving Total Productivity

IMPROVING
TOTAL PRODUCTIVITY

MBO STRATEGIES FOR
BUSINESS, GOVERNMENT,
AND NOT-FOR-PROFIT ORGANIZATIONS

PAUL MALI, Ph.D., CMC.

**Graduate School of Business
University of Hartford
and Paul Mali & Associates**

A WILEY-INTERSCIENCE PUBLICATION
JOHN WILEY & SONS, New York • Chichester • Brisbane • Toronto

This publication is designed to provide accurate and authoritative information in regard
to the subject matter covered. It is sold with the understanding that the publisher is not
engaged in rendering legal, accounting, or other professional service. If legal advice or
other expert assistance is required, the services of a competent professional person
should be sought.

*From a Declaration of Principles jointly adopted by a Committee of the American Bar Association
and a Committee of Publishers.*

Library of Congress Cataloging in Publication Data:
Mali, Paul.
  Improving total productivity.

  "A Wiley-Interscience publication."
  Includes bibliographical references and index.
    1. Industrial productivity.   2. Management by
objectives.   I. Title.

HD56.M33   1978   658.31'42   77-26191
ISBN 0-471-03404-5

Printed in the United States of America

10 9 8 7 6 5 4 3 2 1

DEDICATED TO THE FOLLOWING IDEA . . .

An investment in money for improving the effectiveness of management toward productivity may have a higher rate of return than any other use of an organization's funds.

PREFACE

WHAT MAKES THE ELEPHANT MOVE?

A well-known yarn in management circles is the story of three blind men who were asked to find out "what's an elephant like?" Because each blind man was feeling and analyzing a different part of the huge and complex body, a heated argument developed among them. One had his hands on the tail and claimed the elephant was like a rope. Another had his hands on the body and argued that the animal was a large, soft, and flabby mass. The third had his hands on the legs, leading him to claim it was like the trunk of a tree. Each man was sampling one aspect of the totality, and each failed to grasp the totality in spite of his correct description of his individual sample. The lesson of the story is in the role of the storyteller who, seeing the whole elephant as well as the sampling of each blind man, can see how ridiculous their separate inferences are concerning the complex totality. The storyteller sees the complex geometry and configuration of the whole elephant and is better able to tell what it is like.

This story was told in the 1960s to portray the many efforts to define management. The complex management process was viewed and approached by many specialized "blind" individuals. All put forward their own narrow perspective on its nature. Sales said, "booked orders"; operations said, "getting the work out on time"; personnel said, "handling people"; accounting said, "bottom line." Each department sampled one aspect of the whole, and although each was accurate from a specific viewpoint, each failed to grasp the complex totality of management. Here the role of the storyteller is to see the whole management process as well as the sampling of each specialist. This overview on management enables the storyteller to assess correctly the nature of its complex processes and decision-making options. The storyteller also sees the foolishness of the incomplete solutions that are based on their limited perspectives.

A new twist in the yarn portrays the concern of management of the 1970s and the 1980s. The blind men were asked to find out what makes an elephant move. Because each blind man had hold of only one part of the huge complex body, a heated argument developed among them. The one who had his hands on the tail pulled it. The big elephant moved from side to side. Another who had his hands on the body pinched it and the big large soft wall moved away. The third who had his hands on a leg stepped on it, causing the big leg to move up and away. Each caused the part they had hold of to move, and thought that they had found the way to make the entire elephant move.

Again, the lesson is in the role of the storyteller who sees the entire drama. The storyteller notices that each individual blind man caused a part of the elephant to move, but failed to move the whole elephant. This story portrays the complex processes of an organization as the "elephant". Getting the elephant to move is analogous to achieving productivity in organizations. Programs, individuals, departments, and functions argue that exercising their initiative and process is the way to achieve productivity for the entire organization, but fail to see that real progress toward productivity is the total management approach in organizations.

PRODUCTIVITY: A UNIFYING EXPECTATION!

Productivity has become one of the most overriding concerns in organizations. Economists, politicians, community leaders, government servants, supervisors, and elected officials look to it as the key force to bring jobs, vitality, and growth to our economy. Executives, managers, and businessmen see it as the means for improving profits, competition, and costs. Laborers, workers, and employees see it as the means for enlarging their compensation benefits. Government officers, public administrators, and civil servants hope that it will balance budgets, release more resources, and improve services. Educational administrators, teachers, and researchers look to productivity as a means to reach more students, improve the learning process, and expand budgets.

There is no question about it: productivity improvement appears to be the key to meeting the expectations of many individuals and groups. Productivity is an area where labor, management, and government have strong mutuality of interests. Productivity lags are of great concern to almost all groups in most organizations. To some, productivity creates a veritable crisis. To others, it's a sticky problem that won't go away. But to most, productivity is a challenge that must be met now. The challenge can best be described with questions. Can we get organizations to take "quantum jumps" in productivity improvement? Can we use productivity as a measure of health in an organization? Can we get workers and supervisors with new attitudes and new needs to continue with the traditional work processes in an efficient manner to satisfy their desires for a higher standard of living? Can we get additional productivity from our existing commitments without major changes in plant facilities, processes, equipment, and personnel? If so, how can we do it? Can we use productivity to control inflation? Can we improve our way of managing complexities with innovations in the processes of planning and doing work to experience productivity gains? Can we motivate workers toward productivity?

PURPOSE AND SCOPE

This book intends to answer these questions. It's primary purpose is to provide a clear understanding of the concept of managerial productivity, what it is and how it's measured, and to describe the barriers and trends that prevent its improvement. Productivity in organizations encompasses a wide range of complicated and often controversial issues. This book seeks to expand the awareness and understanding of productivity in a way that will give it prominence in the wide spectrum of concerns in management. A second objective is to describe new skills and proven strategies that can be used for productivity improvement. The book discusses many managerial processes that can be implemented in a number of practical ways in an organization. The book will serve as a practical operating guide for those who wish to introduce productivity improvement into their organizations even though they have never done it before or lack the experience. It will be a text and resource in business schools, management programs, training sessions and development seminars, and workshops on how to develop skills for managing productivity. The book will alert organizational practitioners who are not experiencing productivity difficulties, frustrations, and losses to their causes and the methods to prevent them.

This book is organized into four parts and an epilogue. Part I describes the need to improve productivity. Examples are given of productivity frustrations in various types of organizations. Twelve causes of productivity decline are identified, and the types of trends they generate within an organization are described. Some suggestions are made for their control and reduction. Part II presents managing productivity as a total process. A conceptual framework is developed to help the reader view productivity within the total organization. The principles and measurements that form the basis of its improvement are discussed. Managing productivity by objectives is developed as a viable way to create a system for productivity improvement. Part III describes the management processes for improving the productivity of the changed employee. The existence of white-collar workers, overpaid workers, and affluent employees is introduced as a major issue in organizations, and their effects on productivity are explored. Part IV provides the tools and techniques for achieving greater productivity. Specific managerial techniques and skills for bringing about improved productivity are described and illustrated. The last part, the epilogue, is a presentation of tasks and goals for the immediate future. Specific recommendations are made for the manager who wishes to begin a formal program of productivity improvement in an organization.

There are several areas in this text that are innovative:

1. A matrix showing 12 causes of productivity decline in organizations.
2. A new emphasis and stress on the fact that responsibility for productivity improvement does not rest solely on management, but on all who expect to reap benefits from its success.
3. A discussion of setting productivity objectives for every job in the organization and a demonstration of the way this is done.
4. A strategy for measuring, evaluating, and accounting for productivity in programs, functions, or the organization as a whole.
5. A definitive discussion of managing productivity by objectives (MPBO) and a process for its practice.
6. A discussion of managing productivity that is not confined to the perspective of manufacturing and industry, but includes business, government, education, and health-care facilities.
7. A way of developing motivators using the theory of needs coincident and expectancy alignment.
8. A description of how to set up and conduct a productivity audit in sufficient detail to be of practical use to a practitioner wishing to initiate such a system.
9. Presentations of 18 different processes and 42 actions a practitioner may take for productivity improvement in an organization.
10. How to make a productivity-effectiveness analysis to meet the ever changing needs of the world of "users."

This book, therefore, should be of great help to any managerial practitioner at any organizational level who is responsible for carrying out work in a productive way—executives, managers, supervisors, public administrators, government officials, educators, educational administrators, professionals, health-care administrators, and managers of small businesses.

A WORD ABOUT MANAGEMENT PROCESS OR TECHNIQUES

The era of the casual performer who alone must execute trial-and-error methods until the work is completed has been disappearing for a decade or more. This has resulted in the waste of resources, heavy expenditure of time, and low levels of performance. What is needed is to develop efficient processes to accomplish necessary productivity gains. More attention must be given to the implementation problem or the utilization lag between "knowing" and "doing." Accordingly, the reader will see that many processes or techniques presented in this text are described in a concrete and practical fashion, with suggestions for implementation. I do not intend to present these processes or techniques with rigid guidelines for structured behavior and to stifle individual thinking and innovation. My intention is, rather, to move away from the casual approach to work planning, measuring, and doing that can be reviewed, evaluated, and improved. Productivity improvement is successful when its processes are recorded, examined, scrutinized, appraised, and adopted as a procedure until a better one is developed. The adage "practice makes perfect" is wrong. But practice with feedback, review, analysis, and change does make perfect.

The processes described in this text are intended to encourage the productivity practitioner to think about his or her own process, and to develop what ultimately is the best process for the job at hand. I expect that a process suggested in this text would have to be modified for it to be used effectively in the unique setting of an organization. The tendency of many authors to concentrate heavily on developing new knowledge, without giving suggestions for implementing it has resulted in the utilization lag. Where this book brings out new concepts and new information, a specific process is also described. Because of this reason, many processes are included throughout this book.

SOURCES

The material for this book has been drawn from several sources. It is based on my first two books published by Wiley-Interscience, *Managing by Objectives* and *How to Manage by Objectives*. It includes ideas, solutions, techniques, and approaches interchanged among hundreds of organizations and their practitioners who attended productivity seminars that I have conducted throughout the United States and Canada over a period of years. It is taken from my experience and work assignments as a certified management consultant, dealing directly with problems of productivity, for government and a variety of industries including International Business Machines, Kimberly-Clark Corporation, Emhart Corporation, Combustion Engineering Corporation, Celanese Corporation, General Dynamics Corporation, Sylvania Electric Company, Sun Oil Company,

United Aircraft Corporation, A. C. Nielson Company, Aetna Life & Casualty Company, Connecticut Bank & Trust Company, Scharr Industries, Hartford National Bank Company, Northeast Utilities, University of Maine, University of Connecticut, New Jersey State Department of Education, Methodist Evangelical Hospital, Child Welfare League of America, Saint Joseph's Manor, Waterford Country School, R. R. Donnelly & Sons, Connecticut Corrections Department, Connecticut Research Commission, Norfolk Naval Shipyard, United States Naval Weapons System, United States Naval Underwater Sound Lab, State of Connecticut, Town of Newington, Town of Windsor, Stone & Webster Engineering Company, Peat, Marwick & Mitchell Company.

ACKNOWLEDGMENTS

Management consulting work has a special advantage not found in other types of management work. Instead of remaining with one company and its set of problems, a consultant goes to many companies and confronts a wide diversity of problems. Because of this, I am grateful to the many clients in the United States and Canada whose openness and confidence gave me the intellectual stimulus and substance for this work.

My special thanks are extended to the following colaborers: Michael Fontana for sketches and diagrams, Phyllis Dimpsey for rough manuscript typing, and Dawn Mali Shallieu and Nancy S. Russell as my production managers for the final typewritten words and expediting the manuscript to the publisher.

PAUL MALI

New London, Connecticut

CONTENTS

IMPROVING
TOTAL PRODUCTIVITY

PART ONE

THE NEED TO IMPROVE PRODUCTIVITY

Persistent inflation compounded by an onerous recession within a context of scarcity of materials has threatened the ability of organizations to continue to function and fulfill their obligations. Productivity frustrations abound in both private and public organizations, causing serious economic problems. Part I describes these frustrations and the trends that still continue to generate complicated and challenging issues. The frustrations and trends sharpen the need that something be done!

1

THE PRODUCTIVITY CRISIS
IN ORGANIZATIONS

IN THIS CHAPTER

Productivity development for managers: the ultimate investment.
Crisis as a point of major change.
Four different views of productivity.
Productivity: combination of effectiveness and efficiency.
Managing by objectives—not a fad.
The productivity index.
Types of productivity frustrations in organizations.
Three critical issues in managing productivity.
Thirteen benefits to productivity improvement.

Managing productivity in organizations is in crisis. Everywhere there is talk of the crisis. Managers face difficult choices, and how they choose will determine how well organizations will continue. Ominous signs of crisis emerged in the latter part of the 1960s, but little heed was paid them. Now we are in a predicament that will have profound consequences for employees, management, labor, government, and society. In the 1970s signs continue to emerge. In fact, the rate of productivity growth in the United States has been steadily declining.[1] Between 1960 and 1974 the average annual productivity in the United States was 3.1 percent. In foreign countries it was double this figure and in some cases even higher. Local governments in the United States haven't kept pace with the private sector; they have been averaging 1.5 percent per year. The ability to deliver services and products is severely affected by both recession and persistent inflation. Higher levels of productivity are needed to reverse the trend.

The term *crisis* is intended to mean large troubles that are not necessarily fatal to organizations. However, the troubles are of the kind that could lead to bankruptcy, default, or failure. Most managers consider any sudden trouble a crisis. It is not. The trouble a manager faces at any one time is merely a materialization of symptoms. The crisis itself has been

3

long in the making, usually the result of months or years of delay in facing up to solving problems. Managers put off trouble solving for one of two reasons: Either the cure is painfully slow, or the manager lacks the courage to do what has to be done. The crisis situation seldom arises from a single cause; it comes from many causes, some central and others contributory. But a crisis always requires major changes in the organization. It demands strategies, approaches, and solutions that management has never before applied.

Response to crisis has traditionally been to seek additional revenues through sales or taxes. But higher taxes drive taxpayers and corporations to seek higher wages and prices and other defeating constraints. Another response, cutting services, works hardships on the politically weak and economically disadvantaged. A third option of productivity improvement offers a way of holding down costs while improving and expanding services.

The purpose of this chapter is to (1) identify four different views of productivity that make a single encompassing definition of productivity difficult; (2) define productivity from an organizational standpoint (a comparison is made among goals, performance objectives, performance standards, and productivity objectives); (3) describe the productivity frustrations experienced by five types of organizations—industry, business, government, education, and human services; (4) reveal three factors that indicate what's different about managing productivity today; and (5) describe the benefits an organization may experience when a formal productivity improvement effort is instituted.

FOUR DIFFERENT VIEWS OF PRODUCTIVITY

The views of productivity for purposes of definition and understanding have not been consistent or uniform. In fact, the many views of productivity have contributed to confusion and obscurity about its nature. Fenske has identified 15 different definitions in the literature.[2] Years of seeking productivity growth should have yielded an accepted meaning. This is not the case, probably due to the different positions and emphasis in the economy of the definer, the reference point, and the degrees of skill in interpreting and looking at the productivity processes and measurements. For example, a *national reference point* views the country as a whole. It takes into account, in a simplistic way, the complex interplay of factors such as labor, capital, management, raw materials, and resources as forces influencing economic goods and services. This reference point describes all effects converging in a mix rather than isolating the factors as groups.

Another reference point examines *productivity in industries*. It isolates the factors that relate and affect specific industries such as aerospace, petroleum, steel, education, health care, and transportation. This emphasis concentrates on the factors that bear exclusively on the industry. Obviously, a comparison of firms in different industries be misleading and can lead to difficulty. Still another reference point is the *individual firm or organization*. The organization has a more visible cause-effect relationship of its many factors. Man-hours employed and work produced can be measured and compared to the past or compared with other firms to get a "feel" for how efficient the firm is. Profitability, return on investment, or budget compliance can give a measure of how all resources have been processed to deliver an output. Within an organization, productivity is not determined solely by how hard and how well people work. The importance of technology, equipment, and process factors is sometimes overwhelming, sometimes minor.

A final reference point is the *individual worker*. The productivity of an individual is affected by the work environment and the available tools, processes, and equipment. Here a new factor emerges that is not so visible or measurable—the motivation for productivity. This motivation is highly influenced by the group of which the individual is a member, the interplay with other groups, and the reasons why the individual works.

These varying views of productivity according to reference points is justified because of the purposes and uses intended. They prevent a single, inclusive definition that will encompass all references. At best, the previously described views are only partial views of a complex phenomenon that is difficult to define and measure. The productivity view followed in this book focuses on the organization, its internal processes and individual employees.

WHAT IS PRODUCTIVITY?

Productivity is not production! It is not pushing steel out the front door as fast as possible without regard for safety and quality. Nor is productivity performance! Nor is it results! Production, performance, results are components of a productivity effort, but they are not equivalent terms. Most people associate the concept of productivity with production and manufacturing because that is where it is most visible, tangible, and measurable. Economists have supported this traditional view by defining productivity as output per labor costs. This view must change to incorporate all segments of work life. Government, education, health institutions, service groups, professional groups must be interested in and concerned about productivity. In fact, productivity touches us all as consumers, taxpayers, citizens, and members of organizations. When people say they can no longer afford to repair their cars, meet their weekly food bills, clean up the polluted environment, or handle the rising tax rates, they are talking more than money. What they are talking about is the capacity to utilize our existing resources to meet the ever expanding demands of people. They are talking productivity.

The concept and definition of organizational productivity must be broad enough to include the concerns and interests of employees, because they are inevitably affected by it. Naturally, management has a special interest in it. Therefore:

> *Productivity is the measure of how well resources are brought together in organizations and utilized for accomplishing a set of results. Productivity is reaching the highest level of performance with the least expenditure of resources.*

There are two parts to this definition. The first part is a set of results or performance. Accomplishing a set of results or performing refers to the *effectiveness* in reaching a mission or a planned achievement or a needed value without serious regard for the costs incurred in the process. A Fleetwood Cadillac can be used to deliver a small package three blocks away and can therefore be effective in that mission, but one will argue that its use is a gross misallocation of resources. Effectiveness standards refer to achieving results at all costs or where cost is not a critical problem. The whole productivity question starts with what must be accomplished. *Profits, patient care, budget performance, number of decisions, sales volume, highways completed, student enrollments, production quotas*, and *program completions* are examples of accomplishments. Accomplishing a set of results is by far the most important focus of the productivity concept, because without a set of results there is no productivity. The focus on a set of results for productivity follows closely concepts of managing by objectives (MBO).[3] This strategy is used for managing productivity and is later described in this book as managing productivity by objectives (MPBO). Despite criticism and attacks, MBO has survived and is now being practiced by many organizations. The fact that it is still a popular approach after 40 years proves that it is not a fad; it is here to stay. But it has changed over the years. Managing productivity by objectives is a natural sequel to the basic process of managing by objectives.

The second part of the productivity definition implies consuming resources, without which achievements are not likely to happen and productivity cannot exist. This second part of the productivity concept specifies the number, type, and level of resources needed. Productivity requires resources such as *plant capacity, personnel, costs, raw materials, facilities, capital, technology, budgets, supplies,* and *information.* How well these resources are brought together refers to the efficiency of achieving results with minimal expenditure of these resources. High productivity suggests minimum use of resources. Efficiency implies the attainment of a level or range of results that is acceptable but not necessarily desirable. There is no virtue in delivering a package three blocks away on foot, eliminating the expensive Fleetwood Cadillac, incurring no cost, and using minimal resources if in the process the package arrives too late and the individual needing the package has left. The delivery of the package is efficient but not effective.

George Kuper, acting executive director of the National Commission on Productivity and Work Quality[4] thinks of productivity as a combination of effectiveness and efficiency. To determine productivity one must ask both whether a desired result was achieved (the effectiveness question) and what resources were consumed to achieve it (the efficiency question). There is value in combining these terms since productivity is a concept that relates outcomes with the means that produce these outcomes. Therefore:

Productivity is a combination of effectiveness and efficiency!

Effectiveness related to performance, efficiency to resource utilization. It is achieving the highest results possible while consuming the least amount of resources. How well resources are brought together and utilized is indicated by comparing the magnitude or volume of results, often called output (effectiveness), with the magnitude and volume of the resources, often called input (efficiency). This ratio becomes an index of the definition and measurement of productivity:

$$\frac{\text{productivity}}{\text{index}} = \frac{\text{output obtained}}{\text{input expended}} = \frac{\text{performance achieved}}{\text{resources consumed}} = \frac{\text{effectiveness}}{\text{efficiency}}$$

A basic prerequesite for productivity improvement in an organization is that both the output (performance achievement) and the imput (resources consumed) be measureable. If performance and resources cannot be made measured, its processes must be rearranged so that measurement can be taken. The basic arithmetic of productivity is simple—ratio of some measure of output to some measure in input. The measurement of these two dimensions is crucial in any productivity effort. Furthermore, the productivity index should not be regarded as an abstract ratio that can be justifiably applied in any comparison, which could be misleading.

The productivity index, as a ratio, measures how well resources are expended in the context of accomplishing a mission or a set of objectives.

Note the following differences between a goal, a performance objective, a performance standard, and a productivity objective:

GOAL. *Reduce rework.*
PERFORMANCE OBJECTIVE. *Reduce rework from $40,000 to $20,000 by January 1.*
PERFORMANCE STANDARD. *Performance is satisfactory when rework is not greater than $20,000 per year.*
PRODUCTIVITY OBJECTIVE. *Reduce rework from $40,000 to $20,000 with a new process that costs $2000 (PI = $20,000/ 2000 = 10) by January 1.*

These definitions will be used throughout this book.

PRODUCTIVITY FRUSTRATIONS IN ORGANIZATIONS

Hundreds of organizations from small businesses to giant corporations, from small town governments to large federal agencies, from small public school systems to large universities are experiencing productivity frustrations and losses. Layoffs, hiring freezes, strikes, possible default—the scare headlines out of New York City, San Francisco, Detroit, and Chicago announce unmistakably that the resource strain on organizations is heavy. The once confident management system has been infected with an illness that is yet to be diagnosed accurately and for which no prescriptions have been issued. The management idea of progress, growth, and viability is being shadowed with doubt, restlessness, and disillusionment. Organizations are crisis oriented. Some people even wonder if the free enterprise system as we know it will continue to exist. They wonder if our traditional way of doing things is working at all!

In Industry: Unmanageable Complexities

1. *Miswest Glass Manufacturing Plant.* A glass manufacturing plant in the Midwest instituted a hard cost control program with full support from top management only to experience the largest cost overrun in

history. The direct one-shot cost-cutting slashes seriously reduced revenues which produced new levels of unseen indirect costs.

2. *Chicago Printing Firm.*   A Chicago printing firm could not seem to eliminate work backlog in spite of the fact they had extra capacity to handle it. They simply could not motivate employees to reduce the backlog. Employees kept the backlog up as a form of job security.

3. *Ohio Auto Manufacturing Plant.*   In an auto manufacturing plant in Ohio, a "wildcat" strike occurred because employees reacted against an increased speed of the assembly process. When the boredom that is common in a large assembly plant was intensified through accelerated work processes, a rebellion developed and the plant was shut down.

4. *Connecticut Hardware Manufacturing Company.*   A Connecticut hardware manufacturer wanted to make changes in plant and equipment. The union resisted. These changes, which were intended to improve productivity, were finally abandoned. It was later discovered by outside consultants that the union controlled the company.

5. *Detroit Tire Company.*   Because of lagging new car and truck sales, a Detroit tire company had a large inventory of tires. The company laid off 1400 workers to decrease manufacturing. Prices were increased to make up for the decline in sales.

6. *St. Louis Multidivisional Corporation.*   A multinational firm, headquartered in St. Louis, saw the productivity of one of its divisions stop completely because of the ban on coffee breaks, coffeepots, and hot plates. It seems employees were wasting time and disrupting production over coffee break activities. In an effort to increase the level of efficiency to help assure completion of the work, management posted on bulletin boards the ban on coffee breaks as a way to boost productivity. As soon as the notices went up, all productivity stopped.

In Business: Profit Frustrations

1. *National Restaurant Chain.*   A national restaurant chain, wanting to do "the right thing," adopted social compliance policies. Placing minorities in jobs for which they were not fully qualified did not meet customer expectancies. Customers were lost, and the chain experienced a 12 percent reduction in profits.

2. *Hartford Insurance Firm.*   An insurance firm in Hartford keeps adding clerical staff because the paperwork never gets done. Several attempts to bring about methods changes for efficient paper handling resulted in resistance and low morale. A work handling procedure was abandoned for fear of a work slowdown.

3. *California Wine Producer.* A California wine producer was slapped with an antitrust suit by its own farm workers' union. The suit accuses the company of monopolistic practices. Although this type of suit is common, it is not usually filed by the company's own employees.

4. *San Diego Electronic Firm.* An electronic firm near San Diego gave the psychologists' theories a try by giving the workers more of a voice in how they do their jobs. Among other things, management eliminated assembly lines and time cards. The experiment was a tremendous success until the market pressures became too great. If the president had not reinstituted traditional management techniques, the company would have gone broke. The company believes that the new behavioral theories must be leavened with some regard for the economic realities.

5. *Los Angeles Retail Store.* A retail store in Los Angeles runs spectacular annual sales each year to dump the "junk" the buyer should not have purchased. The annual sales are a losing effort because many customers do not buy the "junk merchandise." It never occurs to the buyer to come out of his office and ask sales clerks what customers want or would prefer. The store could save a good deal of money by developing a working process between the buying and the selling.

6. *Seattle Bank.* A bank in Seattle sets up a 6-month management trainee program to learn all there is to know about the job of a bank executive. The program is regarded as an important development process, at least in the eyes of the program designers. Actually, only 10 percent of the participants stick it out—the rest quit. They are being overtrained for a job that is nothing more than a progression of boring steps, which most of the participants learn early in their placement.

In Government: Budgetary Problems

1. *New York City.* The largest city in the United States is tottering on the brink of financial default. City officials claim that unless the federal government intervenes, they will sink and bring the United States with it. However, the record shows that New York City has the highest wages and salaries in the country, earliest retirement, one of the largest universities free of tuition, a steady stream of unbalanced budgets, massive growth in debts, generous increases in union contracts. The list is never ending. Although these are indicators of bad financial management, they are more. They are resource allocations without managing accountability and productivity.

2. *California Town Government.* During a bargaining period with the employee association for a 35-hour workweek, a town government in California struggled to approve a 10 percent tax increase to maintain levels of services. The 35-hour workweek was only a strategy by the association to get time-and-a-half for the 5 hours to make up the 40-hour workweek.

3. *Connecticut Town Government.* A small town in Connecticut had declared itself bankrupt because the voters refused to adopt the annual budget. The town was on the verge of requesting state takeover when the voters rescinded their decision. But what the voters wanted was clear: Stop the rising taxes even if it means reduced services.

4. *New England Governors.* A Boston conference of New England governors attempted to prevent the president of the United States from imposing tariff hikes on imported crude oil. Legal maneuvers through court action was studied. The issue was whether state governments can bring suit against the federal government for tariff hikes. One governor proposed open revolt against the United States by asking taxpayers to refuse to pay federal income taxes.

5. *Government.* Great Britain spends more than it earns. With industrial plants obsolete, the labor force unproductive, social unheavals continuing, a new question has been raised: Is Britain Dying?[5] Even under the best of circumstances, labor unions in Britain are inspired and organized not for increasing productivity, but for restricting it. A gloomy picture exists for France and Italy. All three countries are experiencing deficits and dropping of currency values. In Italy the currency value may drop to 850 or 1000 lira to the dollar. In France the franc will go to 5 to the dollar. The economies of these three countries are increasing, but inflation, unemployment, and cost problems are increasing at a greater rate than the economy is growing.

6. *Large New England City.* The mayor of a large city in New England has told union leaders that city workers must give up a 4 percent increase they had received earlier or face layoffs. Unless this action is taken, a disastrous budget deficit will be experienced immediately. The mayor insists that layoffs will start unless he receives cooperation for his austerity program to save the city from financial collapse.

7. *Regional Town District.* Small towns in a region that qualify as a consortium for federal funding decided not to apply for a federal grant because the paperwork involved was too great compared to the returns the towns would receive. Even the planning agency agreed that there is too much red tape for Title XX to make it worthwhile.

In Education: Near Bankruptcy from Shrinking Funds

1. *New York Private University.*   A private university in New York experienced a decline in enrollment after increasing tuition rates to meet the demands of the faculty. They faced either a faculty walkout, which meant school shutdown, or a loss of students by increasing tuition. They decided to increase tuition.

2. *Campuses Throughout the United States.*   On college campuses throughout the United States presidents find their assignments precarious. Scare resources, open battles between faculty and trustees, controversies over selection of educational leaders have forced many presidents to resign. On other campuses the battle of the budget continues. From Harvard to Stanford, Florida to Wisconsin, statewide systems of higher education are cutting back deeply. Plans have been laid to reduce faculty size; cut spending; increase charges to students; hold down admissions; and most of all, improve productivity.

3. *Private Colleges.*   A press release put out recently by the Association of American Colleges contains a sort of apocalyptic message:

> Some 365 of the nation's private colleges and universities may be ready to close their doors by 1981 unless immediate aid is forthcoming. Two hundred of these institutions will be exhausting their liquid assets within a year. The financial picture is gravely worse than officials had predicted and even grimmer for the future.

Whether or not colleges and universities deserve their present plight, genuine bankruptcy seems to be real at this time. In his famous speech "Rumal Revisited," James Koerner cites the declining rate of faculty productivity as one of the main reasons.[6] Faculty members with the most seniority teach the fewest students, which translates to lowest productivity. When the highest paid people in an industry have the lowest productivity, cost accountability becomes a farce. Using the criterion of number of students taught in relation to proportion of salary and other costs, productivity has been on a downward slide for the past quarter-century. Unless a new approach is initiated to improve faculty productivity, institutions of higher education may very well be in the "apocalyptic" state.

In Human Services: Inability to Handle Growing Health Needs

1. *Philadelphia Welfare Agency.*   A welfare organization in Philadelphia is committed to a policy of vigorous hiring of minorities in all depart-

ments. Because of a lack of coordination between departments and a "climate" of harassment and disruption, services to recipients are slowed.

2. *Hartford Health-Care Insurance Firm.* A health-care insurance carrier in Hartford cites the growing concern about health-care in America. The central facts of the problem indicate that the health-care system in this nation is in a state of crisis and the condition is worsening. Attempts at correcting and improving are piecemeal, unrealistic, and ineffective.

3. *Dallas Hospital.* Forty years ago a hospital in Dallas had three employees for every 10 patients with an added very low investment per patient. Today, this hospital has 30 employees for every 10 patients with an added very high investment per patient. The percentage of patients who leave the hospital alive has remained substantially the same over the 40 years. The tremendous investment in plant and personnel has not increased the vital output of a hospital.

Other productivity frustrations and difficulties are making headlines— layoffs, growing unemployment lines, increasing material shortages, slow mail delivery, inability of police to protect the citizenry, product recalls due to shoddy quality, inability of welfare services to help the helpless, inability of big organizations to find quality replacements of personnel, schools that can't teach, schedules on which customers cannot depend, and grievances that increase without abatement. No question about it— organizations have troubles like never before, and productivity growth rate is affected by these troubles. Productivity gains in one quarter are offset by losses in the next two quarters. Unless we have a turnabout, we may be faced with the demise of many organizations that have given the American public the highest standard of living in the world. In our affluent society productivity growth is not seen as necessary or important as long as there is affluency. This mistaken impression is noticeable in the low status and priority of productivity. Efforts to solve problems have been mainly monetary, but this approach had led to difficulties and frustrations. The fact that trying to solve all problems with additional money has not worked shows that a new approach—emphasis on a new productivity management—is needed.

WHAT'S DIFFERENT ABOUT PRODUCTIVITY MANAGEMENT TODAY?

Traditionally, productivity is made up of many things: plant, equipment, investment capital, research and development, materials, workers, costs, methods and procedures, goals, and management. These components have always been part of the productivity package. What's new and different lies in many areas but three must be emphasized. First, the workers are different. They have changed. Their needs, wants, attitudes, and personal goals have changed. The type of work they want to do has changed. How far they will allow themselves to be a part of routine, nonfulfilling, repetitive work has changed. The reasons they will work hard have changed. How much they will respond to the pressures and demands of the organization has changed.

What's new in the productivity package with this first factor is *human expectation* in the labor force. In most cases it's gross overexpectation, which has been the underlying reason for the great unrest in our society during the past few years. No matter how much progress is made, the clamor continues for what has not yet been attained. Japan, West Germany, England, and Italy are also experiencing a central change in why workers work and what they expect to get from working hard. Workers are placing a higher value on themselves than they formally did. They feel that what they want is important and not to be lightly denied. Additionally, a strong current is now developing for improvement in the quality of life at work. Strong interest is seen in changes in work climate, conditions, career opportunities, training and development, participation in decision-making, recognition, satisfaction, communications and trust, rewards, safety, collaborative styles in work processes, leisure time, and retirement benefits. The chief component of the quality of work life is the strong desire for workers to influence and have some say in connection with how their own work is planned, distributed, executed, and evaluated. In concept this desire is a desire for "self-supervision," a work situation where workers can feel responsible for significant, important, challenging, and identifiable results. The quality of work life can be summed up as "work with meaning." Redesigning of jobs is looming as a crucial future effort for management, and workers want to be active in the redesign process. As employees become more demanding for quality of work life, social justice, and higher standards of living, managers must pay closer attention to these demands and seek ways of aligning them with the organization's needs. Judson Gooding says that a management innovation of considerable importance is to think of employees in a totally different way.[7] Employees must be thought of as investments in human resources. The magnitude of this investment is great when you think of the costs of recruiting, hiring, training, compensating, coaching, appraising, and retiring. Key questions are posed for the productivity manager: How well are human resources used and maintained? How well are human expectations met? Can management keep up and even lead human expectations? How can we manage productivity with changed employees who have different motivations, values, and attitudes?

New and changing technology is another component that is radically affecting productivity. As technology advances, its impact on established methods, procedures, and processes are disruptive. Technical knowledge in this country has reached levels where no area is unaffected by it. Our technologies have always been far ahead of applications, but the gap between technological usage and technological innovations has widened to a point where we find it nearly impossible to understand and keep up. Consequently, our use of these new innovations is limited compared to what it could be.

When technologies have been applied to the drudgery of life, productivity has always risen. When we are not able to apply them, productivity declines and technological thrust is diminished. Perhaps the United States has reached a technological plateau.[8] Spectacular advances in computers, lasers, light diodes, machine tools, integrated circuits, read-write memories, automated processes, and plastics have come with soaring costs. Will organizations be able to afford these products for their own processes? In some cases *the high costs of these products have forced a curtailment of the very technology that produced the products*! This has meant reduced R & D expenditures. If these reductions continue, productivity in the long run will be affected radically. Other factors that have curtailed technological advances included risk of government regulation, loss suits, minority stockholder action, community boycotts, union intervention, consumerism, and material shortages.

Technology can provide completely new ways and methods of doing work and can save the resources used in doing it. Technology provides the potential for new gains and new breakthroughs. Technology can reach for the ultimate: completely automated factories and work processes with high productivity designed into the system. However, increasing the input of labor, capital, resources, and equipment will not necessarily give us productivity gains: new and better application of technologies toward increasing the effectiveness of these inputs and the efficiency of their transformation will. The productivity manager must be concerned with how well technological resources, equipment and facilities can be used to further productivity and if we can manage complexity to give greater performance while reducing the costs for generating this performance.

Accountability is a third factor that makes productivity different today. The finger of accountability has traditionally been pointed at management. An American Management report of 1960 stated with clear emphasis, "Productivity is a management problem."[9] Joseph Quick, retired chairman of Science Management Corporation, reported that a *New York Times* article stated that productivity rests with management, the burden of its improvement is management's responsibility and consequences of poor productivity is their own and no one else's.[10] It's no wonder that workers, employee unions, and other segments of organization life turn their backs to the productivity question.

Because American workers want quality in the work life and are demanding more from the economy than it can produce, they must accept, along with management, the responsibility for the consequences of their demands. They must join with management for improved productivity. They will share the gains. American workers want a higher standard of living, more leisure time, higher quality of work life, cleaner air, and better education. Merely raising wages, taxes, and prices won't get these, it will only produce inflation. What is needed is to distribute the responsibility for productivity to all parts of our work society. Educators, workers, public officials, union leaders, management, government employees, small businessmen, store clerks, and consumers must be concerned with productivity.

Productivity is no longer a sole responsibility of management. The demands of accountability must be brought to bear on all segments of work life that consume resources. A moral conscience must be developed so that as one draws from the economy, one must make an equal contribution. It's time that the burden of our economy be shifted from some segments to all segments. Productivity must be the area that unites management, labor, government, education, and society in a mutuality of interests. Workers themselves must stop wasteful ways of doing work. They must come to realize that the waste they see and experience will affect their paycheck. I. W. Abel, president of the United Steelworkers of American says that firms nowadays actually expect to scrap 20 percent of what they produce.[11] If we can get American workers to participate with management in productivity improvement as well as productivity gains, a real "dent" can be made in the scrap and waste that goes on daily in the organizational work life.

In short, what is different about managing productivity today can be seen in many areas. But three, *human expectations, changing technology,* and *limited accountability* are the critical ones. Several chapters in this book deal directly with these changes and how the practitioner of managing productivity can handle them. For example, human expectations are changing the traditional methods of motivating employees. A chapter is included to show how new methods of motivating can be applied to the new levels of human expectation. Changing technology is changing work processes and the interconnecting complexities. Several chapters are included on how to manage the complexities of technical work processes. Limited accountability is forcing new formats of planning and budget approvals. Several chapters describe managing productivity by objectives, how to get account-ability and zero-base planning and budgeting. A focus on these three areas does not mean that other factors do not apply to the productivity question. A survey of 2,450 chief executives and 950 industrial relations managers reveals general agreement that the most important factors in improving productivity in an organization depend on (1) better planning, (2) more effective management, (3) improved job procedures, (4) better communi-cations, and (5) more effective human effort and personnel policies. These factors are also dealt with in varying details in the coming chapters. Productivity management is changing, and those who can manage the changes effectively will be those who will reap huge benefits for them-selves as well as for their organizations.

BENEFITS FROM PRODUCTIVITY IMPROVEMENT

The importance of productivity is obvious. In the coming decade produc-tivity will be the primary area of concern in any manager's life. The manager who adopts a productivity strategy and invests the time and effort needed to make it work will experience greater and more favorable results both personally and for the organization.

1. *MPBO Provides "Scorekeeping" Data for Evaluating Organizations, Departments, or Programs.* In most organizations organizational per-formance and evaluation is now critically needed in addition to the traditional financial evaluation. The hit-or-miss approach to this needed form of evaluation is giving way to a more certain, more accurate, and more meaningful approach.

   Managing productivity by objectives (MPBO) provides time-se-quence data through measurement that will allow a scorekeeping process of how well targets and objectives are achieved and how progress is developing. Most organizations are now or will be faced with some form of effectiveness or performance auditing. MPBO provides measured data in a time framework for this needed evalua-tion. MPBO is an aid to tracking the level of productivity and raising it for the purpose of improving performance and savings resources.

2. *MPBO Solves Day-to-Day Operational Problems in a Planning Phase.* Operational problems frequently result from not anticipating a situation. These problems can often be handled effectively and efficiently in the planning context. MPBO forces a "look ahead" to a situation and a surveillance of the type of problems that may exist.

The MPBO process incorporates potential solutions long in advance of its implementation. Through this process, operational problems are held to a minimum. Most are solved in the planning phase.

3. *MPBO Sets up an Accountability Framework for Scarce Resources.* There is a scarcity of resources. Predictions indicate that it will become worse, especially in relation to the rapidly increasing demand for services and products. As a strategy, MPBO sets up a framework in which allocated resources can be traced more easily to the programs and departments that are consuming them. Accounting by department, by program, by function, or by individuals is then possible. In some organizations this is crucial because of the need to account for the legal use of funds to the public and stockholders.

4. *MPBO Gives Better Decision Making for Budget Programming and Control.* Budgets must be flexible. Shifting priorities and needs, curtailment of funds, emerging trends, and spiraling prices indicate the critical need to make judgments related to changing programs and demands. MPBO provides the evaluative measures of program progress and control for more rational handling of changes that are needed for shifting and reallocating resources to new concerns, new needs, or serious cutbacks in a budget. MPBO is flexible in the face of changing demands. MPBO provides an opportunity to take the steps needed to influence emerging trends and direct them into manageable channels.

5. *MPBO Provides a New "Resource" for Critically Needed Funding and New Jobs.* Productivity can be regarded as an untapped resource. Real productivity gains can control spiraling inflation and, in the process, release funds that can be used to finance new and needed social, environmental, and economic goals that have been set. This could create new jobs for the work force entering the labor market. MPBO sets up the process for measuring the level, amount, and expected delivery of productivity possible in a work situation. Productivity gains predicted from these measures can provide the basis for financing other projects and programs.

6. *MPBO Provides Zero-Based Information for Estimating and Formulating Budgets.* Estimates and projections of resource needs have not been too reliable. Traditional budget formulation relies mainly on past performance and expenditures as a base. This performance data is collected, and increments of increases or decreases are added from this base to form the new budget. This approach is merely an extrapolation of the past. MPBO starts out with a zero-based datum

and estimates both performance and resource needs in terms of the volume output or performance effectiveness that is needed and written as an objective. MPBO estimates performance needs as well as a combination of performance and resources. Productivity rates are used as a basis of estimating volume of output and cost of the resources. A more thorough discussion of zero-based budgeting is found in Chapter 8.

7. *MPBO Sets up Incentives for Both Unions and Management.* Unions see productivity as a source for greater pay and benefits for its members. Management sees it as a way of saving effort, money, and other expenditures. MPBO provides the gains that could be achieved in a productivity effort and how much of the gains could be shared with those who produced them. MPBO can create a system for establishing an employee-incentive program. Productivity measures can become imputs into agreed-to targets to be achieved by individuals or groups.

8. *MPBO Evaluates "Trivia" in the Job of Managing.* The job of a manager encompasses a host of activities. Most are trivial—that is, they must be done but do not contribute greatly toward results. As a result, a manager does many things but gets nowhere fast. MPBO helps to separate the activities that count most from those that count least. Expected productivity gains guide the manager to where effort should be applied. Productivity data provide a high degree of clarity as to where time and effort should be concentrated.

9. *MPBO Forces a Search for Unutilized Opportunities.* Probably the most attractive area for productivity improvement is innovation and change. Taking advantage of new opportunities might well be the breakthrough an organization needs. Organizations need to pursue opportunities in a more deliberate way than the "accident" approach.

   Through evaluative measurements MPBO provides an important focus in finding where the greatest gains can be developed. Productivity measures can be arranged into a matrix and assigned an opportunity weight—that is, an area that provides the greatest opportunity for gain. The MPBO practitioner merely scans the matrix and applies the strategy where it gives the greatest payoff.

10. *MPBO Gives an Accurate Assessment of Value of Capital Outlay.* Equipment and facilities are expensive because of spiraling prices and strong competition in markets of the world. The need to assure return value from these purchases is critical. In the face of rising costs top management and the public must be sure that capital

outlay will give the needed return. Heavy capital outlays should improve productivity.

MPBO facilitates evaluative measurements of the levels of productivity before and after installation of new equipment. These measures project the gains throughout the life cycle of the equipment, thus providing a more informed judgment of the value of the equipment. MPBO as a strategy requires the equipment purchased to fit in to a process for achieving productivity objectives. Confidence from funding and budgetary sources is raised since there is greater understanding of what is being done and how well it is being done.

11. *MPBO Provides Better Estimates of Legislative or Policy Changes.* Decision makers, whether they be legislators or organizational policymakers, need to estimate the impact a legislative enactment or a new policy would have on a group, organization, or community. The more accurate this estimate, the more useful the decision. MPBO can be applied, in a preliminary way, to provide meaningful estimates of the effects of a new policy or changes in or elimination of existing policies, now in operation. Thus legislative enactments or new policy changes can be simulated before actual decisions to see whether productivity levels rise or fall.

12. *MPBO Clarifies Relationships in Large Organizations.* Big complex organizations are here to stay. Those who manage these complex structures struggle to create a coordinated and unified system. However, failure in departments, sections, and functions often causes discoordination and imbalance in the whole organization. How resources are flowing and consumed among the subdivisions of an organization is clarified by MPBO. Subdivisions are required to define the productivity levels that will be achieved through an interrelation with other subdivisions. This reduces uncertainty and strengthens the coordinations among these subdivisions.

13. *MPBO Provides a Focus for Cost-Benefit Analysis.* In the past benefit-cost ratios have been used to compare project with project, department with department, or organization with organization. This can be misleading because they reveal nothing about absolutes. MPBO sets up a framework in which benefit-cost ratios are used as a measure toward reaching objectives. The values used in the ratios must be costs derived from a budget allocated toward a given set of objectives. Cost-benefit ratios of different missions or sets of objectives are difficult to compare; but cost-benefit ratios can be compared meaningfully when missions or objectives are aligned.

SUMMARY

This chapter defined productivity as the measure of how well resources are brought together and used for accomplishing a set of results. Four different views were considered in the definition. Productivity is a combination of effectiveness and efficiency and expressed as the productivity index:

$$PI = \frac{output}{input} = \frac{performance\ achievements}{resources\ consumed} = \frac{effectiveness}{efficiency}$$

This chapter provided a perspective from which to view the material that follows. Thus it is little more than an outlined presentation of the issues of managing productivity in organization. We described some of the frustrations now found in industry, business, government, education, and human serivces. Because of human expectations, changing technology, and limited accountability, managing productivity in organizations is different than in the past, and it will continue to be different in the immediate future.

Benefits accrued from productivity improvement using the MPBO strategy are described. The practitioner needs a clear view of these benefits since productivity is a "hard-work" process. The gains must justify the hard work.

MPBO:

1. Provides "scorekeeping" data for evaluation productivity.
2. Solves day-to-day operational problems in a planning phase.
3. Sets up an accountability framework for scarce resources.
4. Gives better decision making for budget programming and control.
5. Provides a new "resource" for critically needed funding and new jobs.
6. Provides zero-based information for estimating and formulating budgets.
7. Sets up incentives for both union and management.
8. Evaluates "trivia" in the job of managing.
9. Forces a search for unutilized opportunities.
10. Gives accurate assessment of value of capital outlay.
11. Provides better estimates of legislative or policy changes.
12. Clarifies relationships in large organizations.
13. Provides a focus for cost-benefit analysis.

QUESTIONS TO THINK ABOUT

1. Does the organizational situation termed *crisis* mean a situation that is beyond managerial recovery? What defines a recoverable situation? How would you regard your organization—in crisis, approaching crisis, not near crisis?

2. Make a list of the types of productivity frustrations that are found in your organization. Give a time line to these frustrations—that is, long-term or short-term frustrations.

3. Identify how managing productivity is different within your organization today from the past.

4. Identify how rising costs within your organization have forced a curtailment of the very products or services that created the organization.

5. Productivity is no longer a sole responsibility of management. What is your position on this statement for you organization? Why?

6. Give a qualitative and quantitative definition of productivity as it might be used in your organization.

7. Indicate a *goal*, a *performance objective,* a *performance standard,* and a *productivity objective* for your organization.

8. Identify the benefits that might accrue in your organization if a formal program of productivity were instituted.

REFERENCES AND NOTES

1. National Commission on Productivity and Work Quality, *Managing Human Resources in Local Government,* U.S. Government Printing Office, Washington, D.C., 1973, p. 1.

2. Russell W. Fenske, *An Analysis of the Meaning of Productivity,* reprint series by the Center for the Study of Productivity Motivation, University of Wisconsin, 1967.

3. Paul Mali, *Managing By Objectives,* Wiley-Interscience Company, New York, 1972, pp. 1–27. I follow closely the MBO approach described in my previous book. The reader is urged to become familiar with this strategy. Other excellent books are: George S. Odiorne, *Management By Objectives,* Pitman Publishing Company, New York, 1965; Dale D. McConkey, *How to Manage By Results,* American Management Association, New York, 1965; Edward C. Schleh, *Management By Results,* McGraw-Hill Book Co., New York, 1961; John W. Humble, *Management By Objectives in Action,* McGraw-Hill Book Co., New York, 1970; W. J. Reddin, *Effective Management By Objectives,* McGraw-Hill Book Co., New York, 1972.

4. George Kuper, "Productivity: A National Concern," *Productivity In Policing,* Police Foundation (established by the Ford Foundation), New York, 1975, pp. 1–3.

5. Roland Gelatt, "Is Britain Dying?" *Saturday Review,* February 8, 1976, pp. 12–16.

6. James D. Koerner, "Rumal Revisited," *Vital Speeches,* January 15, 1976, p. 213.

7. Judson Gooding, *The Job Revolution*, Walker and Company, New York 1972, p. 165.

8. From a special report written by *Business Week* Editors. Readers are urged to read this most provocative document, "Productivity: Our Biggest Undeveloped Resource," *Business Week*, September 9, 1972, pp. 79–124.

9. Frederick J. Bell, *"Productivity: Its Meaning for Management," Meeting the Productivity Challenge*, American Management Report No. 40, New York, 1960, p. 11.

10. Mildred E. Katzell, *"Productivity: The Measure and The Myth,"* American Management Survey Report, New York, 1975, p. 8.

11. Remarks appearing in an editorial advertisement by I. W. Abel, President of United Steelworkers of America, *Fortune*, November 1973, pp. 80–81.

12. Mildred E. Katzell, *op. cit.*, pp. 1–3.

2
ORGANIZATIONAL TRENDS AFFECTING PRODUCTIVITY

IN THIS CHAPTER

Productivity challenge of today
Twelve causes of the productivity crisis in organizations.
Low priority of productivity efforts.
Inflationary generators.
Effect of affluence on the work ethic.
Erosion of management prerogatives.
Foreign productivity centers as a new collaborative competition.
State-level productivity centers.
Voices of requistioners not heard.
The need for commitment toward planned change.

Productivity in any organization—business, education, corporation, government, health care facility, or hospital—does not just happen! Too many complex factors must be arranged, coordinated, and managed for it to occur. Only the right strategy and process will get results. Admittedly, some organizations practice a random, trial-and-error approach with some degree of success. But generally they succeed because the economic cycles favor or do not oppose them. However, panic, high costs, poor schedules, low morale, and near defaults occur when the economic cycles turn against or do not favor them. Reliable productivity requires an awareness of its basic components, an understanding of its processes, and a well thought out strategy. Management personnel must acquire the skills and competence for managing productivity in the unique present-day context.

The purpose of this chapter is to (1) identify 12 causes of productivity decline in organizations; their potential effects in organizational productivity are described and analyzed; (2) describe foreign productivity centers as the emerging new collaborative competition; and (3) cite a direct approach for change to handle the challenge of productivity.

TWELVE CAUSES OF THE PRODUCTIVITY CRISIS IN ORGANIZATIONS

The present productivity crisis is different in both kind and degree from those of the past. It's more pervasive. It's more disruptive. It affects most organizations. It produces reverberations. It cannot be ignored. Many analysts who have looked for the causes of today's productivity crisis have mistakenly sought only one or a few factors. In fact, there are many, causes, each having an effect on the other like the ripples from a pebble dropped into a pond. The productivity crisis we are experiencing within organizations is changing the nature of organizations as well as the way productivity is managed in organizations. the causes of the crisis are regarded as trends and are identified in Figure 2.1. The productivity factors shown are intrinsic to the trends. They are: white-collar workers, rewards, complexities, growth, the attitudes of affluence, scarcity, conflicts, laws and regulations, specialization, rapid changes, leisure, and information. Figure 2.1 shows the effects each action factor has on productivity and the symptoms of the potential problems it creates within the organizations. These trends are interrelated in complex ways: They are congruent at times and at conflict at other times. Each as a cause of low productivity is described briefly here to serve as an introduction for the reader, and they are discussed again in considerable detail in subsequent chapters. Managerial strategies and approaches for coping with each are also suggested in these chapters.

CAUSE ONE.   *Shocking wastes of resources result from our inability to measure, evaluate, and manage the productivity of a growing white-collar work force.*

Manual blue-collar workers are now in the minority. They have been declining in numbers and may become a small segment of our work force. White-collar workers make up the bulk of a growing employment force in the service industries, knowledge jobs, health-care fields, educational institutions, government services, human-services work, research, and the like. These white-collar employees have no tradition of having their work evaluated. Managers in knowledge jobs are not productivity minded and are not trained to measure productivity. Because performance output is not physical or tangible, measurement is difficult. Patrick Haggerty, president of Texas Instruments, has said, "productivity is unknown to lawyers in their work, but service is not since law is a service function. Most leaders in government are lawyers by training thus introducing in ineffectiveness in managing productivity in government."[1] Massive productivity gains in knowledge and service jobs are possible if one can institute

Disruptive Trends	Productivity Action Factors	Effects on Productivity	Potential Organizational Problems
1. Emerging new work force	White-collar workers	Creates evaluation and managing difficulties	Waste of human resources
2. Increasing compensation without equal productivity.	Rewards	Pushes wages and prices up.	Escalation of inflation
3. Developing superorganizations.	Complexities	Decision making and resource accountability	Slow down in reaction time and muddling of resource use
4. Drive toward organizational expansion	Growth	Adding staff reduces productivity.	Soaring costs
5. Rising number of affluent workers.	Affluent attitudes	Changes traditional reasons for working	Low motivation
6. Growing deficiency of materials	Scarcity	Disrupts plans and schedules	Late deliveries
7. Difficulties in cooperation and coordination	Conflicts	Produces unresolved disagreements	Uncoordinated organization
8. Inhibiting effects of antiquated and inadequate laws	Laws and regulation	Increases disruptive legislative intrusions	Excessive and costly constraints
9. Work processes becoming restrictive	Specialization	Produces routine and boring work	Worker dissatisfaction
10. High cost for use of technology	Rapid changes	Affects existing capital investments	Reduction of new opportunities
11. Increasing desire for time off	Leisure	Creates need for discretionary time	Disruption of work commitments
12. Accelerating knowledge	Information	Makes practices outdated	Obsolescence of skills

Figure 2.1 Causes and effects of the productivity crisis.

strategies, productivity mindedness, and measurements for managing white-collar workers.

CAUSE TWO.   *Sprialing inflation results from giving rewards and benefits without requiring the equivalent in productivity and accountability.*

H. E. Markley, president of the Timken Company, points out that during the past 20 years in America productivity has risen approximately 60 percent.[2] During the same period of time the wages of workers increased more than twice as much—135 percent. This means the output of employees has grown significantly, but the compensation for this output has soared. When pay hikes, wage increases, salary adjustments, cost-of-living increments, compensation benefits, and automatic labor contract handouts are given without justifiable increases in productivity, the net difference is made up in price increases. This difference is, by definition, inflation. It plagues us because costs are rising faster than productivity, and prices are increased to equalize the difference. These price increases affect the wage-cost escalators—"inflationary generators"—built in to many labor contracts. As prices increase, wages go up. As wages go up, prices increase. The result is a closed cycle that moves inflation up proportionately while bypassing productivity. Since inflation is a fact in recent years, it is safe to assume employees have been overpaid. Careful control and justifiable increases of wages based on a corresponding productivity and accountability are needed. Productivity data on individuals should be the basis on which to justify price increases, wage hikes, and salary adjustments. Performance contracting with employees rather than time contracting opens up a viable direction to control inflation while providing benefits to organizations and their employees.

CAUSE THREE.   *Delays and time lags result from diffused authority and inefficiency in complex, superorganizations.*

Management skills and the ability to organize on a large scale have suddenly enlarged our capacity to manage size and complexity to achieve great results. For example, well over 100,000 individual contracting firms were required over many years to put the astronauts on the moon. Each of these firms had to be signaled when to plan, execute, and deliver its contribution to the program. But the processes that bring about large projects with large complexities have with them lagging reaction time, authority dilution, and diffused accountability. Harlan Cleveland describes it as "interlaced webs of tension in which control is loose, power diffused, and centers of decision plural."[3] The hidden character of complex procedures must be broken through for productivity gains. Complex procedures must be simplified to bring accountability and reaction time to where decisions and responsibilities are located. Computer systems can contribute greatly for reducing reaction-time delays. Cost centers are needed to aggregate all resources for measurability and accountability.

CAUSE FOUR. *Costs soar from organizational expansion that reduces growth.*

Many organizations have been so busy surviving, developing, and expanding that they scarcely have noticed the drifts toward complexity and the soaring costs that result from organizations growing in the context of this complexity. Costs must be borne: for additional management personnel, more paperwork, government intrusions, more indirect workers, legal and moral contraints, additional employees, more space, unwanted overtime, sensitivity to political pressures, sensitivities, and greater resource use. Parkinson calls it the rising pyramid.[4] A public administrator can spend the entire day in writing and sending a letter to a citizen in the community. It takes a long time because of political constraints — an hour to find out if correspondence on the subject is available; an hour to review statutes that may bear on the subject; half an hour to talk to other officials and gather opinions; an hour and a half to compose with care given to correct expression of good community relations; half an hour to get the letter typed; an additional hour for revisions, restatements, additions, and retyping; and half an hour to make sure the letter gets out in the evening mail. The total effort that would occupy the traditional productive man for 20 minutes takes 6 hours.

The need for additional staff is inevitable, and organizational growth is predictable. The result is cost overruns, high resource usage, wasted time, and burdening paperwork. Productivity suffers when organizations expand without productivity effectiveness and control. Productivity declines if we handle these type of problems in the traditional way. Management has traditionally pushed for organizational growth. We now know this means soaring costs. *What we really want is productivity growth!*

CAUSE FIVE. *Low motivation prevails among a rising number of affluent workers with new attitudes.*

The overwhelming majority of people in the United States are largely free from material want. Abundance seems to be the American birthright, and this abundance continues to increase. As workers and their families achieve relatively high incomes and standards of living, they assume a lifestyle and attitudes characteristic of affluence. Foreign travel, higher education, electronic entertainment, high-style clothes are available to almost anyone who will work for them. This affluence, however, has affected the traditional reasons people work. Long-standing motivators do not seem to be so effective as in the past. A new work ethic, with attending attitudes and motivators, must be developed if productivity is to be gained from the affluent.

CAUSE SIX.   *Late deliveries are caused by schedules that have been disrupted by scarce materials.*

Shortages are manifest! Steel, copper, energy, paper, plastics, glass, food, clothing, paint, oil, gasoline—all are in short supply. One must wait 10 months for delivery of a casting order, 12 months for standard type transformers, 6 months delivery for steel in special applications, 8 months for typewriters. The record shows that the shortages that are now accepted as the norm are causing critical delays that affect productivity. In many cases managers are paying sharply higher prices for materials needed for their operations. Many organizations are coping with the problems as best they can. In some cases drastic reactions have forced owners to close plants or abdicate their businesses. Many new products, processes, equipment, and capital outlays intended for productivity improvement have been placed "on the back burner" until there is some relief. Productivity gains can be realized with new approaches in our shortage economy. Some of these approaches are better use of materials, recycling of materials, substitution of materials, and above all, longer lead-time planning.

CAUSE SEVEN.   *Unresolved human conflicts and difficulties in cooperation result in organizational ineffectiveness.*

Organizations are "driving" managers, supervisors, and employees to set goals and try to accomplish them. This drive is intended to give individuals a sense of direction and a means of deploying their own resources toward these directions. This is good! However, the processes of setting goals and driving toward their completion inevitably involves disparities, disagreements, discoordination, and conflicts. They vary from minor differences of opinions to intensive discord. As organizations continue with their drive for setting and accomplishing goals, the likelihood for minor and major conflicts is assured. When these conflicts are severe, unity of action is seriously disrupted, and organizations often respond to the dominant personalities, while others are forced into the role of "sacrificial lambs." When sales goals conflict with production quotas, a disagreement must be resolved. When human services conflict with budget constraints, a compromise must be made. When union demands exceed organizational resources, a conflict must be removed. In all cases productivity is affected; often it suffers. Unity of action by the total organization, if it occurs, is often accidental! Many organizations respond to numerous one-man random acts of control. Productivity gains are possible through conflict resolution, coordinated goals, and balanced organizational structures.

CAUSE EIGHT. *Management options and prerogatives for productivity are constrained by increasing legislative intrusions or antiquated laws.*

The continued trend toward regimentation and regulation of the free enterprise system has resulted in the reduction and loss of productivity vigor. Social legislation, environmental controls, safety regulations, price and wage controls, and labor-management bargaining constraints have brought about "legalized" participative management. The actions are not negative, for many of them have worth. Organizations must readjust to them. But when the laws and legal constraints enforcing these actions are obsolete or at best marginal in value, the actions are negative. Many of the laws were set up originally to solve problems in a different economic era, under different conditions. Many are now obsolete. To continue these laws when the economy has changed is to intrude on the free play of the marketplace. To constrain managers in the number of decision making options that may be available is to inhibit productivity opportunities. To maintain priorities that were set years ago is to encourage antiproductivity.

In these days of high litigation when anyone seems capable of suing any type of organization, a need has now developed for a complete review of antiquated and costly legislation. Productivity gains are possible if laws that do little except generate costs and constraints are repealed or modified.

CAUSE NINE. *Dissatisfying and boring work has resulted from specialized and restrictive work processes.*

Work satisfaction has steadily decreased over the past several years. For many people, work is no fun at all. Specialization and division of work processes continue to break down jobs into smaller steps to gain efficiency. It also brings tedium and boredom. Work used to be back-breaking for millions of workers; now it's mind-tormenting.

An alarming number of people find their work dissatisfying. Dissatisfying work spreads discontent. The idea of work success is infiltrated with doubt, restlessness, and disillusionment. Pressures to conform, tensions in daily work, and the expectation of compromising personal desires and principles to organizational standards and needs are causing dissatisfaction. Motivators, social interplay, and work processes must be brought into alignment with economic performance. Since the work world is a social world—that is, an opportunity to act and interact with others in groups— productivity gains will be experienced when social behavior can be aligned with economic behavior. Redesigning jobs with new work formats can be a significant factor in eliminating boredom and tedium. Work-enriching approaches and job redesigns can bring about significant steps in productivity improvement.

CAUSE TEN. *New opportunities and innovations are declining from impact of rapid technological change and high costs.*

Technological progress in this country has reached levels where its impact on work processes leaves an unsettling effect, particularly on resources that have been committed to these work processes. Mechanization, mass production, and automation require larger plants and more modern equipment, which usually require heavy outlays of capital. When the technology changes because of an innovation, expensive equipment purchased for the original work process becomes obsolete. Amortization usually takes years to process. When technology changes rapidly, a stress is generated on amortization, cost, time, people, and buildings. When these costs rise, money becomes tight and the future uncertain. Management looks at research and development as the area for cutting costs. This puts a heavy mortgage on the future. Paradoxically, R & D is the function that brought about the technological innovation. R & D usually gets squeezed because it has a long-range value to an organization. The nature of R & D dictates that periodically there is a great breakthrough. They cannot be predicted or anticipated, and they are actually the cummulative product of a long chain of continuous effort by countless workers. To cut down or cut out R & D is to lose the spectacular advances in technology that might well serve productivity in a significant way.

Traditionally, economic squeezes force decisions to maintain a status quo or survive as well as possible with a current situation. With R & D curtailed, new products, new technologies, new processes, new equipment, new machines are placed on the "back burner." Yet, for all its expense, these innovations are vital to the long-range needs of productivity. Since economic squeezes have been with us for some time, cutbacks in R & D programs and expenditures have seriously affected the productivity thrust. This effect is immediate and long range. Productivity gains will be hurt for some time since it will take time for innovative products and processes to be developed and applied. Organizations that invest higher proportions of revenues and time for R & D are the organizations that have a greater leverage toward productivity gain. A continuing and aggressive R & D activity is more vital now than ever before since the price of playing "catch up" is really prohibitive. Government must actively encourage and provide incentives for organizations to see through new ideas in an aggressive R & D program.

CAUSE ELEVEN. *Time commitments are disrupted from the increasing demand of leisure time.*

Social scientists predict that we are moving toward a world of less work and more leisure time. Automation permits the workers of today to produce more in less time than did their predecessors. They are also better compensated for it. The drive for less time and more compensation continues, but it cannot occur unless productivity is increased. Many organizations are experimenting with changing work weeks as a means of giving more time to employees. Flexitime, 4-day workweeks, and reduced traditional workhours are time patterns being examined. The concept of reducing time in exchange for more work seems to motivate. This concept is spreading in many organizations. Riva Poor states that it is critical that we locate, explore, and utilize time innovations such as the 4-day work-week in order to bolster the productivity that has been basic in improving the quality of our lives.[5] She further states that time work schedules will be basic and indispensable to any further improvement. Productivity improvement will occur when motivation for work and its attending time requirements are brought together.

CAUSE TWELVE. *Practitioners become obsolete because of their inability to keep pace with accelerating information and knowledge.*

The swift-moving current of information, knowledge, and skills continues to increase the difficulty for practitioners to keep up and advance with new developments in their fields. These practitioners are in a race between obsolescence and retirement. For many, the best they can hope for is a photo finish. It's tragic to note that many organizations are not even aware of the productivity sickness of obsolescence that results from information growth. Knowledge is moving so rapidly that practitioners are caught in the ambiguous position of being constrained to help bring about knowledge advancement while being inevitably affected by it. Formerly workers could acquire specific skills based on definable attitudes and prescribed knowledge that could be used for their entire worklives. Today the attitudes and knowledge base is continuously changing, causing the process of skill formation to be difficult and incoherent. Because the rate of change is faster than ever before, practitioners who will keep current must change their ways of keeping up more in the next 10 years than they have in the past 50 years. Productivity gains will be realized when renewal, updating, and organizational development are active processes within the organization.

FOREIGN PRODUCTIVITY CENTERS: A NEW COLLABORATIVE COMPETITION

The United States is not the only country in the world that is facing productivity problems. The productivity frustration is a common threat to all nations in the world. Many of these nations have recognized it and are attempting to meet its challenge with unique and innovative approaches. Productivity centers are such an innovative approach. Supported by government, they are collaborative efforts to deal with crisis conditions that prevail or are expected to prevail. Objectives to be reached differ from center to center because conditions in each nation differ, but a primary goal of most centers is to promote meaningful exchange and innovation toward a higher quality of life with the fewest negative consequences. Most intend to stimulate a viable economic growth in their internal industries with the following activities:

1. Disseminate productivity methods to all organizations.
2. Aid in applying new methods to corporate practice.
3. Promote productivity consciousness and rationale to all organizations.
4. Encourage exchange of information on the international level.
5. Educate the public to the value of productivity improvement.
6. Catalog productivity procedures as an information system.
7. Provide the basis for cooperation among management, labor, and government.
8. Extend new productivity expertise.
9. Explore the use of new technologies as productivity aids for old systems.
10. Research ways of measuring and managing productivity improvement.

Filer reports national productivity centers are springing up in many countries of the world.[6] In Europe there are 20 national centers, 17 of which are members of the European Association of National Productivity Centers. The present membership of the European Association includes Belgium, Bulgaria, Denmark, France, West Germany, Greece, Hungary, Iceland, Ireland, Italy, Luxembourg, the Netherlands, Norway, Portugal, Spain, Turkey, and Yugoslavia.

In Asia there are 14 national centers which are members of the Asian Productivity Organization. The present membership of the Asian Organization includes Ceylon, Republic of China, Hong Kong, India, Indonesia, Iran, Japan, Republic of Korea, Nepal, Pakistan, the Philippines, Republic of Singapore, Thailand, and the Republic of Vietnam.

Two of the most successful national centers are those of Japan and West Germany. Both of these centers have been active and useful, resulting in a tremendous influence on the productivity growth of these countries. Since both of these centers were set up in the 1950s, one may surmise that the large productivity growth of these two countries in the past 10 years has been largely from the activities of these centers.

These productivity centers have increased public awareness and understanding of the productivity problem. In many instances they have brought about effective cooperation between management and labor. The centers have been a pivotal point of communicating and distributing research data. They have been a significant input to government for developing new policies and legislation in reordering national priorities. An American productivity center, only recently set up, has not had enough time to gear up for a long-term effort. The new National Center for Productivity and Quality of Working Life is an independent agency of the executive branch of the government. Its mission is to spearhead a national effort to improve the lagging rate of productivity growth and improve the quality of working life in both private and public sectors by encouraging joint labor, industry, and government efforts. The agency will review the impact of government regulations and policies on productivity and efficiency and will seek federal policies with respect to continued productivity growth. We look forward to the agency's helpful interplay with American industries and organizations.

Meanwhile, an American firm must compete in productivity with many companies from several nations who have banded together through productivity centers for a collaborative effort. This is illustrated in Figure 2.2. American firms must go it alone until our own center can be more influential and effective. This may be one of the reasons why foreign competition is outstripping the United States in productivity gains. These countries, with the collaborative effort of government, business, and

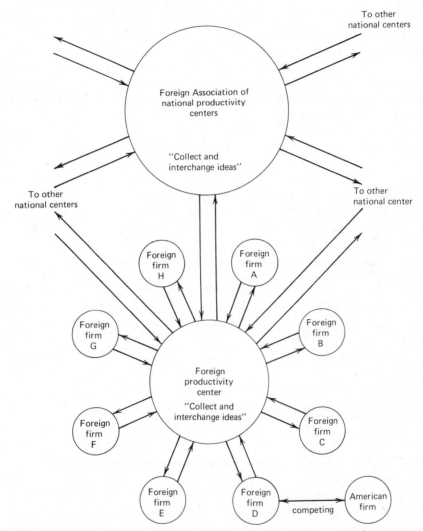

Figure 2.2   American firm competition against foreign firm and the collaborative efforts of national productivity centers.

industry, are bettering the United States' productivity growth by seven times.

Of course, the relationship of federal government and industries in the United States is quite different from other nations and their industries. Foreign countries have more closely managed economies with a closer relationship between business and government. Government even provides financial support. Because of these and other differences, it's not likely that a similar productivity center can be made to operate. Nonetheless, a workable vehicle must be developed to make participative collaboration work for productive growth between the public and private sectors, management and labor, and government and industry. I believe that state productivity centers might be a more practical way to get our national productivity center moving more rapidly and usefully. The intricacies and delicate balance of industry, labor, and government on the national level might best take root on the state level. These state centers might quickly move into the following activities:

1. Popularize the need for productivity growth. Somehow every consumer must understand how important productivity is to the person. American workers have as big a stake in improving productivity as they do in controlling inflation.
2. Communicate new products, technologies, methods, and tools to organizations that could make use of them. Organizations with problems should feel free to air their problems at the center. Technological breakthroughs should be communicated to those who may need them.
3. Develop skills to measure productivity. Where measurement techniques exist, they should be put to better use. Where they do not exist, we must develop them. Few, if any, organizations are using productivity measures.
4. Reemphasize the process of rewarding workers according to their performance where wage increases are connected to productivity.
5. Set up educational programs and seminars that key individuals from labor, management, and government can attend to learn new and innovative approaches to managing productivity.
6. Encourage the use of productivity audits by which an organization may be analyzed from a productivity standpoint and operations may be overhauled and improved.
7. Create a state climate for productivity bargaining—that is, state mediation and arbitration services could offer a service to examine bargaining contracts that are restrictive and unproductive. The service could open up discussions to "bargain away" these clauses in exchange for mutually agreed-upon benefits.
8. Conduct special studies and issue reports on the availability of resources and the prospect of declining resources that are currently being used.

The steps in developing a state-level productivity center are (1) establishing goals and priorities, which will vary from state to state; (2)

instituting a participative vehicle for involving industry, government, management, labor, and education; (3) determining the manner in which the center will conduct its activities and distribute its information. A state-level productivity center would have as a main thrust the promotion and development of productivity growth within the state, but would collaborate and cooperate with other productivity centers in other states. An association of state productivity centers could function similarly to the European Association of National Productivity Centers and the Asian Productivity Organization. A state productivity center could make its greatest contribution by identifying early the potential problems affecting productivity and giving an early assessment of where and how productivity will be affected.

Will there be problems with such centers? Of course there will. Will these centers require outlays of money? Of course they will. Will these centers touch sensitivities among competitors? Of course they will. An innovation of this kind and magnitude will generate a great deal of controversy. But unless we move into a more collaborative effort for productivity improvement like that practiced by foreign national productivity centers, we will not be able to compete in the world marketplace. A systems approach that cuts across industry lines and requires cooperative efforts of many companies and industries seems to be the direction of the future.

NEEDED: COMMITMENT TO CHANGE

The increased concern over the action factors causing lags in productivity has become apparent to government policymakers, business managers, corporate managers, educational administrators, union leaders, and the public. What is needed is change from established routines that don't work, traditional procedures that are ineffective, and comfortable methods that are not efficient. Managing productivity in organizations remains complex and elusive in the present stage of the development of organizations. The most important way to achieve it may be to change significantly the organization itself or close it down and start over. When a company invests substantial resources in a major endeavor and flops, it should! It either wasn't a good idea or wasn't meeting the needs of the consumer. In public organizations this type of discontinuance is not usually considered. One rarely hears of a welfare agency going out of business because it is not effective. Perhaps this is the type of innovation needed. Shut down the organization instead of perpetuating an insatiable consumer of resources! This may be the reason that organizations fear change. No matter how bad things are recognized to be, organizations tend to cling to the old ways for fear that change is an admission that something is wrong. Although people may decide to continue as they are, their actions keep changing to accommodate the new situations and problems confronting us. Unfortunately, there may be no choice about whether to change. Organizations change whether they want to or not. The choice is between a planned change in a desired direction or a forced, haphazard change in an undesired direction. Unplanned, haphazard changes have led us to the productivity crisis we now face.

The strategies, approaches, and solutions described in this book mean commitment to immediate change. Public administrators and private managers—government, business, and the citizenry—must be committed to work for productivity. The extent of our commitment depends upon the productivity challenge we wish to tackle.

The organizations with a wait-and-see attitude on productivity problems will find the problems deeper, more intense, and more complex. Mismanagement, resistance to change, reduced effectiveness, and human failings that affect productivity must be dealt with or they generate secondary problems compounding the initial ones. Most organizations that have been well organized "go by the book"—to follow the rules that have evolved from experience. Yet today doubt is cast on almost every rule, leading us to the idea that changing rules will be the future guide. Judgments based on how things used to be are almost certain to be out of date by the time they take effect. Future-oriented attitudes will be needed for these shifting time lines. Organizations that respond to the need to change will find themselves doing frontier work to ensure survival and growth. Public administrators are beginning to show this frontier work. Instead of relying on larger budgets garnered by emotional pleas before elected councils, public administrators are becoming more reliant on productivity improvement efforts to get the resources needed to meet service demands. Instead of requisitioning additional resources, both private and public administrators are improving productivity skills. Belief that something must happen can actually make it happen. This is the theory of self-fulfilling prophecy. People tend to do what is expected of them. If we believe that productivity increase can or will happen, a change process toward its realization is set in motion.

SUMMARY

Productivity does not just happen. There are too many complex factors that must be arranged and managed. Organizations that deliberately make it occur are the organizations in the best position to bring about its improvement.

This chapter identified 12 causes of productivity decline in organizations. They cannot easily be separated because they have an impact on each other. The 12 causes are:

1. Shocking wastes of resources result from our inability to measure, evaluate and manage the productivity of a growing white-collar work force.
2. Spiraling inflation results from giving rewards and benefits without requiring the equivalent in productivity and accountability.
3. Delays and time lags result from diffused authority and inefficiency in complex, superorganizations.
4. Costs soar from organizational expansion that reduces·productivity growth.
5. Low motivation prevails among a rising number of affluent workers with new attitudes.
6. Late deliveries are caused by schedules that have been disrupted by scarce materials.
7. Unresolved human conflicts and difficulties in cooperation result in organizational ineffectiveness.
8. Management options and prerogatives are constrained by increasing legislative intrusions or antiquated laws.
9. Dissatisfying and boring work has resulted from specialized and restrictive work processes.
10. New opportunities and innovations are declining from impact of rapid technological change and high costs.
11. Time commitments are disrupted from the increasing demand of leisure time.
12. Practitioners become obsolete because of their inability to keep pace with information and knowledge.

The increased concern with productivity frustrations has now pointed to the great need organizations now face—commitment to change. The new situation requires new approaches and strategies to deal with these problems. Foreign countries have recognized this by setting up productivity centers, a concept that could contribute greatly toward survival and productivity growth in organizations.

QUESTIONS TO THINK ABOUT

1. List 12 disruptive trends operating in organizations. Identify any of these trends operating in your organization. List them in order of seriousness together with developing problems.

2. How certain are you that disruptive productivity trends are operating against your organization? What is the evidence or the indicators?

3. Identify the primary disruptive productivity trend in each of the following: corporations, businesses, government, education, and health-care institutions.

4. List the possible benefits that would be feasible in your organization if disruptive productivity trends were controlled or reversed.

5. From a productivity standpoint, is your organization moving toward competition between countries rather than competition between organizations in different countries?

6. Would a state-level productivity center be helpful to your organization? In what way?

7. Is the concept of change incompatible with productivity practices that proved valuable? Why or why not?

REFERENCES

1. Patrick E. Haggerty, "As I See It", *Forbes*, February 1, 1971, p. 43.

2. H. E. Markley, "Survival in the Seventies," *Vital Speeches*, March 15, 1972, p. 344.

3. Harlan Cleveland, *The Future Executive*, Harper & Row Company, New York, 1972, pp. 11–17.

4. C. Northcote Parkinson, *Parkinson's Law*, Ballantine Book Company, New York, 1957, pp. 15–28.

5. Riva Poor, *4 Days, 40 Hours*, New American Library Book Company, New York, 1973, p. xv.

6. Robert J. Filer, "Foreign Productivity Centers," *Management Review*, American Management Association, January 1976, pp. 22–28.

PART TWO

MANAGING PRODUCTIVITY AS A TOTAL PROCESS

A conceptual framework is needed to view productivity in its total perspective. This view gives the manager a way to analyze the multiplicity of facets that are connected and how a change in one causes a reverberation with all the others. Part II, in four chapters, presents managing productivity as a total process in an organization. The frustrations and problems and the need for productivity improvement cited in Part I are best handled in the context of the overall organization. Part II begins to set down the process of managing productivity in our current dilemma. The evaluation and measurement techniques described form the basic core in which to manage the periphery.

3
MANAGING PRODUCTIVITY: A DEVELOPING DISCIPLINE

IN THIS CHAPTER

Productivity as a developing discipline.
The productivity process.
Zero-base planning and budgeting.
Synergistic productivity triangle.
Five guidelines for achieving synergism in an organization.
Complementary value.
Thirty factors in the productivity process.
Ten principles for productivity growth.
Symbiosis of two organizations.
Needs coincidence for developing motivators.
Elasticity of work.

There is evidence that productivity management is developing into a strong discipline. Two reasons are responsible for this: (1) To cope with the long-range prediction that scarce resources will continue to dwindle, managers must develop new attitudes and skills for delivering higher levels of performance with decreasing resources. The tradition of managing to get results is being modified to getting results with the least use of resources—that is, productivity management. (2) There is a growing realization that managing productivity is basic to managing an organization. It is managing both effectiveness and efficiency. Productivity of an organization results when the managerial "weaver" is able to tie together diverse strands of performance and resources to fabricate a meaningful thrust toward productivity. Only the manager who perceives and can handle the impact of reverberations on the "linked performance-resource strands" can manage the organization effectively.

This chapter presents three basic orientations: (1) a conceptual framework of organizational productivity—that is, how to view the productivity process; (2) productivity in the context of a synergistic process—that is, how synergism can be used to improve productivity; and (3) 10 principles of the developing discipline of productivity. The organization is looked at as a total system in a total environment, and managing productivity is executed as a total approach.

CONCEPTUAL FRAMEWORK OF ORGANIZATIONAL PRODUCTIVITY

The most important conceptual view of any organization is the aggregating of resources to achieve desirable goals. These resources (inputs) and goals (outputs) can be stated and diagrammed as follows:

Resources Used (Inputs)	*Goals Achieved (Outputs)*
Monetary ⟶	Profit or loss
Information ⟶	Decision making
Materials ⟶	Products
Equipment ⟶	Work completion
Human ⟶	Role behavior
Energy ⟶	Services
Space ⟶	Capacity

Once these goals are achieved, new goals are set, which may require new resources or a change in existing resources. This goal-achievement, resource-use cycle, established by the goal setters, forces the organization to become what the goal setters want. The organization that experiences a continual series of goal achievement through resource-use is a developing organization. Managing productivity is the process of guiding this continual cycle of goal-achievement through resource use. The process may be random (Figure 3.1) or planned (Figure 3.2).

If random, the end results or ultimate consequences of the process may not be what is desired. If planned, the end results or ultimate consequences of the process may be brought to a high degree of desirability.

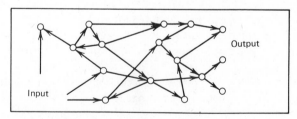

Figure 3.1 A random productivity process.

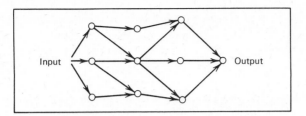

Figure 3.2   A planned productivity process.

Intrinsic to the nature of the concept of process are outcomes that may or may not be desired by the manager.

Productivity in an organization is a managed process that identifies and relates all the events and activities necessary to accomplish productivity objectives. It deliberately seeks an efficient way to transform or convert resources into results, as shown in Figure 3.3.

The systems process begins with a clear understanding of the mission, responsibility, or function of the organization, department, or individual. This is the same as saying the first requirement of any productivity effort is purpose. The purpose is defined, described, and set in terms of expectations. Making a profit is not defined, in my opinion, as purpose. Meeting customer demands and getting customer satisfaction is. Profit is a measure of how well that purpose, customer satisfaction, has been served.

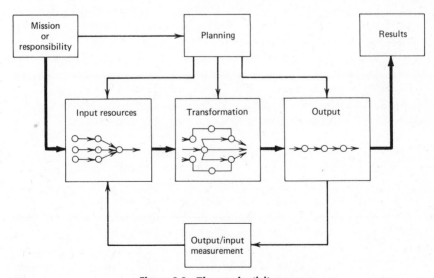

Figure 3.3   The productivity process.

Reaching a 10 percent return on investment from a computer installation is not defined here as purpose. But providing needed computer services is. A 10 percent return is a measure of how well that purpose has been served.

The next step in the process is to plan for the implementation of the purpose. Objectives and goals are set for getting results in the direction needed for the organization. Individual plans are blended toward a large-scale accomplishment within a time frame. In this step productivity is designed into plans by infusing its many dimensions: results, resource utilization, output-input measurement, magnitude, efficiency, pace, and quality. A systems approach must be developed that brings together all the phases of the productivity process and the competencies of people and equipment to handle the functions and subfunctions of the organization .

Input-transformation-output sequences are established in the planning step. A set of work sequences or operations that will deliver results is designed into a process. The work sequences specify and accumulate the type and nature of resources to be utilized. They bring together assembly, conversion, coordination, and operating processes in a time schedule in which an output result is achieved. Throughout the work sequences in-process standards are maintained in order to arrive at the ultimate level of quality with a specific set of results.

Finally, there are the output-input measurements. Actual output results are compared, in a ratio, with input resources as a measure of what actually happened in the transformation of time, materials, personnel, and money. Most situations involving productivity are multidimensional—that is, several measurements must be taken to collect sufficient facts about complicated system of work process sequences. More is said on output-input comparisons as ratio measurement later in this chapter in the section on with the principle of ratio measurement.

To illustrate the concept of the productivity process, four applications are briefly described: (1) hospitals, (2) zero-based planning and budgeting systems, (3) hotels-motels-restaurants, and (4) manufacturing.

Productivity Process in Hospitals

A hospital brings together a concentration of resources for the purpose of providing patient care to sick and injured persons. It also provides facilities for education, training, and development of professional and supportive personnel. New knowledge through scientific research in medicine, nursing, paramedical fields, and hospital administration are also part of its mission. Hospital management includes the planning of community health-care objectives and the execution of policies, resources, equipment, and facilities necessary to provide patient care in relation to these objectives. Managing the hospital elements as a productivity process for mission to results is illustrated in Figure 3.4.

Advances in health technologies, ever-increasing demands for more and better services, expanding population, high costs of living, and the necessity of moving toward competitive wage levels are among the factors that have forced hospitals to look carefully at their productivity and how it can be improved. The modern hospital is an industry of complex services that must be provided day and night, seven days a week. It is keyed to the economic and sociopsychological attitudes of the community it serves.

The hospital manufactures no product yet does considerable processing and fabricating in its dietary department, laundry, central sterile supply, and other departments. Services are diversified and largely nonstandardized. There are few assembly lines, yet hospital procedures have many routine repetitive work sequences that characterize productivity work. There is no doubt that the quality of patient care depends a great deal on how well the productivity processes are being managed in times of limited resources.

The Productivity Process in Zero-Base Planning and Budgeting Systems

Public demand for getting the most for the money expended, in terms of meeting public need, has brought about a systematic process for relating expenditures to the accomplishment of planned objectives. Zero-base planning and budgeting systems (ZBPB), now being utilized by federal, state, and local governments, are a comprehensive budgetary method of setting expense allocations to stated levels of output for established or proposed programs within an agency, without regard to past-year allocations. Each program within a year's planning is defined in terms of objectives to be achieved through government spending, determining the best way to achieve the objectives, minimizing the costs required by the program, maximizing the benefits and analysis for assuring efforts toward stated outcomes. The major value of ZBPB is that it gives an administrator the means to influence more directly and effectively the myriad decisions and order of priorities with accountability that must be made by an organization, while collecting inputs from large segments of diverse groups. Managing ZBPB elements as a productivity process from mission to results is illustrated in Figure 3.5.

The ZBPB system enables administrators to view their fund allocation and decision-making process in terms of ZBPB-generated information rather than the traditional criteria of line-item aggregate accountability

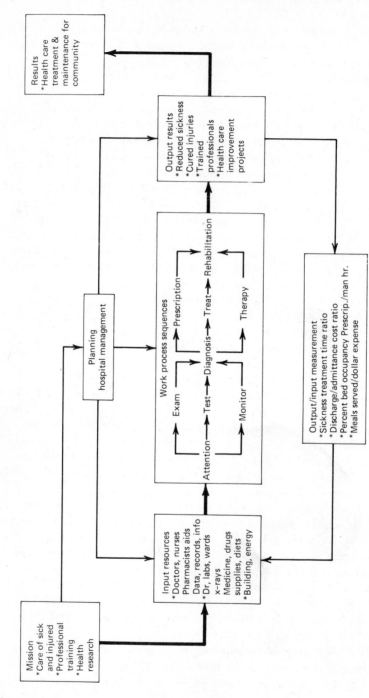

Figure 3.4 The productivity process in hospitals.

48

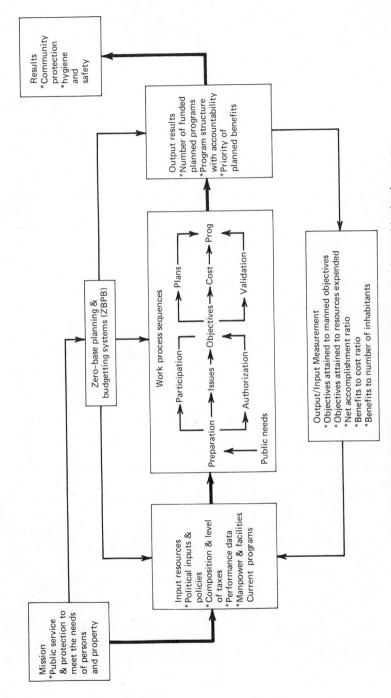

Figure 3.5   The productivity process in zero-base planning and budgeting systems.

49

carried from year to year. The system allows for political inputs into the analysis of policymaking as well as technical and financial inputs. Productivity improvement with ZBPB involves the allocation of funds in such a way that effects of increments (or decrements) within a program have no bearing because the entire program is analyzed from a zero-datum point. On this basis, programs A, B, C, and D are compared and decided for highest benefit for the allocated resources within the budgetary year. Greatest productivity does not occur, for example, between entire blocks of programs or all-or-none propositons, but between increases and decreases in the scale, similarity, and operations of individualized programs. To get the most from limited resources, productivity must delve into alternate ways to carry out tasks or programs, and meaningful quantitative measures must provide indication of gain or cost. ZBPB processes are oriented more toward planning rather than operating, or in other words, *ZBPB processes work out managements' problems in advance and commit them to plans.* Program issues are anticipated in advance, and their solutions are infused into the ZBPB development phases.

Clearly, one of the major aims of ZBPB is to convert the annual routine of preparing a budget into a conscious appraisal and formulation of stated outcomes to the highest benefit possible with the least expenditure of resource. The ZBPB process is spread out over a period of one budgetary phase and requires a level of productivity to bind administrators to policies and plans set by agencies. Because time is scarce, the administrator must act and react during the various phases of preparation, participation, objective-setting, iteration, validation, and formalization with pace, balance, and control. Work efficiency and productivity are no different for the public administrator than for the manufacturing executive or hospital manager. Zero-based planning and budgeting is discussed in more detail in Chapter 8.

Productivity Process in Hotel-Motel-Restaurant Units

Innkeeping is closely tied to the transportation industry. Since the transportation industry has been slowly growing, the innkeeping units have struggled to keep pace. Managing a modern hotel-motel-restaurant unit requires a great deal of sophisticated productivity talent to provide values in hospitality, comfort, and living for travelers and community needs. Hotel-motel-restaurant management of yesteryear relied a great deal on personality, flair, showmanship, and dedicated followers. Today almost without exception the problems of rising costs, declining occupancy, slender profits, and low productivity are being handled by management techniques and processes found in any other industry. Productivity processes in the hotel-motel-restaurant units refer to the planning of customer satisfaction and the use of total facilities to meet this objective. Profits and net earnings are measures of how well this objective has been met. Managing the elements of an inn as a productivity process from mission to results is illustrated in Figure 3.6.

The innkeeping industry anticipates an undreamed of number of new travelers, vacationers, and people seeking recreation to use hotel-motel-restaurant facilities. The need to keep pace with this growing demand is stronger than ever. The demand will be for higher quality rooms, food, and services at lower prices. Managers of the units will search for new methods to cope with this demand. Closing down for one or more days of the week is one innovation for reducing costs on a per-time basis. Self-service is another. Guests may actually be willing to serve themselves in a way that maintains their value of hospitality and comfort. Automation of services is a third. Direct-dial telephones, push-button elevators, precut and preportioned foods, and prearranged service packages are but a few examples of automated processes. Productivity processes are moving more and more into innkeeping management and operations.

The Productivity Process in Manufacturing

Manufacturing encompasses all the transformation procedures that fit the output-input concept discussed in this section. The problems found in manufacturing more often concern how to interconnect sets of output-input subsystems so that the large system can perform productivity in a satisfactory manner. The larger the manufacturing system, the more likely that the subsystems will not be interconnected. Lower productivity results. High productivity prevails when there is a successful synthesizing process. This is illustrated in Figure 3.7.

Various raw materials may be sent through a number of processing operations performed at varying rates. The outputs of each individual work element become the input of the succeeding element. The transformation process is the output-input interconnection of a series of elements from component inventory to finished goods inventory.

Undoubtedly, the most challenging problem for manufacturing management has been the subsystem interconnector of people with machines. Machines cannot be used during the "set up" and "put away" operations, and they cannot be used when raw material supplies are not available or when a person decides to shut down the machine for personal reasons. These are the conditions that disrupt productivity in the process.

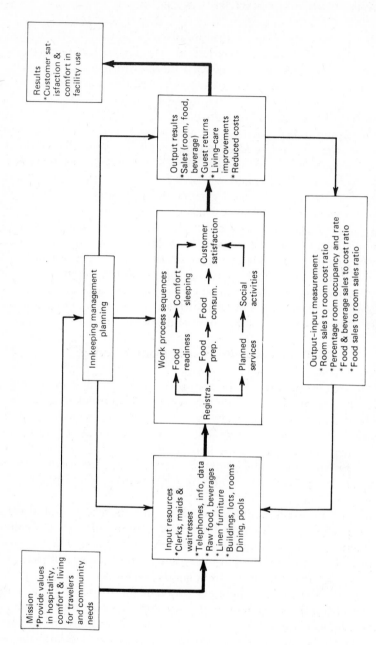

Figure 3.6 The productivity process in innkeeping.

52

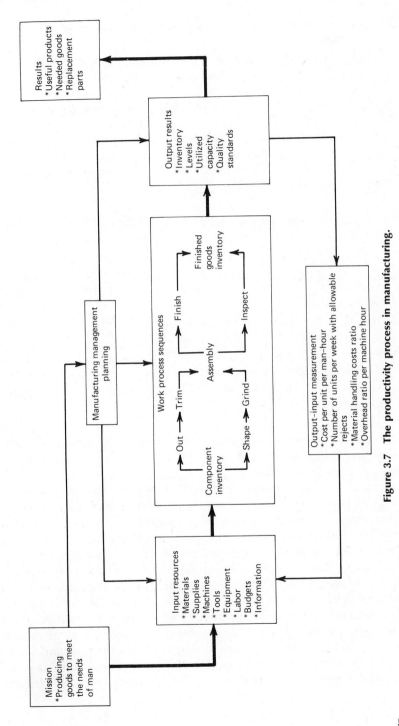

Figure 3.7 The productivity process in manufacturing.

PRODUCTIVITY IS A SYNERGISTIC PROCESS

Synergism is the combining of parts or factors in a process so that its operating whole is quite different from a simple sum or addition of these same parts. In other words, when two parts are changed or added together synergistically, instead of getting two, one may get three, four, or five. A new element emerges in the synergistic combination. Examples of parts are method, equipment, attitude, skills, leadership, costs, awareness, and policies. The basic phenomena related to synergism are interactions, interdependence, and linked interfaces. These phenomena will operate in an organization if the following actions can be made:

1. Change any one part if the change produces far-reaching positive reverberations to other parts of the process. The change could mean to modify or remove the part.
2. Control the role of a part if the part loses the strength of its interactions with other parts. This works against productivity "drifts" in the process.
3. Include a new part if its inclusion will disturb the original pattern of segmentation for better and not for worse.
4. Remove any parts that do not coordinate, link, or give the whole process an effectiveness or efficiency toward achieving objectives.
5. Set the same priority for all parts in a process that has been deployed toward achieving an objective.

Unused capacity, stored potential, or low level of effectiveness are released or greatly enhanced when the parts or factors of the synergistic phenomena are made to work well.

At least 30 parts or factors directly or indirectly affect the management of productivity in an organization. Productivity is increased or enhanced when these factors are combined synergistically in such a way as to multiply their effects greater than each would do independently. Take, for example, the factors of cost and performance. If situational factors are changed so that costs are reduced, but the effects also reduce performance, the situational factors are not synergistically changed. However, if situational factors are changed so that costs are reduced but the effects increase performance, the situational factors are synergistically changed. Managing productivity in an organization is arranging and combining 30 or more factors that would yield the highest level of performance with the least expenditure of resources. This is the sum and substance of the concept of productivity. The combination of effectiveness and efficiency is another way of stating the synergistic combination of parts in the productivity process. Effectiveness and efficiency are the results of the interaction and interdependence of many factors rather than one.

The 30 factors that directly or indirectly affect productivity are shown in the productivity triangle of Figure 3.8. The factors are identified by levels as follows:

Fourth-Level Factors (Affect Productivity Most Directly). Effectiveness (performance), efficiency (resource usage).

Third-Level Factors. Skills, motivation, methods, costs.

Second-Level Factors. Leadership, experience, climate, incentives, schedules, organizational structure, technology and materials.

First-Level Factors (Affect Productivity Least Directly). Abilities, style, training, knowledge, physical conditions, unions, social awareness, aspiration levels, processes, job design, goals, policies, R & D, plant and equipment, standards and quality.

From the synergistic productivity triangle, the following guidelines should be kept in mind in developing synergistic combinations and reverberations:

1. Importance of each factor on each level will probably be different for each organization, department, or individual. An organization should assess the factors that dominate and are critical to a productivity process from those that merely contribute.

2. The factors on each level are more apt to affect the factors on the same level before having an impact on other levels. For example, changing the organizational structure on Level Two is 'more apt to change the climate on Level Two before it will affect skills on Level Three or policies on Level One.

3. The factors that are on the lower level of directness are less apt to influence productivity than the factors on the higher levels of directness. Costs, motivation, or methods on Level Three are more apt to change the type and amount of productivity than physical conditions, training, policies, or job design on Level One. This does not preclude the influence of any factor on any level on productivity. They all influence productivity.

4. The factors in each level have the potential of affecting directly the factors on the next level, which may in turn affect the factors in the next level, and so on. How well productivity is managed is based on how these factors are uniquely and synergistically changed to bring about an ultimate improvement in productivity. When training on Level One is changed, it reverberates experience on Level Two, which has an impact on skills on Level Three. When the changes in these

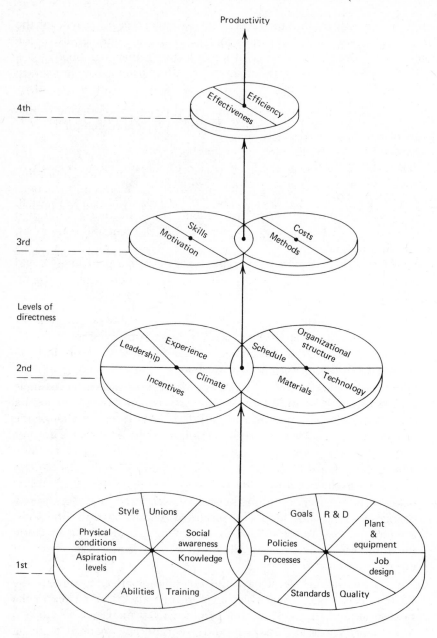

Figure 3.8 The synergistic productivity triangle.

factors on different levels are made in the right combination, sequence, and timing, the factors of effectiveness and efficiency are also changed.

5. The factors on all levels are highly affected by time, for time itself will cause changes in directions that are not desired or directions that are needed. This means the "productivity drifts" are found in all organizations. For organizations that do not control or hold the working factors correctly combined, productivity will drift in type and amount.

Each organization will require a differently managed combination and reverberation of the factors of the triangle suggesting that overall productivity of an organization is largely determined by the actions and reactions of its management personnel. This is not to say they have total responsibility. It is to say that ideas, judgment changes, and innovations are more likely to be implemented by this group than any other group. Management's attitudes and personal example must pervade and infect all others in the organization. The following example, the admitting and discharge operation of a hospital, will give some insight to the synergistic process.

Case Example: Hospital Admitting Department

The Mercy Hospital in Connecticut is a general hospital serving approximately 30 communities. The hospital has 375 beds plus 40 baby bassinets. The hospital's main source of revenue is from patients' stays. The annual budget of $9 million is used mainly for salaries. Therefore, the hospital is always interested in finding ways to increase revenues, maintain high census ratios, or simply lower costs. The admitting department is most responsible for maintaining a high level of room utilization. Any attempt to improve the admitting-discharge procedure has a positive reverberation throughout the whole hospital, treatment care, and patient handling process. The productivity index that could be used to measure the effects of any changes is as follows:

$$\frac{\text{admission cost per}}{\text{patient per week}} = \frac{\text{salaries} + \text{machine rentals} + \text{form processing costs}}{\text{number of patients admitted weekly}}$$

The admission process from bookings to discharge at Mercy Hospital is charted in the upper diagram of Figure 3.9. This process requires one chief of admitting, seven registered nurses, one secretary typist, five cycles of form handling of six copies, and one addressograph machine. The cost of this entire process, based on 325 admissions, is as follows:

$$\frac{\text{admission cost per}}{\text{patient per week}} = \frac{\$1500 + \$65 + \$32}{325 \text{ patients}} = \$4.91 \text{ per patient per week}$$

Changes were made in the process to gain benefits for the department as well as the hospital. The changes were to replace three admitting nurses with two clerk-typists, replace addressograph machine with Friden Data Processor Flexowriters, restrict elective admissions to scheduled hours, reduce number and cycle of forms and make available quicker data processing information to treatment and care staff. The cost of this entire process, based on 325 admissions, is as follows:

$$\frac{\text{admission cost per}}{\text{patient per week}} = \frac{\$850 + \$100 + \$16}{325 \text{ patients}} = \$2.97 \text{ per patient per week}$$

The admission process from bookings to discharge with the changes and the level of synergistic directness is charted in the lower diagram of Figure 3.9. This synergistic process has brought about an annual total savings of $20,000 per year.

An alternate approach in getting a synergistic reverberation toward productivity improvement is through *adding complement value to how capacity is organized in the firm.* If the organization conducts its operation so that labor and labor-connected services are primary, the organization is said to be labor intensive. If the organization conducts its operation so that equipment and equipment-connected procedures are primary, the organization is said to be equipment intensive. Synergistic changes are more easily made when equipment or equipment-connected procedures are added to labor-intensive organizations. This is complementing value to the parts. Similarly, synergistic changes are more easily made when labor or labor-connected services are added to equipment-intensive organizations. This also is complementing value to the parts. For example, when automated equipment can be added to an organization experiencing high labor costs, effectiveness or performance output can be gained while reducing the overall costs. When improved human relations or behavioral factors can be added to an organization experiencing low morale and poor attitudes, efficiency or better use of resources can be gained while improving on overall performance. The 30 factors that directly or indirectly influence productivity can now be viewed in terms of labor or equipment-intensive organization as shown in Figures 3.10 and 3.11. The factors to the left of the triangle should be emphasized for equipment-intensive organizations and those to the right, labor-intensive organizations. The significance of the synergistic insight can be another important

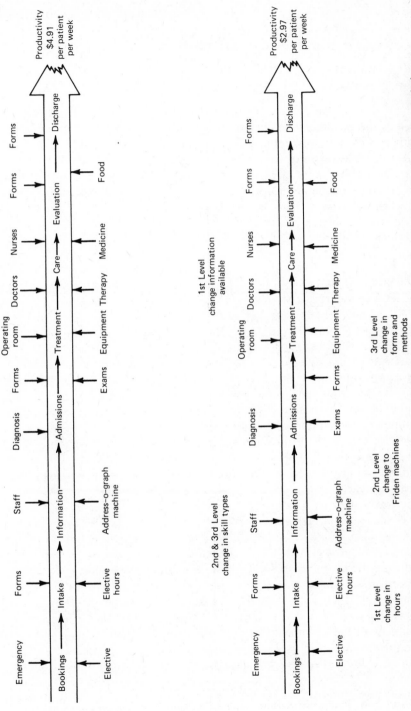

Figure 3.9 Synergistic admission process for a hospital. (*a*) Existing admission process. (*b*) Synergistic changes in the admission process.

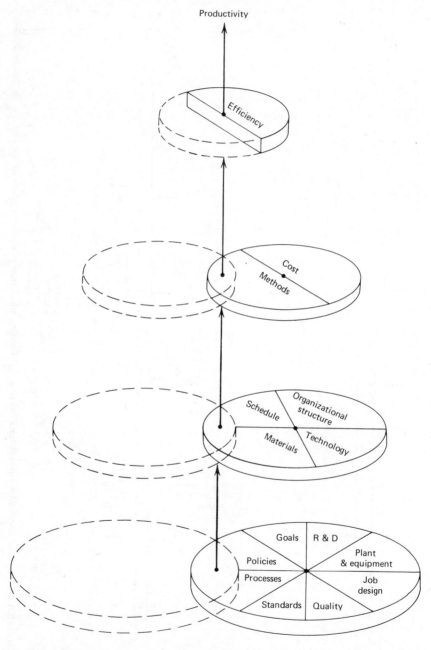

Figure 3.10 Productivity factors emphasis for labor-intensive organizations.

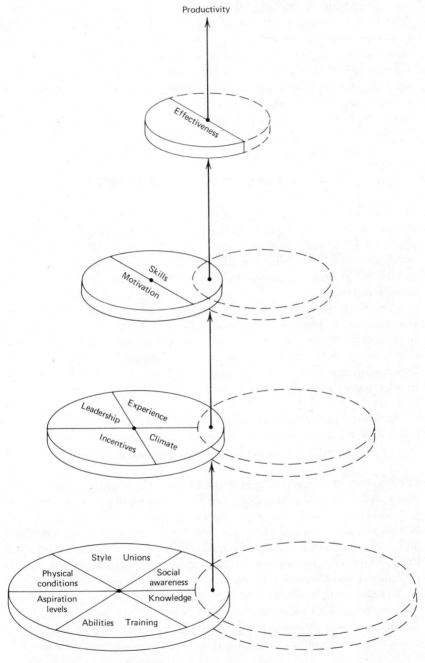

Figure 3.11 Productivity factors emphasis for equipment-intensive organizations.

view of production management as a total process. The advantage in viewing the organization in this manner is to see the effects on the whole operation when any of its parts or types of parts are changed, or to see what changes can be made in any parts or type of parts of an organization to bring about positive effects to the total. Additionally, labor-intensive organizations will find productivity improvement more conducive by adding equipment in place of labor. Similarly, equipment-intensive organizations will find productivity improvement more conducive by changing the quality or skills of labor.

PRINCIPLES OF PRODUCTIVITY GROWTH

Principles convey a notion that they are fundamental truths to be followed rigidly. Those who accept them as such claim they have universal application. Actually most traditional principles lack data to support or verify their universal existence. If data are supplied they are of contemporary value under a set of conditions that become invalid when the conditions change.

The 10 principles described in this section are guides for thought, planning, and productivity growth. They should help the reader to understand the concept of organizational productivity and the processes that bring it about. As management of productivity matures and experience accumulates, some of these guides may be superseded by new guides in adapting to a changing set of needs.

1. **PRINCIPLE OF RATIO TIME MEASUREMENT.** *Productivity is more likely to improve when expected results are measured and made greater in the same time frame that expected resources are measured and made less.*

Lord Kelvin once said, "When you can measure what you are speaking about and express it in numbers, you know something about it; but when you cannot measure it, cannot express it in numbers, your knowledge of it is meager and unsatisfactory." Productivity compares output with input and in the process reveals the magnitude or volume of the comparison. Productivity can be intensified and raised in magnitude or can be diminished and lowered in magnitude. More output without a proportionate increase in the magnitude of the input is a primary goal in productivity improvement. This measures how well resources are being utilized. It is the main thrust in product improvement. The measure of output over input must be made at the same time or in the same period and held constant throughout the operating schedule. Greenberg, who was the executive director of the National Commission on Productivity from 1970 to 1972 and was charged, along with the 32-member tripartite commission, by the president to develop conclusions and recommendations, stresses this point: "An important criterion of the productivity ratio is that the output and the imput be expressed in constant terms over the selected time period."[1]

Since productivity is a ratio of comparison within a period of time, the productivity index described earlier can be a basis of measurement. Thus the index can be improved by operating on the top (numerator), the bottom (denominator), or both. Productivity increases when the net difference becomes greater in any one of these three operations. When this difference is measured, checked, scored, and improved at the same time that resources are consumed, productivity is being managed. This principle is illustrated as follows:

$$\frac{\text{productivity}}{\text{index}} = \frac{\text{results}}{\text{resources}} = \frac{\text{sales}}{\text{employees}} = \frac{\$600,000}{10}$$
$$= \$60,000 \text{ sales per employee}$$

Case 1: Increase results; hold resources constant; productivity goes up!

$$\frac{\text{productivity}}{\text{index}} = \frac{\text{sales (up)}}{\text{employees (hold)}} = \frac{\$700,000}{10}$$
$$= \$70,000 \text{ sales per employee}$$

Case 2: Hold results constant; decrease resources; productivity goes up!

$$\frac{\text{productivity}}{\text{index}} = \frac{\text{sales (hold)}}{\text{employees (down)}} = \frac{\$600,000}{8}$$
$$= \$75,000 \text{ sales per employee}$$

Case 3: Increase results; decrease resources; productivity goes up!

$$\frac{\text{productivity}}{\text{index}} = \frac{\text{sales (up)}}{\text{employees (down)}} = \frac{\$630,000}{9}$$
$$= \$70,000 \text{ sales per employee}$$

Case 4: Increase both results and resources but disportionately; productivity goes up!

$$\frac{\text{productivity}}{\text{index}} = \frac{\text{sales (up)}}{\text{employees (up)}} = \frac{\$900,000}{12}$$
$$= \$75,000 \text{ sales per employee}$$

Case 5: Decrease both results and resources but disproportionately; productivity goes up!

$$\frac{\text{productivity}}{\text{index}} = \frac{\text{sales (down)}}{\text{employees (down)}} = \frac{\$400,000}{5}$$
$$= \$80,000 \text{ sales per employee}$$

Productivity would remain unchanged if results (numerator) and resources (denominator) are both doubled and halved in the same proportion. The principle of ratio measurement specifies that productivity is improved by getting a greater *net difference* in the ratio. The net difference can be also obtained by increasing or decreasing disproportionately one of the factors of the ratio. A $1000 increase in sales may increase profits by $100, but a $100 decrease in costs is equivalent to a $1000 increase in sales, since reduced costs as a resource has an effect on sales as performance. The principle of ratio-time measurement indicates that productivity growth is likely to happen when an evaluative measure, such as the productivity index, that can relate performance and resources in the same time period is applied.

✓2. PRINCIPLE OF SHARED GAIN. *Productivity increases rapidly when its expected benefits are shared with those who will produce it.*

In biology, symbiosis (living togetherness) is a state in which two or more dissimilar or different organisms or species live together to mutual advantage.[2] There is a shared gain between the two organisms. When one organism begins to gain more at the expense of the other, a parasitic relationship emerges. The parasite becomes the predator upon the victim. The parasite can grow to huge dimensions, taking all its nutrition from the main organism and doing nothing in return. If this process continues for a long time, the organism that is unable to sustain both dies. This termination is lethal to the dependent parasite.

Symbiotic states in organizational worklife tend to increase productivity. Examples of states where shared gain is mutually beneficial are:

(a) Collective bargaining that mutually benefits labor and management.
(b) Viable budgets that favor both taxpayers and government.
(c) Fee demands that are worthwhile to both patients and doctors.
(d) Tuition assessments that are fair to both students and faculty.
(e) Merit increases that recognize both employee and supervisor.
(f) Negotiated agreements in annual plans for both top and lower management.

When one organization, group, or individual benefits at the expense of the other, a parasitic state, which disrupts productivity, emerges. One becomes the prey and the other the predator. When the parasitic state is permitted to exist for a long time, productivity declines seriously, and both organizations, both groups, or both individuals eventually cease to exist. When two functions, two departments, two groups or two individuals relate together for mutual, balanced advantage, productivity increases. Thus productivity can be a measure of the health and vigor of an organization.

3. PRINCIPLE OF EXPECTANCY ALIGNMENT. *The greater the alignment of employee expectancies (needs) with organizational objectives (targets), the greater the motivation to accomplish both.*

Employees work primarily for themselves and only secondarily for their employers. They work to meet their needs and personal goals. When these goals and needs are closely aligned to organizational needs and goals so that both are achieved, motivation to accomplish both increases. This alignment is "needs coincidence"—that is, needs of both organization and individuals are met. When there is recognition and reinforcement of this needs coincidence, motivation intensifies. The closer the alignment, the more intense the motivation. Employees see and feel that they are meeting their needs as well as meeting the needs of their employer. Examples of expectancy alignment (needs coincidence) are:

Organizational Need	Employee Need
1. Need to get commitments to complete work before work commences.	Need to know what is going on and why and an opportunity to exert an influence.
2. Need results that are significant and worthwhile.	Need to be recognized for achieving work that is important.
3. Need for employees who can handle new and different types of job assignments.	Need for work that fascinates and generates intense interest.

Motivation for productivity can be developed when situations are created to allow for this alignment of needs coincidence.[3] Job methods, content, and techniques should be designed and redesigned toward this end.

4. PRINCIPLE OF WORKER ACCOUNTABILITY. *Accountability for productivity is more likely to happen when employees understand, participate in, and are held responsible for productivity objectives, measurement, and evaluation.*

Since everyone benefits from productivity, productivity improvement is everyone's responsibility, not solely management's. Those receiving the greatest benefits from productivity are the ones who should assume greatest responsibility for its continuance and improvement. The greater the benefit one receives from productivity gains, the greater the responsibility to assure the improvement of its processes. Employees who are responsible for greater productivity are apt to feel more accountable when they participate wholeheartedly in the selection, development, and execution of productivity objectives. Here is a case where the democratic processes should prevail. Get everyone into the act. Get people making suggestions and proposals in their areas of responsibilities. They will feel and be moved to accomplish results when they know their ideas are being pursued. But participation is only a first step in accountability. The others are expectancy, achievement, and reporting. The following are illustrations of this principle:

	Method	Participation	Expectancy	Achievement	Reporting
1.	Job description	Employee and supervisor	Performance standards written for each duty	Annual results	Results in annual appraisal
2.	Operational planning	All supervisors	Objectives and action plans with names	Quarterly and annual results	Results in quarterly and annual report
3.	Suggestion system	All employees	Usable ideas	When implemented	Results in newspaper or newsletter

Allowing participation does not mean that managers abdicate their accountability. They still reserve the right to make the final decision. Nor does participation mean involvement in every decision. Participation should be encouraged where contributions can be made by those who are willing to make them.

5. **PRINCIPLE OF FOCUS.**   *The greater the focus toward productivity objectives on a time scale, the greater the likelihood of achieving these objectives.*

An organization spreads its time, effort, and resources across a large and intricate spectrum of demands. This spreading often means doing many things but not necessarily doing them well. Managers similarly give more time and attention to many items over a wider spectrum of activities.

They literally "spread themselves thin" over many activities, most of which are trivial. As a result, dilution could mean ineffectiveness or waste. When the organization proceeds to sort, select, and concentrate on the critical demands that carry productivity gain, the more likelihood there is for productivity growth. This allows the deployment of limited resources to be more effective toward the critical few objectives that contribute greatly toward productivity. The principle of focus requires the assignment of priorities and weights to productivity objectives that are most important to the organization. An organization that has 10 objectives, all demanding equal priority, ignores the principle of focus and assumes all objectives have equal benefits. A major study by the National Industrial Conference Board show, that the organizations with high concentrations in few areas have high productivity, while organizations that practice low concentration tend to have low productivity. The guide to follow in selecting objectives that will yield the greatest productivity gain is to determine the benefits and the likelihood (risk factors) of achieving these benefits. The following relationship holds true:

$$\text{potential benefits} \times \text{probability of occurrence} = \text{expected benefits}$$

This is illustrated in the following example:

Desired Results	Potential Benefits (B)	Probability of Occurrence in Same Time Frame (P)	Expected Benefits (P × B)
1. Sales volume	$10,000	0.30%	$3000
2. Cost reduction	6,000	0.60	3600
3. Rework reduction	5,000	0.90	4500
4. Scheduled improvement	2,500	0.80	2000
5. Obsolete inventory	1,500	0.70	1050
6. Value improvement	4,000	0.40	1600

Risk is always present when deciding on some future event or some expected value. The higher the risk of failure, the lower the expected value. Conversely, the lower the risk of failure, the higher the expected value. Thus many attractive opportunities must be analyzed to see the greatest benefit possible within an existing time frame. A concerted effort to focus on the objectives with highest expected benefits would give greatest results.

6. PRINCIPLE OF CREATING POTENTIAL PRODUCTIVITY. *Productivity gains are more likely to be achieved from situations where the potential for productivity gain is created.*

Productivity gains and potential for gain are interrelated and inseparable. Each is a determinant of the other. When productivity gain is increasing, potential is unfolding. Productivity growth starts as a "look-ahead" to search out and identify the potential situations for gain. This search and identity is not so much finding where productivity gain has never been experienced as it is creating new situations for which productivity gain may occur. In other words, the manager should look at a situation as a potential for creating productivity—what changes could be made, what procedures could be adopted, what new resources or equipment can be used for raising the existing productivity level. Not all productivity opportunities are visible. The greatest breakthroughs are hidden. I think that the greatest productivity breakthrough will occur with two general approaches: Labor-intensive organizations will make greater use of technology, equipment, mechanized processes, and capital plant; equipment-intensive organizations will make greater use of human relations, motivational processes, and work incentives. When these approaches are brought into the situation major changes may have to be made for productivity gains to emerge. Take for example the expensive regional meetings held monthly by a multidivisional firm. These meetings of six regional managers were vital to coordinate and cooperate their efforts. But the frequency of being away from their offices and the expense of travel forced a careful examination of how this coordination and cooperation effort could be carried out with less expense. The following illustrates how this situation was analyzed for creating productivity.

OBJECTIVE. *Complete 12 coordination meetings of six managers for 3000 clients by January 1.*

The decision was made to replace the expensive monthly regional meetings with a monthly 4-hour coordination conference using a telephone conference connection with six managers in six different regions of the firm. The following are other examples of how traditional situations are modified to reach for gains with the principle of creating potential

Reasons for Decisions (Priority Rank)

Alternatives	Less Risk	Bigger Benefit	Quicker Benefit	Related Benefit	Long-Term Benefit	Total	Best Compromise Rank
1. Hold meetings as they are	1	6	2	3	3	15	
2. Hold meetings to a minimum	3	3	5	4	5	20	
3. Cut down on meetings	6	1	6	5	6	24	
4. Use written report system	5	5	4	6	4	24	
5. Use telephone system	2	2	1	1	1	7	
6. Use "delegate" representation system	4	4	3	2	2	15	1

productivity:

(a) Recommended use of automated equipment generating heavy resistance is being replaced by feasibility and use studies by the people the equipment is to replace.

(b) The difficult and slow method of harvesting grapes for winemaking in California is being replaced by growing and training the vines for high production harvesting.

(c) Long wait in doctors' offices for diagnosing is being replaced by multiroom structures for doctors to circulate while assistants complete work.

(d) Expensive and time-consuming sorting of mail that is thrown into a mailbox is being replaced by several mailbox receptacles that force mail separation when the customer deposits the mail.

7. PRINCIPLE OF CONTINUANCE. *Productivity tends to continue when achieving an objective does not incapacitate or destroy any of the factors which produced it.*

Productivity is determined by factors such as technology, personnel, materials quality, and work processes. These factors are needed for productivity to exist. Productivity levels that have been reached will continue when these factors are arranged and used in such a way that objectives are met without incapacitating or destroying the factors. When productivity is gained by incapacitating any of its producing factors, short-term benefits are received at the sacrifice of longer-term gains. The one factor most often affected by short-term productivity gains is quality. Productivity gains attained at the sacrifice of quality are only temporary and often result in scrap, rework, rejects, returns, and losses. These in turn force costs to increase which eventually causes productivity to decline. *Productivity cannot be obtained at the expense of quality.* Therefore, a series of appropriate additional indicators of the quality of output should be used as a monitor to assure that the needed quality level exists. The following are examples of indicators for maintaining quality levels when achieving productivity objectives:

(a) Completion ratio in treatment plans.

(b) Percentage of errors in filling orders.

(c) Percentage of learning items in a learning checklist.

(d) Percentage of scrap, waste, or incompleted paperwork.

(e) Mean on range of equipment downtime.

(*f*) Damage claims as a percentage of sales levels and orders.

(*g*) Percentage of patient-care items in a patient-care checklist.

(*h*) Percentage of rework.

(*i*) Overshipment and undershipment ratios.

(*j*) Defect-correction ratio.

(*k*) Delivery-delay ratios.

8. PRINCIPLE OF WORK JUSTICE.   *Productivity is more likely to continue when employees are given equal pay for equal work; when employers are given equal work for equal pay.*

"Pay the job and not the person" is a cause of productivity decline. "Pay the person and not the job" is another cause of productivity decline. On a given job it is not unusual for one employee to produce one-quarter more than another employee or for another employee to produce one-half less than another while both are getting the same pay. Poor employees may get as much reward as good employees. It is also not unusual for employers to underpay employees when their productivity is greater than a prior time. Productivity gains occur when those who do the most get the most pay, when earnings and benefits are directly connected to individual output. Marion Kellogg speaks of this in different words:

> The problem for the manager lies in the fact that he is expected to get results, to make certain defined contributions to the organization. But he is not expected to do this at all costs. And so his money resources must be carefully and skillfully handled as other resources. But the key to his achieving needed results is the employee who, by his ingenuity and commitment, produces these results. If the employee is to give his best, he must feel he is being fairly treated. If the manager is to live up to his own principles, he also has a need to feel that he is treating the employee fairly.[5]

A method that illustrates that pay should follow the amount of contribution is using the Objective Completion Pay Rating Scale (Figure 3.12).

9. PRINCIPLE OF ELASTICITY.   *Productivity tends to increase when the same amount of work is achieved in a shorter period of time.*

Since work is elastic and time is not, work normally will be stretched to fit the time set for its completion. Many of you will recognize this as

Rating Scale	Low Performance (%) 1	Below-Average Performance (%) 2	Average Performance (%) 3	Above-Average Performance (%) 4	Outstanding (%) 5
Percentage of prime objectives completed	60	80	100	Quality Point one 150	Quality Point two 200
Merit pay increase	0	2	4	6	8
General increase (across the board)	2	2	2	2	2
Total pay increase	2	4	6	8	10

Figure 3.12 Objectives completion pay rating scale. Performance that falls between rating scales must be interpolated.

Parkinson's Law.[6] Productivity objectives must be managed against this scarce resource of time. Managers cannot delay the clock, therefore they must play the clock. They can only use it to gauge and pace their activities. The pace-setting nature of time is the same whether work is accomplished or not. Productivity requires a timetable for the allocation, arrangement, and use of resources to reach a set of objectives. Time deadlines signal individuals to perform what's needed. It is not just achieving a reduction of 15 percent in operating costs but performing this by the end of the operating quarter. Setting expected results within a schedule or deadline is to set a pace stance that is normal to productivity processes. A results output of processing 10 orders per individual per month is to build a pace stance or productivity into the work process. Productivity tends to increase when the time expectancy for a given amount of work is shortened and the same level of quality is maintained. Productivity increases when work's elasticity is compressed by advancing it to shorter intervals of time.

$$\frac{\text{productivity}}{\text{index}} = \frac{\text{benefits for completing project}}{\text{time to complete project}} = \frac{\$20,000}{4 \text{ weeks}}$$
$$= \$5000 \text{ per week}$$

Case 1: Hold benefits constant, decrease time one-half week.

$$\frac{\text{productivity}}{\text{index}} = \frac{\$20,000}{3.5 \text{ weeks}} = \$5714 \text{ per week}$$

Case 2: Hold benefits constant, decrease time full week.

$$\frac{\text{productivity}}{\text{index}} = \frac{\$20,000}{3 \text{ weeks}} = \$6667 \text{ per week}$$

10. PRINCIPLE OF RESOURCE PRIORITY. *Productivity increases when objectives for productivity set the priorities for resource allocation.*

Resources are scarce! They will always be scarce. The deployment of limited resources for organizational objectives does not automatically assure their efficient use. Since the limited amount of resources tends to change, usually becomes scarcer, productivity will be affected greatly on how these changing limitations are handled. Productivity is maintained and often increased when priorities of resource use follow closely the priorities of benefits from productivity objectives. Resources influence objectives. Benefits influence both objectives and resources. When benefits set the priorities for resource allocation, productivity is more likely to occur. When resources set the priorities of the type of objectives that should be pursued, productivity becomes a matter of trial-and-error. It's like cost reduction slashes without regard to the effects on objectives. More often than not, a one-shot cost reduction move by the manager may save money resources but may lose much more in performance output. Cost reduction efforts work when they are made in the context of performance maintenance or controlled performance reduction. The important point to keep in mind is that benefits and resource allocations should have the same priorities. The rank-order correlation coefficient that is a measure of association between two sets of priorities is the degree of agreement or disagreement between the two array of priorities. The calculation and interpretation of this correlation is as follows:

Step 1. Ten objectives are listed for a department. The benefits that will be achieved for each objective are ranked by consensus, from 1 to 10.

Step 2. Resource allocations in terms of availability, conflicts with other commitments, and value to other programs and departments are ranked for each objective.

Step 3. The rank-order correlation is calculated using the rank-order correlation formula (ρ = rho).

$$\rho = 1 - \frac{6 \sum d^2}{N(N^2 - 1)}$$

where N is the number of objectives that are ranked, d is the difference between the ranks, and Σ is the summing of the differences squared.

Step 4. Interpret the correlation coefficient. The size or magnitude of the coefficient of correlation can be interpreted as the strength of association of a set of benefits with its resource allocation priorities. A positive perfect correlation, $\rho = +1$ means perfect alignment of priorities. A negative perfect correlation, $\rho = -1$ means perfect inverse alignment of priorities. A zero correlation, $\rho = 0$ means no association between the priorities. Values between limits may be interpreted as follows:

Size of ρ	Priority Alignment
.00 to .20	Little or no alignment
.20 to .40	Slight association, doubtful utility
.40 to .60	Useful priorities, well aligned
.60 to .80	Substantially useful, very well aligned
.80 to 1.00	Very high and definite alignment

The value of the correlation coefficient will signal the decision maker to proceed with the differences in priorities or make an attempt to reorder the priorities. In any event, productivity will be high when priorities of resource allocations are closely aligned with the benefits in each objective. Example:

Social Service Department's Objectives	Ranks			
	Benefits	Resource Allocation	d	d^2
1. Diagnostic counseling	1	2	−5	25
2. Financial assistance	2	3	−1	1
3. Short-term counseling	3	7	−4	16
4. Housing for elderly	4	2	2	4
5. Transportation for the aged	5	1	4	16
6. Senior citizens' program	6	8	−2	4
7. Information services	7	4	3	9
8. Senior citizens' nutrition	8	9	−1	1
9. Referral to other agencies	9	5	4	16
10. Employment referral	10	10	0	0

$$\sum d^2 = 92$$

$$\rho = 1 - \frac{6 \times 92}{10\,(100 - 1)} = .442$$

Priorities of benefits and resource allocations are useful and well aligned.

SUMMARY

Productivity is a developing discipline. Unique knowledge and skills are emerging on its behalf. This discipline will continue for some time since scarcity will be a long-term concern. Besides, managing an organization is managing its productivity.

The conceptual view of managing productivity is to view resources in an organization as aggregated to achieve desirable goals and thereby fulfill a mission. Once a level of these goals is achieved, new levels are set. This goal-achievement, resource-use cycle forces the organization to become what the setters want. The productivity process is a planned series of steps from input through transformation to output with a feedback measurement on how well the outcomes were achieved in terms of the resources used.

Productivity is a synergistic process. That is, a change in one part in the process may set up a series of positive reverberations throughout the process so that it's better than it was originally. Thirty factors were identified as parts of the synergistic productivity process. These factors have varying degrees of directness in productivity. Complementary value is a synergistic approach to add equipment and technology to labor-intensive organizations and to add motivation and human factors to equipment-intensive organizations.

Ten principles were introduced as guides to the practitioner as aids in the productivity situation. These principles guide the application of the productivity index and set the stage for a managerial strategy for productivity improvement. The 10 principles are: ratio measurements; shared gain; goal alignment; worker accountability; focus; creating potential productivity; continuance; work justice; elasticity; resource priority.

QUESTIONS TO THINK ABOUT

1. Identify in your organization the types of resources that are becoming difficult to obtain and the effects this is having on organizational productivity. Which ones can best be handled by long-lead procurement?
2. Conceptualize for your organization the productivity process—input-transformation-output sequences—as described in Figure 3.3. Does your organization have a clear understanding of its mission, targeted results, resources needed, work process sequences, and output/input measurements?

3. Think about why a zero-based planning and budgeting system would or wouldn't work for your organization.

4. Describe at least five synergistic processes acting in your organization. Identify five potential ones that could be proposed.

5. How many of the 30 factors in Figure 3.8 directly or indirectly affect productivity in your organization. Which are direct and critical? Are you satisfied that there is sufficient quality in the management of these direct and critical factors?.

6. Identify five synergistic reverberations in your organization. In your analysis of a synergistic reverberation, do you notice that changes are often made in one element without regard to the effects in the others? How can changes best be handled in a situation such as this?

7. Identify if your organization is labor or equipment intensive. How can complementary value be used by your organization?

8. If your organization plans to move from equipment intensive to labor intensive or labor intensive to equipment intensive, how would the 30 factors of productivity determination be handled?

9. How many of the 10 principles of productivity growth are working in your organization?

10. Give five examples of symbiotic states in your organizations.

11. List five organizational needs with five individual needs for your organization that depict needs coincidence.

12. Give some examples of accountability management as defined by the author.

REFERENCES

1. Leon Geenberg, *A Practical Guide to Productivity Measurement,* Bureau of National Affairs, Inc., Washington, D.C., 1973, p. 4.

2. Helen Curtis, *Invitation to Biology,* Worth Publishers, Inc., New York, 1972, p. 460.

3. Paul Mali, *Managing by Objectives,* Wiley-Interscience, New York, 1972, pp. 55–61, pp. 192.

4. Betty Bock and Jack Farkas, *Concentration and Productivity,* National Industrial Conference Board, New York, 1969, pp. 1–13.

5. Marion S. Kellogg, *What To Do About Performance Appraisal,* rev. ed., American Management Association, New York, 1975, p. 87.

6. Northcote Parkinson, *Parkinson's Law,* Houghton Mifflin, New York, 1967, pp. 2–8.

4

MEASUREMENT: THE PRODUCTIVITY BREAKTHROUGH

IN THIS CHAPTER

Pervasiveness of measured productivity.
Five reasons why productivity measurement is avoided.
Quantifying work expectations.
Ratio of qualitative and quantitative factors.
Measurement using productivity ratios.
Measurement using total-factor productivity.
Measurement using management by objectives.
Measurement using productivity check-list indicators.
Measurement using productivity audits.

The need to manage productivity with measurement is found in nearly every work process of nearly every organization and therefore represents a primary goal of the firm. The machinist who grinds 10 flange faces on a pipe per day needs measured productivity to complete his work within a schedule. The waitress who takes the customer's order and fills it within 15 minutes requires measured productivity of a high order to meet customer satisfaction. The medical intern who is confronted with an accident victim gushing blood needs the highest measured productivity in five seconds to stop the bleeding before life ends. The government official who analyzes budget performances of contracting vendors needs measured productivity to make the analysis within a responsive time period for correction in order to avoid overruns. The manager who makes a decision to enter a new market with new products and commits his organization to additional personnel, increased plant capacity, and capital expenditure must use measured productivity to achieve a set of results within an expected period of time. Examples of measured productivity within work processes are endless. Each is a case of delivering a measurable set of results (output) from committed resources (input) within a specified period of time.

If measured productivity is pervasive in organizations and represents a significant goal, it also must be the primary goal of the individual manager. The manager must acquire a positive attitude that initiating improvements is the sum and substance of the job. The manager must mobilize resources and knowledge to make productivity gains happen. The manager must proceed with a measurement system for these gains. A manager should achieve, on a continuing basis, a better ratio of output to input in executing responsibilities that are expected to be carried out. The manager must be able to evaluate this ratio since measurement will be the gauge of progress and achievement within a period of time. The manager must do this while achieving required levels of quality.

This chapter focuses on the core of productivity improvement—its measurement. To be effective any system of productivity requires evaluation—evaluation readily understood, simple to implement, easy to administer, and clearly cost effective. This means that the evaluation system must have a basis of measurement—measurement that must be agreed upon and designed into the system for evaluation to work. Several topics regarding evaluation and measurement are presented in this chapter: (1) who productivity measurement is difficult and what have been the barriers; (2) the value of quantifying work expectations and how this sets up productivity measurement; and (3) measurement techniques that can be used to design an evaluation system for assessing the level of productivity achieved. Four techniques are presented: (1) productivity ratios, (2) total-factor productivity, (3) measurement using management by objectives, and (4) measurement using productivity checklist indicators. A fifth form of measurement, the audit with productivity standards, is a significant enough topic to warrant a separate chapter. Therefore, the productivity audit will be the subject of Chapter 6. These five techniques of measuring productivity form the basis to evaluate productivity in organizations. These measurement techniques are used more fully in other chapters dealing with critical topics in productivity.

WHY PRODUCTIVITY MEASUREMENT IS DIFFICULT

The measurement of productivity as a discipline has clearly been slow. Few, if any, organizations use productivity measurements as a day-to-day, week-to-week, or month-to-month tool. There are several reasons for this.

1. *Work Processes Are Complex and Unwieldy.* Any measure used tends to

oversimplify the real complexity of workflow, equipment, people, and technical processes. Much of a workflow process is submerged and out of sight. It is seldom as perceptible or dramatic as a scrap pile, shut down machine, absent employee, or variances in the budget. Casual observation or surface information will not make it evident. A single yardstick to measure this complexity is clearly an oversimplification. For example, output per manhour is too much of an oversimplification. As work complexes grow in size and number, the single yardstick becomes virtually useless. One way to overcome this disadvantage is to use several yardsticks or measures. The greater the number of ratio indexes used for measurement, the greater the validity of productivity measurement. In his excellent book, Westwick stressed that several ratios must be developed for one organization, with additional ratios for different levels of management.[1] This would mean each organization would have its own "model of measurement" that would be unique and not very useful for other organizations.

2. *Measurements Are Made After Work is in Process.* Traditionally, work is designed and implemented for functional reasons, and ways are sought to measure it later. Most organizations have had their work processes instituted for years, making it difficult to incorporate evaluative measures. An open work design procedure is needed to overcome this problem by building in measures for productivity before the work processes are implemented. Furthermore, work processes already in operation will need to be revised for productivity measurement. A future requirement for work design processes will no doubt demand evaluative measures for productivity purposes. No work should be planned or carried out unless its productivity can be measured and evaluated.

3. *Generalized Terms Inhibit the Use of Evaluative Measures.* Most work processes are described in such language that a variety of meanings are implied. This is not intentional! Uncertainties, lack of information, and generalizations have prevented pinning down exactly what's happening and what's required. Examples of words whose meanings are difficult to understand are: *streamline, economic, quality, growth, service, morale, attitude, timely,* and so on. These terms cover such an elusive broad range that assigning quantitative measures is difficult or impossible. Although these terms are an acceptable part of our day-to-day language in management, they should not be used when expressing an evaluative measure for productivity. Measuring productivity will move more rapidly when terms that indicate how much or to what extent are used. Generalized terms should be accompanied or modified by *percentages, ratios, averages, index numbers, time units, cost units, degrees,*

and so on. Examples of these are: *increase 10 percent, reduce 10 rejects per person, hold expenses to 5 percent of sales,* and so on.

4. *Measurements Have Been Activity Oriented Rather Than Output Oriented.* A failure to focus on the output of workflow tends to cause a loss of direction and forces a drift toward the hustle and bustle of activities. Since many activities are needed in a work process, it takes little effort to become engrossed within them. As a result, the "activity trap"— conducting activities for the sake of activities—emerges. This measurement flow can be overcome by defining the work processes in terms of what the organization is trying to achieve rather than the activities it can conduct. Measurements defined and incorporated at the output phases of a work process tend to give more precise and meaningful evaluations of productivity of the process.

5. *Measurements Are Used at the Macrolevel of Economy.* Productivity as a concept and measurement has traditionally been in the domain of the economist. Like GNP, productivity is viewed as a comparison between the total quantity of goods and services produced in the economy in turning out goods and services. This view is much too broad and nebulous to be useful for a single organization. Measurements are needed that relate and are useful at the firm level, measurements that evaluate the productivity processes within the organization. Any generalized measurements will fall short of the mark.

THE VALUE OF QUANTIFYING WORK EXPECTATIONS

Attempts to measure productivity have been varied and usually limited in scope—like checking the temperature of the human body and declaring, when it is a certain level, that a life is in excellent shape. Quantifiable factors in the productivity process such as costs, time, and performance can be evaluated, yet the experienced practitioner knows that everything cannot be measured—at least with our present knowledge. This would suggest that evaluations of complex productivity processes should be made with caution—they should be decision-making tools only.

For evaluative purposes, productivity can and should be quantified. The evaluations can be costly or inexpensive, technically or loosely defined, comprehensive or selective in coverage, tailored or generalized to the needs of the organization. The organization should choose to select and construct its form of evaluation with the aim of assessing the amount of productivity change over time. There are many advantages to quantifying productivity change in work expectations. Let's examine each one.

1. Quantified work expectations define and clarify the elements of expected results better than any verbal description. They provide a better configuration of what is expected. "To improve morale" is a generalization, but "to improve morale by reducing monthly grievance rate from 10 to 5" is a quantified target and a specific way to evaluate it.

2. Quantified work expectations build in measures of effectiveness and efficiency. The process of evaluating progress toward an end result is difficult, if not impossible, with qualitative statements. Using an evaluative measure to describe a future result provides a way of evaluating the current activities that will make it happen. Management can see the relationships among data, resources, and skills needed to deal with specific situations. The reduction of the grievance rate from 10 to 5 to improve morale suggests the relationship among several skills and activities, such as handling people, knowing the labor contract, and being able to "nip trouble in the bud."

3. Quantified work expectations can be enlarged or reduced for progressive performance stretches. This is hardly possible with generalizations. To improve morale by reducing the grievance rate from 10 to 5 for the first year implies a second-year effort to reduce the rate from 5 to 3. Reducing costs 10 percent for the first year suggests a progressive reduction for subsequent years. Quantitative techniques give work statements an intrinsic manipulative value—what is, results can be manipulated both to direction and the speed at which they are achieved.

4. Quantitative work expectations offer a means of keeping unknowns and uncertainties at a given level; the quantitative feature helps us see the effects the results will have on other areas. To reduce the grievance rate from 10 to 5 implies the need for a sharper and better level of supervision. If training is necessary, how much will it cost? When can it be conducted? What will the program consist of? Implications derived from quantitative statements tend to make unknowns more knowable.

The value of quantified work expectations cannot be overestimated. It is a most effective way to increase the rationality of decision making and managing. With quantified work expectations on the outcomes of projects, programs, and tasks, judgments of many kinds can be made in budget allocations and priorities, program planning and accountability, and need assessments and focus. But all work cannot be quantified; therefore, qualitative assessments often prove useful to evaluate productivity. As a guide, highly structured, repetitive tasks tend to be suited to quantitative evaluation. However, creative, abstract, nonrepetitive tasks tend to be better suited to qualitative evaluation. Between these two extremes there is always a mix of quantitative and qualitative measures. Instead of considering quantitative and qualitative evaluation as mutually exclusive, the evaluator should regard them interdependent—that is, productivity evaluations can be made by both quantitative and qualitative assessment as shown in Figure 4.1.

The experienced practitioner need not to be convinced that the nature of work in real organizational situations will contain both quantitative and qualitative factors. Hence, evaluating productivity will require combinations of the two: qualitative assessment (*a*) and quantitative assessment (*b*). In either event, measurement or evaluation in itself is not results. Measurements that center on results is what is wanted.

MEASUREMENT USING PRODUCTIVITY RATIOS

The concept of productivity stressed in this book is that productivity is not solely performance or solely good utilization of resources. It is the combination of both. Its measurement compares these two important

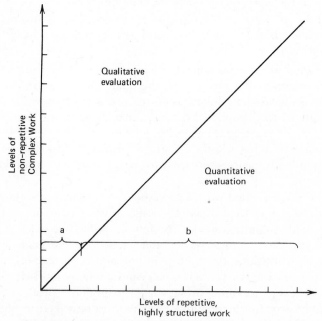

Figure 4.1 Evaluating productivity requires both quantitative and qualitative factors.

variables in a ratio of their magnitudes. Productivity is the highest performance possible with the least utilization of resources. A special study of the federal sector conducted by representatives of the Civil Service Commission, General Accounting Offices, and the Office of Management and Audit have stressed this important point.[2] This is illustrated in Figure 4.2, which shows the wide changes in results (output) and resources (man-years) for industrial services. Nonetheless, productivity, the net difference, has increased.

The productivity index and the principle of ratio-time measurement described in previous chapters sets the basis of evaluating productivity using ratios. The comparison of the two variables may be made as a ratio of single parameters such as labor and labor, dollars and dollars, hours and hours, incidents and incidents, or complaints and complaints; or it may be made with several parameters such as net outputs when several inputs are required, man-hours of labor, machine time, amount of material, and capacity utilization. According to Westwick, the number of productivity ratios that are possible in a firm are unlimited with this ratio concept.[3] How they are interpreted and related to the overall operations can be controversial, but they are the same as financial ratios, which have the same controversial interpretation. Practice, comparative use, and historic validation are methods for giving productivity ratios meaning and validity. They could never give precision and accuracy. Single ratios

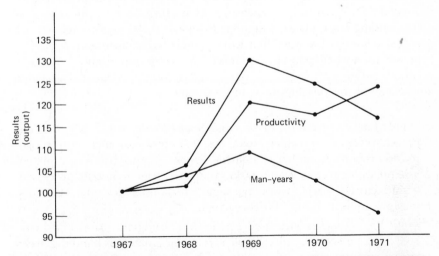

Figure 4.2   Changes in productivity in industrial services (1967–1971). Productivity =
$$\frac{\text{results}}{\text{resources}}.$$

should never be used. Using many ratios, as a group, is a method of guiding managerial judgments and analysis. These ratios show the comparisons of how resources are being utilized within an organization and between organizations of comparable size. Against this qualification, then, several key ratios can be developed for evaluating productivity in an organization. In summary, to use these ratios meaningfully, the following guidelines are suggested:

1. Use several ratios that have historic validity for the organization.
2. Build in ratio measures while the work processes for productivity are being designed, planned, and developed.
3. Change general terms to quantified expressions that tell how much and what is needed.
4. Focus the ratio toward the output of the process rather than its activities.
5. Select ratios that are useful at the firm level rather than at the macrolevel of the economy.

We suggest five categories of ratios representing the productivity index: (1) overall indexes—measures of the final outputs of the entire organization related to the resource inputs, (2) objectives ratios—measures of the achievements of individual managers or departments at the end of a schedule related to the objectives that were planned at the beginning of the schedule, (3) cost ratios—measures of performance output related to corresponding costs, (4) work standards—measures of work units or work packages achieved by individual work centers or departments related to expected or normal standards practiced in other organizations, (5) time standards ratios—measures of performance output related to needed time. Some of the variables used in these ratios are:

1. *Output Variables (Results, Performance, and Effectiveness).* Services rendered, revenues, products sold, cost benefits, customers, units produced, reports completed, failures generated, programs completed, assemblies, deliveries made, tasks completed, raw materials processed, manufactured parts, work packages, responsibilities met, benefits, machine utilization, standards reached.
2. *Input Variables (Resources and Efficiency).* Budgets, space, land, payroll, costs, personnel, time, supplies, fees paid, materials handling, work orders, compensation, rent, equipment, computers, required standards, raw materials.

The five categories of measurement of the productivity index are illustrated in Figures 4.3 to 4.8. These are examples only! Once the reader grasps the basic concept of productivity, an endless variety of ratios is possible. They can be used within a planned time period or as a reference in some time period to be chosen as a base period. The formula to be used for a base period follows:

$$\frac{\text{productivity}}{\text{index}} = \frac{\text{productivity, current year}}{\text{productivity, base year}}$$

$$= \frac{\dfrac{\text{results, current year}}{\text{resources, current year}}}{\dfrac{\text{results, base year}}{\text{resources, base year}}} \times 100$$

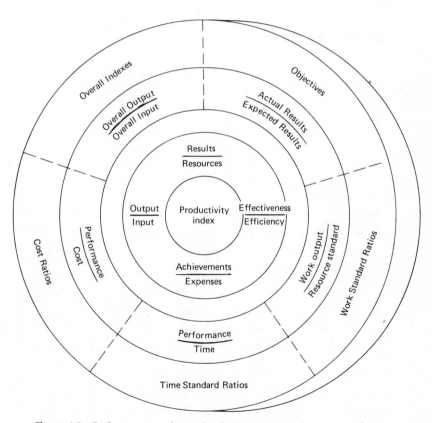

Figure 4.3   Ratio measures for evaluating productivity in an organization.

1. *Business and industry*

   (a) $\dfrac{\text{Sales}}{\text{Employees}}$

   (b) $\dfrac{\text{Space utilized}}{\text{Space available}}$

   (c) $\dfrac{\text{Market share now}}{\text{Market share in base year}}$

   (d) $\dfrac{\text{Sales lost}}{\text{Customer complaints}}$

   (e) $\dfrac{\text{Profit}}{\text{Equity capitol}}$

   (f) $\dfrac{\text{Actual price paid}}{\text{Market price}}$

2. *Government*

   (a) $\dfrac{\text{Benefits}}{\text{Costs}}$

   (b) $\dfrac{\text{Legislation authorized}}{\text{Legislation proposed}}$

   (c) $\dfrac{\text{Quits}}{\text{Employees}}$

   (d) $\dfrac{\text{Budget performance}}{\text{Authorized budget}}$

   (e) $\dfrac{\text{Prices now}}{\text{Prices at base year}}$

   (f) $\dfrac{\text{Gains from legislative enactments}}{\text{Cost of enactments}}$

3. *Education*

   (a) $\dfrac{\text{Enrollment}}{\text{Faculty}}$

   (b) $\dfrac{\text{Class count} \times \text{credit hours}}{\text{Direct costs}}$

   (c) $\dfrac{\text{Personnel costs}}{\text{Employees}}$

   (d) $\dfrac{\text{Income/expense}}{\text{Faculty}}$

   (e) $\dfrac{\text{Research projects completed}}{\text{Costs of projects}}$

   (f) $\dfrac{\text{Tuition}}{\text{Administrative staff}}$

4. *Health and human services*

   (a) $\dfrac{\text{Cost of patient care}}{\text{Number admitted}}$

   (b) $\dfrac{\text{Treatment plans implemented}}{\text{Total treatment plans}}$

   (c) $\dfrac{\text{Client caseload}}{\text{Professional staff}}$

   (d) $\dfrac{\text{Beds occupied}}{\text{Beds available}}$

   (e) $\dfrac{\text{Revenues}}{\text{Patients}}$

   (f) $\dfrac{\text{Training costs}}{\text{Employees}}$

Figure 4.4 Overall indexes.

1. *Business and industry*

   (a) $\dfrac{\text{Projects completed}}{\text{Projects planned}}$

   (b) $\dfrac{\text{Progress in labor negotiations}}{\text{Expected schedule}}$

   (c) $\dfrac{\text{Marketing products adopted}}{\text{Feasible ideas}}$

   (d) $\dfrac{\text{Work packages}}{\text{Expected work packages}}$

   (e) $\dfrac{\text{Sales level}}{\text{Expected inventory}}$

   (f) $\dfrac{\text{Quits}}{\text{Desired level of quits}}$

2. *Government*

   (a) $\dfrac{\text{Highways built}}{\text{Highways needed}}$

   (b) $\dfrac{\text{Actual contributed value}}{\text{Expected contributed value}}$

   (c) $\dfrac{\text{Settlement of claims}}{\text{Total claims}}$

   (d) $\dfrac{\text{Convictions}}{\text{Arrests}}$

   (e) $\dfrac{\text{Benefits}}{\text{Expected benefits}}$

   (f) $\dfrac{\text{Contracts renegotiated}}{\text{Needed renegotiations}}$

3. *Education*

   (a) $\dfrac{\text{Benefits from research projects}}{\text{Expected benefits}}$

   (b) $\dfrac{\text{Skills prevailing}}{\text{Skills needed}}$

   (c) $\dfrac{\text{Behavioral outcomes}}{\text{Behavioral outcome desired}}$

   (d) $\dfrac{\text{Handicapped children trained}}{\text{Total to be trained}}$

   (e) $\dfrac{\text{Minorities completing program}}{\text{Expected completions}}$

   (f) $\dfrac{\text{Faculty ratings in current year}}{\text{Expected ratings}}$

4. *Health and human services*

   (a) $\dfrac{\text{Steps completed in treatment}}{\text{Total steps}}$

   (b) $\dfrac{\text{Treatment plans}}{\text{Budget allocation}}$

   (c) $\dfrac{\text{Prescriptions filled}}{\text{Expected prescriptions filled}}$

   (d) $\dfrac{\text{Preventive medical programs}}{\text{Total desired}}$

   (e) $\dfrac{\text{Client caseloads}}{\text{Expected total}}$

   (f) $\dfrac{\text{Patients admitted}}{\text{Patients needed}}$

Figure 4.5 Objectives ratios.

1. *Business and industry*

   (a) $\dfrac{\text{Sales}}{\text{Operating costs}}$

   (b) $\dfrac{\text{Borrowed capitol}}{\text{Borrowing costs}}$

   (c) $\dfrac{\text{Inventory}}{\text{Advertising costs}}$

   (d) $\dfrac{\text{Rejects}}{\text{Costs}}$

   (e) $\dfrac{\text{Turnover}}{\text{Costs}}$

   (f) $\dfrac{\text{Rework}}{\text{Costs}}$

2. *Government*

   (a) $\dfrac{\text{Transactions}}{\text{D P costs}}$

   (b) $\dfrac{\text{renegotiated contracts}}{\text{Cost of renegotiations}}$

   (c) $\dfrac{\text{Recruits selected}}{\text{Costs}}$

   (d) $\dfrac{\text{Mail processed}}{\text{Payroll cost}}$

   (e) $\dfrac{\text{Benefits from proposal}}{\text{Cost of proposal}}$

   (f) $\dfrac{\text{Legislative enactments}}{\text{Cost of enactments}}$

3. *Education*

   (a) $\dfrac{\text{Tuition generated}}{\text{Cost of generation}}$

   (b) $\dfrac{\text{Dropouts}}{\text{Cost of enrollment}}$

   (c) $\dfrac{\text{Benefits of research projects}}{\text{Cost of projects}}$

   (d) $\dfrac{\text{Students graduating}}{\text{Annual costs}}$

   (e) $\dfrac{\text{Budget value}}{\text{Allocated budget}}$

   (f) $\dfrac{\text{Meals served}}{\text{Cost of cafeteria operation}}$

4. *Health and human services*

   (a) $\dfrac{\text{Trainees completing programs}}{\text{Training costs}}$

   (b) $\dfrac{\text{Design of therapeutic treatment}}{\text{Cost of design}}$

   (c) $\dfrac{\text{Research reports}}{\text{Allocated budget}}$

   (d) $\dfrac{\text{Client caseloads}}{\text{Cost of interviews}}$

   (e) $\dfrac{\text{Beds occupied}}{\text{Cost of bed occupancy}}$

   (f) $\dfrac{\text{Patients admitted}}{\text{Cost of admission}}$

Figure 4.6 Cost ratios.

1. *Business and industry*

   (a) $\dfrac{\text{Machines operating}}{\text{Setup time}}$

   (b) $\dfrac{\text{Value of returned goods}}{\text{Purchases}}$

   (c) $\dfrac{\text{Grievances settled}}{\text{Grievances investigated}}$

   (d) $\dfrac{\text{Workload assignments}}{\text{Engineering staff}}$

   (e) $\dfrac{\text{Actual labor per unit}}{\text{Scheduled labor per unit}}$

   (f) $\dfrac{\text{Accepted products}}{\text{Products produced}}$

2. *Government*

   (a) $\dfrac{\text{Benefits from a project}}{\text{Total task required}}$

   (b) $\dfrac{\text{Settlement of unfair labor charges}}{\text{Investigation of charges}}$

   (c) $\dfrac{\text{Compliance of board orders}}{\text{Investigation of on-compliance}}$

   (d) $\dfrac{\text{Board adjudications}}{\text{Total hearings}}$

   (e) $\dfrac{\text{Buying costs}}{\text{Purchases}}$

   (f) $\dfrac{\text{Value added}}{\text{Contract changes}}$

3. *Education*

   (a) $\dfrac{\text{Research projects completed}}{\text{Procedure used}}$

   (b) $\dfrac{\text{Achievement attainment}}{\text{Standardized test}}$

   (c) $\dfrac{\text{Graduates}}{\text{Standardized curriculum}}$

   (d) $\dfrac{\text{Graduates reading in 50th percent}}{\text{Standardized reading test}}$

   (e) $\dfrac{\text{Implemented recommendations}}{\text{Committees}}$

   (f) $\dfrac{\text{Graduates}}{\text{Curriculums}}$

4. *Health and human services*

   (a) $\dfrac{\text{Client caseload}}{\text{Standard caseload}}$

   (b) $\dfrac{\text{Prescriptions filled}}{\text{Standard procedure}}$

   (c) $\dfrac{\text{Patients admitted}}{\text{Standard admissions}}$

   (d) $\dfrac{\text{Absenteeism}}{\text{Industry standard}}$

   (e) $\dfrac{\text{Skills displayed in a situation}}{\text{Skills trained for in a procedure}}$

   (f) $\dfrac{\text{Rework backlog}}{\text{Rework procedure}}$

Figure 4.7 Work standards.

1. *Business and industry*

   (a) $\dfrac{\text{Production}}{\text{Working days}}$

       $\dfrac{\text{Actual machine hours per unit}}{\text{Scheduled machine hours per unit}}$

   (b) $\dfrac{\text{Reject work}}{\text{Standard hours to produce}}$

   (d) $\dfrac{\text{Inventory buildup}}{\text{Average daily purchases}}$

   (e) $\dfrac{\text{Overtime hours}}{\text{Total hours}}$

   (f) $\dfrac{\text{Rework}}{\text{Time for rework}}$

2. *Government*

   (a) $\dfrac{\text{Working time}}{\text{Total time}}$

   (b) $\dfrac{\text{Man-days lost}}{\text{Man-days worked}}$

   (c) $\dfrac{\text{Gains from legislative enactments}}{\text{Time period of the gain}}$

   (d) $\dfrac{\text{Service to noncrime calls}}{\text{Time devoted to noncrime calls}}$

   (e) $\dfrac{\text{Benefits from project}}{\text{Time to complete project}}$

   (f) $\dfrac{\text{Renegotiated contracts}}{\text{Time for renegotiation}}$

3. *Education*

   (a) $\dfrac{\text{Teaching days in a schedule}}{\text{Teaching days lost}}$

   (b) $\dfrac{\text{Research projects completed}}{\text{Time required}}$

   (c) $\dfrac{\text{Faculty plans submitted}}{\text{Time required}}$

   (d) $\dfrac{\text{Minorities in program}}{\text{Standard time required}}$

   (e) $\dfrac{\text{Skills level attained}}{\text{Standard time required}}$

   (f) $\dfrac{\text{Benefits from project}}{\text{Total hours}}$

4. *Health and human services*

   (a) $\dfrac{\text{Meals served}}{\text{Standard time}}$

   (b) $\dfrac{\text{Implementation of new therapeutic treatment}}{\text{Manhours to complement}}$

   (c) $\dfrac{\text{Prescriptions filled}}{\text{Average man-hours}}$

   (d) $\dfrac{\text{Patients admitted}}{\text{Man-hours to admit}}$

   (e) $\dfrac{\text{Client caseloads}}{\text{Man-hours to complete}}$

   (f) $\dfrac{\text{Sickness treatment}}{\text{Standard time}}$

Figure 4.8 Time standard ratios.

A productivity index can be established to indicate the percentage change that has occurred relative to the base period. This base period allows comparison of two or more sets of productivity in two or more areas.

MEASUREMENT USING TOTAL-FACTOR PRODUCTIVITY

In principle, total-factor productivity is a ratio of output to *all* inputs required to deliver the output. This ratio concept moves closer to the realities of productivity in a work process since all resources are "factored" in the calculation. Thus there is currently a great deal of interest in its use. Takeuchi at Harvard completed a massive study of supermarket productivity, formulating a total-factor index to measure productivity in supermarkets based on the time needed to perform 60 different tasks in 100 product categories.[4] The ratio used was selected components of standard time to labor hours. The study revealed that sales as a measure of output was too biased because of different price structures. With the time-standard index, the only problem is to see how efficiently labor is being used. Takeuchi uses his study to determine the most efficient size of a large supermarket chain. For example, he claims productivity starts to go down after the size of the store reaches 27,000 square feet, has more than nine checkout counters, remains open more than 88 hours per week, and is older than six years. This measurement of productivity can provide significant decisions related to growth, expansion, and efficiency.

Because of the complexities of a situation, the total-factor productivity ratio relates output to labor and/or selected components of capital, space, supplies, and so on. This suggests that total-factor productivity must be developed within the firm or within the industry using critical and significant factors. Total-factor ratio is as follows:

$$\frac{\text{total-factor}}{\text{productivity}} = \frac{\text{output}}{\text{all inputs}} = \frac{\text{output}}{\text{labor} + \text{capital} + \text{resources} + \text{miscellaneous}}$$

The ratio is useful to larger views of the economy or larger organizations whose complex interplay of variables affecting productivity is not easily seen. The ratio is especially useful when there is a need to evaluate changes that may occur in production, sales, budgets, wages and salaries, cost measures, inventories, plant investment, and other inputs. Output may be related to one, several, or all measurable inputs, depending on the purpose and type of comparisons to be made. Frequently output is physical volume of a series of products. Labor input can be direct labor, indirect labor, salaried personnel, utilities labor, or any service departments directly supporting the output. Captial as a component of input would consist of investment, equipment depreciation, securities, or other forms of capital.

Tracking and charting the changes that occur in different time periods is the most useful application of total-factor productivity. Organizations construct and use indexes of total-factor productivity by first breaking it down into each of its components such as output per unit of labor, output per unit of capital, output per unit of materials, and so on. This allows the organization to analyze the changing costs of the inputs when combined or when separated in terms of both their prices and quantities. The essential requirement is that input be expressed or combined in constant-dollar terms. This means value of labor and capital must be expressed in values of base-year comparisons. If this is not done, an undue amount of weight may be given to one or another.

An example of the use of total-factor productivity in a small manufacturing organization follows:

	1975 (Base Year)	1976	1977
Output			
Sales (adjusted for inventory)	$800,000	$940,000	$1,110,000
Input			
Materials and supplies	290,000	305,000	325,000
Purchased services	80,000	82,000	86,000
Depreciation	16,000	16,500	17,100
Interest	12,000	12,600	17,200
Labor (wages and salaries)	285,000	294,000	301,000
Capital investment income	96,000	101,000	105,000
Total all inputs	$779,000	$811,100	$ 851,300
Productivity-factor ratios			
All inputs	1.03	.16	1.30
Labor only	2.81	3.19	3.69
Labor plus capital	2.09	2.38	2.73

Figures used in this calculation of total-factor productivity are taken from balance-sheet and income-statement statistics. As one can see from the ratios, there is a healthy growth in productivity in this small firm from the period 1975 to 1977.

A variation of the total-factor productivity is to use a "total productivity link series." This is the sum of a series of productivity ratios of various units or departments within an organization. This is expressed as follows:

$$\begin{array}{c} \text{total productivity} \\ \text{link series} \end{array} = \sum_{n=1}^{k} \left(\frac{P_1}{R_1} + \frac{P_2}{R_2} + \frac{P_3}{R_3} + \cdots \frac{P_k}{R_k} \right)$$

Where P is the performance factor of unique departments and R is the resource factor of these same departments, the ratio P/R is the productivity index. This can be illustrated with a town government as follows:

Library

$$PI = \frac{\text{books checked out}}{\text{library staff}} = \frac{30,000}{10} = 3000$$

Police

$$PI = \frac{\text{class II crimes solved}}{\text{total number of retailers}} = \frac{2400}{600} = 4.0$$

Social services

$$PI = \frac{\text{number of clients served}}{\text{social service staff}} = \frac{400}{2} = 200$$

Public works

$$PI = \frac{\text{tons of refuse disposed}}{\text{population}} = \frac{270,000}{30,000} = 9$$

Health services

$$PI = \frac{\text{number of restaurants} \times \text{quality check list}}{\text{number of staff}} = \frac{60 \times 4}{3} = 80$$

Recreation

$$PI = \frac{\text{programs} \times \text{users}}{\text{facility area}} = \frac{20 \times 20,000}{50,000} = 8$$

The chief use of the total productivity link series is not in the absolute values of each of the ratios; it is in the relative comparison during intervals of time. Tracking the total productivity value with changes can give a sense of total productivity of the organization. Reducing each ratio to an integer, the link series becomes:

$$\begin{array}{c} \text{total productivity} \\ \text{link series} \end{array} = 3000 + 4.0 + 200 + 9 + 80 + 8.0 = 3301$$

MEASUREMENT USING MANAGING BY OBJECTIVES

Managing by objectives (MBO) as a process[5] has given managers a variety of benefits in its use—for example, planning, performance appraisals, motivation of subordinates, management development, coordinated teamwork. An advantage of its use that is not frequently mentioned is its "yardstick" ability to provide evaluation of achievement and evaluation of progress toward achievement. This means that the MBO process can set up measures of effectiveness (output) and efficiency (input) in the context of a planned work process from start to finish. This implies planning for and control of productivity. MBO as a measurement process forces recognition of the possibilities of how to increase efficiency while incurring a cost of effectiveness or how to increase effectiveness while incurring a cost of efficiency. Either way, the process will reveal the gains while dealing with attendant losses. This ensures that planned work will not, in fact, prove counterproductive.

There are numerous variations of MBO, but all seem to possess certain elements in common. In general, MBO attempts to plan future results by involving managers and subordinates in the areas of responsibility. It identifies the organization's mission and goals and uses them to guide the individual manager to formulate individual objectives. When completed, they represent measures of performance on how well the individual has met responsibilities and furthered the organization in its mission. MBO is based on several assumptions that seems to hold true:

1. People perform better when they know where they are going and how to get there.
2. People perform better when they are allowed to influence the decision about where they are going.
3. People perform better when they receive some indication of performance.
4. People perform better when they see others formally attempting to improve their performance.
5. People perform better when rewards are given in direct relation to performance efforts.
6. People perform better when there is a feeling of achievement, recognition, and growth in their work.

The MBO process as a way of managing productivity is discussed further in the next chapter. This section is to give the basic format of using MBO as an evaluative productivity measure. As such, managing by objectives can also be considered as measurement by objectives. This is outlined in the following steps, along with an example.

Steps	Method	Example
1. Identify duty or expectancy	Goals, mission statements, or job descriptions	Rehabilitate emotionally disturbed children
2. Determine performance factors, resources to be used, and required quality level	Treatment programs, clinicians, therapeutic procedures	10 clinical actions completed, 2 clinicians to do work, regressions held to 4
3. Calculate productivity index	$PI = \dfrac{effectiveness}{efficiency} = \dfrac{high\ performance}{best\ use\ of\ resources}$	$PI = \dfrac{10\ clinical\ actions}{2\ clinicians} = 5$ $PI = \dfrac{4\ regressions}{10\ clinical\ actions}$ $= .40$ regression rate
4. Formulate objective with evaluative productivity measure	Supervisor and subordinate communicate and agree	Complete 10 clinical actions on a treatment plan with no more than 4 regressions by January 1 using 2 clinicians
5. Set up progress milestones	Suitable timeline	Complete 2 clinical actions per month

To use this MBO format will require the ability to identify key responsibilities and translate them into a measurable objective. Since not all responsibilities can be quantified into measurable objectives, qualitative measures could provide an indirect form of measurement. The following list illustrates both quantitative and qualitative evaluative productivity measures.

Duties and Responsibilities	Measurable Objectives
1. Install electrical installations in accordance with customer specifications	Complete 1400 installations with no more than 2 personnel $PI = \dfrac{1400}{2} = \dfrac{700\ installation}{person}$
2. Supervise transportation system to meet the needs of the citizenry of the city	Achieve an administrative performance to keep incidents no greater than 10 from the checklist of incidents: (a) Complaints by customers

(b) Start vehicles on schedule

(c) Vehicle breakdown

(d) Vehicle accidents

$$PI = \frac{9 \text{ incidents}}{10 \text{ incidents}} = 90\%$$

3. Develop and process computer programs

Complete 10 programs with an average of 10 days to complete

$$PI = \frac{10 \text{ programs}}{10 \text{ days}} = \frac{1 \text{ program}}{\text{day}}$$

4. Process corporate records for central storage

Complete process of 35,000 boxes with no more than 5% error using 12 employees

$$PI = \frac{1700 \text{ boxes}}{12 \text{ employees}} = \frac{142 \text{ boxes}}{\text{employees}}$$

5. Teach talented or gifted children in 8th and 9th grades

Complete 10 learning projects within a year with no more than 2 incomplete projects; achievement level no less than 80%

$$PI = \frac{8 \text{ completed projects}}{10 \text{ planned projects}}$$

$$= .80 \text{ completion rate}$$

$$PI = \frac{.20 \text{ unattainable}}{8 \text{ completed projects}}$$

$$= .25 \text{ unattainable rate}$$

6. Provide mechanical designs of rotating and static hardware in aircraft engines

Submit 3 designs to reduce weight from 2 pounds to 5 pounds

$$PI = \frac{2.0 \text{ reduced weight}}{5.0 \text{ expected weight}} = .40 \text{ ratio}$$

7. Redetermine eligibility of welfare recipients

Process 100 redetermination interviews with no more than 5 workers

$$PI = \frac{100 \text{ interviews}}{5 \text{ workers}} = \frac{20 \text{ interviews}}{\text{worker}}$$

8. Instruct new employees to broaden abilities of workers to new product knowledge areas

Increase employee product knowledge 25% over previous year with pre- and post-tests

(a) Learning seminars—1 per month

(b) Weekly rap sessions

(c) Required selected readings and discussion

(d) Selected job assignments

$$PI = \frac{1.25 \text{ post-test performance}}{1.00 \text{ pretest performance}}$$

= .25 increase in product knowledge

9. Prepare regional profit plans from corporate goals and objectives

Complete regional profit plan with no less than 20% net contribution

$$PI = \frac{\$500,000 \text{ sales}}{\$400,000 \text{ expenses}}$$

= 20% net contribution

10. Assist other departments to prepare their departmental budgets

Complete 8 departmental budgets within 30 days with no more than 1 reworked budget

$$PI = \frac{30 \text{ days}}{8 \text{ budgets}} = \frac{3.75 \text{ days}}{\text{budget}}$$

$$PI = \frac{1 \text{ reworked budget}}{8 \text{ budgets}}$$

= .125 rework rate

11. Receive and process distributor quotations through accounting, purchasing, and engineering departments

Complete 5 quotations with an average of 15 days for each quotation & no more than 1% error

$$PI = \frac{5 \text{ quotes}}{15 \text{ days}} = \frac{1 \text{ quote}}{3 \text{ days}}$$

$$PI = \frac{1200 \text{ accepted orders}}{1212 \text{ total orders}}$$

= .99 acceptance rate

12. Assist with language and negotiations in collective bargaining contracts

Complete negotiation strategies checklist of 26 items with no more than two incomplete or repeat items by March 1

$$PI = \frac{2 \text{ incomplete items}}{26 \text{ checklist items}}$$

= .076 repeat rate

13. Provide coverage to broad media on company's traffic safety program

Complete 30 newspaper or TV press releases mentioning company's safety program with 80% actually accepted for release to public

$$PI = \frac{24 \text{ acceptances}}{30 \text{ total released}}$$

= 80% acceptance rate

14. Increase home office mi-
    norities in management

Increase minorities in management from
25 to 28 by end of 3 years

$$PI = \frac{10 \text{ new hires}}{25 \text{ minority employment}}$$

= 40% increase in minorities

$$PI = \frac{3 \text{ new managers}}{3 \text{ years}} = \frac{1 \text{ manager}}{\text{year}}$$

15. Prepare factual and statis-
    tical reports for manage-
    ment information system

Complete all reports and correspondence
as requested with no more than 60%
error completion rate

$$PI = \frac{10 \text{ completed reports}}{6 \text{ errors} \times 10 \text{ reports}}$$

= .16 rate

16. Prepare reports as re-
    quired by investment offi-
    cer

Complete all required reports with no
more than 20% of allocated time. *Report
checklist:*
(a) Cash flow report
(b) Investment income report
(c) Investment description on securities
(d) Report on public securities
(e) Document research reports
(f) Field trip information trips

$$PI = \frac{160 \text{ total hours}}{32 \text{ report hours}}$$

= 5.0 rate of total

17. Maintain required inven-
    tory of math materials,
    supplies equipment, text-
    books, and learning aids

Complete 10-item checklist of inventories
for all math classrooms

$$PI = \frac{10 \text{ inventory items} \times 10 \text{ rooms}}{10 \text{ classrooms}}$$

= 10 readiness rate

18. Assist evaluators in moni-
    toring teaching objectives

Complete 10 observations per month for
9 months

$$PI = \frac{90 \text{ observations}}{9 \text{ months}} = \frac{10 \text{ observation}}{\text{month}}$$

19. Prepare architectural site
    drawings

Complete architectual site drawings with
drawings standards
(a) High detailed—60 hours
(b) Average detail—40 hours

(c) Simple detail—20 hours

$$PI = \frac{60 \text{ high detail hours}}{50 \text{ actual hours}}$$

= 1.2 rate

20. Practice epidemiology in accordance with current practice

Complete interviews on 12 infectious VD cases assigned to clinic on monthly basis

$$PI = \frac{12 \text{ cases interviewed}}{12 \text{ cases assigned/month}}$$

= 1.0

$$PI = \frac{1 \text{ case incompleted}}{12 \text{ cases assigned/month}}$$

= .1 reinterview rate

$$PI = \frac{24 \text{ contacts located}}{30 \text{ contacts named}}$$

= .80 infected brought to medical attention

MEASUREMENT USING PRODUCTIVITY CHECKLIST INDICATORS

Quantitative measurement of productivity in many phases of work life is often difficult, if not impossible. However, through experience and informal guidelines, many practitioners have developed indicators for identifying productivity actions that would lead to high levels of productivity. Productivity checklist indicators represent "judged actions" by senior or experienced practitioners that would to the job needed. Checklist indicators may represent a consensus of several practitioners on the important steps or items that would solve a problem or lead to the needed level of productivity. Thus the checklist format is particularly useful in presenting these steps or items. Checklist indicators usually itemize what the worker should do. They do not specify how or why the work should be done. It's a framework to ensure that all that needs to be taken into account before the entire project or task is considered completed. Incidentally, checklist indicators serve as excellent thought provokers. Seeing a list gives an overview but suggests omissions and deletions. The lists are usually easily understood and can be used by inexperienced employees. Checklists, however, should be used with caution since they imply completeness and directness.

Evaluations using checklist indicators can, in an indirect way, measure productivity by specifying the actions to be taken that can measure both performance effectiveness and resource efficiency. The productivity index is calculated as follows:

$$\text{productivity index} = \frac{\text{Checklist indicators completed}}{\text{Total indicators}}$$

When using this format of evaluation, the situation must be carefully analyzed to assure the indicators truly scope a qualitative assessment. The following examples illustrate this type of productivity evaluation.

MENTAL HEALTH WORKER FOR CHILDREN

Responsibilities That Yield High Productivity	Observed in Worker
1. Sets an example of the behavior wanted	
2. Helps children learn desirable health habits	X
3. Enriches the care environment for social opportunities	X
4. Cooperates and assists other personnel and programs	X
5. Involves children in meaningful routine work	X
6. Teaches safety habits	X
7. Develops desirable self-control personality traits	
8. Encourages children to try	X
9. Helps children to try	X
10. Does not expect more or less than child's ability	X
11. Gives children choices	X
12. Helps children to be accepted by his or her group	X
13. Continually seeks causes of behavior	X
14. Requests for a child to do something are one at a time	X
15. Disciplines as necessary, but never punishes children	X
16. Respects children's privacy	X
17. Does not discuss children's problems in presence of others	
18. Radiates infectious attitudes of enthusiasm and optimism	X
19. Always puts children's best interests first	X
20. Avoids a condescending or inferior manner	

$$PI = \frac{16 \text{ indicators observed in worker}}{20 \text{ required responsibilities}} = 80\%$$

MOTOR MAINTENANCE PROCEDURE

Actions for a High-Productivity Motor Procedure	Actually Completed
1. Checks voltage at terminals with name plate ratings	X
2. Tightens terminal lead connections	X
3. Checks heat of overload control box	X
4. Rotates shaft to feel if bearings are stiff	X
5. Tightens coupling bolts securely	X
6. Checks vibration and noise when motor is unloaded	
7. Pokes shaft punchings to see if loose	X
8. Checks to see if rotor rubbing on stator	X
9. Checks restricted ventilation in winding passages	X
10. Rotates shaft to see if grease is stiff	X
11. Assures no foreign materials is in grease	X
12. Checks the proper grade of grease used	X
13. Checks bearings if clogged with dirt	X
14. Checks for poor ground connections	X
15. Sees that the commentator is smooth	X
16. Checks adjustment of governor	X
17. Checks to see if brushes return to commentator	X
18. Checks frequency at terminals with name plate ratings	
19. Checks for worn and sticky brushes	X
20. Checks for proper brush setting	X

$$PI = \frac{18 \text{ actions completed}}{20 \text{ required actions}} = 90\%$$

RESEARCH AND DEVELOPMENT EMPLOYEE

Indicators of a High-Producing Employee	Observed with Employee
1. Looks for improvement	X
2. Has record of accomplishments	X
3. Learns a new assignment quickly	X
4. Has a strong will to work, keep busy	
5. Has good work habits	X

6.	Has a strong sense of commitment to completing work	
7.	Is cooperative in teamwork	X
8.	Is open to ideas and listens well	X
9.	Uses time effectively	X
10.	Takes initiative to do things	
11.	Is cost minded	X
12.	Has a strong sense of urgency	
13.	Gets satisfaction from a job well done	X
14.	Contributes beyond what is expected	X
15.	Knows the job well	X
16.	Sees things to be done and takes action	
17.	Is considered valuable by supervisor	
18.	Interacts effectively with other people	X
19.	Understands organizations and their objectives	X
20.	Believes in a fair day's work for a fair day's pay	X

$$PI = \frac{14 \text{ Indicators observed with employee}}{20 \text{ Total indicators}} = 70\%$$

Note: The value of this assessment occurs with a comparison over two or more different periods of time.

MEASUREMENT USING PRODUCTIVITY AUDITS

Measurement using productivity audits is our fifth method for the measurement of productivity. Since the concept of managing productivity in organizations stressed in this book is a total process in the total organization, the productivity audit is such an important assessment for the productivity practitioner that it warrants a separate chapter. Accordingly, Chapter 6 describes in considerable detail how to set up productivity standards and ways of conducting an audit in terms of these standards.

SUMMARY

The need to manage productivity with measurement is found in nearly every work process of nearly every organization. The key step in the improvement of productivity is to assess the existing productivity level of the organization. This book stresses the idea that productivity must be measured before it can be improved. Five reasons have been cited why measurement of productivity has been slow: (1) work processes are complex and unwieldy; (2) measurements are difficult to make after work is in process; (3) use of generalized terms inhibit the evaluative process; (4) measurements are made on activities rather than on results; (5) measurements are made toward a macrolevel of utilization in the economy. These five barriers to measuring productivity point to the need to quantify work expectations. Evaluations are made easier when quantitative factors are built in the complex productivity processes.

Five measurement techniques were introduced in this chapter:

1. *Measurement Using Productivity Ratios.* The productivity ratio is developed further into five categories: (*a*) overall indexes; (*b*) objective ratios; (*c*) cost ratios; (*d*) work-standards ratios; and (*e*) time-standard ratios.
2. *Measurement Using Total-Factor Productivity.* The productivity ratio is expanded to incorporate all inputs that are required to produce an output.
3. *Measurement Using Managing by Objectives.* The productivity ratio is expressed as a measure of effectiveness and efficiency and is used in the MBO work process from start to finish.
4. *Measurement Using Productivity Checklist Indicators.* The productivity ratio is expressed in an indirect qualitative way as a checklist of items completed in relation to total items expected.
5. *Measurement Using Productivity Audits.* The productivity ratio is applied to the organization as a total approach in meeting standards that have been set by those who are expected to meet them.

QUESTIONS TO THINK ABOUT

1. List the reasons why the measurement of productivity has been slow and difficult in your organization.
2. What would be the principal action your organization would have to take to start to measure the work in progress for productivity purposes?
3. List the terms used in your organization that make evaluation difficult and controversial.
4. What value do you see in quantifying work expectations in your organization?

5. Develop six ratios that would completely measure the productivity in your department.

6. Of the five measurement techniques suggested in the chapter, which would be most useful in your organization? Least useful?

7. What can be done to the least useful work process or measurement technique to make the measuring process more useful?

8. Which of the following actions would improve the productivity ratio in your organization? Which ones would reduce it?

   (a) Purchase of materials and supplies

   (b) Payment of a current debt

   (c) Taking a tax refund

   (d) Short-term borrowing

   (e) Not hiring three personnel replacements

   (f) Instituting a performance evaluation system

   (g) Rental of more space

   (h) Increasing the level of inventory

   (i) Training of subordinates

9. For your organization, collect the figures for the following: monthly cash flow, accounts receivable, inventory start, inventory end, total sales, employees, rejects, and returns. Develop ratios for your organization; calculate the productivity levels; and develop a plan for productivity improvement.

REFERENCES

1. C. A. Westwick, *How to Use Management Ratios,* Halsted Book, Wiley, New York, 1976.

2. Joint Economic Committee of the Congress of the United States, *Measuring and Enhancing Productivity in the Federal Sector,* U.S. Government Printing Office, Washington, D.C., 1972, pp. 22–24.

3. C. A. Westwick, *op. cit.,* pp. 1–8.

4. *Business Week,* "What Cuts Efficiency at the Supermarket," March 7, 1977, p. 55.

5. For a better understanding of the systems approach for interlocking manager's commitments by levels, review Paul Mali, *Managing by Objectives,* Wiley-Interscience, New York, 1972, pp. 47, 127–135, 229.

5
MANAGING PRODUCTIVITY BY OBJECTIVES

IN THIS CHAPTER

Demands for accountability.
Extending MBO into productivity.
Ten guidelines to formulating productivity objectives.
MPBO as a process.
Milestones of progress.
Evaluating productivity.
Creating a productivity system.
Interlocking ratios.
The future organization.

The steady demand for new, better, and improved effectiveness and efficiency within organizations is unprecedented in history. Organizations have responded to the demands in a variety of ways, creating elaborate structures with interlocking departments, branches, sections and people. In addition, people who are concerned with the financial operation of an organization, are asking for information about the actual level of effectiveness and efficiency practiced in an organization. They are asking for purposes of programs, resources used in the programs, methods of accomplishment, contribution or gain from the program. Would the funds or budget be better used in other programs or projects? This demand for accountability is in reality a demand for a better system of managing productivity. The paramount idea in productivity is simple enough: Does it increase the net between output and input? Does it increase effectiveness while utilizing less resources in the process? If the management system in an organization is not structured for productivity, those who achieve it are just plain lucky.

Managing by objectives (MBO) is one of the most striking developments in the managerial art of getting results. It replaces the "lucky factors" with "planned factors." Hundreds of organizations report astounding accomplishments with this strategy. Although MBO was originally thought to be a fad, organizations continue to adopt it. George Odiorne estimates eight out of ten United States businesses are managed by objectives.[1] The basic reason for the growth of MBO in organizations is that the practitioners see it as a deliberate way to measure and improve their own effectiveness in organizational life. But many have not seen and understood how MBO can be extended into improving efficiency in resource utilization or the optimal combination of effectiveness and efficiency—productivity.

This chapter deals with this concept of how MPBO can be used to manage productivity directly and deliberately. The measurement techniques described in the previous chapter form its basic idea. Several topics are covered in this chapter: (1) formulating productivity objectives—10 guidelines are included for setting up productivity objectives; (2) strategy, steps, and examples of managing productivity by objectives (MPBO); and (3) how MPBO creates a management system for productivity improvement.

FORMULATING PRODUCTIVITY OBJECTIVES

Managers and administrators have tended to regard setting objectives as a relatively simple process. However, it is deceptive. The formalization of a statement of productivity objectives requires precision of thinking, forecasting, and work measurement. It also requires making commitments involving others. Most managers are not accustomed to such practices. Many companies report that statements are often fuzzy collections of commitments that result in misunderstandings and misinterpretations. Many are ambiguous. They incorporate ways to escape the commitment. The selection of words in the statement is critical, since even commonplace words carry different meanings for different people, depending on where or when they are used and who uses them. Words such as *total systems, input, quality, effectiveness,* and hundreds of others pose interpretive problems in meaning and usage. Reddin identifies job descriptions that sound good but are not very useful as operating commitments.[2] The descriptive phrases that are intended to show the manager's job (e.g., *administers, maintains, organizes, plans, schedules, reports to, coordinates, authorizes, and delegates)* are useful for communications and discussions, but they are not specific enough for statements of commitment and evaluation. A statement of objectives cannot be structured generally and worded ambiguously and ignore the fact that people of diverse backgrounds are involved. A statement must relate to the feelings, thoughts, and experiences of those involved.

Formulating meaningful statements of productivity objectives takes careful thought and analysis. The intention of the objective must be clear, and its focus must be understandable. The formal statement must specify the action to be taken and its measurement for progress control and evaluation in the work-flow process. As Peter Drucker emphasizes:

> Work is a process and a process needs to be controlled. To make work productive, therefore, requires building the appropriate controls into the process of work. Specifically the process of production needs built-in controls in respect to: its direction; its quality; its quantity; its standards; its efficiency.[3]

Ten guidelines should be followed to assure careful formulation of productivity objectives and the means of its control in the work-flow process.

1. *Productivity Objectives Must Be Measurable.*   The productivity index is used to quantify the ratio of effectiveness and efficiency. Other measurement techniques may be used if the work is not quantifiable. This is the heart of an objective that is to be controlled and evaluated.

2. *Productivity Objectives Must Achieve Single-Ended Results.*   The tendency to achieve several possibilities within an objective should be discouraged. A single-ended combination of effectiveness and efficiency is ideal. Multiple directions confuse the focus and allocation of resources.

3. *Deadlines for Productivity Objectives Must Be Set.*   Deadlines are set to limit the result to when the organization needs it. A productivity objective that is achieved beyond its timeline automatically loses its productivity because time as a resource has been lost. Time must be recognized as one of our most precious resources.

4. *Productivity Objectives Must Be Attainable.*   Challenges are necessary for productivity improvement, but a challenge must be within the range of performance capability and resource availability. To reach for productivity that is not realistic and achievable is "playing games" in organizational life.

5. *Productivity Objectives Must Be Opportunistic.*   Productivity improvement comes about when innovative opportunities are deliberately sought and exploited. Greatest productivity is a leap forward in performance with the same resources or the same performance with considerable reduction in resources. The search for new ways must be intense.

6. *Productivity Objectives Must Motivate Those Who Will Achieve Them.*

Motivational processes, such as participation, must be used in the formation of the objective. The objective must be important and have value to both the organization and the individual who will achieve it. In an article on ways to kill MBO Dale McConkey wrote: Instead of getting subordinates involved in their commitments, write the objectives yourself and hand them out to each subordinate.[4]

7. *Productivity Objectives Must Be Supportable by the Organization.* Productivity targets must coincide with availability of resources, facilities, skills, and equipment. Although an objective may be properly set, it is merely an exercise unless resources are available. This supports the idea that greatest results from MPBO occur when the total organization is committed to the process.

8. *Productivity Objectives Must Be Controllable.* Productivity targets must be reducible into milestones of progress to allow for control and correction during the implementation phase. Measurable objectives easily lend themselves to this divisability. Evaluation of productivity can never happen unless it is built into productivity targets.

9. *Productivity Objectives Must Have Assigned Accountability.* An individual, identified by name, must be accountable for an agreed-to objective and its required action. Not only presidents, heads of departments, managers of sections, and directors are to be held accountable; specific individuals, by name and position, are part of the ultimate accountability.

10. *Productivity Objectives Must Be Evaluative.* The results sought in an objective must be communicated terms that are understood by the people who will authorize the "go ahead." A tentative evaluation of results must be given to these sources before there is authorization to proceed. Generalized terms or "motherhoods" must be challenged in order to arrive at the specific level and amount of productivity that will be accomplished.

Productivity objectives are the results an organization needs for continuing success. Samples of productivity objectives for major functions of a private firm with their respective Evaluative Productivity Measure (EPM) are illustrated as follows:

1. *Productivity Objectives for the Presidential Function*
   (a) Achieve a 12 percent return on equity within four operating quarters.
$$\left(\text{EPM} = \frac{24 \text{ million} \times 7\%}{12 \text{ months}}\right)$$

(b)   Complete 10-item checklist of requirements for board of directors in preparation of annual stockholders' meeting.

$$\left(EPM = \frac{\text{completed items}}{\text{10 required items}}\right)$$

(c)   Achieve three validated large-scale improvement objectives from each of the five functions of the firm by November 15.

$$\left(EPM = \frac{\text{actual objectives completed}}{\text{15 expected objectives}}\right)$$

(d)   Implement all policies established by the board and its committees within a calendar year.

$$\left(EPM = \frac{\text{actually implemented}}{\text{all developed policies}}\right)$$

(e)   Reduce capital expenditures in the coming year, priority B, from $350,000 to $150,000 while maintaining production of four million parts.

$$\left(EPM = \frac{\text{4 million parts}}{\$150,000 \text{ capital}}\right)$$

(f)   Complete annual operational plan of 10 percent profit growth of the company in time for the board's May meeting.

$$\left(EPM = \frac{10\% + \text{current (sales costs)}}{\text{current (sales} - \text{costs)}}\right)$$

(g)   *Complete management controls systems with five standards of performance in 24 key areas of the company by December 1.*

$$\left(EPM = \frac{\text{number of standards implemented}}{\text{120 standards required}}\right)$$

(h)   improve current asset to current debt ratio from 3.0 to 4.0 for the next fiscal year.

$$\left(EPM = \frac{\text{24 million current assets}}{\text{6 million current debts}}\right)$$

(i)   Improve sales per employee to 60,000 during the next 3-year profit plan.

$$\left(EPM = \frac{\text{30 million total sales}}{\text{500 employees}}\right)$$

(j)   Achieve an improved public image of the company with personal completion of 31 newspaper articles, 5 community speeches, and 10 attendances at community functions within the coming year.

$$\left(\text{EPM} = \frac{\text{completed activities}}{18 \text{ planned activities}} \right)$$

2. *Productivity Objectives for the Finance Function*

(a)   Achieve a budget reporting system so that variations between budgeted performance and actual results are analyzed for corrective actions within 10 working days.

$$\left(\text{EPM} = \frac{\text{days variance reported}}{10 \text{ days expectancy}} \right)$$

(b)   Reduce aging of accounts receivable within the next quarter from 60 days to 40 days while maintaining a staff of 10.

$$\left(\text{EPM} = \frac{\text{new monthly 40 days aging}}{\text{present monthly 60 days aging}} \right)$$

(c)   Reduce total costs of operating while maintaining the present margins on all products.

$$\left(\text{EPM} = \frac{\$24 \text{ million total costs}}{6 \text{ million present margin}} \right)$$

(d)   Complete 5-year study with index of expense trends for 24 key departments by budget preparation time.

$$\left(\text{EPM} = \frac{\text{actual indexes completed}}{24 \text{ expense indices}} \right)$$

(e)   Collect ten suggested cost-reduction ideas per month from each of six operating managers.

$$\left(\text{EPM} = \frac{60 \text{ suggestions}}{4 \text{ weeks}} \right)$$

(f)   Complete and distribute cost-reduction manual within 2 months.

$$\left(\text{EPM} = \frac{24 \text{ sections}}{8 \text{ weeks}} \right)$$

(g)   Improve profits to payroll margin from 5 percent to 10 percent within the next four profit sharing quarters.

$$\left(\text{EPM} = \frac{\text{profit to payroll margin}}{4 \text{ operating quarters}}\right)$$

(h)   Collect from six operating managers long distance telephone call and control analysis for 10 percent reduction by January 1.

$$\left(\text{EPM} = \frac{\$12,000 \text{ cost of calls}}{1450 \text{ number of calls}}\right)$$

(i)   Complete training (15 item checklist) of 3 replacements for key positions in accounting with cost not to exceed $3000.

$$\left(\text{EPM} = \frac{\$3000 \text{ cost of training}}{45 \text{ items of training}}\right)$$

3. *Productivity Objectives in the Marketing Function*

(a)   Increase market position within the coming year for nondefense sales from 15 to 30 percent while maintaining current total employees of 500.

$$\left(\text{EPM} = \frac{10 \text{ million total nondefense sales}}{500 \text{ employees}}\right)$$

(b)   Hold sales expenses this year to 3 percent of total sales while increasing total sales 10 percent.

$$\left(\text{EPM} = \frac{30 \text{ million total sales}}{900,000 \text{ cost of sales}}\right)$$

(c)   Reduce number of monthly customer complaints on commercial business from 24 to 10 of total orders booked.

$$\left(\text{EPM} = \frac{14 \text{ reduced complaints}}{24 \text{ total complaints}}\right)$$

(d)   Complete a sales strategy statement for defense sales to meet a 10-item criteria checklist by January 1.

$$\left(\text{EPM} = \frac{\text{actual items completed}}{\text{total 10-item checklist}}\right)$$

(e)   Complete 75 percent follow-up calls of new inquires with no more than three sales representatives within 3 days of initial inquiry.

$$\left(\text{EPM} = \frac{60 \text{ follow-up calls}}{3 \text{ sales representatives}} \right)$$

(f)   Achieve 100 percent distribution in markets D, E, and F within 3 months of authorization.

$$\left(\text{EPM} = \frac{900,000 \text{ parts}}{12 \text{ months}} \right)$$

(g)   Increase sales of new product in district 3 while holding advertising expense to current levels.

$$\left(\text{EPM} = \frac{\$3 \text{ million sales}}{\$20,000 \text{ advertising costs}} \right)$$

(h)   Increase advance sales bookings relative to demand bookings 10 percent within the coming year.

$$\left(\text{EPM} = \frac{\$16 \text{ million advance bookings}}{\$14 \text{ million demand bookings}} \right)$$

(i)   Complete training program for 30 district representatives with pre- and post-test results ratio to be greater than 4.0.

$$\left(\text{EPM} = \frac{\text{posttest mean } 90}{\text{pretest mean } 20} \right)$$

4. *Productivity Objectives for the Research and Development Function*

(a)   Achieve a research effort to feasible idea ratio of 10 for marketability within the current year.

$$\left(\text{EPM} = \frac{100 \text{ feasible proposals}}{10 \text{ marketable proposals}} \right)$$

(b)   Complete design and development of new prototype in 14 months within cost of $140,000 without farm-out work to vendors.

$$\left(\text{EPM} = \frac{\$140,000 \text{ prototype costs}}{14 \text{ months}} \right)$$

(c) Supply three new products to marketing within the coming fiscal year with forecasted sales not less than 1.5 million.

$$\left(\text{EPM} = \frac{\$1.5 \text{ million forecasted sales}}{52 \text{ weeks}}\right)$$

(d) Complete PERT layout (35 work packages) for contract B within the 4-week prebudgetary planning period.

$$\left(\text{EPM} = \frac{35 \text{ work packages}}{4 \text{ weeks}}\right)$$

(e) Achieve $500,000 savings from value analysis for three engineering sections using six people per section.

$$\left(\text{EPM} = \frac{\$500,000 \text{ savings}}{18 \text{ personnel}}\right)$$

(f) Collect 10 patentable ideas from literature and patent search sources using no more than 2 man-years.

$$\left(\text{EPM} = \frac{10 \text{ patentable ideas}}{2 \text{ man-years}}\right)$$

(g) Improve research know-how in department A by increasing Ph.D. hires 20 percent by July 1.

$$\left(\text{EPM} = \frac{24 \text{ Ph.D. expected employment}}{20 \text{ Ph.D. present employment}}\right)$$

(h) Develop new technological capability (10-item criteria list) within 6 months of the current operating year.

$$\left(\text{EPM} = \frac{10 \text{ item technological capability}}{24 \text{ weeks}}\right)$$

(i) Achieve a product line mix in which 80 percent of sales is made by no more than 20 percent of R & D projects.

$$\left(\text{EPM} = \frac{\$6 \text{ million sales}}{400 \text{ R \& D projects}}\right)$$

5. *Productivity Objectives for the Production Function*

(a) Hold plant operating costs to $4 per 10 unit lots while reducing production force to 375.

$$\left(\text{EPM} = \frac{\$24 \text{ million total costs}}{375}\right)$$

(b) Complete construction of 5000 square feet, two-story approved addition to existing plant within cost of $125,000 by March 1.

$$\left(\text{EPM} = \frac{\$125,000 \text{ cost of addition}}{28 \text{ weeks}}\right)$$

(c) Reduce cost of pump and engine repairs from $10,000 to $5000 per year per mechanic.

$$\left(\text{EPM} = \frac{\$50,000 \text{ cost of repairs}}{10 \text{ mechanics}}\right)$$

(d) Maintain a once-a-day contact with all subordinates at their work stations.

$$\left(\text{EPM} = \frac{\text{total number of no-contacts reported}}{40 \text{ subordinates at stations}}\right)$$

(e) Improve morale in the work force through better union relations.

$$\left(\text{EPM} = \frac{\text{total number of written grievances this year}}{\text{total number of written grievances last year}}\right)$$

(f) Master 10 techniques in work simplification for 30 supervisors in a 2-week training period.

$$\left(\text{EPM} = \frac{10 \text{ techniques} \times 30 \text{ supervisors}}{2 \text{ weeks}}\right)$$

(g) Achieve a delivery of 16 units per day for less than $45 unit cost to shipping point B.

$$\left(\text{EPM} = \frac{\$45 \text{ cost} \times \text{number of units}}{16 \text{ units} \times 360 \text{ days}}\right)$$

(h) Complete by next year a vendor-quality rating system to maintain price, delivery, and reliability at or below an index established for the past 5-year record.

$$\left(\text{EPM} = \frac{\text{number of unsatisfactory incidents}}{5\text{-year index of 3 items}}\right)$$

(i) Reduce master schedule slippage from 3 weeks to 2 weeks within the next four operating quarters.

$$\left(\text{EPM} = \frac{2 \text{ weeks slippage}}{3 \text{ weeks present slippage}}\right)$$

6. *Productivity Objectives for the Personnel Function*

    (a)   Achieve a termination rate of 30 quits per year by January 1.

$$EPM = \frac{450 \text{ total employees}}{30 \text{ quits per year}}$$

    (b)   Reduce absenteeism record for next year from 16 to 8 percent.

$$EPM = \frac{\text{actual absences}}{\text{targeted absences}}$$

    (c)   Complete study by December 1 of company's hiring wage to assess 15-point criteria in three labor markets.

$$EPM = \frac{15 \text{ points} \times 3 \text{ labor markets}}{\$4000 \text{ cost}}$$

    (d)   Complete for distribution within 2 months a 20-page, 10-topic industrial relations policy manual for newly hired employees.

$$EPM = \frac{20 \text{ pages} \times 10 \text{ topics}}{8 \text{ weeks}}$$

    (e)   Complete training by December; 2-day seminars on MPBO for all 120 supervisors in the company.

$$EPM = \frac{120 \text{ supervisors} \times 2 \text{ days}}{20 \text{ days to complete}}$$

    (f)   Complete planning, organization, and installation of an employee suggestion at the start of next year's cost-reduction program.

$$EPM = \frac{6\text{-item criteria system} \times 20 \text{ locations}}{3 \text{ personnel}}$$

    (g)   Complete within 3 months an attitude survey of labor–management relations among employees within cost of $1800.

$$EPM = \frac{\text{number of prevailing attitudes}}{\text{number of desired attitudes}}$$

    (h)   Achieve and validate 12 standards of qualifications for new hourly employees by January 1.

$$EPM = \frac{12 \text{ hiring standards} \times 50 \text{ annual hires}}{\$6,000 \text{ cost}}$$

(i)   Read 12 new books in management by the end of a year.

$$\left(\text{EPM} = \frac{12 \text{ new books}}{12 \text{ months}}\right)$$

HOW TO MANAGE PRODUCTIVITY BY OBJECTIVES

Many organizations have adopted the strategy of MBO as a way of managerial life. The precise extent to which it has been adapted within the organization is difficult to measure because many pieces of the MBO system have been around for many years. Setting objectives and developing plans for reaching objectives is hardly a new activity. What is new about MBO is that it is a formal system for translating participation from organization members to a commitment format for a common goal. This requires a timetable for blending the individual contributions into an overall set of results. The participation and commitment process provides a desire and willingness to achieve that tends to be motivational. In many ways the concept of MBO is inseparable from other management essentials. In fact, in its theoretical meaning MBO is eclectic. That is, the management essentials of planning, delegating, organizing, decision making, performance appraisals, budgeting, policymaking, controlling, forecasting, and so on are selected and banded together into a strategy for getting results in the organization. The strategy works through a sequence of steps that must be taken in a certain order to lead to its intended results.

Managing productivity by objectives (MPBO) is an adaptation of managing by objectives. Managing by objectives can be thought of as measurement by objectives since productivity closely follows a measurement concept. MPBO is a six-step process. It does not exclude additional steps required in the process. Additional steps are incorporated in one or more of the following main steps:

1. Identify potential productivity areas.
2. Quantify productivity level desired.
3. Specify a measurable productivity objective.
4. Develop a plan for attaining objectives.
5. Control with milestones of progress.
6. Evaluate productivity reached.

The flow diagram (Figure 5.1) shows that all steps are sequentially related

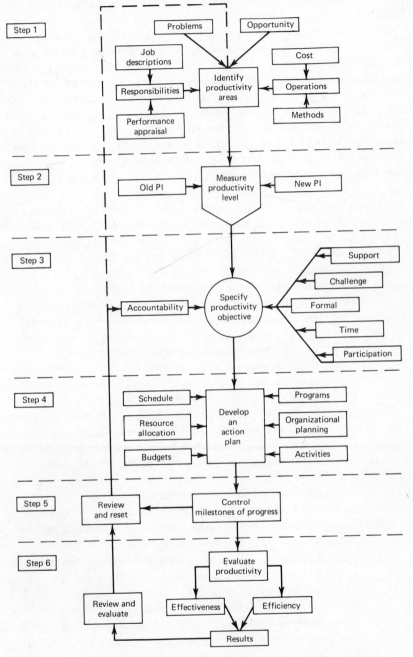

Figure 5.1 The strategy of managing productivity by objectives (MPBO).

117

for a start-to-finish cycle. Repetitive cycles can be generated, making the process unending.

MPBO as a strategy should not be considered in the narrow or limited sense of a technique or tool but rather a managerial process for directing the total organization to what it wants to achieve during a particular period. Its totality is important because productivity as a ratio of effectiveness with efficiency reaches for total effectiveness and total efficiency of the organization. This does not exclude departmental or sectional productivity concerns, but planned productivity is for the organization as a whole. It attempts to achieve the greatest benefit/cost ratio for all expenditures. When practiced as a process by members of management, the six steps help to create a management system for achieving productivity.

Step 1. Identify Potential Areas for Productivity Improvement. Productivity improvement starts with a deliverate and systematic examination of potential areas where improvement is needed for survival, growth, or budget justification. Five areas should be examined.

(a) Operations. Large number of employees who perform routine and repetitive tasks, organizational functions that consume large numbers of man-hours or dominate the budget, and loosely connected and ill-defined work processes are situations that need to be improved.

(b) Responsibilities. If employees are not meeting their responsibilities, or performance levels are steadily declining or departments have high unit costs and large backlogs of work, the sources of these problems may be job descriptions, performance evaluations, or operational plans. If formal lists of responsibilities are not available, an individual or a department should list the major responsibilities to be met.

(c) Problems. Problems emerge because the total work system is not functioning smoothly or because outside factors influence inside factors to a critical degree, or because the total work system has antiproductivity barriers.

(d) Traditions. The same old way of doing things has been followed for years, or innovations have not been permitted because of empires or perpetuating "hobbies", or the resistance to change is so great that the climate for doing work in a different way is not permitted.

(e) Opportunities. If a new opportunity has not been pursued because of uncertainty or because levels of effectiveness cannot be forecasted in terms of the committed resources, the capacity of the organization has not been utilized.

The manager must give this first step considerable time and analysis because this is the stage at which drift, aimless tendencies, or failing productivity levels are noted for redirection.

Step 2. *Quantify Productivity Level Desired.* The broad areas of potentially usable targets identified in Step 1 provide the basis for the measurement of productivity. It starts with the search for the performance level that prevails and the resources that are consumed in the process. A productivity ratio is established for the prevailing productivity level, and from it a new productivity ratio is developed in terms of what level the manager desires. The principle of ratio measurement is to be used as a guide. Precise and accurate measurements are not intended in this step. We are looking for a measurement, even limited, that provides a mark of how effectiveness is to be directed and existing resources are to be reduced. "Before and after" productivity indexes are established in this step.

Step 3. *Specify a Measurable Productivity Improvement Objective.* The new productivity level provides the basis for adapting and setting a productivity objective. This objective is stated and written as a formal commitment by an individual, a group, a department, or the entire organization. It is most effective when it is originated by those who must execute the work involved. The statement is shared with top management and coordinated with other groups. Most important, the immediate supervisor participates in the setting of the objective and agrees to it. Setting productivity support and participation by those responsible for its implementation. It is set within the range of challenge consistent with available resources, is based on realistic schedules, and is designed to achieve the results needed by the firm. Accountability for the achievement of the objective is identified in this step, and the immediate supervisor agrees to the level and scope of this accountability.

Step 4. *Develop Plans for Attaining the Objective.* Once a statement of productivity commitment has been made and agreed upon, plans are developed to implement completion of the commitment. These plans pull together the activities and tasks that are necessary to fulfill the commitment. Studies of viable alternatives assure that the best plan for reaching the objective is selected. The plan includes sufficient detail of time required to reach the objectives. Tasks and increments of work that have common boundaries are readily identifiable and controllable. Contingency actions are developed for coping with potential problems if they emerge. A special effort must be made in this step because planning for productivity improvement requires a high degree of competence with which committed people focus the exact amount of their resources of time, skill, effort, and money to reach the needed productivity levels.

Step 5. *Control with Milestones of Progress Toward Objectives.* Progress can be measured only in terms of the objective one is trying to achieve. This step sets up all activities and tasks on a schedule to measure and report the status of and the progress made toward completing the objective. Task completion must relate to cost and schedule criteria. During the controlling and reporting process, deviations of actual progress from expected progress are detected and reported for corrective action. Progress reviews could be monthly, quarterly, or semiannually. Two essentials are needed for this progress reporting system to work: Productivity level desired must be broken into milestones, and feedback reports must be made to correct deviations. Deviations must remain within acceptable limits. A "down" in one period must be compensated for by an "up" in the next period. Regular periodic discussion regarding progressions or regressions take place between individuals and managers.

Step 6. *Evaluate Productivity Reached.* The results of the entire productivity effort are evaluated to see how well objectives have been reached. The evaluation procedure is both a rating for how well results have been achieved and a means of ensuring that the managerial productivity processes are established and operating. Results of the evaluation provide the basis of accountability. The data also become the basis for future planning and object setting.

The six sequential steps of MPBO productivity strategy provide a framework within which to think about and perform the job of improving productivity. This framework helps to meet the large and complex productivity challenges in an organized way. Examples of how this strategy is applied are given in the following three illustrations. Further illustrations are given in Chapter 7, which discusses the management of white-collar workers.

SUPERVISOR

Step 1.   *Identify Productivity Area*
(a) *Responsibility.*   Welding production.
(b) *Performance.*   Weld 40 plates, 50 assemblies weekly with no more than two plate rejects (5%).
(c) *Resources.*   Two men, welding machine, 40 hours per week.

Step 2.   *Quantify Productivity*
(a) *Before:*
$$PI = \frac{40 \text{ plates}}{2 \text{ men}} = \frac{20 \text{ plates}}{\text{man}}$$
$$PI = \frac{2 \text{ rejects}}{40 \text{ plates}} = .05 \text{ reject } (5\%) \text{ rate}$$
(b) *After:*
$$PI = \frac{60 \text{ plates}}{2 \text{ men}} = \frac{30 \text{ plates}}{\text{man}}$$
$$PI = \frac{2 \text{ rejects}}{60 \text{ plates}} = .03 \text{ reject } (3 \%) \text{ rate}$$

Step 3.   *Specify Productivity Objective.*   Achieve 60 plate-welding results weekly.
(30 plates)/(Man)
with no more than two plate rejects (3%) by January 1.

Step 4.   *Develop a Plan.*   Install new semiautomatic welding machine and provide 80 hours training for welders.

Step 5.   *Control with Milestones of Progress*

July	September	January
40 plates/man	50 plates/man	60 plates/man

Step 6.   *Evaluate Productivity.*   By January 1, 60 plates are welded in 40 hours. (50% productivity improvement) while maintaining a two-plate reject rate (40% quality improvement).

PUBLIC ADMINISTRATOR

Step 1.   *Identify Productivity Area*
(a) *Responsibility.*   Maintain clean streets.
(b) *Performance.*   Twenty streets swept once a week with no visible paper debris.

   (c) Resources. Five men, one machine, 14 hours per week.

Step 2. *Quantify Productivity*
   (a) Before:

$$PI = \frac{20 \text{ streets}}{14 \text{ hours}} = \frac{1.5 \text{ streets}}{1 \text{ hour}}$$

   (b) After:

$$PI = \frac{40 \text{ streets}}{10 \text{ hours}} = \frac{4 \text{ streets}}{\text{hour}}$$

Step 3. *Specify Productivity Objective.* Reduce cleaning all 450 streets in town from 300 hours to 100 hours (4 streets/hour) by September 1.

Step 4. *Develop a Plan.* Organize into a team approach—two paper pickers, one manual sweeper, one machine sweeper, one follow-up and inspector.

Step 5. *Control with Milestones of Progress*

March	May	July	September
|	|	|	|
1.5 streets/hour	2 streets/hour	3 streets/hour	4 streets/hou

Step 6. *Evaluate Productivity.* By September 1, 450 streets are cleaned within 100 hours (160% productivity improvement).

EDUCATIONAL ADMINISTRATOR

Step 1. *Identify Productivity Area*
   (a) Responsibility. Admitting students.
   (b) Performance. 500 students accepted as enrolled from 1000 applications. (50% acceptance rate).

Step 2. *Quantify Productivity*
   (a) Before:

$$PI = \frac{\$100,000 \text{ budget}}{500 \text{ acceptances}} = \frac{\$200}{\text{student acceptance}}$$

   (b) After:

$$PI = \frac{\$90,000 \text{ budget}}{600 \text{ acceptances}} = \frac{\$150}{\text{student acceptance}}$$

Step 3. *Specify Productivity Objecgive.* Achieve a 600-student acceptance while reducing budget $10,000 ($1500 per student) by October 1.

Step 4.   *Develop a Plan.* Institute new information processing center
             with procedures for information handling, storage, and re-
             trieval. Institute interview training for staff.

Step 5.   *Control with Milestones of Progress*

        January   March   June   October
        | | | |
        $200/student $180/student $160/studnet $150/student

Step 6.   *Evaluate Productivity.* By October 1, 600 students will be
             accepted (20% productivity improvement) while operating
             under a 10% budget reduction (25% productivity improve-
             ment).

MPBO: A MANAGEMENT SYSTEM FOR PRODUCTIVITY

The whole point of a management system is to coordinate all the available
resources and efforts of people toward agreed-upon goals and objectives.
The goals, objectives, and purposes determine how relationships, activities,
and methods are to be set up. The goals, objectives, and purposes change
unrelated resources to related resources, disorganized facilities to organized facilities, unused skills to used skills. The goals, objectives, and
activities—with processes—create the framework to fit all parts together to
accomplish the purpose. Complex systems of management imply complex
coordination for reaching multiplicity of goals. Government, multidivisional corporations, national and global chains all imply huge quantities of
resources and functions that are highly influenced by economical, political,
and social powers. Managers within these organizations must design and
integrate all elements to guide, synthesize, and control all resources toward
purposes. If the management system has many purposes but does not
focus on productivity, the system is bypassing a chief concern of the
organization. Any productivity that is experienced is accidental. However,
if the purpose of the management system is to accomplish higher levels of
productivity, managers within the system arrange unrelated and nondi-
rected employees, money facilities, equipment, supplies, shifts, and available time within the framework to reach these levels of productivity. The
overall output of the system is what is most significant to the manager.
Thus the manager looks at the big picture—the overall system—rather
than focusing on its constituent parts.

    MPBO and the productivity index provide a measurement format for
creating a management system to improve productivity. It sets up the

potential of synergistic links of individual managers to the entire organization. It interlocks departmental contributions with managerial levels. It provides individual participation for large-scale accomplishment. It signals the start and stop of individual contributions in the productivity flow process. It blends performance outputs of several flow processes. It aggregates all costs within cost centers. For example, a marketing manager in a private enterprise not only heads the function of marketing and sales but must create a system within his function for the kinds of results he wishes to achieve. How he interlocks and coordinates the relationships of the various levels in the function determines to a great degree how well a system will prevail for sales productivity. The productivity ratio does provide a way in which the results, the amount of results, the kind of results, the timing of the results can be interlocked as a network of individual actions, reactions, and interactions. The index becomes the "pulse" for the manager to know by levels whether a productivity system prevails. If properly developed and implemented the interlocking nature of the productivity ratio, along with the coordinating features of a schedule, should create a productivity system within an organization. The interlocking of MPBO and the productivity index within the function of marketing is illustrated in Figure 5.2. Use of the productivity index for an entire organization is illustrated in Figure 5.3.

The value of a productivity system lies in how easily a manager can grasp how the real situation can produce the desired productivity. This becomes a form of validation to predict the success or failure of venturing into the uncertain productivity future. The manager who gives considerable time to the connecting and interconnecting of the productivity index by levels not only builds confidence in reaching overall productivity but can make the desired result happen. That is, productivity generates a host of secondary benefits such as profitability, morale, and rewards. How well the manager foresees the implications of his productivity objectives for the implementation phases should determine the degree of his willingness to be committed to a set of results. The manager is wise to simulate the future situation as nearly as he can. He should simulate different aspects of the situation, such as information, time, cost, experience, and equipment support, to help predict the success or failure of the productivity system. This is a way to validate the productivity plan for a system before the plan is implemented.[5] The manipulation of the productivity index in the validation can take several forms (see Figure 5.4). Whichever form is explored and analyzed, it must actually validate the existence of a management system for delivering productivity.

This idea of the creation of a management system is viewed as the future of the new management by Gruber and Niles.[6] The future

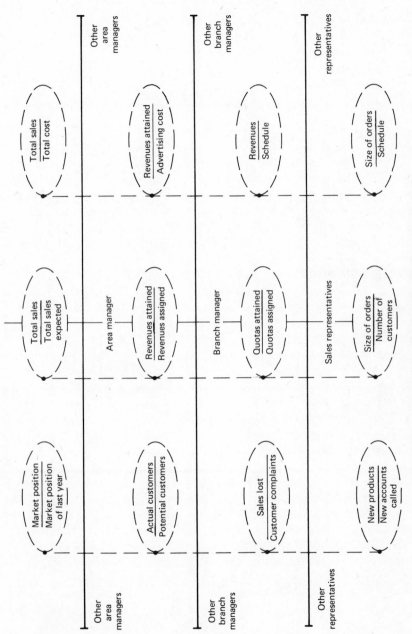

Figure 5.2 Interlocking ratios within organizational levels.

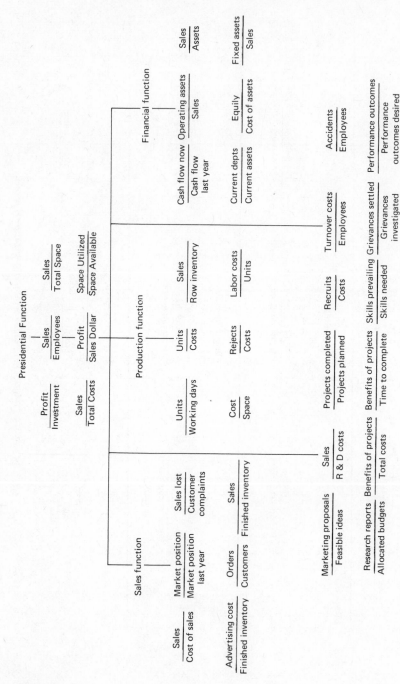

Figure 5.3 Productivity index applied to functions in an organization.

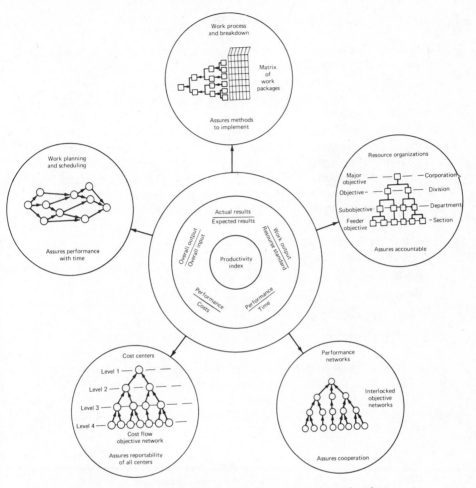

Figure 5.4 The productivity index sets up a management system.

organization will have an effective monitoring and planning system for both long- and short-range capability. This monitory and planning system will survey and retrieve information, produce innovations upon request, and be able to use alternate resources when existing resources run out. In many ways the firm of the future must move its organization based on tradition and experience toward a system based on innovation and experimentation. The scarcity of resources such as oil, copper, steel, food, wood, metals, and gas will force us to sharpen the need to manage productivity with alternate resources.

SUMMARY

The steady demand for new, better, and improved effectiveness and efficiency within organization is unprecedented. This demand has been accompanied by a demand for information about the actual *level* of effectiveness and efficiency practiced in an organization. This demand is a demand for a better system of managing productivity, a system that makes productivity less an accident and more a deliberate effort.

This chapter presented productivity as a process—a series of steps that are organized in a deliberate way to achieve productivity. When the process is deliberately organized for reaching objectives, a strategy emerges. This chapter introduced the strategy of how to manage productivity by objectives (MPBO). Six steps form the strategy:

1. Identify potential productivity areas.
2. Quantify productivity level desired.
3. Specify a measurable productivity objective.
4. Develop plans for attaining objectives.
5. Control with milestones of progress.
6. Evaluate productivity reached.

These six sequential steps of MPBO provide a framework within which to think about and perform the job of improving productivity. The key to the proper execution of the strategy lies in the formulation and setting of objectives. Ten guidelines were suggested for effective formulation of objectives:

1. Productivity objectives must be measurable.
2. Productivity objectives achieve single-ended results.
3. Productivity objectives must be set against deadlines.
4. Productivity objectives must be attainable.
5. Productivity objectives must be opportunistic.
6. Productivity objectives must motivate those who will achieve them.
7. Productivity objectives must be supportable by the organization.
8. Productivity objectives must be controllable.
9. Productivity objectives must have assigned accountability.
10. Productivity objectives must be evaluated.

MPBO creates a management system for productivity if objectives and the means of measuring them are interlocked and interconnected by levels and functions. Complex coordination will mean complex interlocking of goals and commitments. Yet if the system is to be flexible, this interlocking among objectives must change to meet unexpected challenges from within and without the organization.

QUESTIONS TO THINK ABOUT

1. List the kinds of demands required to keep your organization viable and healthy. How many of these demands directly or indirectly relate to productivity?
2. Is your organization practicing MPBO? If yes, has it been moved toward managing productivity? If not, why not? Would MPBO help you to reach your needed levels of productivity? What changes would you make in MPBO?
3. Write six statements of objectives for your job. Apply the 10 rules suggested in this chapter for producing good statements of objectives. What improvement may be needed?
4. Using the MPBO strategy, develop a job framework for achieving productivity as suggested in the examples of supervisor, public administrator, and educator in this chapter.
5. Write interlocking ratios between your job and your supervisor, and your job and your subordinates.
6. Take the organization chart of your firm and suggest productivity ratios from the top down that may give rise to a coordinated system.

REFERENCES AND NOTES

1. George Odiorne, *Management By Objectives' Newsletter,* Westfield, Mass., Vol. VI, No. 11, November 1976.
2. W. J. Reddin, *Effective Management By Objectives,* McGraw-Hill Book Company, New York, 1971, pp. 6–8.
3. Peter Drucker, *Management: Tasks, Responsibilities, Practices,* Harper & Row Company, New York, 1974, p. 217.
4. Dale D. McConkey, "20 Ways to Kill Management By Objectives," *Management Review,* American Management Association, Vol. 61, No. 10, October 1972, pp. 4–13.
5. Several methods for validating a proposed plan for creating productivity are described in Paul Mali, *Managing By Objectives,* Wiley-Interscience, New York, 1972, Ch. 5.
6. William H. Gruber and John S. Niles, *The New Management:* McGraw-Hill Book Company, New York, 1976, pp. 213–232.

6

THE PRODUCTIVITY AUDIT

IN THIS CHAPTER

Productivity auditing.
Seven types of auditing.
Model for evaluating productivity.
Standards for measuring productivity vigor.
Audit traps.
Productivity audit reports.
Thirty-one productivity practices found in organizations.
Forty-two actions for improving productivity.

Historically productivity has been the driving force that has led to our high standard of living and our high quality of work life. Kendrick has found that productivity accounted for 75 percent of the fourfold increase in real net national product per capita in the United States from 1889 to 1957.[1] The long-range benefits from productivity have resulted primarily from technological innovations, along with new processes, greater investment in capital equipment on a per-worker basis, improved managerial techniques, and improved skills of workers. But the climate has changed. Suddenly we are faced with conditions such as shortages of resources, changed attitudes of workers. In the coming decade there will be a sharply increased demand for information about organizational productivity and how to improve it. Organizations will have to formalize their efforts to monitor, evaluate, and improve productivity. Admittedly, the greatest productivity gains during this period have been due to technological advances with its associated equipment and process. But few organizations will have to formalize their efforts to monitor, evaluate, and improve productivity at an organizational function in a deliberate way. Most efforts are piecemeal, happenstance and last minute desperate moves. Some organizations don't ever know what productivity is all about even though they may be practicing parts of its process. Other organizations who do know what productivity is assume that it will come out right if good general management is practiced. Productivity must be planned, controlled, and appraised. Barriers to it must be removed. The greatest effort will be the formal effort to investigate, evaluate, and expose productivity practices, which will be developed into a mechanism for holding key personnel accountable. One definition of this formal mechanism will be the evaluation or productivity audit.

Productivity auditing should be a primary practice of funding organizations (government, private foundation), boards of directors (private, elected public, public appointed), program directors, clients, customers, prime contractors, and taxpayers. They should be fully aware of what a productivity audit is and how to conduct one. It is an important part of the accountability process because it provides an independent evaluation of the validity and credibility of statements made by managers of the results achieved and the manner in which they were achieved. Auditing serves to check on the abilities of management on all levels of all facets of the organization and the degree of effectiveness they are having in managing productivity. On a much broader scale, the greatest value of the services of an independent auditor, according to Howard Stettler, is furthering the public interest and assuring proper accounting for public resources and concerns.[2]

This chapter provides a general approach to productivity auditing as an evaluation process for assuring that productivity factors are found in organizations. It will show how the audit can be used as a tool for continuous evaluation of productivity performance in all areas of the organization. More specifically, the chapter is divided into three sections: (1) the productivity audit—what it is, what it can do, and how it differs from other forms of auditing; (2) the productivity audit model, which serves to give an evaluation procedure for a function, a program, or the organization itself—four phases are described in this model with a section on productivity standards; and (3) productivity practices that organizations have actually adopted to bring about productivity improvement. Thirty-two such practices from organizations throughout the United States are briefly identified. Forty-two actions for managing productivity are also included.

PRODUCTIVITY AUDITING: WHAT IT IS

Productivity auditing rises out of the need for management to have specific information on the level and progress of productivity in an organization in order to take action as needed. After all, if you're going to manage productivity in an organization, detailed information is needed concerning the vigor and thrust of the effort. This information will be requested, not because something went sour in the organization, but rather to prevent something from going sour. Most organizations and programs consume resources as they complete objectives. Information about what level of productivity will be required in an organization or a program to justify its continuance should be collected in advance. What level of performance can be predicted for a period of time when resources are committed for the same period of time? What is the greatest return on effort and resources that can be expected when selecting an option from among many that may be available? The productivity audit uncovers organizational factors contributing to poor use of resources, lack of concerted and unified effort, high costs, potential problems, and mediocre performance. It "cuts into" the elaborate structure of interlocking relationships among all levels to discover and evaluate and generate information on the quality of the productivity effort. It also collects and aggregates decision-making information needed for correction and improvement. The aim of productivity auditing is to seek out and define these factors so that management can act.

Productivity auditing is a process of monitoring and evaluating organizational practices to determine whether functional units, programs, and the organization itself are utilizing their resources effectively and efficiently to accomplish objectives. Where this is not being achieved, productivity auditing recommends necessary action to correct and adjust shortcomings, poor results, and system deficiencies.

Productivity auditing should not be confused with other traditional audit practices. The use of auditing techniques in nonfinancial areas has increased considerably in recent years due to the recognition that other factors are as important as financial factors. A brief comparison of these practices will serve to clarify each role.

Financial Auditing

Financial auditing is an objective appraisal by a independent auditor that certifies that the records and reports of an organization reflect the true financial condition and operating results. It determines whether financial operations and practices are properly conducted according to applicable laws and regulations. This type of audit is conducted as a matter of routine and is therefore both corrective and preventive.

Program Auditing

Program auditing is an appraisal undertaken to detemine whether the desired results or benefits are being achieved within a program. Its principle focus is on how well results compare to expected results specified in program objectives. This type of audit is not routine. It is usually conducted because something is wrong or is suspected to be wrong. It may also be conducted if a firm or organization intends to carry out two or more programs, each having different program requirements. This assures differences among programs are maintained in spite of their completion by the same personnel.

Operations Auditing

Operations auditing is a technique for routinely and systematically appraising unit or function effectiveness against corporate and industry standards, utilizing nonspecialist personnel, with the objective of assuring a given management that its aims are being carried out or identifying conditions that could be involved through more intensive and specialized attention.[3] It seeks out the performance level in all facets of operations. This audit is conducted to discover what could go wrong.

Compliance Auditing

Compliance auditing is an appraisal undertaken to ensure that practices, specified procedures, and adopted standards are followed according to intent or legal requirements. Legal requirements or standards are set up in policies, and an assessment is made to determine how well these policies are carried out. This may be an audit mandated by an agency or a legal source. Auditors are charged with the responsibilities of identifying differences between plans and policies and actual practice only. They would not be responsible for making recommendations for improvement. A weakness in this type of audit is that the experience of auditors is often ignored.

Social Auditing

Social auditing is an appraisal to ascertain how an organization impacts, interplays, and contributes to the social health and vitality of individuals employed by the organization and the communities they live in. This is a controversial new form of auditing that seeks to determine the negative or positive impact a corporation may have on its environment. An organization will conduct this type of auditing infrequently. Both professional auditors and an array of representatives from an organization, government, and the community may form the audit task group.

Management Auditing

Management auditing is a diagnostic appraisal process for analyzing goals, plans, policies, and activities in every phase of operation to uncover unsuspected weaknesses and to develop ideas for improvement in areas that have escaped management attention.[4] Its emphasis is primarily the quality of total management of an organization. It is largely a preventative measure to spot problems before they break out. When corrective action is proposed, it is to make actual practice conform with stated procedures and to point out the weaknesses in policies and procedures that require changes.

Common Factors

Among the common factors of auditing are: auditing seems to use predetermined and significant and agreed upon standards; auditing requires the evaluation by an independent auditor; auditing is tailored to the organization in question; and auditing requires a deductive and comparative analysis for measurement and evaluation. There are also important differences. Some are shown in Figure 6.1.

MODEL FOR EVALUATING PRODUCTIVITY

The scope of any evaluation may be wide or narrow. Since organizations vary and functions and programs are diverse, a specific method of evaluation to fit the evaluation needs for all is nearly impossible. Motorola conducted a productivity audit with a worldwide employee population of 56,000 on a design plan unique to its requirements.[5] Some main items in the audit were: (1) use of allowances and how they were being applied by each facility and how Motorola compares with competitors, (2) accuracy of standards in the shop, (3) bench methods, (4) observed productivity versus reported productivity, (5) accuracy of production and operation counts, (6) technical ability of engineering staff, (7) critique of training programs, (8) dollar amount of cost improvement. The results of the audit in reducing direct labor alone was estimated at $6.5 million. A different audit design was developed for indirect labor; it is still being conducted. This unique audit could never be duplicated in another organization .

The all-purpose auditing model is a myth. The best that can be done is to set up a basic approach that puts the evaluation process into general steps but allows each evaluator to formulate additional steps or include substeps. Yet to be effective any system of evaluation must be readily

Type of Audit	Scope of Evaluation	Evaluation Focus	Resources to be Evaluated	Comparison Method
Productivity audit	Organization, functions, departments, programs, individuals	Level and amount of productivity in organization	Money, personnel, equipment, space, time, procedures	Objectives and standards
Financial audit	Organization	Verification and certification of financial condition	Money	Standards and ratios
Program audit	Programs	Effectiveness in achieving program results	Money, personnel	Program objectives
Operations audit	Organization, functions, departments	Level and amount of performance effectiveness	Money, personnel, equipment, procedures	Standards and procedures
Compliance audit	Organization	Adherence to legal requirements	Personnel	Policies and standards
Social audit	Organization	Social contributions to individual and community	Money, personnel	Past performance
Management audit	Organization, functions	Quality and effectiveness of management	Management, personnel, policies	Other organizations

Figure 6.1 Audit comparisons.

understood, simple to implement, easy to administer, and clearly cost effective. The time, effort, and cost involved to conduct the evaluation must be equal to or less than the worth or value the audit can deliver. It must require minimal paperwork, and any competent and reasonable manager must be able to conduct it. Many audits conducted in organizations are not only expensive but require specialists who alone can interpret the results. Attempts to evaluate should take into account employee response to that evaluation. Most employees will be uneasy about a critical evaluation of their productivity. The whole effort could be counterproductive. In many cases group evaluation may be far easier to accomplish than individual evaluation.

The model for evaluating productivity suggested in this section follows the idea of simplicity, clarity, and managability. It can be conducted internally. At best, it's a generalized model, but can be adapted and adjusted to a specific organization, function, or program based on purposes and goals an evaluator wishes to achieve. The evaluation model would have five separate and distinct phases for conducting an audit as follows:

1. *Determine purpose* to be achieved by the audit.
2. *Select standards* as criteria for measurement.
3. *Use measures and compare* with standards. Several cycles may be necessary.
4. *Correct* for significant deviations and variances.
5. *Compile results* into a written report.

These phases are interrelated to give the evaluation process a systems flow from purpose through selecting standards through measuring, comparing, correcting, and reporting as shown in Figure 6.2. Let's examine each of the steps in greater detail.

Determining the Purpose of the Audit

The purpose of the audit determines the steps that follow. It shapes the standards, methods, measures and type of corrective feedback to be employed. An evaluator must make a choice about the use the evaluation will serve. Some purposes may conflict or be incompatible with others. For example, the market review and assessment of wages and salaries as they relate to employing and retaining manpower resources may conflict with cost of wages and salaries as it relates to productivity processes. How this conflict is resolved depends on how the audit is used relative to the

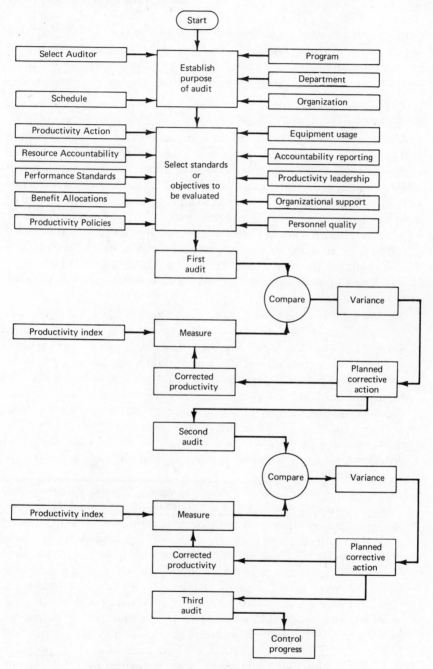

Figure 6.2 Model for evaluating productivity.

purpose it is expected to accomplish. Perhaps the reason that there are several types of audits and audit methods is because there are various purposes for evaluation procedures. Let's examine briefly some typical audit purposes for an organization.

1. *To Continue or Discontinue an Organization, a Function, a Program.* A productivity audit can provide significant and decisive information on which to base a decision to continue or discontinue an organization, a division, a function, or a program. Information about performance and its related resource utilization determines the level that prevails and indicates the amount of additional performance and related resources needed to raise the level to an acceptable standard compared to the market or competing organizations. If the performance and the need for resources are too great to bring productivity levels to standard within a given period of time, an evaluator may recommend a decision to discontinue and start fresh. To admit a wrong start and begin over with a new approach may be a hard decision, but it may cost less than to continue in an ineffective way.

2. *To Allocate Resources Among Competing Organizations, Functions, and Programs.* Resources are limited and probably will become even more limited. Careful analysis must be made to avoid overstaffing in relation to the work being done, inefficient or uneconomical use of equipment, waste and rework, and duplication of efforts by employees or between functional units. Information is needed to determine proper resource allocation among competing activities, functions, and programs. Productivity evaluation accounts for present allocation and provides the basis for a reallocation benefit analysis. It determines the degree of effectiveness a set of resources is achieving in a program, a function, or an organization.

3. *To Improve Practices and Procedures Among Competing Organizations, Functions, and Programs.* Program approaches, functional techniques, and organizational practices must be continuously evaluated to determine their effectiveness and efficiency. Adding and dropping techniques, approaches, procedures, and practices, based on productivity information, gives the organization the opportunity to maintain itself and even grow in the face of changing conditions and challenges. Careful analysis is necessary to discover procedures and policies that are ineffective, unsuitable, or more costly than justified; performance of work that serves little or no useful purpose; faulty buying practices and accumulation of unneeded or excess quantities of property, materials, equipment, or supplies; and the extent to which current managerial controls are effective. Although the productivity evaluation

can be staffed, structured, and concluded in many ways, its purpose will provide the guideline for its arrangements.

Selecting Standards as Criteria for Measurement

Standards are reference points by which performance, resource utilization, or productivity can be measured or compared. Standards provide a logical basis for assessment. A reference point is needed for taking action. Tell a manager, "Your productivity is 3.4." He will ask, "Is that good or bad?" Knowledge of performance or productivity is not enough. There must be a basis for comparison before a judgment can be made. Standards represent the only forms of reference that give sufficient universality for comparing different units of time. The concept of accountability is woven into the basic premises supporting these standards. They give work scope to the audit and suggest correct actions that need to be taken. The application of standards is not limited to quantitative information and ratio assessments, such as cost performance, scheduled shipments, percent program attainment, and the hundreds of possible ratios (see Chapter 4). The concept of standards extends to practices, methods, procedures, and techniques. Various terms such as *budget, specification, quota,* or *schedule* have been used for standards. *Objectives* may also be used as standards since they represent targets to be "hit." A productivity objective would serve as a criterion for indicating how practitioners must apply themselves for expected results to prevail. A *plan* may also constitute a standard since it represents the kind of work, activities, and results that must be attained.

Another way of expressing standards is to recognize key organizational practices that are vital to productivity. Katzell conducted a major survey for the American Management Association and revealed 10 primary factors that must be taken into account if an organization is to achieve systemwide changes that are essential to raising its productivity.[6]

1. Employee compensation tied to performance and to sharing in productivity gains.
2. Participation of workers in decisions affecting their own and related jobs.
3. Job enlargement, including challenge, variety, wholeness, and self-regulation.
4. Employee sense of involvement in the total organization.
5. Adequate safety conditions, pay, fringe benefits, and working conditions.
6. Simplification of channels of communication and authority.

7. Resources at worker's disposal to facilitate work effectiveness and reduce frustration associated with getting the job done.

8. Improved work methods that workers have been involved in planning and implementing.

9. Opportunities for greater employee stewardship—that is, direct care of and attention to customer, client, and co-worker needs.

10. Allowance for flexibility in relation to type of incentive and authority patterns.

These factors suggest that productivity is not a simple matter of cause and effect. Organizational changes to meet these factors must be extensive, or whatever effort is made will be slight and temporary. Simplistic approaches will not suffice. A total organizational approach that takes into consideration the unique requirements of the organization is a must.

Standards for Evaluating Productivity. Organizational standards are evaluative criteria against which an organization is measured and compared. Functional standards are evaluative criteria against which functions of an organization, such as engineering, accounting, admissions, or operations, are measured and compared. Program standards are evaluative criteria against which programs of an organization, such as cost reduction program, occupational therapy program, and quality improvement program, are measured and compared.

The following list of standards that could be used in a productivity audit is not comprehensive. They can be applied in total or in part for the total organization, a department, or a program. The reader should identify and formulate standards that would suit and fit a given set of audit objectives.

PRODUCTIVITY ACTIONS

1. All key individuals manage and have made a commitment to do their work according to well defined, properly stated, and precisely measurable productivity objectives and goals. These objectives are written and open for review.

2. Productivity objectives are consistent with mission statements and other objectives of the organization.

3. Productivity objectives are set at levels similar to or greater than previous levels.

4. Productivity effort exhibits indicators that distinguishes it from other efforts needed and practiced in the organization.

5. Productivity progress toward meeting performance, cost, and schedule

milestones can be assessed for early detection and timely correction of problems.

RESOURCE ACCOUNTABILITY

1. All resources are aggregated and accounted for in budgets located at well organized cost centers that are responsible for achievement of plans and objectives.
2. Time is viewed as a critical resource and managing it is clearly visible with priority systems, schedules, and avoidance of work on trivia.
3. Cost centers account through a budgeting information system for resource utilization and waste for the whole organization.
4. Resources are at workers' disposal at the time needed to facilitate work.
5. Cost centers are closely aligned with functional authority of the organization structure. That is, cost centers are tied to the decision-making process of budget formulation and adoption.

PERFORMANCE STANDARDS

1. Individuals are aware of trained-for, expected performance before they start work.
2. Performance standards are clearly defined, attainable, accurate, and measurable.
3. Individuals are aware of and have controls on the amount of resources they are to use in completing performance standards.
4. Performance measures are made and aggregated within cost centers.
5. Productivity is measured with resource and performance results at cost centers.

BENEFIT ALLOCATIONS

1. Cost of benefits are precisely identified and assigned in cost centers.
2. Reward and benefit system is based on performance and productivity data. Increased benefits are given only with increased productivity.
3. Benefits to be achieved are clearly stated for each program, project, or plan.
4. Planned benefit allocations are accompanied by planned productivity improvement.
5. Productivity is a criterion during negotiations and trade-offs.

PRODUCTIVITY POLICIES

1. A productivity mission statement is issued, actively pursued, and given high priority by top management.
2. Managers must submit formal productivity plans to be integrated into an overall productivity plan.
3. Productivity results are formally evaluated once a year.
4. Gains resulting from increased productivity are shared with those responsible for the increase.
5. Productivity improvement is practiced within all cost centers or departments of the organization.

EQUIPMENT USAGE AND TECHNOLOGY

1. Equipment purchase is justified by data of productivity improvement or by the savings it institutes.
2. Of available equipment options, planned usage of equipment is shown to be best for productivity.
3. Technological innovations and the use of technological aids are visible in practice.
4. Equipment purchase, use, and expenditures are controlled and reported through cost centers.
5. Short-range trade-off benefits should not outweigh long-range benefit expectations.

ACCOUNTABILITY REPORTING

1. A system exists for reporting to accountability sources total variances from an established plan of productivity improvement.
2. Required productivity is delegated and can be traced to a specific person in the organization.
3. Observed productivity is in fact the same as reported productivity.
4. Status reporting system is self-correcting through feedback to workers.
5. A formal annual report on productivity progress is submitted to top management.

PRODUCTIVITY LEADERSHIP

1. Leaders operate and manage in an action-research manner for productivity improvements. They "tune-up" the organization, searching for ways to improve. There is a high *esprit de corps*.

2. Leaders operate a system to seek and implement work improvement innovations from workers.
3. Leaders allow high "clashes" in productivity ideas but low "clashes" in interpersonal relations. Competition is encouraged for results but is not encouraged among personalities.
4. Leaders delegate work responsibilities accompanied by accountability.
5. Leaders conduct and make use of periodic productivity audits.

ORGANIZATIONAL SUPPORT

1. Power structure is recognizable and close to the formal plan of organization. All unnecessary or marginal functions are eliminated.
2. Decision making is delegated to the most critical point of productivity action or cost centers—where work is accomplished and the impact is greatest.
3. Balanced effort from all significant units prevails.
4. Employees are allowed to participate in decisions affecting their own and related jobs.
5. Research and development are a formal and deliberate effort in the organization.

PERSONNEL QUALITY

1. Individuals are open to and express a positive attitude toward productivity improvement.
2. Self-renewal, obsolescence, and low performance are personal concerns.
3. Orientation, training, and coaching for abilities and skills for productivity are provided.
4. System of personnel backups prevail to continue level of productivity when turnover occurs.
5. Productivity skills are a primary criterion in the recruiting and hiring of personnel.

Measuring Productivity and Comparing with Standards

Productivity evaluation control and adjustments requires measurements. Several types of measurements were suggested and illustrated in Chapter

4. More must be developed especially in the important areas such as morale, safety, and perseverance. Our use of the word *measurement* is not intended to convey the precision one might gather from its definition. Our measurements are for quantity of productivity results—"how much." The numbers in ratios, indexes, percentages, amounts, frequency rates, averages, degrees, and proportions specify exactly what is intended and how well it is completed. Measurement gives the bench marks so that practitioners can tell whether they are moving toward objectives and standards or away from them. These bench marks tell whether their programs will hit their targets within required units of time. For example, a productivity standard of 20 percent cost reduction in office supplies within 4 months can be allocated at 5 percent per month, and a progress chart can be developed to show present status and progress toward reaching the standard. Quantitative measurements may not always be possible. In this case a checklist of items to be completed for desirable results can be used.

Measurements provide a basis for comparing with standards. Visual comparison is especially desirable. Cold figures come to life when they are portrayed graphically. A simple display, chart, matrix, or profile that is well prepared, easily understood, and kept up to date should do the job. Examples are bar charts, target charts, trend lines, percentage completion charts, checklists, and comparative tables.

Comparison may show a variance from the standard. Variance can be positive (ahead of standards), negative (behind standards), or zero (meeting standards exactly). Evaluating the significance of the variance might be guided by historical records, experience, and observation of other organizations. The 10 standards suggested in the previous section can be placed in an evaluative auditing procedure in which points can be assigned to each category and a judgment made on an organization, a function, or a program. The procedure suggested here follows in concept the procedure used by the American Institute of Management in evaluating organizational managements. The American Institute of Management has conducted this audit over many years and has published the results in *Manual of Excellent Managements*.[7]

The productivity audit attempts to provide a quantified evaluation of how well an organization, a function, or a program meets the expectancies of each standard. Consequently, the productivity audit is an evaluative process based on comparing it with standards. The 10 standards are grouped; points are assigned; and relative weights, based on the total productivity audit, are specified. The points, weights, and minimum rating for productivity vigor are shown as follows:

Standards	Maximum Rating Possible	Minimum Rating for Productivity Vigor
1. Productivity actions	150	120
2. Resource accountability	75	50
3. Performance standards	100	75
4. Benefit allocations	125	100
5. Productivity policies	100	75
6. Equipment usage and technology	150	110
7. Accountability reporting	50	35
8. Productivity leadership	125	100
9. Organizational support	50	35
10. Personnel quality	75	50
Total points	1000	750 (approximate)

Points to be assigned for five bench marks within each standard can be obtained by dividing the maximum rating possible for each standard by five. Managers who conduct this audit internally should use information and personal judgment to determine how well each standard is achieved.

Correction of Significant Deviations

The next step in the productivity audit is to plan for and take actions that will correct the variances. Herein lies the value of the audit and the auditor. The auditor must have the ability to develop the actions that will correlate what is with what is wanted. The task of developing an improvement is not always easy, and correction cannot be achieved overnight. The productivity deficiency will usually require significant actions and a long period for correction. Changing the organization, purchasing equipment, and shifting or releasing personnel are typical required efforts. The proposed plan will be to institute whatever is needed to bring the organization, the function, or the program up to acceptable levels. This action step is significant in the feedback loop seen in Figure 6.2. The decision to act on the variance and deviations is transmitted to the individuals who manage the programs, function, or organization. They are the ones who can and should act. The audit is virtually useless if the first three steps are taken without completing the fourth. The first three steps indicate that the organization must get back on a productivity track; the fourth step is the place to do something about it immediately.

This is another way of implementing the concept of follow-up and follow-through for assuring that productivity reaches the desired standard. The concept of the audit model emphasizes repeating two or more cycles of auditing as follow-up to assure that the actions taken are implemented and operating. This follow-up recycled process retraces exactly the steps taken in the first cycle. Comparisons of the second audit with the first or the third audit with the first gives a valid measure of the changes in operating productivity practices.

The extent of necessary follow-up or follow-through depends largely on whether the actions to be taken are reversible. If the action is to get rid of a piece of equipment and install a new one, there should be no question in the follow-up. Either equipment usage has been corrected or it has not. However, if the action is a change in personnel practices, a question may arise of backsliding. Here follow-up, follow-through, and second and third auditing with periodic checks are needed to assure that new practices and improved actions are well rooted. Several audit traps should be avoided when developing improvements.

1. Proposing a correction for an organization without first assessing its impact on coordination and cooperation.
2. Proposing the purchase of new equipment without assessing its indirect effects on other departments.
3. Proposing a change in work procedure without noticing the impact it will have on other departments.
4. Proposing a change in equipment, work procedure, or schedule without studying the effects it will have on morale, training, and confidence.
5. Proposing a change in a department without considering the objectives and plans the department is pursuing.
6. Proposing any kind of change based on data that is suspect, faulty, or inaccurate.
7. Proposing any kind of change without sampling the reactions of those who will be affected by the change.

The plan for correcting the deviations and variances follows closely the guidelines for productivity planning suggested in earlier chapters.

Compiling Results into a Written Report

A most important effort in the productivity audit is the gathering of all information and recording it for visibility, review, analysis, and accountability. The written report formalizes the entire audit. It establishes significant relationships and facilitates further analysis. It makes the audit less susceptible to misunderstanding. The information recorded is intended to establish the validity and reliability of the facts of performance in relation to resources utilization. With a written report, the results of the audit can be widely communicated for greatest advantage. The written report renders a full accounting of how responsibilities and resources have been executed and applied in the organization.

Gathering and recording the information should be done so that another independent auditor, conducting the same audit, would come up with approximately the same results. The written report facilitates follow-up work. Forms, documents, files, charts, appraisals, tables, tests, letters, policies, procedures, directives, layouts, interviews, and statistical analysis related to and in support of the audit appraisal and its subsequent analysis should be included.

An outline of the written report that includes all information and reports the results is suggested.

OUTLINE OF PRODUCTIVITY AUDIT REPORT

1. *Summary (Single-Page)*
   (a) Purpose and objectives of the audit.
   (b) Results obtained.
   (c) Recommendations for improvement.
   (d) Brief description of qualification of auditor.
2. *Main Contents*
   (a) Introduction and background.
   (b) Purpose and objectives of the audit.
   (c) Why the audit was conducted—facts, current practices, and the evaluation.
   (d) Procedure for conducting the audit.
   (e) Analysis and measurements of facts and information.
   (f) Results obtained.
   (g) Conclusions and recommendations.
3. *Appendix*
   (a) Tables or calculations.
   (b) Graphs of diagrams.
   (c) Supporting documents.
   (d) Qualification of auditor.

The written report should be sent to the individuals who have authorized its development. But this should not limit or prevent discussions of findings, judgments, conclusions, and recommendations with persons who have responsibilities involving the area being audited. On the contrary, this kind of discussion is encouraged. The following three cases illustrate how the concept of a productivity audit can be used to assess productivity vigor in a city garbage collection program, a product-oriented manufacturing company, and a nonprofit health-care facility.

Garbage Collection Program in a City Government: A Case History

Located in the northeastern part of the country, New Rome is a city of 210,000 citizens established in 1830. It is agriculturally oriented, and most of the revenues collected are derived from agricultural products. There are also some industries. The city operates under a council-manager form of government with the mayor and four councilmen elected at large. The city manager is appointed and hired by the council. The council makes final decisions on planning and zoning matters, holds hearings on items of public interest, reviews and adopts the annual budget, determines appropriations of bond funds, grants franchises, and awards contracts.

During a department meeting three years ago the director of public works reported that the cost of garbage and trash collection had skyrocketed because more routes had been added which resulted in less efficiency and higher labor costs. In addition, the director had received many complaints about residential garbage collection from citizens, the health department, and the sanitation department workers. The public works director was assigned to head a three-man study team to formalize a garbage collection program to reduce the high costs and eliminate complaints. The actions that were formulated were:

1. Levy an assessment for removing garbage and trash.
2. Specify the types and sizes of containers.
3. Define the system of routing, collecting, and disposing.
4. Develop an ordinance that would satisfy all groups in the city.
5. Organize a public relations program to inform citizenry.
6. Set up the administration of the program to keep it efficient and low in operating costs.

After nine months of hearings, public reaction, and passage of the ordinance, the program was set up and operating. After two years of operations, the city manager wanted a productivity audit to be conducted to determine the effectiveness and efficiency of the program. The results are tabulated in Figure 6.3. From the audit, a policy was instituted to put the entire program on an effectiveness plan using MPBO. Changes and improvements were made to reach for productivity, and a second audit was conducted 6 months later (Figure 6.3). The overall productivity improvement was 112 percent.

This improved productivity was accomplished with the following action items:

1. The entire program was set under an MPBO basis—that is, all results needed or desired were specified in objectives, and a schedule was developed by supervisors.

2. All costs were aggregated in a program cost center to determine their magnitude and location. Cost control efforts were focused at the sources. For example, disposal of solid wastes at the land-filled area was separated by private contractors into recycled and nonrecycled wastes. This had an effect on capacity and recycling uses.

3. Disposal capacity of the land-filled areas was set up on a time-controlled schedule to give the council status reports on potential capacity, usable capacity, and filled capacity. These were tabulated and correlated with population growth. The city council was given monthly reports on program status.

4. Garbage collection routes were formalized, and performance standards were set up—that is, sections of the city that should be covered on a per-day basis by truck. Size and type of containers were specified to reduce number of trips.

5. Crews were allowed to set their own schedule, provided they met their productivity standards. For example, in the summer they start at 5:30 and are finished at 1:30.

6. Preventive maintenance procedures were instituted to reduce the truck breakdown rate from 30 to 10 percent.

7. A system of personnel backups were developed to assure all trucks were fully manned and operating to meet productivity standards.

8. The three supervisors in the program were given special training and development in time management for crew and truck usage handling.

9. A number of workers were cut from the payroll and the remaining workers were given higher wages for meeting their productivity standards. This resulted in a reduced annual payroll.

Standards	First-Year Point Rating			Second-Year Point Rating			Productivity Improvement (%)
	Maximum	Minimum	Actual	Maximum	Minimum	Actual	
1. Productivity actions	150	120	30	150	120	80	167
2. Resource accountability	75	50	10	75	50	20	100
3. Performance standards	100	75	10	100	75	40	300
4. Benefit allocations	125	100	20	125	100	20	0
5. Productivity policies	100	75	10	100	75	50	400
6. Equipment usage	150	110	10	150	110	80	700
7. Accountability reporting	50	35	10	50	35	40	300
8. Productivity leadership	125	100	80	125	100	100	25
9. Organizational support	50	35	30	50	35	40	34
10. Personnel quality	75	50	35	75	50	50	43
Total	1000	750	245	1000	750	520	112

Figure 6.3   Productivity audit: productivity vigor of the garbage collection program in a city government.

Olympic Manufacturing Company: A Case History

The Olympic Manufacturing Company is a nonunionized manufacturer of several lines of outdoor sports equipment. Ninety percent of its revenue is generated by the sales of snowmobiles, skis, tennis rackets, and fishing equipment. It markets its products to sporting goods stores in the eastern half of the United States through a system of representatives. When the plant first opened, 200 employees were hired. Over a period of years the plant operation has grown at the existing plant site to 800 employees—four times its original size. The company has not been able to keep pace with the fast growing demand for its products. Sales forecasts predict an even greater demand in each of the next five years, due largely to the average American having more leisure time, more disposable income, and a growing interest in sports.

Under a new policy direction of the president to improve all its internal systems, a productivity audit was conducted to discover what the "productivity vigor" might be and the problems preventing it in the operation. The results are tabulated in Figure 6.4. The problems uncovered were:

1. Employee productivity was down 40 percent from the previous year and was steadily declining.
2. Absenteeism was up 30 percent from the previous year.
3. Discontent and low morale prevailed for no apparent reason. Plenty of overtime ws available, but few took advantage of it.
4. Turnover was high. Recruitment efforts were on a continuous schedule due to the high rate and the low labor market yield.

The president proceeded to institute changes recommended by a committee set up within the company. These changes were given one year to operate after which an evaluation would be made on the progress and new changes would be made if needed.

One year later a second audit was taken, and significant progress was noted. Two years later a third audit was taken, and the company appeared to be heading toward becoming a highly productive operation. The results of the third audit are tabulated in Figure 6.4. The overall productivity improvement was 183 percent. The improved productivity was accomplished with the following action items.:

1. All department managers were to submit annual productivity plans with specific objectives for reaching higher levels of productivity.
2. Productivity standards were to be set in all job stations and employees

Standards	First-Year Point Rating			Third-Year Point Rating			Productivity Improvement (%)
	Maximum	Minimum	Actual	Maximum	Minimum	Actual	
1. Productivity actions	150	120	20	150	120	120	500
2. Resources accountability	75	50	30	75	50	40	33
3. Performance standards	100	75	20	100	75	80	300
4. Benefit allocations	125	100	20	125	100	80	300
5. Productivity policies	100	75	10	100	75	80	700
6. Equipment usage	150	110	80	150	110	120	50
7. Accountability reporting	50	35	10	50	35	40	300
8. Productivity leadership	125	100	20	125	100	100	400
9. Organizational support	50	35	20	50	35	40	100
10. Personnel quality	75	50	40	75	50	65	63
Total	1000	750	240	1000	750	765	183

Figure 6.4 Productivity audit: productivity vigor changes in the Olympic Manufacturing Company.

were to be oriented and trained to the new standards. Employees were expected to participate in the setting of standards. The standards were set to meet existing and growing inventory demands set by sales.

3. The company went on a short and reduced workweek schedule. A 9-hour, 4-day workweek was instituted as compensation for reaching the higher levels of productivity standards.

4. The reduced workweek had an intense motivational effect on the operation. Leisure time for the employees was accepted so overwhelmingly that turnover and absenteeism dropped to an insignificant level. Morale improved greatly. It was later discovered that those working in a leisure product industry are adversely affected if they themselves do not have sufficient leisure time.

5. The high gains of the new productivity standards and the reduction of turnover and absenteeism bought about a cost performance that compensated for the reduced workweek, reached the inventory quotas expected by sales, and brought about significant gains in profitability.

The Clinic Memorial Hospital: A Case History

The Clinic Memorial Hospital had its beginnings in the 1920s when it first started as a out-patient day clinic. Over the years the clinic expanded and eventually facilities were added so that it operates as a full-fledged open-staff hospital administered on a nonprofit basis. This means all financing is from patient fees. All monies received in excess of operating costs are applied directly toward expansion or are used for taking care of charity patients. The 350-bed hospital employing 700 full-time employees and 110 part-time employees is accredited and accepted by the medical profession.

The hospital has operated under a traditional dichotomous management system where doctors and administrators were often on opposite sides of decision making about hospital services and care. The hospital operated on a budget form of management. All decisions on expenditures were based on if the budget would allow them or if they were in the budget when it was approved. There are 15 department heads in the hospital. Since the "budget rule" dominated all decision making, the supervisors who head the departments were totally lacking in responsibility and performed poorly. The budget was the "supervisor." As a result several critical problems emerged:

1. Supervisors were not getting optimal performance out of employees.
2. There were no budget overruns, but improved services and care could not be instituted because of lack of new funding.

3. Supervisors would not take responsibility, make decisions, and institute improvements.

4. The prevailing "climate" was geared toward getting along with others rather than improving the quality of patient care and adding vitally needed services.

5. Friction between physicians who needed support services and hospital staff who held to the budget had become serious.

The chief hospital administrators had attempted several times to bring about improvement, but the system caused them to fail. They decided that a new management system was needed to turn the operations around. With this in mind, a productivity audit was conducted. The results are tabulated in Figure 6.5. A series of seminars were developed to put all personnel on a new management system of MPBO.

1. All supervisors were to set annual objectives for the results needed for the hospital. All supervisors would be evaluated on these results for their merit increases, promotions, transfers, demotions, or terminations.

2. All supervisors were given the authority, within their allocated budgets, to decide all matters for reaching and completing their objectives.

3. A new emphasis was to be placed on improvement of services and quality of care. Innovations were encouraged.

4. Productivity standards for services and care needs were instituted, and employees were "educated" about why and how they were to be reached.

5. The budget was still important, but greater stress was placed on accomplishments even if the budget had to be changed.

6. Regular meetings were set up between hospital staff and the physicians to iron out their differences. Communications were developed to understand the needs of both sides.

At the end of the first year, a second audit was conducted to note the changes in productivity vigor. The results are tabulated in Figure 6.5. Overall productivity improved 178 percent.

PRODUCTIVITY IMPROVEMENT PRACTICES

The following checklist represents productivity practices that organizations throughout the United States have actually adopted to bring about increased

Standards	First-Year Point Rating Maximum	Minimum	Actual	Second-Year Point Rating Maximum	Minimum	Actual	Productivity Improvement (%)
1. Productivity actions	150	120	10	150	120	80	700
2. Resources accountability	75	50	40	75	50	60	50
3. Performance standards	100	75	10	100	75	60	500
4. Benefit allocations	125	100	10	125	100	20	100
5. Productivity policies	100	75	10	100	75	80	700
6. Equipment usage	150	110	100	150	110	120	20
7. Accountability reporting	50	35	20	50	35	40	100
8. Productivity leadership	125	100	10	125	100	100	900
9. Organizational support	50	35	10	50	35	40	300
10. Personnel quality	75	50	10	75	50	40	300
	1000	750	230	1000	750	640	178

Figure 6.5 Productivity audit: productivity vigor change in the Clinic Memorial Hospital.

productivity. Names of the companies have been omitted; only the type of organization has been included. In most instances productivity figures have been estimated. My experience has been that only a few organizations have arrived at productivity maturity where a quantitative value can be measured.

1. *Chemical Manufacturer.* Use of digital computers with special programs to lay out the design of piping systems. This reduced design time considerably. Productivity improvement: 30 percent.

2. *Retail Chain Store.* Use of part-time workers in busy periods to replace full-time workers. Full-time workers given job enlargement. Transferred lower-rated employees to job formerly handled by higher-priced employees. Productivity gains resulted from smaller compensation packages to lower operating budgets. Productivity improvement: 22 percent.

3. *Construction Compnay.* Shifting an 8-hour schedule (8:30–4:30) from the hot hours of the day to the cool hours of the morning (5:30–1:00) in outside construction work. Productivity improvement: 35 percent.

4. *Large Corporate Bank.* Focused efforts on improving personnel through accelerated use of training, greater morale aids, and special incentives. Training was intensive to assure skills and to teach the best methods for performing jobs. Morale was improved by making a more comfortable environment and work stations. Rewards were made more liberal with better insurance, more benefits, and greater investment options. Productivity improvement: 12 percent.

5. *Small Machinery Manufacturer.* Used a special raw material inventory system with specialized and sophisticated machinery and equipment. The system reduced inventories from four million to less than two million, resulting in greater flexibility and space. Productivity improvement: 60 percent.

6. *Large Hospital.* Set up work standards, job scheduling priorities and better equipment usage policies to experience a reduction of resource utilization with no apparent change in services. Trained department heads in work planning, scheduling, sampling, time-and-motion and problem-solving approaches. Productivity improvement: 45 percent.

7. *Government Agency.* Agreeing on priorities, eliminating needless chores, and streamlining a decision-making approach among several departments resulted in sharp reductions of backlog and doubled each department's output. Productivity improvement: 65 percent.

8. *Defense Contractor.* Use of PERT (program evaluation review technique) and RAMPS (resource allocation and multi-project scheduling) as capacity schedules improved effectiveness of allocating existing unknown capacity while drastically reducing costs. Productivity improvement: 46 percent.

9. *Small Tool Manufacturer.* Initiated a 3-day, 12-hour-per-day week for 1200 employees to optimize equipment usage and scheduling. Idle time reduced considerably, while quality went up with reduced waste and scrap. Productivity improvement: 16 percent.

10. *Garbage Collections in Large City.* Instituted incentive pay to complete garbage collection without the use of overtime. Workers saw this as a chance to make more money but go home earlier. Productivity improvement: 24 percent.

11. *Airline Carrier.* Introduced cost centers as basis for aggregating resources. Performance was interwoven and related to these cost centers. Productivity improvement: 38 percent.

12. *Hose Manufacturer.* Initiating 4-day, 9½-hour-per-day workweek for a plant of 400 employees increased total production by cutting the absenteeism rate. Productivity improvement: 10 percent.

13. *Construction Company.* Specialized computers programmed for estimating proposals reduced staff from 103 to 56 at $0.5 million a year less expense. Productivity improvement: 85 percent.

14. *Large Residential Treatment Center.* Instituted position guides that incorporated job descriptions and methods of evaluating each responsibility in the description. Productivity improvement: 20 percent.

15. *Steel Stamp Company.* Converted useless scrap material into a useful, highly marketable production part. Scrap recycling and reutilization has driven cost downward. Productivity improvement: 55 percent.

16. *Corporate Bank with Branches.* Shut down some branch offices, combined operations, and reached for optimal number of operators. Reducing number of employees and general overhead caused a reduction in costs. Productivity improvement: 20 percent.

17. *Police Department of Medium-Size City.* Instituted incentive pay and bonuses for reduction of crime. The plan amounted to $45 per man, but saved the city and taxpayers approximately $150,000 from burglaries alone. Productivity improvement: 18 percent.

18. *Power Equipment Manufacturer.* Instituted monthly participating efficiency bonuses based on the ratio of payroll costs to production value. The new program of bonus awards based on productivity lowered absenteeism and tardiness. Productivity improvement: 85 percent.

19. *New York City Bank.* Instituted a check-clearing system by giving each clerk the complete clearing process for a bank check from start to finish. The clerk was responsible for all discrepancies and handling of checks. Productivity improvement: 25 percent.

20. *Health-Care Facility.* Used "job pairing" in which two part-time employees are responsible for a whole job, not just half. This reduced turnover and absenteeism. Productivity improvement: 30 percent.

21. *Food Supplier.* Instituted a 4-day workweek for all food distribution units. Overtime was reduced to near zero, while quality of services increased. Productivity improvement: 18 percent.

22. *Overseas Chemical Industry.* Instituted a plan affecting 55,000 workers in 75 plants in which workers participated in the planning and selection of production techniques and were responsible for their own quality. These techniques were productivity bargaining, elimination of restrictive work practices in jobs, elimination of distribution between white-collar and blue-collar workers, and special morale-increasing programs. Productivity improvement: 13 percent.

23. *Food Producer.* Use of project-team approach where several members of a team identify the task, schedule and plan their own work, and execute the responsibilities necessary within the team. With this approach morale increased, absenteeism decreased, and quality was improved. Productivity improvement: 40 percent.

24. *Large Midwest Government Agency.* Instituted an effective absence-control program through quarterly reporting and recognition of perfect attendance. For every 1 percent decrease in absenteeism, 10 fewer people are needed on payroll. New hires were reduced. Productivity improvement: 35 percent.

25. *Insurance Company.* Instituted a job enrichment program for key-punch operators and secretaries who were experiencing high absenteeism, low morale, and poor productivity. Jobs were broadened; operators were made responsible for their work; and a firm operator-customer relationship was developed. Secretaries were given administrative responsibilities. Productivity improvement: 26 percent.

26. *Visiting Nurse's Association.* Used a four-level horizontal promotion plan in which professional work was aggregated into four levels, and rewards and promotions were connected to these levels. The visiting nurse association had been experiencing maximum professional growth, but there was nowhere to go in the agency. Productivity improvement: 30 percent.

27. *Large New York Office.* Developed work measurement for clerical

standards. Reevaluated and reorganized jobs with new standards. Productivity improvement: 45 percent.

28. *Medium-Sized Town.* Used a minicomputer to institute a management information system for forwarding data and information to individual departments more quickly than before. Productivity improvement: 20 percent.

29. *Parks Department of a Large City.* Instituted a work planning and scheduling system that had not been used before to relate personnel, equipment, crew specialization, and work standards to the large backlog of work usually experienced in the summer when staff is at an all-time low. Productivity improvement: 18 percent.

30. *Hospital in Medium-Sized City.* Scrapped the automatic 5 percent rate step increments and revised methods of compensation. Instituted new appraisal system that focuses on the individual results. Productivity improvement: 12 percent.

31. *Assembly Manufacturing Firm.* Convinced union in the middle of a contract's life to have operators learn more than one job under a new job classification program. This gave employees more money and more security through flexibility and enlarged opportunities. Productivity improvement: 28 percent.

The challenge of management in productivity improvement can be seen in two ways. First, recognize that productivity improvement is not a common effort in our prevailing work ethic. Productivity is not usually considered when pursuing other managerial concerns. Attitudes toward productivity are changing, but they are not ideal. Second, to experience improvement in productivity requires a level of competence and ability comparable to other functions that make organizations work.

ACTIONS FOR MANAGING PRODUCTIVITY

Specific actions can be taken by management to improve productivity.

1. Encourage and give incentives for technological innovations and the use of mechanical aids.
2. Increase productivity mindedness among workers and "tune-up" the climate for better ways to complete work.
3. Develop and apply measures for evaluating white-collar performance.
4. Develop "work-smarter-and-harder" policies.

5. Grant wage increase only with recorded justified equivalent productivity contribution.

6. Move away from time contracting or giving rewards based on "time triggers" toward performance contracting.

7. Use computer systems or time-sharing terminals to decrease reaction time needed in decision making or aiding in cost estimating, design analysis, drafting, testing, or preparing reports.

8. Motivate the work force toward productivity objectives.

9. Match employees with jobs for which they are best suited.

10. Review and improve such basic managerial processes as planning, organizing, staffing, directing, and controlling.

11. Use effective work thinking and planning before the work starts.

12. Evaluate effectiveness of programs and functions and eliminate those that are marginal and cannot be improved.

13. Repeal or modify laws that only generate costs and provide unneeded and unnecessary constraints.

14. Enrich work for challenge and variety and redesign jobs for interest and productivity.

15. Increase R & D activities for productivity breakthroughs.

16. Increase capital investments for lowering unit costs. Amortize the investment through productivity savings.

17. Manage time like other managerial concerns and bring time usage and waste under control.

18. Encourage healthy competition among groups and between organizations.

19. Eliminate "nice to have" but "not needed" functions, programs, personnel, space, equipment, and facilities.

20. Get away from emphasis on cost control into the area of effectiveness and efficiency.

21. Train for new skills and abilities with in-house education and training programs.

22. Complex procedures must be simplified to bring accountability and reaction time into a focus where decisions and responsibilities are located.

23. Develop jobs to allow for individual enrichment and personal satisfaction.

24. Develop a new work ethic with its attending attitudes and motivators.

25. Balance organization structures so that no one function or department dominates the budget or the entire organization.

26. Improve the total organization with formal renewal, updating, and development programs.
27. Shorten time expectancy for a given amount of work while still maintaining quality.
28. Priorities in resource allocation must follow priorities of productivity objectives.
29. Use equipment and facility aids in service-intensive organizations.
30. Use human relations skills and process in equipment-intensive organizations.
31. Increase discretionary content of jobs for white-collar workers.
32. Replace performance appraisals with productivity appraisals.
33. Move away from time contracting toward performance contracting.
34. Give rewards and benefits only for the equivalent in productivity.
35. Link compensation with work output.
36. Discourage the practice of giving general across-the-board wage increases.
37. Discourage the practice of giving the same benefits in the same amount to all employees.
38. Pay for jobs rather than for time.
39. Hold regular employee meetings to encourage communication. Emphasize employee productivity—both performance and resources—and its relationship to pay reviews and benefits.
40. Have people initiate workload studies to eliminate unproductive time in their own jobs.
41. Create a receptive environment for labor and management to work toward efficiency improvement.
42. Get employees involved in the concept that higher productivity means higher profits or better budget performance, which means better pay and benefit rewards.

The managerial practitioner steers productivity efforts toward the desirable goals of the organization. This leadership role requires superior methods that are sharpened continuously to keep the effort progressive and significant. The productivity audit contributes to this end.

SUMMARY

Productivity has been the driving force that has led to our high standard of living and our high quality of work life. Any function or process that has had such a beneficial impact over such a long period of time is certainly worth major consideration and attention by all organizations. Few organizations have formalized their efforts toward productivity improvement.

This chapter described how an organization can conduct a productivity audit. The definition of the audit was given:

Productivity auditing is a process of monitoring and evaluating organizational practices to determine whether functions, programs, and the organization itself are utilizing their resources effectively and efficiently to accomplish objectives.

Productivity auditing should not be confused with other traditional forms of auditing such as financial auditing, social auditing, compliance auditing, operations auditing, and management auditing. There are many common features, but there are some important differences. These differences were noted and placed in a table for comparison.

The model for evaluating productivity is a general one. That is, it provides the concept for conducting an audit but should not be used as a detailed procedure for extensive or comprehenisve evaluation. There are four separate and distinct phases to the evaluation model:

1. Establishing the purpose to be achieved by audit.
2. Selecting standards as criteria for measurement.
3. Using measures and comparing with standards.
4. Correcting for significant deviations and variances.

These phases are interrelated to give the evaluation process a systems flow from purpose through standards through measuring, comparing, correcting, and reporting. Ten audit standards were described for evaluating the productivity process in a function, a program, an organization.

1. Productivity actions.
2. Resource accountability.
3. Performance standards.
4. Benefit allocations.
5. Productivity policies.
6. Equipment usage.
7. Accountability reporting.
8. Productivity leadership.

9. Organizational support.
10. Personnel quality.

Productivity improvement practices were also described in this chapter. Thirty-one productivity practices from 25 organizations were briefly described. Forty-two actions were also described. They indicate that the whole effort in productivity management in organizations is maturing.

QUESTIONS TO THINK ABOUT

1. Does your organization conduct any type of auditing? Which type? Why? Is productivity auditing conducted? Why or why not?
2. If you are conducting productivity auditing either formally or informally, have the results furthered the productivity effort?
3. Would the model for productivity auditing shown in Figure 6.2 work for your organization? Why or why not? What steps could be added? What steps should be removed?
4. If the standards of the productivity audit in Figure 6.2 could not apply to your organization, what changes would you suggest?
5. List the productivity improvement practices conducted in your organization last year. Does such a list exist for the coming year?

REFERENCES AND NOTES

1. John W. Kendrick, *Productivity Trends in the United States*, Princeton University Press, New Jersey 1976.
2. Howard F. Stettler, *Systems Based Independent Audits*, Prentice Hall Book Company, Englewood Cliffs, N.J., 1974, p. 22.
3. Roy A. Lindberg, "Operations Auditing: What It Is", *Management Review*, American Management Association, December 1969, p. 5.
4. *The Management Audit*, American Institute of Management, New York, 1966.
5. Walter B. Scott, "Motorola's Program for Improved Productivity," *Management Review*, Vol. 63, American Management Association, January 1974, pp. 56–58.
6. M. E. Katzell, *Productivity: The Measure and the Myth*, A Survey Report, American Management Association, New York, 1975, p. 1.
7. *Manual of Excellent Managements*, American Institute of Management, New York, 1970.

PART THREE

MANAGING THE CHANGED EMPLOYEE FOR PRODUCTIVITY IMPROVEMENT

Productivity has been changing because employees have changed. The worker of today has far greater economic impact in the organization than any workers in the past. But what are these changes? How have these changes produced the productivity frustrations? Part III discusses managing the changed employee for productivity improvement. The value of viewing the organization as a total process described in Part II must be coupled with new abilities for managing the new employee in organizations.

7
MANAGING
WHITE-COLLAR WORKERS

IN THIS CHAPTER

Differences between white-collar and blue-collar workers.
Management implications for handling white-collar work force.
Productivity mindedness.
Attitudes as a barrier to productivity.
Equipment aids for labor-intensive organizations.
Discretionary versus prescriptive job content.
Productivity appraisals.
Methods for designing jobs.
Time management.
Twenty examples of using MPBO with white-collar workers.

Traditional management methods for handling white-collar workers are inadequate and are counterproductive in some organizations. The typical white-collar worker's productivity ranges between 50 and 60 percent when there is no measurement of productivity.[1] Increases to 90 percent are possible when measurement and good management are applied. Total employment costs for salaried employees are higher than for wage earners and are growing more rapidly on a per capita basis. Productivity of salaried workers is an area for experiencing great gains. Who are the white-collar employees? How important a group are they? Are there special ways of managing this group? Would these ways improve productivity? Could we release the 30 to 40 percent stored productivity potential within this group?

The purpose of this chapter is to (1) define the white-collar work force, its growth, and significance for productivity, (2) identify the implications this work force has for management and its approaches for handling employees, (3) describe some of the management methods that are useful for achieving higher productivity from these type of workers. Six strategies are described: developing productivity mindedness, using equipment aids, increasing discretionary content of jobs, replacing performance appraisals with productivity appraisals, giving time-management training, motivation, and managing productivity by objectives.

WHO ARE THE WHITE-COLLAR WORKERS?

The year 1956 represents a significant milestone in the history of personnel management.[2] It was the first time the number of white-collar workers in the United States was equal to the number of blue-collar workers. The size of this work group has grown and is now the largest segment of the personnel market. The limits for this group are not in sight. When parity occurred, there were no press conferences, no news releases, no special announcements. Yet it marked a new era in personnel management. The special needs of this group and their unique character-istics demand new approaches for managing them toward productivity. The percentage of this group compared to other groups, according to the government's latest figures, and projections to 1985, are shown in Figure 7.1. The number of white-collar workers continues to increase; the number of blue-collar workers is decreasing; the number of service workers is increasing slowly. These trends may account for the recent decline in productivity in the United States. Between 1850 and 1889, when the country was predominately agricultural and beginning to industrialize, the annual productivity rate increased to 1.5 percent. Be-tween 1889 to 1919, as industrialization progressed, the rise advanced to 1.6. After World War II the productivity rate averaged close to 3.5 percent per year.[3] In recent years—at about the same time when the large white-collar work force emerged—the productivity rate has dropped to about 3 percent. We are now in transition from a predominately indus-trialized economy to an industrialized and service economy.

Worker Group	Percentage of Total			
	1960	1972	1980	1985
White-collar	43.1	47.8	51.5	52.9
Blue-collar	36.3	35.0	33.1	32.3
Service	12.7	13.4	13.3	13.2
Farm	7.9	3.8	2.1	1.6

Figure 7.1 Manpower workers in the United States in 1974.[4]

Some insight into the type of jobs within each worker group follows:

1. *White-Collar Workers.* Professional and technical workers—executives, teachers, accountants, engineers, medical doctors, nurses, lawyers, managers, supervisors, public administrators, government workers, social workers, real estate agents, quality control staff, draftsmen, technicians, salaried workers, tellers, data programmers, computer analysts, administrators, self-employed workers, sales workers, and clerical workers.

2. *Blue-Collar Workers.* Craft and vocational workers—carpenters, mechanics, machinists, construction workers, repairers, printers, metal workers, equipment and machine operators, assembly workers, transportation and shipping workers, deliverers, nonfarm laborers.

3. *Service Workers.* Food workers—waiters, cashiers, clerks, cooks, bartenders, hotel workers, firefighters, police officers, guards and security personnel, health service workers, nursing aides, hospital employees, hairdressers, psychiatric and social aides, housekeeping employees, and private household workers.

4. *Farm Workers.* Farmers—farm laborers, farm equipment operators, foremen, and managers.

Some insight into the growth of some selected jobs of the white-collar worker is shown in Figure 7.2. These selected professional occupations show huge increases, and the end is not in sight.

Let's compare some of the unique features white-collar workers with the traditional blue-collar group.

Occupation	1962	1964	1975	Percent Increase 1964–1975
1. Accountants	517,000	572,000	847,000	48
2. Engineers	1,002,000	1,059,000	2,031,000	92
3. Lawyers	247,000	258,000	407,000	58
4. Nurses	590,000	592,000	1,091,000	84
5. Doctors	238,000	246,000	402,000	63
6. Public administrators	176,000	215,000	423,000	97

Figure 7.2 Percent increase in selected professional occupations.[5]

Blue-Collar Characteristics	White-Collar Characteristics
1. Equipment-oriented	Service-oriented
2. Physical workers	Knowledge workers
3. Works with hardware	Works with people and information
4. Vocational education	College education
5. Nonprofessional	Professional
6. Goes to a place of work	Work can be completed regardless of the place
7. Output easily inventoried	Output not easily inventoried
8. Nonexempt compensation	Exempt compensation
9. Loyalty to unions	Loyalty to the profession
10. Focuses on monetary rewards in acceptable work	Focuses on challenging work with acceptable monetary rewards
11. Equipment and tools needed for productivity	Skill, information, and time needed for productivity
12. Productivity can be forced since work is visible and tangible	Productivity cannot be forced since work is not visible and intangible.
13. Results are immediate and short range	Results are delayed and long range

Because of the differences between white-collar workers and blue-collar workers, approaches toward managing these two groups must necessarily differ. What has been successful in the management of blue-collar workers cannot be carried over into white-collar work.

IMPLICATIONS FOR MANAGING WHITE-COLLAR WORKERS

The growth of the white-collar work force has many implications for managers in organizations.

1. *Women Will Compete on More Nearly Equal Terms with Men.* Women have been entering the labor force today at a greater rate than ever before. In 1950 they were 29 percent of the work force. Today, they are 38 percent of the work force.[6] Because white-collar work does not make demands for characteristically male qualities, such as physical strength, more women will enter these types of jobs and compete on

more nearly equal terms with men. Considering the Civil Rights Act of 1964, which assured equal opportunity for women, it is safe to conclude that women eventually will occupy approximately 50 percent of this work force.

2. *Part-Time Older Workers are a New Growth Sector of the Work Force.* The nature of white-collar work can allow for part-time employment in peak or busy periods. Since physical strength or endurance is not characteristic of the white-collar work, the older employee will remain in the labor force longer or reenter in a different capacity even it is is on a part-time basis. Part-time employment has emerged as an attractive employment method. Work is accomplished without a total compensation package and job benefits. Older workers view part-time work as a means of enlarging their leisure activities while maintaining a needed income level.

3. *Strategies in Handling White-Collar Unions Will Be Different from Those for Blue-Collar Unions.* Since there is a vast difference between white-collar and blue-collar characteristics and work habits, there is a vast difference in attitudes toward these workers. Unionism has spread to white-collar workers. But walkouts by teachers, government employees, nurses, and hospital employees provoke more comment and intervention than much longer strikes by workers in mining, manufacturing, construction, or repair, probably due to the intangible nature of the service output. This means that the traditional approaches to collective bargaining must be modified to deal with this new type of worker. Pressure for compulsory arbitration and third-party intervention will grow. But collective bargaining is only one example. Other successful managerial approaches in the blue-collar arena will not be effective for white-collar work when there is an attempt for carryover.

4. *Work of White-Collar Workers Must Be Focused More on Individuals.* Employees in white-collar jobs are closely related to their work. They often render a highly individualized service that reflects the exercise of personal skills that are the result of many years of training and development. Personal identification with the work is essential. They will not accept the loss of personal identification with the work as blue-collar workers have. Blue-collar workers have allowed the final fruit of their labor to be broken up so that a craft-oriented group has become a mass-production work force. Loss of personal identification with the work by blue-collar workers is one reason for alienation of blue-collar workers from their product output. The white-collar worker requires personal identification with the service rendered. Social scientists have identified four elements that causes alienation among white-

collar workers: powerlessness, meaninglessness, isolation, and self-estrangement.[7]

5. *The Line Between Work and Leisure Is Difficult to Define.*   White-collar workers derive a great deal of satisfaction from a job well done. Pride in one's work is not only a part of the professional "process," but in many cases it becomes a goal to be reached. The work is rewarding, and the line between work and leisure activity is often difficult to define or even identify. Teachers who enjoy their work find it fun to engage in school activities nights and weekends. Engineers who are bent on a new design will devote seven days a week to the search because it fascinates them. The same case can be made of accountants, social workers, supervisors, lawyers, public administrators. White-collar workers concentrate on challenging and satisfying pursuits in which they derive value for both work and leisure. Highly educated individuals with specialized skills are generally more loyal to their professions than to the organizations that employ them.

STRATEGIES FOR ACHIEVING HIGHER PRODUCTIVITY

Organizations of white-collar workers need to increase productivity more rapidly than in recent years. These workers must be convinced of the high value and importance of productivity. As Galbraith cogently points out, "Productivity, by its overpowering importance and its incalculable difficulty is the central problem of our lives."[8] Strategies must be examined and adopted to meet the increasing demand for benefits inherent in productivity improvement.

A First Step: Develop Productivity Mindedness

The rise of the white-collar worker means that today's organizations are being infiltrated by men and women who have an entirely different concept of what organizations are all about or what they should be. In effect, these workers are outsiders working within the system. The worker is not the true "organization man" because loyalties are tied to widely dispersed contemporaries who are as a group highly mobile and loyal to the profession.

In addition, many of these people have the notion that productivity is what the other fellow ought to deliver. White-collar workers must be sold—sold hard—and resold on the benefits for productivity improvement. The white-collar worker not only must be persuaded but must be enthusiastic. A Harris poll asked people in various kinds of work whether their own productivity could be increased. Most people thought not. Among white-collar workers less than one person out of three said yes.

Productivity attitudes may have been shaped by a broad process of many informal influences. These influences are the actions and results that occur in connection with a frustrating job, educational experiences, group membership, or social activities. Whatever the source may be, they mold the attitudes of the individual. Some negative attitudes—that is, attitudes that work against productivity improvement—follow:

> You can't measure my work since its largely conceptual.
> If it's a service, the taxpayers will want it.
> Don't ask me; the supervisor is supposed to do it.
> I quit. The company doesn't pay enough.
> It's impossible to write quality objectives.
> This is a lousy place to work. All they think about is costs.
> You cannot manage people like machines.
> I don't like our negotiated package; let's appeal to the courts.

Productivity mindedness is a frame of mind noticed in employees in which continued interest is shown in wanting to improve work and productivity. Productivity mindedness is more than a matter of lip service. It is a genuine interest noticed in attitudes and borne out by action. Some positive attitudes—that is, attitudes that work for productivity improvement—follow:

> I would like to try this measure for evaluating my work.
> We've got to make a persuasive presentation if the council is to buy it.
> Solving problems and improving productivity is part of my job.
> I'd like to try MBO to see if it works.
> Let's do something about these guys who won't cooperate.
> We got as much as we could at the negotiations.

Attitudes that prevent contributions toward greater productivity must be dealt with in a deliberate way. Productivity mindedness can be developed among white-collar workers. It must be developed. Five practices are suggested here for supervisors that would contribute toward this development. These practices are illustrated in Figure 7.3.

1. *Supervisors Must Give Facts and Information to Counter Negative Attitudes.* The greatest influence in an employee's work life is the supervisor. When a supervisor allows freedom of discussion in face-to-face relationships, certain attitudes will emerge. The supervisor must

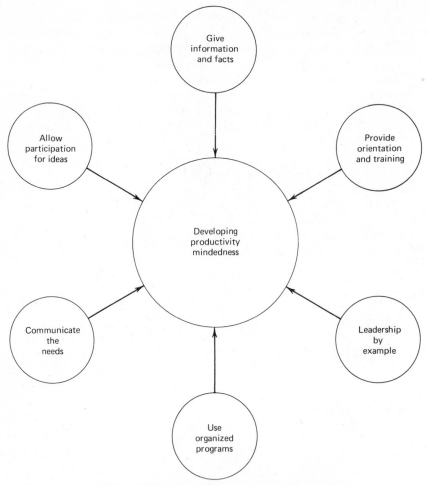

Figure 7.3 Supervisory actions for developing productivity mindedness.

make every effort to get these attitudes to surface since exposing negative attitudes is the first step in dealing with them. The supervisor proceeds to identify the sources of the attitudes and collects contradictory information. For example, an employee utters a negative attitude: "This is a lousy place to work." The supervisor proceeds to find out why this attitude exists. He might note the source is from union influences. He proceeds to show the improvements made over the years, points out the changes that are expected to be made, and compares the organization with other organizations. He tries to get the employee thinking, "This isn't such a bad place to work." Thus this person receives new information. Employees should be made to realize that excessive absenteeism, tardiness, turnover, waste, idleness, and overtime leads to the decline of customer services which eventually affects the benefits they receive. Supervisors should give information that will counteract these negative productivity practices.

2. *Supervisors Themselves Must Be Examples of Productivity Mindedness.*   Productivity experts are convinced that massive percentage gains are possible in the productivity of supervisors and managers. The time they waste is pretty shocking. In addition, the example they set can greatly affect the productivity of their employees. The most earthshaking pronouncement in support of productivity fades into nothingness for employees when they see their supervisors behaving in a manner that reduces productivity. All of us tend to resist rules and restrictions that are not imposed on everyone. Employees especially resist a responsibility when supervisors are not included. Supervisors must understand and be committed to concepts and practices for productivity improvement. As members of management they can do much to set the tone of productivity mindedness in the organization by displaying attitudes, behavior, and actions in behalf of sound productivity performance. Employees take their cues from management. Management personnel must clearly convey the feeling of the importance of productivity and a strong desire to see active productivity improvement efforts.

3. *Give Productivity Orientation and Training to Employees.*   White-collar adult men and women in organizational life will learn and retain only the things that they need to know, that they genuinely believe will help them in their work. They will acquire attitudes and skills that they think will be most likely to help them to solve daily problems. These needs stir an interest in learning. These needs emerge sharply at the time of employment. This is the time for productivity orientation. It should be followed with regularly scheduled courses in productivity for both supervisors and employees. An examination of in-house courses conducted by many organizations shows a wide range of courses and training programs, but few organizations schedule courses or programs in productivity—what it is and how can it be improved.

4. *Communicate Concern and Need for Productivity Improvement to Employees.*   Every employee must be conscious of the fact that his or her job security, benefits, and satisfaction depend to a great extent on the organization's ability to maintain or improve its reputation for greater results in productivity. There is a sad failure to do this! A number of

media can be used to educate employees about productivity minded-ness—memoranda, short writeups in employees newspapers, special letters, cartoons in newsletters, poster displays in work areas, productivity slogans, and suggestion awards for productivity improvement. They should be used intensively over a predetermined period to make an impact on the organization.

5. *Allow Participation in Productivity Decision Making.*   White-collar workers find great satisfaction and need fulfillment when they actively participate in plans and activities that affect them. The extent to which widespread participation in productivity should be allowed in the organization depends on the definition of the situation and the styles existing in management. White-collar workers are usually professionals who need to get involved in the decisions that affect their work life. They have ideas to offer. They are, as a group, highly creative. They can understand what is needed in a situation and respond in a meaningful way. If productivity improvement is to be a concern of all members of the organization, each member must be involved. In a significant study managers were asked what it means to get employees involved and participating.[9] The study revealed that managers had a relatively consistent idea of the meaning of participation. These were the agreements among these managers about participation:

(a) Give subordinates a share in decision making.

(b). Keep subordinates informed of the time situation, good or bad, under all circumstances.

(c) Be alert to morale and do everything possible to keep it high.

Participation and involvement do not mean that individuals make separate decisions on what to do, however. It means that management shares the opportunity to make a decision that affects everyone. This is a viable way to develop productivity mindedness.

6. *Use Organized Programs.*   The following would be, in approximate order, the steps to be taken for implementing an organized program for developing productivity mindedness.

(a)   A memorandum or letter from the president, chief administrator, or organizational head sent to all employees indicating the productivity improvement program.

(b)   A series of articles on productivity in newsletters or employees' paper giving an understanding of what productivity is, its relationship to job security, and what it means personally for each employee.

(c) A productivity improvement slogan contest offering cash prizes or other incentives.

(d) A series of displays showing how waste, rejected materials, customer complaints, and poor attitudes affect productivity.

(e) A productivity comparison profile showing how different departments compare. (This can be only done when ratios are comparable.)

(f) A special organizationwide committee to study and examine ways and means of improving productivity. This committee would be charged with responsibility for identifying productivity problems and ways of handling these problems and for following the progress made in their solution.

(g) A series of special films or slides for showing to employees. These should cover objectives of a productivity improvement program and how its results could benefit employees.

(h) A special orientation presentation given to all new employees at the time of employment, intended to describe how new employees can perform work for maximum productivity.

(i) A special series of courses for supervisors and managers presenting in considerable detail the nature of productivity, how to manage it, how to measure it, how to improve it, and how to control it.

A Second Step: Use Equipment Aids Where Possible

White-collar workers are, for the most part, labor intensive. That is, personal time, skill, and information are the tools for accomplishing work. If these employees are working at their peaks, a natural recourse is to turn to labor time-saving devices. As a general rule, equipment aids are attractive applications in labor-intensive jobs. This was brought out in Chapter 3 with the synergistic productivity triangle. Conversely, human relations aids are attractive applications in equipment-intensive jobs.

There are three guidelines to follow when selecting equipment:

1. Equipment that reduces the amount of time and resources consumed or wastes created.
2. Equipment that increases the performance output of the worker.
3. Equipment that improves the quality of the output.

Of course, the usual concern of costs, maintenance, and return on investment are also considered. How far and how much equipment is to be used will depend on the combination of human effort and mechanical aids that gives the greatest productivity. When machines or equipment are inexpensive and can be effectively applied, productivity increases radially. When machines or equipment are expensive and marginal in their effectiveness, productivity drops significantly. When applying equipment aids to white-collar work processes, a maximum machine application and utilization must be obtained.

A Third Step: Increase Discretionary Content of Jobs

In spite of the great advances in equipment aids, computers, and mechanized technology, knowledge workers will continue to use time, skill, and information as their basic tools. Therefore a special focus should be made in the design and redesign of jobs to better utilize these tools. This means that the two broad areas in designing white-collar jobs—content and methods—should be analyzed for prescriptive and discretionary approaches. The prescriptive (P) approach connotes the idea that duties, techniques, responsibilities, processes, methods, and objectives are unilaterally required of the employee and communicated to him as a matter of policy. The discretionary (D) approach means duties, techniques, responsibilities, processes, methods, and objectives are open for participation and individual judgment. To redesign a job means to develop an optimal combination of these two variables. The number of prescriptive and discretionary options available in a job is illustrated in Figure 7.4. Job methods identified in the matrix of Figure 7.4 are defined as follows:

1. *Specialization.* Job loading or restructuring which reduces the variability of duties and responsibilities so that one assignment can be delegated. Work content is concentrated on a specific process or end.
2. *Simplification.* Job loading or restructuring which reduces the complexities of duties and responsibilities before delegation or assignments. Work content is made simpler, plainer, and easier.
3. *Standardization.* Job loading or restructuring which selects duties and responsibilities for consistency and similarity. Work content is made uniform and regular.
4. *Enrichment.* Vertical job loading or restructuring to permit responsibilities and duties to be delegated from higher management. Work content is given greater value due to elements from authoritative positions in the organization.
5. *Enlargement.* Horizontal job loading or restructuring to permit re-

Job content \ Job methods	Specialization	Simplification	Standardization	Enrichment	Enlargement	Logical Sequence	Time Sequence	Cause-Effect
Designs	P		P			P	D	P
Products		D		D		D		D
Man–hours		D	P		P		P	P
Human factors	D				P			
Machines & equip.		P	P			P		
Processes			D	P		P		
Supplies	P	P		P	P			D
Standards	P			D	P	D	P	P

Figure 7.4 Balancing prescriptive (p) and discretionary (D) options in a job.

sponsibilities and duties to be interchanged and rotated from peers or similar job classifications. Work content is expanded in size, length, or volume for interest purposes.

6. *Logical Sequence.* Job loading or restructuring which selects duties and responsibilities for a logical sequence in the work execution process. Work content is systemized and interconnected because of good and natural relationships.

7. *Time Sequence.* Job loading or restructuring which selects duties and responsibilities for a time sequence in the work execution process. Work content is systemized and interconnected because of time relationships.

8. *Cause-Effect.* Job loading or restructuring which selects duties and responsibilities for a cause-effect sequence in the work execution process. Work content is systemized and interconnected because of a producing-result relationship.

The prescriptive approach to job design has dominated for years. It is the approach generally followed with blue-collar workers. The spillover effect to white-collar workers has been clearly visible. This must change. Because of their special work characteristics and skills, white-collar workers need more chances for decision making in their jobs. They need more independent judgment opportunities for both content and method.

Effective management of white-collar workers requires an increase in the discretionary features of a job.

A Fourth Step: Replace Performance Appraisals With Productivity Appraisals

The traditional practice of performance appraisals relies heavily on supervisory judgment and perception of the output of the employee. In most cases this has been a guessing game. This process makes the supervisor reluctant and uncomfortable. The process makes the employee defensive and insecure. There are three criticisms one can observe about the traditional form of appraisals. First, it is unilateral. That is, it is what the supervisor does with the employee. The employee merely receives this judgment—either condemnation or praise. There is little or no participation. Second, performance appraisals examine the output or results the employee delivers in the situation. This is not bad! But it does not bring into focus the resources that were consumed in the process. When performance achievement and resources consumed are both examined and evaluated in the same time context, productivity is appraised. Performance appraisals evaluate achievements only. *Productivity appraisals evaluate both achievements and the consumed resoruces.* Third, performance appraisals are not generally based on measurements. The process does not begin with quantitative targets to be reached. Productivity appraisals as a process begin with the employee participating in determining targets and the measurement that will be used to know they have been reached.

Productivity appraisals as a process incorporate the three essential ingredients of an appraisal: employee participation, evaluation of both performance and resources, and productivity measurement. This subject of productivity appraisals is examined in greater detail as a process in Chapter 8. It is introduced at this point to assure the reader of its importance in the managing of white-collar workers.

A Fifth Step: Give Time Management Training.

Time is one of the biggest resources of the white-collar worker. If it is wasted or ineffectively utilized, low productivity results. Most white-collar workers are salaried, which means that time is a variable and costs are constant. Whether a great deal of time or little time is contributed in the work process, the cost will remain essentially the same. What remains is to assure that time is productivity utilized. Three general approaches to time utilization have been observed among white-collar workers:

1. Search for more hours.
2. Search for timesaving aids.
3. Search for effectiveness.

These searches are appropriate because time utilization has great implications for productivity. Furthermore, the pressures on the white-collar worker for more time are increasing. Managing white-collar workers for greater productivity means better utilization of time. Several techniques are suggested:

1. Improve the planning and scheduling skills of the white-collar worker.
2. Prepare a list of time-robbers. Most employees are not aware of these.
3. Give meaningful time management training.

The subject of time management is critical for many phases of the total productivity effort. It is taken up again in greater detail in Chapter 11.

A Sixth Step: Motivate.

Motivation is a key process in the managing of white-collar employees as with all employees in the work force. The major difficulty in the motivation of white-collar employees is the lack of a systematic approach. Current motivational practices tend to be day-to-day chances. Few motivators are applied to employees while they are engaged in work. Those who apply these motivators wait for diminishing effects before applying new motivators. This results in inconsistent motivation. A period of no motivation could be very damaging to employee morale and confidence.

A planned motivational approach is a systematic approach that anticipates the need for motivation and the diminishing effects of existing motivators.[10] Motivators are applied according to a schedule along with the work so that they are not left to chance. Motivators are fitted among organizational objectives, employee needs, and the constraints of the work environment. The use of a planned motivational model suggests that the problem of managing white-collar workers is managing both the work and the desire to complete the work. They are complementary! The manager does not proceed with one unless the other has been properly fitted and adjusted. The three variables of organizational objectives, employees needs, and the constraints of the work environment are so closely interrelated that to assure productivity each must be examined in the context of its effects on the other. The planned motivation concept is taken up again in considerable detail in Chapter 9. At this point suffice it to say that motivating as a process is an absolute must for managing productivity improvement with white-collar workers.

A Seventh Step: Manage Productivity by Objectives (MPBO).

The success that managing by objectives (MBO) has had in organizations is a matter of record. Managers and supervisors have found that it is an approach that brings about improvement. It is a systematic method for achieving desired ends. But a key question has been raised. Where is MBO going? Has the process reached the pinnacle of utilization? Can the process be "sharpened" as a tool to penetrate deeper in the thrust for solving managerial problems? The answers to these questions lie in the context of combining productivity with MBO. This combination has been introduced and described in the previous chapter. Managing productivity by objectives (MPBO) provides a process for improving the productivity of white-collar workers. The 20 jobs that follow are examples of how MPBO can be applied.

PSYCHOTHERAPIST

1. *Productivity Responsibility*
   (a) *Duty.* Rehabilitate emotionally disturbed children.
   (b) *Performance.* Complete 10 clinical actions on a treatment plan for 12 children with no more than four regressions.
   (c) *Resources.* Three clinical staff, residential treatment centers, $10,000 annual budget allocation per child.
2. *Productivity Measurement*
   (a) *Before:*

$$PI = \frac{4 \text{ regressions}}{10 \text{ clinical actions}} = .40 \text{ regression rate}$$

$$PI = \frac{12 \text{ children}}{3 \text{ clinical staff}} = \frac{4 \text{ children}}{\text{staff}}$$

   (b) *After:*

$$PI = \frac{2 \text{ regressions}}{10 \text{ clinical actions}} = .20 \text{ regression rate}$$

$$PI = \frac{15 \text{ children}}{3 \text{ clinical staff}} = \frac{5 \text{ children}}{\text{staff}}$$

3. *Productivity Objective.* Complete 15 treatment plans annually (5 children/staff) with no more than two regressions (20%) by December 30.

4. *Plan for Productivity Improvement.* Institute therapeutic milieu programs and support procedures with clinical support from special community groups.

5. *Productivity Control Points.* Schedule:

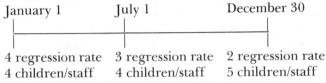

January 1	July 1	December 30
4 regression rate	3 regression rate	2 regression rate
4 children/staff	4 children/staff	5 children/staff

6. *Productivity Evaluation.* By December 30, 15 children will have their treatment plans complete (25% productivity improvement) while reducing the regression rate to 20 percent (50% productivity improvement). All resources are held at the prior budgetary period.

COMPUTER PROGRAMMER

1. *Productivity Responsibility*

   (a) *Duty.* Develop and process computer programs.

   (b) *Performance.* Complete 10 programs that average 15 days to complete and $250 in machine expenses. One workday equivalent to $100 in wages, benefits, and supplies.

   (c) *Resources.* Computer programmer and computer facility.

2. *Productivity Measurement*

   (a) *Before:*

$$PI = \frac{performance}{resources}$$

$$= \frac{10 \text{ completed programs}}{150 \text{ days} + \dfrac{\$2500 \text{ cost}}{\$100 \text{ cost/day}}}$$

$$= \frac{10}{175} = .06 \text{ program completion rate}$$

   (b) *After:*

$$PI = \frac{10 \text{ completed programs}}{100 \text{ days} + \dfrac{\$2000 \text{ costs}}{\$100 \text{ cost/day}}}$$

$$= \frac{10}{120} = .083 \text{ program completion rate}$$

3. *Productivity Objective.*   Complete 10 programs with average working of 10 days each using no more than $2000 as total machine expense.

4. *Plan for Productivity Improvement.*   Initiate time-sharing facility rather than normal batch testing operation which consumes "wait-days."

5. *Productivity Controls Points.*   Schedule:

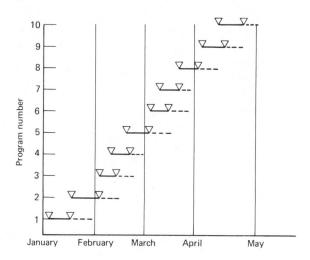

6. *Productivity Evaluation.*   By May 10 computer programs are to be completed in 100 days (33% productivity improvement) while reducing machine expenses to $2000.

ENGINEERING SUPERVISOR

1. *Productivity Responsibility*

   (a)   Duty.   Install time standards in plant for direct labor-incentive workers.

   (b)   Performance.   Install 475 time standards in the plant for 20 employees with no more than 25 union grievances.

   (c)   Resources.   Four staff engineers budgeted at $45,000 annually.

2. *Productivity Measurement*

   (a)   Before:

$$PI = \frac{25 \text{ grievances}}{475 \text{ time standards}} = .05 \text{ grievance rate}$$

$$PI = \frac{20 \text{ workers}}{4 \text{ engineers}} = \frac{5 \text{ workers}}{\text{engineer}}$$

$$PI = \frac{\$45,000 \text{ budget}}{475 \text{ time standard}} = \frac{\$95 \text{ cost}}{\text{time standard}}$$

(b)   After:

$$PI = \frac{15 \text{ grievances}}{550 \text{ time standards}} = .03 \text{ grievance rate}$$

$$PI = \frac{28 \text{ workers}}{5 \text{ engineers/clear}} = \frac{5.6 \text{ workers}}{\text{engineers/clerk}}$$

$$PI = \frac{\$51,000 \text{ budget}}{550 \text{ time standards}} = \frac{\$93 \text{ cost}}{\text{time standard}}$$

3. *Productivity Objective.*   Complete 550 time standards for 28 employees annually while reducing grievance rate to 3%.

4. *Plan for Productivity Improvement.*   Institute job enrichment program to improve quality of work life with union; hire additional clerk for processing information; organize engineers by time standard categories.

5. *Productivity Control Points*

	January		July		December
Grievance rate	|	|	|	|	|
	.05	.04	.03	.03	.03
Cost per standard	\$95	\$95	\$95	\$94	\$93

6. *Productivity Evaluation.*   By end of year, 55 time standards will be implemented (16% productivity) with no more than 15 union grievances (40% productivity improvement) while reducing cost per standard to $93 (2% productivity improvement).

STOCKBROKER

1. *Productivity Responsibility*

    (a)   Duty.   Maintain and acquire stock purchase clients.

    (b)   Performance.   Make contact with 50 clients per week, 20 of whom make a transaction of greater than 1000 shares, 5 of whom are new clients.

    (c)   Resources.   Stockbroker in brokerage house with necessary facilities.

2. *Productivity Measurement*

    (a)   Before:

$$PI = \frac{20 \text{ client transactions}}{50 \text{ clients contacted}} = .04 \text{ client transaction ratio}$$

$$PI = \frac{5 \text{ new client transactions}}{20 \text{ clients contacted}} = .25 \text{ new client transaction ratio}$$

(b)   After:

$$PI = \frac{30 \text{ client transactions}}{50 \text{ client contacted}} = .60 \text{ client transaction ratio}$$

$$PI = \frac{12 \text{ new client transactions}}{30 \text{ clients contacted}} = .4 \text{ new client transaction ratio}$$

3. *Productivity Objective.*   Achieve 60% client transaction ratio and 40% new client transaction ratio over 12 month period beginning June 1.

4. *Plan for Productivity Improvement.*   Direct mail campaign through new marketing plan soliciting two potential clients from each client reached.

5. *Productivity Control Points.*   At 2-month intervals transaction ratios, both existing and new clients, should progress 3 to 4 percentage points.

6. *Productivity Evaluation.*   Complete over 1500 shares of transactions annually with 60% client transaction ratio (50% productivity improvement) and 40% new client transactions (60% productivity improvement). All resources are held constant.

SALESPERSON

1. *Productivity Responsibility*

    (a)   Duty.   Sell machinery and equipment.

    (b)   Performance.   Achieve $800,000 sales volume per year through 1000 customer contacts and calls.

    (c)   Resources.   Budget salary and expenses not to exceed $26,000.

2. *Productivity Measurement*

    (a)   Before:

$$PI = \frac{\$800,000 \text{ sales volume}}{26,000 \text{ budgeted expenses}} = \frac{\$31 \text{ sales dollar}}{\text{budgeted dollar}}$$

$$PI = \frac{1000 \text{ customer contacts}}{50 \text{ weeks}} = \frac{20 \text{ customer contacts}}{\text{week}}$$

    (b)   After:

$$PI = \frac{\$1,000,000 \text{ sales volume}}{30,000 \text{ budgeted expenses}} = \frac{\$33 \text{ sales dollar}}{\text{budgeted dollar}}$$

$$PI = \frac{1200 \text{ customer contacts}}{50 \text{ weeks}} = \frac{24 \text{ customer contacts}}{\text{week}}$$

3. *Productivity Objective.*   Achieve a sales volume of $1000 million per year while holding budgeted expenses to $30,000 annually to yield $33 sales per budgeted dollar.

4. *Plan for Productivity Improvement.* Reorganize territorial accounts by potential payoff separating critical from trivial by geography and density of manufacturing plants.

5. *Productivity Control Points*

	January	April	June	October	November 25
Contact increase	⌐	|	|	|	⌐
	1000	1200	1200	1200	1200
% sales increase	0	0	10	15	20

6. *Productivity Evaluation.* By November 25 sales volume will reach $1000 million (20% productivity increase) yielding $33 sales per budgeted dollar.

RECORDS ANALYST

1. *Productivity Responsibility*

   (a) *Duty.* Process corporate records for central storage.

   (b) *Performance.* Process 35,000 boxes annually with assigned retention, destruction, and update periods with no more than 5% error rate.

   (c) *Resources.* Twelve record clerks annually.

2. *Productivity Measurement*

   (a) *Before:*

   $$PI = \frac{35,000 \text{ boxes}}{12 \text{ employees}} = \frac{2900 \text{ boxes}}{\text{employee}}$$

   $$PI = \frac{1750 \text{ boxes in error}}{12 \text{ employees}} = \frac{146 \text{ boxes in error}}{\text{employee}}$$

   (b) *After:*

   $$PI = \frac{50,000 \text{ boxes}}{15 \text{ employees}} = \frac{3334 \text{ boxes}}{\text{employee}}$$

   $$PI = \frac{15 \text{ boxes in error}}{15 \text{ employees}} = \frac{100 \text{ boxes in error}}{\text{employee}}$$

3. *Productivity Objective.* Complete processing of 50,000 boxes annually of all corporate records to central storage with no more than 1500 boxes in error (3% error rate) by December 30.

4. *Plan for Productivity Improvement.* Institute a locator and retrieval system for accurate labeling of disposition, dates, and inventory control.

5. *Productivity Control Points.* Schedule:

January 1	July 1	December 30
35,000 boxes	40,000 boxes	50,000 boxes
150 box errors	100 box errors	100 box errors

6. *Productivity Evaluation.* By December 30, 50,000 boxes of corporate records will be processed in a retrieval system (43% productivity improvement) while reducing the error rate to 100 boxes (34% productivity improvement). Three additional clerks are hired.

TEACHER

1. *Productivity Responsibility*
   (a) *Duty.*   Teach talented or gifted children (8th and 9th grades).
   (b) *Performance.*   Complete 10 independent learning projects within the academic year with no more than four incomplete projects.
2. *Productivity Measurement*
   (a) *Before:*

   $$PI = \frac{6 \text{ projects completed}}{10 \text{ planned projects}} = .60 \text{ project completion rate}$$

   $$PI = \frac{12 \text{ items completed in project}}{20 \text{ tasks learning items}} = .60 \text{ learning completion rate}$$

   (b) *After:*

   $$PI = \frac{8 \text{ completed projects}}{10 \text{ planned projects}} = .80 \text{ project completion rate}$$

   $$PI = \frac{18 \text{ items completed in project}}{20 \text{ task learning items}} = .90 \text{ learning completion rate}$$

3. *Productivity Objective.* Complete eight learning projects with gifted children while increasing the learning completion rate to 90%.
4. *Plan for Productivity Improvement.* Provide students with options to select; motivate students through participation in project selection and formulation; set up mutually agreed schedule; provide early feedback on project work; display projects in library.
5. *Productivity Control Points.* Schedule:

	September	November	January	April	June
Projects completed	0	2	4	6	8
Item completed	0	5	9	12	18

6. *Productivity Evaluation.*   Achieve eight completed projects (33% productivity improvement) while increasing the learning completion rate to .90 (50% productivity improvement).

DESIGN ENGINEER

1. *Productivity Responsibility*
   (a)   Duty.   Provide mechanical designs of rotating and static hardware in aircraft engines.
   (b)   Performance.   Propose designs to reduce weight from 2 pounds to as close as 5 pounds, to reduce costs from $800 to as close as $1500, to increase test performance ratio from 0.1 to as close as 0.4.
   (c)   Resources.   Design team of three; engineering facility and budget for project $50,000.
2. *Productivity Measurement*
   (a)   Before:

   $$PI = \frac{2.0 \text{ actual reduced weight}}{5.0 \text{ expected reduced weight}} = .40 \text{ weight ratio reduction}$$

   $$PI = \frac{\$800 \text{ reduced costs}}{\$1500 \text{ expected costs}} = .53 \text{ cost ratio reduction}$$

   $$PI = \frac{0.1 \text{ actual performance}}{0.4 \text{ expected performance}} = .25 \text{ test performance ratio}$$

   (b)   After:

   $$PI = \frac{4.0 \text{ planned reduced weight}}{5.0 \text{ expected reduced weight}} = .80 \text{ weight ratio reduction}$$

   $$PI = \frac{\$1100 \text{ reduced costs}}{\$1500 \text{ expected costs}} = .73 \text{ cost ratio reduction}$$

   $$PI = \frac{0.3 \text{ actual performance}}{0.4 \text{ expected performance}} = .75 \text{ increased test performance ratio}$$

3. *Productivity Objective.*   Complete five possible designs that will reduce engine weight by two pounds, cost by $300, and increase test performance to 3%.
4. *Plan for Productivity Improvement.*   Alter design procedures to allow for computerized analytical support and test the use of five substitute materials.

5. *Productivity Control Points.*   Schedule:

January	July	December
2 pounds	3 pounds	4 pounds
$800	$1000	$1100
0.1	0.2	0.3

6. *Productivity Evaluation.* By December 30 new mechanical part will weigh two pounds less (100% productivity improvement), cost $300 less (38% productivity improvement), and increase its test performance to 0.3 units.

ESTIMATOR

1. *Productivity Responsibility*

   (a) Duty.   Submit proposals for building cost estimates.

   (b) Performance.   Complete 60 building cost proposals in one year with no more than 20 rejects.

   (c) Resources.   Three estimating staff and part-time terminal operator.

2. *Productivity Measurement*

   (a) Before:

   $$PI = \frac{35 \text{ proposal awards}}{60 \text{ cost proposals submitted}} = .58 \text{ proposal award rate}$$

   $$PI = \frac{26{,}000 \text{ budget for proposal work}}{60 \text{ proposals}} = \frac{\$434 \text{ cost}}{\text{proposal}}$$

   $$PI = \frac{\$2{,}500{,}000 \text{ proposal value}}{35 \text{ awards}} = \frac{\$7143 \text{ dollar value}}{\text{awarded proposal}}$$

   (b) After:

   $$PI = \frac{55 \text{ proposal awards}}{65 \text{ proposals submitted}} = .85 \text{ proposal award rate}$$

   $$PI = \frac{\$29{,}000 \text{ proposal budget}}{65 \text{ proposals}} = \frac{\$446 \text{ cost}}{\text{proposal}}$$

   $$PI = \frac{\$5{,}500{,}000 \text{ proposal value}}{55 \text{ awards}} = \frac{\$10{,}000 \text{ dollar value}}{\text{awarded proposal}}$$

3. *Productivity Objective.*   Complete 65 proposal submittals annually with a proposal award rate of 85 percent.

4. *Plan for Productivity Improvement.*   Allow for overtime work during critical proposal deadlines; specialize staff into proposal categories and set up proposal "model" as guideline.

5. *Productivity Control Points.*   Schedule:

	January	April	July	October	December
Award rate	.58	.48	.68	.78	.85
Dollar value	$7143		$8500		$10,000

6. *Productivity Evaluation.*   By end of year, 65 proposals will be submitted on an annual basis (8% productivity improvement) with dollar value per awarded proposal increasing to $100,000 (39% productivity improvement).

SURGEON

1. *Productivity Responsibility*
   (a) *Duty.*   Diagnose patients and perform surgical operations.
   (b) *Performance.*   Accept 12 patients monthly for operations with no more than one unsuccessful operation.
   (c) *Resources.*   Two office nurses, hospital facilities, budget for total nursing staff $15,000.

2. *Productivity Measurement*
   (a) *Before:*

   $$PI = \frac{8 \text{ patients in office}}{4 \text{ hours}} = \frac{2 \text{ patients}}{\text{hour}}$$

   $$PI = \frac{9 \text{ successful operations}}{12 \text{ total}} = .75 \text{ success rate}$$

   $$PI = \frac{10 \text{ operations}}{30 \text{ days}} = \frac{1 \text{ operation}}{3 \text{ days}}$$

   (b) *After:*

   $$PI = \frac{15 \text{ patients in office}}{4 \text{ hours}} = \frac{3.8 \text{ patients}}{\text{hour}}$$

   $$PI = \frac{13 \text{ successful operations}}{15 \text{ total}} = .87 \text{ success rate}$$

   $$PI = \frac{15 \text{ operations}}{30 \text{ days}} = \frac{1 \text{ operation}}{2 \text{ days}}$$

3. *Productivity Objective.*   Complete 15 operations monthly with an 87% success rate.

4. *Plan for Productivity Improvement.*   Increase preoperation planning time; organize and train nurses to handle routines of office visits; eliminate unnecessary consultations.

5. *Productivity Control Points.*   Schedule:

Now	Midyear	End of Year
12 operations month	15 operations month	15 operations month
3 unsuccessful	3 unsuccessful	2 successful

6. *Productivity Evaluation.*   Complete by end of year 15 surgical operations with 87% success rate (25% productivity improvement).

RENTAL CAR MANAGER

1. *Productivity Responsibility*
   - (a) *Duty.*   Rent safe, quality cars to customers at a profit with a minimum of complaints.
   - (b) *Performance.*   Complete 3950 rental agreements per month with no more than eight complaints.
   - (c) *Resources.*   Inventory of 500 cars.
2. *Productivity Measurement*
   - (a) *Before:*

$$PI = \frac{3950 \text{ rental agreements}}{500 \text{ cars}} = 7.9 \text{ frequency rate}$$

$$PI = \frac{8 \text{ complaints}}{3950 \text{ rental agreements}} = .002 \text{ complaint ratio}$$

   - (b) *After:*

$$PI = \frac{4200 \text{ rental agreements}}{500 \text{ cars}} = 8.4 \text{ frequency rate}$$

$$PI = \frac{6 \text{ complaints}}{4200 \text{ rental agreements}} = .001 \text{ complaint ratio}$$

3. *Productivity Objective.*   Close out 4200 rental agreements with no more than six complaints by April 1.
4. *Plan for Productivity Improvement.*   Implement a 20-point checklist on each rented car before rental and formalize customer usage rating sheet.
5. *Productivity Control Points.*   Schedule:

December	February	April
3950 rentals	4100 rentals	4200 rentals
8 complaints	7 complaints	6 complaints

6. *Productivity Evaluation.* By April complete 4200 transactions per month (6% productivity improvement) while lowering the complaint ratio to .1%.

1. *Productivity Responsibility*
   (a) *Duty.* Redetermine eligibility of welfare recipients.
   (b) *Performance.* Process 100 redetermination interviews per week with budget computations and forms while holding to error rate of 20 cases.
   (c) *Resources.* Supervisor and five eligibility process workers.
2. *ProductivityMeasurement*
   (a) *Before:*

   $$PI = \frac{100 \text{ interviews}}{5 \text{ workers}} = \frac{20 \text{ interviews}}{\text{worker per week}}$$

   $$PI = \frac{20 \text{ cases with errors}}{100 \text{ cases}} = .20 \text{ case error rate}$$

   (b) *After:*

   $$PI = \frac{120 \text{ interviews}}{5 \text{ workers}} = \frac{24 \text{ interviews}}{\text{worker per week}}$$

   $$PI = \frac{12 \text{ cases with errors}}{120 \text{ cases}} = .10 \text{ case error rate}$$

3. *Productivity Objective.* Complete 120 redetermination cases per week with no more than 12 cases containing errors.
4. *Plan for Productivity Improvement.* Survey causes of errors; institute skills training; develop checklist and interview guidelines; provide feedback survey.
5. *Productivity Control Points*

	January	April	July	October	December
Interviews	100	100	110	120	120
Error rate	.20	.15	.15	.15	.10

6. *Productivity Evaluation.* Achieve 120 redetermination cases per week by December 30 (20% productivity per week) while decreasing cases containing errors to 12 per week (67% productivity improvement).

CITY PERSONNEL DIRECTOR

1. *Productivity Responsibility*
   (a) *Duty.* Assure appointment of the most qualified person to municipal positions.
   (b) *Performance.* Process eight merit examinations to fill eight classified positions.
   (c) *Resources.* Two professional staff for test construction and administration. Budget of $12,000.

2. *Productivity Measurement*
   (a) *Before:*

$$PI = \frac{\$12,000 \text{ budget}}{8 \text{ exams}} = \frac{\$1500 \text{ cost}}{\text{exam}}$$

$$PI = \frac{8 \text{ positions}}{12 \text{ months}} = \frac{.67 \text{ positions}}{\text{month}}$$

$$PI = \frac{8 \text{ exams}}{2 \text{ employees}} = \frac{4 \text{ exams}}{\text{employee}}$$

   (b) *After:*

$$PI = \frac{\$12,000 \text{ budget}}{10 \text{ exams}} = \frac{\$1200 \text{ cost}}{\text{exam}}$$

$$PI = \frac{10 \text{ positions}}{12 \text{ months}} = \frac{0.83 \text{ positions}}{\text{month}}$$

$$PI = \frac{10 \text{ exams}}{2 \text{ employees}} = \frac{5 \text{ exams}}{\text{employee}}$$

3. *Productivity Objective.* Complete 10 exams to fill 10 merit system positions annually with two professional staff by December 30.

4. *Plan for Productivity Improvement.* Formalize recruiting, screening, and testing processes of all employees.

5. *Productivity Control Points.* Schedule:

	January	April	July	October	December
Exams	0	5	7	10	0
Filled positions	0	2	5	7	10

6. *Productivity Evaluation.* By December 30, 10 examinations have been completed (25% productivity improvement) and 10 positions have been filled while holding the budget at prior levels.

DATA PROCESSOR ANALYST

1. *Productivity Responsibility*
   (a) *Duty.* Complete data processing requests to enhance trust system.
   (b) *Performance.* Complete DPRs that require five to seven different programs to be changed within 10 working days and free from production problems.
   (c) *Resources.* Two programmers on each team and machine cost less than $300.
2. *Productivity Measurement*
   (a) *Before:*

$$PI = \frac{14 \text{ working days}}{2 \text{ programmers}} = \frac{7 \text{ days}}{\text{programmer}}$$

$$PI = \frac{\$300 \text{ machine cost}}{6 \text{ programs}} = \frac{\$50 \text{ cost}}{\text{program}}$$

$$PI = \frac{12 \text{ production problems}}{8 \text{ DPRs}} = 1.5 \text{ production problem ratio}$$

   (b) *After:*

$$PI = \frac{10 \text{ working days}}{2 \text{ programmers}} = \frac{5 \text{ days}}{\text{programmer}}$$

$$PI = \frac{\$200 \text{ machine cost}}{6 \text{ programs}} = \frac{\$33 \text{ cost}}{\text{program}}$$

$$PI = \frac{2 \text{ production problems}}{8 \text{ DPRs}} = .25 \text{ production problem ratio}$$

3. *Productivity Objective.* Reduce working days on DPRs to 10 while reducing production problems to no more than two by March 1.
4. *Plan for Productivity Improvement.* Divide programming unit into teams; identify those DPRs requiring five to seven different programs; allow for one compiler for each program changed; schedule testing to adequate level; monitor production.
5. *Productivity Control Points.* Schedule:

	January	February	March
Working days	14	12	10
Cost per program	$50	$40	$33

6. *Productivity Evaluation.* By March, working days on DPRs are re-

duced to 10 (29% productivity improvement) while reducing production problems ratio to 25%.

1. *Productivity Responsibility*
   (a) *Duty.* Coordinate group home activities toward more independent situations for mentally retarded.
   (b) *Performance.* Provide or arrange comprehensive treatment services to 110 mental retardants which generates movement of 10% to more independent living with no more than 4% returnees.
   (c) *Resources.* 35 direct care staff members.
2. *Productivity Measurement*
   (a) *Before:*
   $$PI = \frac{11 \text{ resident movements}}{110 \text{ residents}} = .10 \text{ progression rate}$$
   $$PI = \frac{4 \text{ returnees}}{110 \text{ residents}} = .04 \text{ regression rate}$$
   $$PI = \frac{110 \text{ residents}}{35 \text{ staff}} = \frac{3.1 \text{ residents}}{\text{staff}}$$
   (b) *After:*
   $$PI = \frac{25 \text{ resident movements}}{120 \text{ residents}} = .21 \text{ progression rate}$$
   $$PI = \frac{4 \text{ returnees}}{120 \text{ residents}} = 0.03 \text{ regression rate}$$
   $$PI = \frac{120 \text{ residents}}{35 \text{ staff}} = \frac{3.4 \text{ residents}}{\text{staff}}$$
3. *Productivity Objective.* Complete 25 resident movements to independent living while reducing the regression rate to 3%.
4. *Plan for Productivity Improvement.* Institute formal individual plan for each resident; establish prescriptive tasks for each individual; provide short-time feedback corrections.
5. *Productivity Control Points.* Schedule:

	January	April	July	October	December
Resident movement	0	7	13	18	25
Regressions	.04	.04	.03	.03	.03

6. *Productivity Evaluation.* By end of year, residents have been increased to 120 (9% productivity improvement) while increasing resident move-

ments to 25 (130% productivity improvement). Regression rate reduced to 3%.

COST ACCOUNTANT

1. *Productivity Responsibility*
   - (a) *Duty.* Install new cost standards for future fiscal periods in the organization.
   - (b) *Performance.* Install 100 cost standards annually with no more than a $15,000 budget.
   - (c) *Resources.* Two cost accountants.

2. *Productivity Measurement*
   - (a) *Before:*

$$PI = \frac{100 \text{ cost standards}}{2 \text{ accountants}} = \frac{50 \text{ cost standards}}{\text{employee}}$$

$$PI = \frac{\$15,000 \text{ budget}}{100 \text{ standards}} = \frac{\$150 \text{ cost}}{\text{standard}}$$

$$PI = \frac{15 \text{ errors}}{100 \text{ cost standards}} = .15 \text{ error ratio}$$

   - (b) *After:*

$$PI = \frac{150 \text{ cost standards}}{2 \text{ accountants}} = \frac{75 \text{ cost standard}}{\text{employee}}$$

$$PI = \frac{\$18,000 \text{ budget}}{150 \text{ standards}} = \frac{\$120 \text{ cost}}{\text{standard}}$$

$$PI = \frac{10 \text{ errors}}{150 \text{ cost standards}} = .07 \text{ error ratio}$$

3. *Productivity Objective.* Formulate 150 new cost standards by December 30 with an error factor of 7%.

4. *Plan for Productivity Improvement.* Eliminate duplication effort; allow some overtime to complete work on time; develop model and process cost standard.

5. *Productivity Control Points.* Schedule:

August	October	December
100 cost standards	125 cost standards	150 cost standards
$150 cost/standard	$135 cost/standard	$120 cost/standard
15% error rate	11% error rate	7% error rate

6. *Productivity Evaluation.* By December, 150 cost standards have been formulated and installed (50% productivity improvement) while the error rate was decreased to 7%. Budget was allowed to increase $3000.

Project test engineer

1. *Productivity Responsibility*
   (a) *Duty.* Evaluate fan blade designs for resistance to impact.
   (b) *Performance.* Complete 15 tests in the coming year with no more than three test deficiencies.
   (c) *Resources.* Project budget for engineer, technician, cameraman, and facility usage is $45,000.
2. *Productivity Measurement*
   (a) *Before:*

$$PI = \frac{3 \text{ test deficiencies}}{15 \text{ tests}} = .20 \text{ error rate}$$

$$PI = \frac{\$45,000 \text{ budget}}{12 \text{ valid tests}} = \frac{\$3750 \text{ cost}}{\text{valid test}}$$

   (b) *After:*

$$PI = \frac{2 \text{ test deficiencies}}{15 \text{ tests}} = .13 \text{ error rate}$$

$$PI = \frac{\$36,000 \text{ budget}}{13 \text{ valid tests}} = \frac{\$2769 \text{ cost}}{\text{valid test}}$$

3. *Productivity Objective.* Conduct in the coming year 15 tests with no more than two test deficiencies.
4. *Plan for Productivity Improvement.* Development test procedure that allows for any team member to conduct; increase preplanning test analysis.
5. *Productivity Control Points.* Schedule:

	January	July	December
Error rate	.20	.16	.13
Cost per valid test	$3750	$3000	$2769

6. *Productivity Evaluation.* By December 30, 15 tests will be conducted in which the error rate will be held to 2 (35% productivity improvement).

PSYCHOLOGICAL TEST EXAMINER

1. *Productivity Responsibility*
   (a) *Duty.* Construct and validate reliable competitive merit examination.
   (b) *Performance.* Construct and validate five examinations a year with three examinations having a reliability index of .85.

(c) Resources. Five hundred professional man-hours yearly at an average rate of 15 per hour.

2. *Productivity Measurement*

   (a) Before:

$$PI = \frac{3 \text{ examinations with index of } .85}{5 \text{ total examinations}} = .60 \text{ examination reliability rate}$$

$$PI = \frac{\$7500 \text{ examination costs}}{5 \text{ examinations}} = \frac{\$1500 \text{ cost}}{\text{examination}}$$

   (b) After:

$$PI = \frac{6 \text{ examinations with index of } .85}{8 \text{ total examinations}} = .75 \text{ examination reliability rate}$$

$$PI = \frac{\$8000 \text{ examination costs}}{8 \text{ examinations}} = \frac{\$1000 \text{ cost}}{\text{examination}}$$

3. *Productivity Objective.* Construct and validate eight examinations per year with six examinations having a reliability index of .85 or greater.

4. *Plan for Productivity Improvement.* Construct a common core (model) examination based on job level with a distribution of options; administer and validate examinations for a broadbanded group.

5. *Productivity Control Points.* Schedule:

January	July	December
3 examinations with .85	5 examinations with .85	6 examinations with .85
5 examinations	6 examinations	8 examinations

6. *Productivity Evaluation.* By December 30, eight examinations have been constructed and validated (34% productivity improvement) with at least six having a reliability index of .85 or greater. Budget change with new targets reduces cost per exam to $1000 (34% productivity improvement).

INSURANCE UNDERWRITER

1. *Productivity Responsibility*

   (a) Duty. Underwrite and issue life insurance policies.

   (b) Performance. Underwrite 600 life insurance policies annually (approve-decline-postpone).

   (c) Resources. Twenty underwriters.

2. *Productivity Measurement*

   (a) *Before:*

$$PI = \frac{600 \text{ applications}}{12 \text{ months}} = \frac{50 \text{ applications}}{\text{month}}$$

$$PI = \frac{600 \text{ application} \times 55 \text{ days to process}}{20 \text{ underwriters}}$$

$$PI = \frac{1650 \text{ days to process}}{\text{underwriter}}$$

   (b) *After:*

$$PI = \frac{800 \text{ applications}}{12 \text{ months}} = \frac{66.7 \text{ applications}}{\text{month}}$$

$$PI = \frac{800 \text{ applications} \times 40 \text{ days to process}}{20 \text{ underwriters}}$$

$$= \frac{1600 \text{ days to process}}{\text{underwriter}}$$

3. *Productivity Objective.* Complete annually 800 applications for life insurance while keeping the days to process each application to 40.

4. *Plan for Productivity Improvement.* Separate clerical from underwriting; institute an information retrieval system; provide specific training.

5. *Productivity Control Points.* Schedule:

	January	July	December
Applications	600	700	800
Process days	55	48	40

6. *Productivity Evaluation.* By December 30, 800 applications for life insurance will be processed annually (33% productivity improvement) while reducing process time for each application to 40 days (27% productivity improvement).

PURCHASING AGENT

1. *Productivity Responsibility*

   (a) *Duty.* Procure materials, supplies and tools.

   (b) *Performance.* Procure $400,000 tools inventory to support a sales volume of $36 million.

   (c) *Resources.* Purchasing administrator and two clerks.

2. *Productivity Measurement*

   (a) *Before:*

$$PI = \frac{180 \text{ stockout orders}}{12 \text{ months}} = \frac{15 \text{ stockouts}}{\text{month}}$$

$$PI = \frac{\$36,000,000 \text{ sales}}{180 \text{ stockouts}} = \frac{\$200,000 \text{ sales}}{\text{stockout}}$$

   (b) *After:*

$$PI = \frac{120 \text{ stockout orders}}{12 \text{ months}} = \frac{10 \text{ stockouts}}{\text{month}}$$

$$PI = \frac{\$36,000,000 \text{ sales}}{120 \text{ stockouts}} = \frac{\$300,000 \text{ sales}}{\text{stockout}}$$

3. *Productivity Objective.* Achieve a stockout reduction annual rate to 120.
4. *Plan for Productivity Improvement.* Institute the system contracting method and identify alternate buying sources for shorter delivery time.
5. *Productivity Control Points.* Schedule:

	January	July	December
Stockouts/month	15	13	10

6. *Productivity Evaluation.* By December 30, annual stockouts have been reduced to 120 (34% productivity improvement) raising the sales to stockout ratio 50%.

SUMMARY

White-collar workers cannot be managed with the traditional management methods used with blue-collar workers. The attempt to do so must cease because it's causing a waste of these employees as an important resource in the organization. This waste contributes to low productivity.

This chapter provided a specific focus on the white-collar worker. These workers are service oriented; college educated; use information, skills, and time as their basic tools; and their professional work needs are concentrated on challenging and meaningful work. They are quite different from other groups of workers. The growth of this group has many implications: (1) women will compete on more nearly equal terms with men; (2) part-time older workers will reenter this work force; (3) strategies in handling white-collar unions will be different from strategies used with blue-collar unions; (4) work of the white-collar worker will be focused more closely to the individual; (5) the line between work and leisure is difficult to define for this group.

Special strategies for managing this group to higher levels of productivity are needed. This chapter presented seven strategies toward this end:

1. Develop productivity mindedness.
2. Use equipment aids where possible.
3. Increase discretionary content of jobs.
4. Replace performance appraisals with productivity appraisals.
5. Give time management training.
6. Motivate.
7. Manage productivity by objectives.

The last strategy of MPBO is unique in the management of this type of worker. Twenty examples using MPBO in white-collar jobs were described: psychotherapist, computer programmer, engineering supervisor, stockbroker, salesperson, records analyst, teacher, design engineer, estimator, surgeon, rental car manager, welfare eligibility supervisor, city personnel director, data processor analyst, social worker, cost accountant, project test engineer, psychological test examiner, insurance underwriter, and purchasing agent.

QUESTIONS TO THINK ABOUT

1. If there has been wasteful use of white-collar workers in your organization, make a list of them.
2. How fast is the number of white-collar workers growing in your organization compared with blue-collar workers: What is the implication of this growth?
3. Characterize the white-collar worker in your organization.
4. Describe the kinds of strategies that could work for improving productivity in your organization.
5. Would productivity mindedness work for your organization? Why or why not?
6. Of the eight methods described in Figure 7.4, which would be most useful for your organization?
7. Analyze and record the MPBO approach to your job.
8. From your job description, identify the prescriptive duties from

discretionary duties. Which items would you change? How would you change them?

REFERENCES AND NOTES

1. William M. Aiken, "Work Measurement and Incentives," in H. B. Maynard, *Handbook of Business Administration,* McGraw-Hill Book Company, New York, pp. 7-136.
2. J. D. Dunn and Elvis C. Stephens, *Management of Personnel,* McGraw-Hill Book Company, New York, 1972, p. 66.
3. Gilbert Burck, "The Still Bright Promise of Productivity," *Fortune,* Vol. 78, October 1968, p. 134.
4. *Statistical Abstract of the United States.* 95th Annual Edition, U. S. Department of Commerce, Washington, 1974, p. 350.
5. *Ibid.,* p. 352.
6. Leonard A. Lecht, *Manpower Needs for National Goals in the 1970's.* New York, Praeger, 1969.
7. HEW Special Task Force, *Work In America,* MIT Press, Cambridge, p. 22.
8. John K. Galbraith, *The Affluent Society,* New American Library, New York, p. 32.
9. Larry E. Greiner, "What Managers Think of Participative Management," *Harvard Business Review,* March-April, 1973, p. 114.
10. Paul Mali, *Managing By Objectives.* Wiley-Interscience, New York, 1972, pp. 168-176.

8

MANAGING THE
OVERPAID EMPLOYEE

IN THIS CHAPTER

Concept of the overpaid employee.
Managing productivity into the inflation cycle.
Fair day's pay for fair day's work.
Fringe benefits reporting similar to wages and salaries.
Compensation links to productivity.
How to get accountability.
Zero-based Budgeting.
Appraisal methods not applicable to productivity evaluation.
An example of a productivity plan, measurement, and evaluation.
Performance contracting compared to time contracting.

Inflation increases when monetary rewards and benefits are given without requiring the equivalent in productivity! Every time a negotiation is completed or a strike is settled with no apparent increase in productivity, a jump in inflation occurs. The cost of higher wages or salaries without an equivalent contribution in performance must be made up somehow. Organizations make it up by increasing prices which furthers the pace of inflation. If productivity continues its approximate 3 percent annual rise and wage increases average 7 percent and more, we can expect prices to rise by at least 4 percent. Since organizations practice the distribution of rewards and benefits without first requiring careful justification from productivity data, it is safe to say that these organizations overpay their employees and make up the difference in prices. The consumer pays. In one country after another, in one organization after another, wages continue their upward thrust in response to widespread discontent and the drive to better individual economic status. The effect of these forces is inflation; the rate of inflation is four times greater than that experienced between 1949 and 1974. The causes and cures of the complex problem of inflation are discussed in books, magazines, journals, and the daily newspapers. Managing productivity is one solution for the problems of inflation.

This chapter (1) shows how the discrepancy between compensation and productivity has "fired" the wage-cost upward swing to cause never-ending inflation; (2) defines the overpaid employee and the conditions that indicate that an organization overpaying employees; (3) describes the new concept of accountability—what it is and how to establish it in an organization; (4) describes traditional appraisal processes, their weaknesses and strengths, and how MPBO as a multipurpose appraisal process provides a meaningful evaluation base; and (5) explains performance contracting as an emerging new method most likely to succeed the old time contracting system that causes never-ending inflation.

NEVER-ENDING INFLATION?

Everyone is waiting for inflation to end. Their wait may be endless unless the cycle that relates the factors that cause inflation is broken or controlled or productivity requirements are introduced. Although the exact starting point of an inflationary cycle is sometimes difficult to identify, its progression is simple and clear. Increase in prices triggers a demand for increased wages which in turn raises costs of production and eventually brings about another increase in prices. Irving Friedman discusses this cycle in terms of "demand-pull" and "cost-push" which incidently has worldwide impact.[1] According to Friedman, there are two highly related cycles. Demand-pull characterizes inflation when total demand exceeds total supply, creating an "inflationary gap" which is closed through price increases. Cost-push characterizes inflation when wages rise to push costs toward prices of products and services. This push squeezes the profit gap. Organizations that need the profit will raise prices to close the profit gap. The difference between the profit gap and new levels of prices is the inflationary rise. Note that productivity has been ignored in this process, but there is a strong link between productivity and profitability. These cycles are illustrated in Figure 8.1.

When pay hikes, wage increases, salary adjustments, larger compensation, new catch-up boosts, merit raises, and cost-of-living grants are given without a corresponding equivalent in productivity, inflation moves up proportionately. When supplies, services, materials, and products are not produced to meet customer demands or taxpayers needs, productivity declines, which moves inflation up proportionately. In either case price levels will change to accommodate cost changes or supply deficiencies. Prices rise because productivity improvement has not absorbed the cost

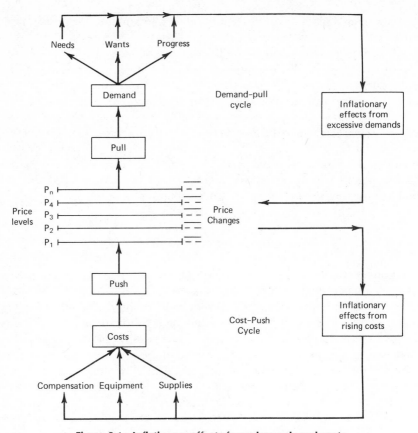

Figure 8.1 Inflationary effects from demands and costs.

changes or supply deficiencies. In fact, an argument can be made that for every increment that productivity drops, there is a corresponding increase in prices, which in turn causes a corresponding increase in inflation. Increased wages can be offset by increased productivity which gives lower costs per unit of production. Furthermore, increased production means that heavy demand can also be met. Thus productivity is a way to control the cycle of demand and costs.

If, for example, welders get a 10 percent hike in pay but don't raise their output of weldments by a quarter of that amount, the employer's costs are pushed up, and the price of the product is raised to cover the higher costs of welder's wages. This is inflationary. However, if after the 10 percent hike, welders produce more weldments to be equivalent to the increase in wages, prices need not be increased because production has gone up and more weldments are sold. This discourages inflation. This sensitive relationship among demand, prices, costs, and productivity is the reason for the guideline introduced by the National Council of Economic Advisors: *"The general guide for non-inflationary wage behavior is that the rate of increase in wage rates (including fringe benefits) in each industry be equal to the trend rate of over-all productivity increase."*[2] The underlying principle of this guideline is based on a widely accepted observation. General acceptance of this guide would maintain stability of labor cost per unit for the economy as a whole, though not of course for individual industries.

The rationale is based on the idea that employees will accept a more moderate wage increase in exchange for more stable prices. Organizations would accept stable prices as a part of the bargain because costs are not increasing because of wages and salaries. The guideline worked well initially, through the Eisenhower, Kennedy, and Johnson administrations. It later was ignored when war broke out, after war effects caused unemployment to rise. The guideline was later modified to take into account variations in productivity found in different industries.

In spite of the guideline, the traditional approach to ending inflation has been to either reduce the level of general demand relative to supply to hold prices down, or control wage increases relative to products by holding prices at certain levels. This traditional approach has not always been successful for two reasons: The fact that demand-pull and cost-push have an impact on each other has been ignored. They are not independent. Exerting effort in one area without controls in the other is like trying to dig a hole on the beach when the tide is coming in. What productivity is doing in the cycle has also been ignored. Productivity is the means of connecting the push-pull feature of the cycle so that efforts made to meet growing demand should be accompanied with equivalent productivity and not increased prices. Including productivity as part of the cycle would allow prices to rise somewhat to meet demand but in a productivity controlled way. Similarly, when productivity is part of the cycle, cost increases will be offset by productivity increases. Prices can rise to meet some growing costs, but in a productivity controlled way. *Demand should not be suppressed! Compensation for efforts should not be denied!* Productivity can pull in the slack of cost and price differentials. *Productivity becomes the equalizer between changing demand and higher compensation.* The disconnection between these two variables is the reason inflation is perpetual. The failure to measure and include productivity in the cycle has been a huge reason for the vague and imprecise manner of making adjustments for changes in costs and demands.

FAIR DAY'S PAY FOR FAIR DAY'S WORK

Are employees overpaid? *Overpaid* is defined here as compensation above an employee's value, worth, or contribution to the organization. Some people fall into the trap of thinking that organizations do not overpay their employees because they do not "go broke." They fail to see that overpayments can be subsidized by increased prices to customers or increased taxes to taxpayers. This may well be the history of inflation. The organization cannot afford to pay its employees because of its declining productivity. Hence, it passes the increased cost to the customer or the taxpayer.

The question of overpaid employees is a loaded one because neither employee or employer will often admit that it is true. The employee will seldom admit his low contribution relative to his compensation package. Some do, however, in termination interviews. The employer will not admit retaining an employee whose value is less than his contribution. Some do, however, during collective bargaining periods. This is a sensitive and emotional issue. Nonetheless it must be brought out into the open.

Pay should not be thought of as simply money taken home weekly, biweekly, or monthly. *Pay* is a loose term. To be accurate, the total compensation earned by an employee consists of both wages and benefits. Wages are the visible portion and benefits are the hidden portion. *The organization dispenses both visible and hidden portions of the package in payment for an employee's contribution.* The hidden portion of the package has often been termed *fringe benefits* since an ad hoc effort is often exerted in its management. But are fringe benefits of an ad hoc nature? A study of potential changes in employee benefits revealed that American companies spent over $100 billion on employee benefits.[3] This is a huge outlay! This amount is equivalent to 13 percent of the United States gross national product. It is also 25 percent of the entire amount spent by employers on wages and salaries. This study further indicated that benefits dispensed averaged 10 percent each year compared to 4 percent each year of dispensed wages and salaries. *Benefits given to employees are a big business*! This big business continues to grow at a spectacular rate. The National Association of Manufactures has identified fringe benefits allocated in organizations. The following are selected items from that list:

Premium payments	Medical insurance
Shift differentials	Accident and sickness insurance
Cost of living bonus	Workmen's compensation
Paid holidays	Disability insurance
Retirement plans	Old-age insurance

Social security payments
Profit-sharing plans
Savings plans
Group life insurance
Rest periods
Call-in time
Call-back time
Downtime
Sick and maternity leaves
Paid vacations
Paid leaves—military
Voting time
Witness time

Unemployment compensation
Time for jury duty
Excused absence—personal
Wash-up time
Severance pay
Dressing time
Portal-to-portal time
Wet time
Credit unions
Parking space operation
Contest awards
Educational reimbursements
Laundry allowance

Niels Nielsen of the Allis-Chalmers Company reported the cost of benefits in his company increased 11 percent a year during a 10-year period.[4] This represented twice the rate of growth in sales and two and one-half times the growth of wages and salaries. The growth of benefits is startling. It is no longer a matter of fringe costs! Yet, there is still a general feeling that employee benefits are "fringes." This attitude is evident from the way benefit plans are designed, administered, and managed.

Because benefits represent a significant cost outlay they must be managed and controlled beyond a mere ad hoc effort. Benefit management must be brought into the productivity picture. A fair day's pay must include both wages and benefits. A fair day's work must be a productivity contribution to cover both. This also means that different individual productivity contributions will require different treatments. If wages are given to employees equally—that is, they are paid a day's wage for a day's work but benefits are ignored—the increase in benefit cost can be regarded as the equivalent loss in productivity. Compensating employees equally is not synonomous with compensating them equitably. This is an important view! Honeywell Information System exhibits this view by compensating for individual differences.[5] This unequal compensation means unequal treatment because there are unequal productivity contributions.

These concerns lead one to raise questions about the overpayment problem with employees. Is there a way an organization may know whether they are overpaying their employees? Here is a list of conditions that might serve to *indicate* that employees are being overpayed. They are not intended to be a definitive measure.

1. *No Link Between Compensation and Work Output.* Most appraisal

systems are *oriented* toward work performance. But few collect and analyze productivity data and use it as a basis for making a decision for increasing wages, salaries, or benefits. There is little or no careful appraisal in connecting the individual's work contribution to dispensed financial rewards. Fringe benefits such as life and health insurance and retirement funds seem to have little relation to productivity. Organizations get a poor return for their huge investments in these benefits, although they help to attract and hold the valuable employee. Most employees view benefits as "rights" rather than compensation for employment and performance. I would even suggest a new practice for organizations. The weekly, biweekly, or monthly paycheck should be accompanied by a weekly, biweekly, or monthly statement of allocation of benefits to the employees.

2. *General Wage Increases Are Given Across the Board.* Organizations still practice the general increases for all employees. Individual differences and contributions are often ignored. Employees who contribute much are given the same financial rewards with those who contribute little. One may argue that general increases are necessary to keep employees from becoming underpaid. Cost of living adjustments should not be regarded as general increases. General increases confuse employees. They are not sure whether they are cost of living increases, merit increases, or benefits of employment. General wage increases work against productivity.

3. *Benefits Are Allocated in the Same Amount to All Employees.* Here again, organizations dispense benefits to all employees regardless of responsibilities and contributions. One reason for this practice is the gains received from economies of scale. Insurance, for example, is less expensive if all employees are included instead of only a segment. However, some groups, such as executives, receive a benefit differentiation. In any event, few organizations break down the benefits to the individual on a per-hour basis. Employees who do not understand the type and amount of benefits they are receiving will demand more benefits.

4. *Time as the Basis for Increasing Compensation.* For most organizations, time periods have become the basis for signaling when additional compensation is to be awarded. It is either at appraisal time or contract negotiation time. An examination of 12 labor contract agreements of organizations in Connecticut revealed that benefits are programmed for distribution at certain intervals of time regardless of performance or productivity. One organization, in fact, that went bankrupt still has a scheduled increase for the first part of next year!

5. *Compensation Is Dispensed from Power Moves, Threats, or Legal Acts.* Probably the most common basis of dispensing compensation results from power moves by unions, legislative enactments by government, or termination threats by individuals. When organizations yield to these pressures, compensation is dispensed without regard to productivity. Organizations react to demands or circumstances. If an organization has had this practice, it's safe to assume that customers or taxpayers have been "footing the bill." From an organizations standpoint, they are overpaid.

6. *The Practice of Paternalism.* Organizations that practice paternalism— provide care and concern over employees as a "family"—will dispense compensation because of success in the marketplace in which economic cycles favor them. Or paternalistic managers will dispense of financial rewards to keep the level of morale high enough to prevent dissatisfaction in the "family." Benefits are developed independently and along traditional lines instead of interdependently and on a productivity-oriented basis.

7. *Compensation "Automatically" Allocated from "Escalators."* The age of "escalators" has arrived—*cost-of-living escalators, price escalators, retirement benefit escalators, tax escalators, new catch-up escalators, automatic percentage rental escalators,* and others. Escalators are inflationary generators. They fire up the engines for past prices to catch up which automatically trigger other escalators to move ahead. This innovative economic device has become popular because of uncertain economic trends and conditions. In spite of the confidence and security they provide for an uncertain future; they also encourage a sloppy and inefficient control of prices and costs. They obviously move prices and wages ahead regardless of the level of productivity. Escalators tied to productivity are not known to exist. Probably the major reason for this is the difficulty in productivity measurement. In addition, labor unions are now demanding escalators on the basis of equality to other industries, social need, and government regulations without regard to the productivity requirement of the organization. Inflation continues to "fire up".

8. *Appraisal Systems Are Highly Subjective.* When the appraisal system does not limit the role and influence of past obligations, "halo" effects, friendships, power plays, or personal factors, compensation is allocated with these criteria as guides. The appraisal system must assess in an objective way the productivity delivered by an individual at the assessment time and must link this assessment with the financial rewards to be allocated. Careful consideration of this entire process

reveals that many supervisors, managers, and administrators may not have the skill to do this effectively. Consequently, productivity as a primary criterion for advancement may take a back seat. The starting point in improving the equitable allocation of wages and benefits is to recognize the effects this allocation has on the productivity of an organization. The reader is reminded of the basic concept of productivity:

$$\text{productivity} = \frac{\text{output}}{\text{input}} = \frac{\text{performance achievement}}{\text{resources allocated}}$$
$$= \frac{\text{actual performance}}{\text{expected performance}}$$

When wages and benefits are increased while output or performance is at the same level, productivity drops in the same proportion. When wages and benefits are increased at a faster rate than the increases in performance; productivity still drops. Productivity grows when wages and benefits are held at a level or reduced while performance or output is increased. A second point in improving the equitable allocation of wages and benefits is to make an important connection with appraisals. This means that performance appraisals must evolve to a higher level of use by incorporating productivity needs. *In fact, in view of the inequities of pay in relation to performance and rising inflation, in the future productivity data on an individual's performance may be the only basis that will justify price increases, wage hikes, or salary adjustments!*

ACCOUNTABILITY: WHAT IS IT? HOW TO GET IT?

A new demand for accountability in education, human service institutes, government, and business has emerged. It derives from a fundamental right of a democratic society that holds that those entrusted with public resources, sell to a consumer market and give returns to stockholder, and extract a fee for educating, curing, and developing people, have a responsibility to give a full account of what they did and how well they did it. This demand for accountability is not coming from supervisors, managers, top levels of management, or boards who direct organizations. The new demand for accountability is coming from consumers who cannot understand why prices continually change, from funding sources who want to know exactly what was accomplished from given support, from taxpayers who see an ever-expanding budget to meet, from retirees whose fixed incomes are dwarfed by the cost of living, and from stockholders whose dividends are eroded by the high costs of operating a company.

The new demand for accountability is raising fundamental questions. Has the huge amount of money and support given to our educational systems failed to accomplish its mission in education? America's public education budget in 1948 was $6.5 billion and rose to $68 billion in 1969. That's a little over 20 years. Can we account for how that money was spent in results? At the present growth rate, spending on education will eventually equal the United States gross national product. Has the huge amount of money and support used for welfare, social action, and poverty programs given these individuals the leverage they needed to become responsible citizens in society? Has the huge amount of money and support given to our government failed to bring the quality and efficiency that government must have? Has the huge amount of money extracted by big business and industry in the form of increased prices and products been used for capital expansion and increased employment, or has it been used to line the coffers and pockets of the greedy? Has the huge amount of money and support given to our penal systems failed to reform prisoners? There is a demand to know what was accomplished, who accomplished it, what resources were consumed in the process, and if it could be accomplished with fewer resources? Hundreds of billions of dollars are being spent, yet do conditions improve in proportion? What are we getting for our money?

Accountability as a concept has always been with us. Traditionally it meant to explain and give reasons on what, how, and why responsibilities are discharged or executed in the manner they are. Traditionally accountability meant to answer in judgment of the reasons, causes, and explanation of performance that has occurred within a period of time. This traditional concept would mean that educators would explain and justify the expenditure of funds for education, legislators would explain and justify the expenditure of budgets for government and social action, and businessmen would explain and justify the reinvestment of money for capitalization and expansion. This traditional view of accountability of controlling and reporting is only partially adequate for today. New dimensions have been added. *They are expectancy and achievement. The new concept of accountability is evaluation based on an agreed-upon role of expectation.* This new concept of accountability is seen as reporting achievements at a needed and expected level. It involves funding and budgeting by agreed-upon levels of expected results. The traditional concept of accountability has depended on authoritarian styles with crude coercion and threats, which are no longer legal effective. A new style of managing is needed.

The process of making all employees accountable for productivity continues through all phases of a worker's career. It begins with education in understanding how and why our economy operates. But these are generalized methods of establishing accountability in preemployment activities. Suggestions on how to establish accountability in organizations and among employees during employment follow:

1. Broad, nebulous, and elusive goals of organizations must be replaced with definable, specific, and measurable objectives. This gives definition to expectancy!

2. Loosely assigned responsibilities assumed by departments, agencies, and organizations must give way to well-defined commitments from individuals by name and position. Job descriptions must be written so that each responsibility has a measurable evaluator to indicate effectiveness in completing the responsibility. This relates individual commitments to levels of expectancy.

3. Subjective and highly opinionated judgments must be replaced by evaluations based on measurable achievements that are agreed to by those responsible for the achievements. This incorporates evaluative measures into participative planning.

4. "Pointing the finger at the other person" must be discouraged. Individuals must hold themselves accountable. Productivity must be a personal goal rather than an organizational goal imposed upon employees. The attitude that the person who plans the action, creates the action, and follows through on the action is accountable must be developed.

5. Nebulous and unrelated incentives must be replaced with "motivators" that encourage employee commitment to personal accountability. The conditions of the organization should motivate employees to honor their commitments.

There can never be accountability for results unless there are commitments to purpose. There can never be commitments to purpose unless there is a clear understanding and competence of process on how to transform resources to expected levels of performance. MPBO provides a model for this process to take place. MPBO is a meaningful way to meet the demands of the new accountability.

ZERO-BASE PLANNING AND BUDGETING—A RISING STAR!

If the new demand for accountability is saying anything it's saying that commitment to the past must cease. Perpetuating programs because of their historic value will be analyzed in terms of current critical priorities. Spending will not be allowed on the basis of a past decision but on an agreed-upon level of expectations of needs and results.

Traditional line-item budgeting, which tends to perpetuate commitments that have had their origins in the past, is a prevalent practice in both private and public organizations. This budgeting practice begins with the past level of expenditures as a base and concentrates on projected increases or decreases from that base. Historical data is related to the budget year. Such a procedure leads to an examination of only a small portion of the overall budget, the increases or decreases, rather than a close scrutiny of every facet of it. This means budget analysis concentrates on justifying increases only. This traditional approach is based on the assumption that every function being performed is effective and essential. It provides an "institutionalized framework" for perpetuating past commitments. In many cases the past is 20, 30, or 40 years ago. The assumptions were valid for priorities and concerns that existed at the time they were initiated. They may not be valid in terms of new priorities and concerns. Previous methods for performing tasks may have become inefficient, outdated, or unnecessary. Funding and decision-making sources are asking how many of the existing functions and programs can be eliminated to provide funds for new and vital programs. This is not to say that all existing projects, programs, and commitments do not have value, but limited resources must be allocated to new concerns and priorities.

Zero-base budgeting is a new formal process, which does not carry over past commitments or perpetuate a base budget that has been "institutionalized." The process starts with a zero base or a zero datum and requires each program or functional manager to demonstrate precisely and convincingly the need for the function, department, program, or project under his or her supervision before funds are provided. The manager must delineate the results of achievements that will be delivered if funding and support are given. Distinct units of work or projects are analyzed, ranked in order of priority, and set up under a program cost center. The program cost center has identified goals or missions. These units of work have been variously termed *work packages,* such as used in PERT scheduling networks, or *achievement packages,* such as used in MBO systems, or what Peter Pyhrr refers to as *decision packages.*[6] A decision package is a document that contains all the information needed by funding sources to approve or disapprove it for budget entry. The decision package is definitive enough for managers to evaluate its benefits compared to other packages. The information in a decision package would vary from organization to organization, but generally would contain the following information and would be classified under a program cost center whose mission or goals are clearly delineated.

1. Objective to be pursued.
2. Measures of effectiveness and efficiency.
3. Alternative courses of action and the reason for selecting the best course.
4. Benefits when objective is achieved.
5. Consequences if objective is not pursued or existing activity is eliminated.
6. Costs.
7. Time schedule.

The following illustrates a decision package in zero-base planning and budgeting.

NAME OF DECISION PACKAGE: REDUCTION IN MUGGINGS

Program Cost Center: Police precinct
Goal of Center: Reduce crime in 30th blocks

1. *Objective.* Reduce muggings 20% in the 30th blocks while reducing 10% costs by January 1.
2. *Measurement*
   (a) *Before:*
   $$PI = \frac{80 \text{ to } 70 \text{ muggings}}{8 \text{ officers (4 patrol cars)}} = \frac{1.25 \text{ muggings}}{\text{officer}}$$
   (b) *After:*
   $$PI = \frac{70 \text{ to } 56 \text{ muggings}}{6 \text{ officers (patrolmen)}} = \frac{2.33 \text{ muggings}}{\text{officer}}$$
3. *Courses of Action*
   (a) Increase number of patrol car surveillances.
   (b) Set up foot-officer surveillance.
   (c) Install new street lights for better illumination.
   (d) Institute awareness program through TV, radio, and newspapers.
   (e) *Best course of action:* Foot-officer surveillance is the most effective way to pursue young muggers through off-street alleyways.

4. *Benefits*
   (a) Reduction in mugging rate.
   (b) Rehabilitation is more likely for a young mugger than for an older hardened criminal.
   (c) Contribute toward safer street.
   (d) Avoid potential loss of life.
5. *Consequences*
   (a) Mugging rate increases.
   (b) Nonapprehended mugger is encouraged to continue.
   (c) People refusing to walk and shop will affect sales tax potential.
   (d) Accidental killings are more likely.
6. *Costs.*   Costs reduced from $96,000 to $72,000.
7. *Schedule.*   To be fully operational by January 1.

The decision packages are aggregated under each program cost center and ranked in value and benefit to the organization. A manager can then determine the benefits at a certain level of expenditure to meet existing or new priorities. Consequences of not carrying out the activities at these levels can also be viewed. The following illustrates in conceptual form benefit analysis for different decision packages. The benefit analysis follows the analysis described in Chapter 3 under the principle of creating potential productivity.

A mosquito-control program under a health department cost center of a town may have as many as six decision packages, each dealing with mosquito control but on different levels. The first level may be a $10,000 budget covering 50 acres and benefiting 62 families. The second level may be $24,000 covering 120 acres and benefiting 155 families. The third level may be $42,000 covering 320 acres and benefiting 489 families. Thus the decision package array continues providing for the decision maker the amount of benefits possible with different levels of expenditure. The value of zero-base planning and budgeting in its potential for canceling old commitments that have little or marginal value for the new and promising opportunities and prospects that give the organization a chance for improvement. Additionally, it puts the decision maker in the position of "shopping" for the "best buy" of benefits with a given level of expenditure.

Zero-base planning and budgeting as a process sharpens accountability. It puts managers in a position of accounting for how resources will be consumed and the benefits to be derived in advance of decisions and actual implementation. This is good planning. It puts the funder, tax-

Benefits Analysis

Program Cost Center	Decision Packages	Level of Costs	Bigger Benefits	Quicker Benefits	Related Benefits	Long-Range Benefits	Best Decision
A	DP-1	C_1			Benefit costs		
	DP-2	C_2					
	DP-3	C_3			or		
	DP-4	C_4					
	DP-5	C_5		benefit ranking			
B	DP-1	C_1			Benefit costs		
	DP-2	C_2					
	DP-3	C_3			or		
	DP-4	C_4					
	DP-5	C_5		benefit ranking			
...	...	...					

218

payer, customer, or client in the "shopper's seat" to buy desired results from a large array of possibilities. This means that boards of directors, boards of education, city or town councils can make reasonable and responsible decisions regarding how to set up and allocate a limited budget toward a wide range of priorities. A comparison between traditional line-item budgeting and the new zero-base budgeting is as follows:

	Traditional Line-Item Budgeting	Zero-Base Program Budgeting
Program	A	A
Last year	$350,000	0
Proposed changes	10%	Total number of decision packages for the coming year
Proposed budget	$385,000	$325,000

Several advantages are experienced with the zero-base budgeting process:

1. Decision maker given a better view to pinpoint where budget cuts can be made to align costs with existing funds.
2. Decision makers given a better view of how to eliminate low priority functions, activities, and programs, and provide funds for new and vital projects.
3. Decision makers given a better view of how to balance decisions in terms of risk, cost, service, and multiple requirements of multiple departments and groups.
4. Decision makers given a better view of how costs are consolidated into cost centers for control, forecasting, and productivity measurement.
5. Decision makers given a better view of where to institute changes of flexibility and applications of funding based on new service demands that have recently emerged.
6. Decision makers given a better view of how iteration between many levels of an organization is taking place for coordination and optimization of the entire organization.
7. Decision makers given a better view of supporting documentation that clarifies evaluation and accountability of results and expenditures.

The Southern California Edison Company began experimenting with zero-base planning and budgeting in 1974.[7] The problems of fuel shortages, rising prices, and reduced sales pointed to projected earnings substantially below 1974 goals. Consequently, department managers were directed to submit estimates of activities that could be reduced. But this caused an arbitrariness of "crash" reductions that proved inflexible. The company proceded to test the zero-base process and found it to be an enlightening process. In 1975 the ZBPB process was extended to the entire company and the results were:

1. Personnel reductions saved 9 percent of the budget.
2. Decision packages gave a better way to set priorities.
3. Permanent dollar savings were significant.
4. Planning and budgeting improved in areas of responsibility.
5. Surveillance by senior management over proposed activities was better for the coming budgetary year.

Zero-base planning and budgeting is not the total answer for handling the problems of an accounting and budgeting system but it comes close to it. The decision package concept allows for both planning of productivity and the inclusions of these plans in the resource allocations of a budget. What more could you ask?

APPRAISAL METHODS DO NOT EVALUATE PRODUCTIVITY!

Almost everyone will agree that current performance appraisal methods need a great deal of improvement! Winstanley of the Xerox Corporation goes even further to say most organizations would do better without them. He urges we must make some effort to clean up the "mess."[8] He is not the only one who had a low regard for performance appraisals. Others have voiced similar reactions. The reason for the low value placed on appraisal methods is due to its wide practice between two extremes: (1) informal, random, slipshod, and highly opinionated judgments of one individual by another, and (2) formal, well-organized objective criteria in systems for precise assessment of results. An appraisal process can fall anywhere between these two extremes. But wherever it falls, it seems to fail the purpose it intends. Some managers even play "games" with the appraisal process. Managers who dislike the process of confronting employees with their inadequacies because of the lack of evidence to prove their position may resort to approaches such as "peer evaluation." Peer evaluation is an ill conceived practice in an organization where competitive pressures are high. In other cases managers go through the exercise of the appraisal process but do little or nothing at all with it. If the appraisal effort is not going to have an effect on decisions, practices, or development, it is a futile exercise. Nonetheless, in spite of imperfections, inconsistencies, and variations in application, appraisals seem to be here to stay. But they do need considerable improvement. Formal appraisal systems adopted by many organizations are at least a commendable attempt to evaluate precisely the contributions made by individuals. This evaluation forms the information base for decisions about rewards, promotions, and remuneration. Formal appraisal methods seem to be in a continual stage of development. Perhaps we're merely sampling an evolutionary process. An examination of the eight appraisal methods currently employed in organizations reveals they fall within four categories.

At the risk of oversimplification, these eight appraisal methods will not be described in these categories. For purposes of descriptions, these methods are treated as if they are used singly. In actual practice, features of several of them are combined eclectically to meet the evaluative needs of the organization.

Appraisals That Focus On Behavior and Personality

1. *Trait Appraisals (Graphic Rating Scale).* The most widely used performance evaluation technique is the trait appraisal or graphic rating scale. The evaluator is presented with a series of traits or behavior-related characteristics on a scale and asked to rate employees on each trait or characteristic shown. Examples of traits are leadership, communications, initiative, dependability, cooperation, and personality. Advantages are that it is simple, easy, and uncomplicated; it reaches for human qualities that are known to be important in getting results; it recognizes that all organizations where people are banded together are social organizations requiring certain characteristics to make them work. Disadvantages are that supervisors are reluctant to label deficiencies and criticism without foolproof evidence; it is unilateral—the employee is not involved; supervisors have a tendency to remember recent or negative incidents; and definitions of traits are not always clear.

2. *Essay Appraisals.* Not so widely used as the trait appraisal, the essay appraisal is one or more paragraphs about the employee's strengths, weaknesses, and behavior on the job. The information, as complete as is deemed necessary by the evaluator, is used to decide pay increases, promotion, or termination. The fact that the evaluation is written makes it a formal entry for present or former employees. Advantages are that it allows in-depth evaluation of job factors that are vital for the employer; it is easy to use for jobs that are changing; it eliminates a

fixed set of expectancies and allows a broad focus to meet individual differences. Disadvantages are that its variability in length and content prevents meaningful comparisons among employees; it is unilateral; it requires the evaluator to possess communications skills for an accurate description.

3. *Process Appraisals.* Interest in process appraisals has recently been high because of "due process" requirements of civil and individual rights. The method requires a series of descriptive and quantitative statements that represent standards of effective behavior on the job. The difference between process behavior standards and actual behavior is the strength or weakness of the behavior. Examples of process behavior standards are absenteeism, tardiness, alcoholism, and violation of rules covering, for example, coffee breaks, safety, and insubordination. Advantages are that it controls behavioral activities directly needed for the job; it specifies the human behavior that will lead to job effectiveness; it provides data that are critically needed for "due process" procedures. Disadvantages are that human behavior is too broad to describe levels of effectiveness; not all behavior can be externally controlled; and employees with terrible behavior patterns can perform well.

Appraisals That Focus on Work Activities

4. *Critical-Incident Appraisals.* Not often used, critical-incident appraisals attempt to observe and record both positive and negative factual incidents of an employee. The incidents are recorded in a log of some type, often daily, so that they are not forgotten. This record is often termed the "little black book." For example, an employee has a disastrous experience with a client and hostilities were exchanged. The supervisor records the incident. Advantages are that relates closely to performance elements of the job; it records work incidents that are never known with any degree of specificity; it overcomes partial remembering or latest incident remembering. Disadvantages are that the log tends to have a "police" adjudication image; there is a tendency to identify more negative than positive incidents, and employees not usually involved in this appraisal method.

5. *Standards of Performance Appraisals.* Many organizations are greatly interested in standards of performance appraisals. The method requires a series of descriptive and quantitative statements that represent standards of effective performance on jobs. For example, a performance standard for a supervisor is that overtime hours are controlled to less than 4 percent of scheduled hours. Advantages are that it directly

relates to the requirement of the job; it specifies the level and consistency of effort necessary for job effectiveness; and subjective judgments are minimal. Disadvantages are that there is little or no participation by the employee in the standards or the evaluation; not all important areas can be quantified; and it can be used only where work does not change frequently.

Appraisals That Focus on Comparisons

6. *Ranking Appraisals.* This approach recognizes that an individual must at some point be compared with other individuals, especially when limited wage increases are to be given to a few employees and not to all. The method involves a ranking technique of employees from top to bottom. Supervisors are asked to choose the "most valuable" and the "least valuable." Paired-comparison rankings or normal distribution ranks are two popular methods for this procedure. Advantages are that it provides a way to compare people who work for different departments and supervisors; it allows an overall judgment that includes additional facts and impressions; pooled judgments are possible—that is, a ranking may be developed from the rankings of several supervisors. Disadvantages are that there is no standard form or way to replicate the judgment that was executed; minor and insignificant impressions may take a strong priority in the evaluation; it lacks the focus that is needed for important job elements.

7. *Forced-Choice Appraisals.* Designed to reduce the bias and prejudices of the evaluator, forced-choice appraisals set up standards of comparison among individuals. The evaluator is asked to choose from categories of statements those that accurately fit the individual being rated. Also, the evaluator is forced to select statements that least fit the "evaluatee." The statements are then weighted or scored. Employees with high scores are, by definition, the better employees. Those with low scores are the poorer ones. Advantages are that a high degree of reliability is possible with this method—that is, the judgment of the evaluator can be repeated and compared with himself over a period of time; it tends to be more objective since the evaluator does not know the scoring; the designer of the statements can incorporate almost any essential element required for the job. Disadvantages are that evaluators are forced to select one or another statement with no choice between; "halo" effect may operate in which the evaluator may be appraising a model employee and not the actual employee; the method is unilateral—the employee does not participate in either the statements

or the evaluation; the method is expensive to formulate, validate, and execute.

Appraisals That Focus on Results

8. *Managing by Objectives Appraisals (MBO).* Because it focuses on outputs or results of the employees' efforts in the organization, MBO has developed a great deal of interest by organizations. The method requires a supervisor and subordinate to agree during a planning period on the results to be achieved during the period.[9] These are written as objectives. At the end of the period both evaluate the output or results. An example of an objective for an educational administrator is to achieve an admission acceptance level of 1500 students (60 percent of applicants) by April 1 of an admitting year. Advantages are that it is future oriented, does not have to follow past practices; it is not passive—that is, it involves supervisor and subordinate; the role of evaluator changes from a defensive role to a supportive role; it is highly connected to results needed and expected by the organization; when used properly, it will motivate the staff. Disadvantages are that targeted results can be influenced and changed by uncontrollable factors; it ignores personal traits, activities, and work habits that are deemed important; it does not purposely and precisely connect inputs or resources with the output or results (productivity) with feedback and feedforward progress controls.

This brief analysis of methods currently practiced in managing and evaluating employees and their results may help to decide on one or more of the methods for the task of evaluative contributions. Few, if any, of the methods evaluate productivity as a direct managerial effort and give it the priority it deserves. Organizations that practice the all-purpose appraisals are pursuing a mythical effort that's costing time, money, and effort.

PRODUCTIVITY EVALUATION IN PERFORMANCE APPRAISALS

Appraisal is an elastic word that stretches to cover evaluations of many kinds and types. If an appraisal does not affect decision making or change, it's an exercise in futility. Each of the eight appraisal methods has its own combination or strengths and weaknesses. Yet, the purpose of the appraisal, in large part, shapes the criteria, method, measures, and type of corrective feedback to be employed. The effectiveness of the appraisal will depend on how it is used relative to the purpose it is expected to accomplish. Perhaps the reason for the development of several methods is the varying uses and purposes appraisal procedures are intended to accomplish. Let's examine breifly what some of these appraisal purposes are in an organization:

1. *To Justify Pay Increases.* Performance appraisals provide the framework and procedure for comparing and evaluating employees' performances in levels and categories of equity for increasing wages or salaries. Acceptable performance on the job is the sole basis for compensation.

2. *To Evaluate Results.* Performance appraisals provide an evaluative procedure for assessing the precise and meaningful results contributed by an employee. The stress is on actual results. Important as activities may be, results are the ultimate criteria.

3. *To Account for Productivity.* Performance appraisals provide an evaluative procedure for review of employee accomplishments and contributions in relation to the resources consumed in the process. Accountability for productivity must link results and resources. The appraisal process evaluates both in the same context and time.

4. *To Set up Conditions for Achievement Motivation.* When properly developed, performance appraisals provide the basis for motivating staff and employees to reach higher levels of performance through a plan-do-achievement cycle. Communicating in a climate of openness and participation engenders a meeting of the minds before work commences.

5. *To Set up a Feedback for Organizational Change.* Performance appraisals provide feedback on how well the managerial processes are operating with the staff and what changes are required. What may appear to be weaknesses in the individual often may be weaknesses in the organization.

6. *To Develop Personnel for Positional Changes.* Performance appraisals provide better data for making decisions on promotions, transfers, or demotions. It is a long-range process for planning the development of employees to occupy higher levels in the organization.

7. *To Identify Employees with Hidden Potential.* Performance appraisals provide a formal way to identify high-potential employees who are assigned jobs that are not utilizing their potential.

Many have attempted to devise the multipurpose appraisal process to encompass at least the major purposes cited earlier. This has resulted in giving productivity concerns either low priority or complete omission in the evaluation process. When the appraisal methods are listed in a matrix with the many purposes they are expected to achieve, the low priority of accountability for productivity is easily noted (Figure 8.2).

Managing Productivity By Objectives (MPBO) as an appraisal method is not innovative—that is, it's not an entirely new approach. It is a modification of MBO with the addition of the evaluation of resource utilization toward achieving a set of objectives. It requires a measurement of productivity during the planning phase and a similar measure of productivity during the evaluation phase. MPBO as an appraisal method has several distinct advantages:

1. *Gives Focus on Productivity.* MPBO shifts the priority in a multipurpose appraisal process from a lesser concern and need to a higher concern and need for productivity improvement and justified compensation allocation. The focus gives resource utilization equal evaluation with performance. MPBO is highly connected to productivity expectancies for individuals and the organization. MPBO will encourage the development of attitudes that productivity improvement is expected in the organization.

2. *Institutes Controls for Resource Allocations.* MPBO controls costs and

Appraisal Methods	Pay increases	Delivering results	Accountability for productivity	Achievement motivation	Individual development	Organizational development	Assessment of potential
Traits				X			
Process				X	X		
Critical incident		X		X			
Standards of performance	X	X			X		
Ranking				X	X	X	
Forced choice				X	X	X	
MBO	X	X		X	X	X	
MPBO	X	X	X	X	X	X	

Figure 8.2 Appraisal methods' low priority in evaluation of productivity.

other resources by ensuring that compensation dollars are paid for actual results produced. MPBO develops an information base for justifying compensation allocations. A connection or link is formed between compensation and productivity.

3. *Forces Evaluative Measures into Plans.* MPBO requires evaluative measurements to be built in to the MPBO document of commitments during the planning phase. This ensures a basis of evaluating results when results are said to have been delivered. Evaluation is made easier and more certain. MPBO stimulates the improvement of individual performance because bench marks are available in its evaluative measures to encourage performance stretches.

4. *Provides Accountability for Resources Consumed.* MPBO is a highly structured process that identifies the resources to be used in an action plan and who is responsible for the results. *MPBO provides good accountability of both resources and results!* This gives more precision to the appraisal process and makes it more objective. Evidence·is now given to supervisors for justifying deficiencies and assisting in the elimination of these deficiencies.

5. *Increases Productivity-Mindedness.* MPBO raises the level of awareness of the need and value of productivity in a group, department, or organization. When productivity expectancies are initiated in an early period, measured in progress periods, and evaluated at an end period, an employee's awareness of productivity results is increased.

6. *Heightens Motivation for Productivity.* When practiced as a participative form of management, MPBO "sharpens" the personal role in formulating commitments that tend to motivate employees. The sense of participation, feeling of accomplishment, and recognition of worth form a potent motivational base on which the organization can rely to help it reach its goals. Unlike other appraisal systems, there are no unilateral actions. This enhances agreement, communication, and commitments.

7. *Encourages "Preventive" rather than "Corrective" Managerial Work.* MPBO demands a high degree of planning and anticipating skills. This opens the opportunity to shift operational problems to the planning phase of a manager or supervisor's job. In this manner many problems are solved during the planning phase rather than the operational phase.

8. *Forms a Natural Vehicle for Progress and Evaluation Reviews.* MPBO requires the supervisor and employee to agree on the objectives to be reached. It also requires evaluation periods to assess progress on how things are going. This formal periodic evaluation process encourages

feedback of corrective steps to be taken as a target is reached. The involvement of both supervisor and subordinate is active and positive, unlike other appraisal methods in which it is passive and defensive. Both supervisor and subordinate track progress and evaluative results.

MPBO as an appraisal method has several distinct disadvantages:

1. *Requires Skills in Making the Appraisal.* MPBO requires both a qualitative and quantitative judgment about a person's contribution on the job. It will not work well unless the supervisor understands the purposes and procedures of productivity and its assessment. MPBO can be used only by people who are competent and skillful. Training can minimize this disadvantage.

2. *More Time Required in the Planning Phase.* MPBO is a participative process that leads to a set of commitments between a supervisor and subordinates. The process demands a careful infusion of productivity measurements into action plans or job responsibilities. This will take time. Those who do not have the time or will not take the time to do this will find the planning phase too demanding. A convincing argument can be made that shifting more time into this period may greatly reduce the time for correcting problems in an operational phase.

3. *Gives Personal Traits and Behavior a Low Priority.* MPBO focuses on results, output, resource conservation, and productivity. Human relations, human qualities, and necessary behavior may be treated with lower priority. These important human and social considerations could be ignored with MPBO. One way to minimize this disadvantage is to add to the MPBO appraisal qualities and behavior that are deemed to be important. The supervisor and manager then assesses both productivity and behavior. This might be termed the eclectic approach.

MPBO as an appraisal process has advantages and disadvantages. An organization that is experiencing productivity problems will find that the advantages far outweigh the disadvantages. However, certain features must prevail to make MPBO an effective appraisal system: The system must have management support at all levels and must be applicable to all levels. The system should allow evaluation based on the employee's overall contribution during the entire rating period. This does not preclude day-to-day informal observations of performance, timely feedback, and constructive suggestions for improvement. It means the supervisor should look for the large, significant accomplishments made by the employee.

Finally, MPBO requires that supervisor and employee work together to establish what productivity goals must be pursued and the degree of priority they have in relation to other organizational concerns. A complete sample guide on how to practice MPBO is described at the end of this chapter (pp. 237–245).

ARE WE MOVING TOWARD PERFORMANCE CONTRACTING?

Traditionally, employees have been hired on a time basis. That is, they are hired for so many hours a day, so many days a week. Compensation is allocated when the agreed-upon units of time have been consumed. Wages are dollars per hour or dollars per week: salaries are dollars per month or dollars per year. In return for the compensation per unit of time, the employee agrees to do what the employer requires during the pay period. This traditional basis of employment might be termed "time contracting." It is contractual because an employee agrees to put in time and the employer agrees to pay for this time. The contract is broken when either party fails to uphold the commitment.

Over the years management has had to assume responsibility for ensuring that pay is connected to performance and productivity. Managers have had to be skillful enough to get a fair day's work for a fair day's pay. Management has obtained a high degree of success for both organization and the individual employee.

Recently, however, some startling trends have raised the question of whether time contracting, which does not relate pay to performance and productivity, has outlived its usefulness. A major study by a special task force on work in America, emphasized that inflation is generated when rising wages and salaries are not tied to productivity.[10] Negotiated contracts in the United States from the period 1969–1970 awarded compensation increases to labor in the range of 7 to 15 percent, while the national productivity was increasing only 0.5 per unit in 1969 and 0.9 percent in 1970. Other years have similar startling statistics! The inflationary effect of the lack of connection between productivity and reward is only partially reversible. Wages and salaries that are flexible upward will move upward, but become rigid and inflexible downward. Wages and salaries that are flexible upward and downward will move in this way according to time contract agreements. But upward and downward flexibility for wages and salaries is the exception, not the rule.

The traditional time contracting form of employment is gradually being replaced—in a small way, to be sure—by a new form of employment— "performance contracting." This type of employee-employer agreement is relatively new and ties compensation to the performance contribution of productivity improvement. Some employees are being hired on the basis of performance rather than time. They are hired to do a particular job, a specific project, or a definable task. Compensation is agreed to during the planning and contractual phase and allocated when performance is complete and productivity is delivered. Thus fees or wages are dollars per job, dollars per project, dollars per production output, or dollars per assignment. In return for the compensation per project or assignment, the employee agrees to do the work without using time as the basis. This gives the employee a great deal of independence and discretionary prerogatives of when day-to-day work must be completed. Salesmen, contractors, consultants, laywers, teachers, and other professionals are practicing performance contracting.

A comparison of time contracting with performance contracting may be made as follows:

Time Contracting	Performance Contracting
1. Pay for time worked	Pay for jobs completed
2. Pay not held up if work not completed	Pay held up if work not completed
3. Continuous availability of workers	Discontinuous availability of workers
4. Close process supervision required	Little or no process supervision required
5. Supervisor and evaluator are one	Evaluators required
6. Work for the organization	Work for self
7. Projects or tasks are on-going and routine, often never ending	Projects or tasks are "chunked" for each to have a start-stop cycle
8. Work is stretched to fill the time allocated	Work is compressed to get it done
9. Wage and salary increases are annual projects	Fee increases are negotiated based on productivity improvement
10. Benefits are automatically paid regardless of actual productivity	Benefits are not paid; individual arranges individualized benefits
11. Unemployment benefits are assured	Unemployment benefits are not assured
12. Escalators are triggered on the basis of time and other indirect factors	Escalators do not exist

Time Contracting	Performance Contracting
13. Organization develops employees to avoid obsolescence	Individual uses "free time" to develop himself
14. Jobbers are not required for third-party intervention	Jobbers for third-party intervention will add their fees
15. Accountability centers on being at a place within a period of time	Accountability clauses can be written for a wide range of requirements
16. Money is a weak base for motivation	Money is a strong base for motivation
17. Idle time exists and is expensive	Idle time is eliminated
18. All jobs can be time contracted	Not all jobs can be performance contracted

This partial list of differences between time contracting and performance contracting implies that there are advantages and disadvantages to each approach. But as the proportion of white-collar workers grows in relation to blue-collar workers, the need for a flexible compensation system linked to productivity will increase. Performance contracting appears to satisfy the conditions for compensation for productivity. Highly successful internal consultants in companies such as General Electric, Gulf and Western Industries, and Stanley Works are showing that performance contracting can work.

The question remains whether performance contracting can work with nonprofessional workers as it does for professional workers. One possibility that could make it practical for both groups of workers is to use both

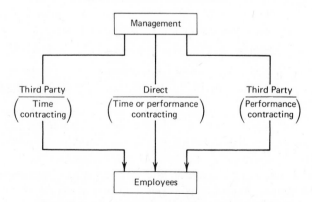

Figure 8.3 Performance and time contraction mode.

performance and time contracting. A third-party intervenor could help determine in which situations each type of contracting would be feasible and agreeable. Unions already act as third-party intervenors for time contracting, and jobbers are available to act as third-party intervenors for performance contracting. This is illustrated in Figure 8.3.

SUMMARY

This chapter provided a focus on how the lack of managing productivity in organizations is resulting in a never-ending inflation. The cycle of demand-pull or cost-push can be managed and controlled by including the productivity variable in the cycle. Demand should not be suppressed. Increased productivity should produce an adequate supply to match demand. Compensation for efforts should not be denied. Increased productivity should allow prices to rise, but in a cost-controlled way. The lack of connection among prices, costs, and productivity is causing inflation.

Organizations practice the distribution of rewards and benefits without careful justification of productivity. Since the difference must be made up in increased prices, it is safe to say that these organizations overpay their employees. The difference fires inflation. It could be controlled by allocating compensation only when productivity data allow it.

Runaway inflation has caused the tradition of a fair day's pay for a fair day's work to become an issue. Benefits for employees must be included in the "day's pay." The allocation of benefits is running far ahead of productivity. Here is a list of conditions that indicate that an organization may be practicing overpayment of employees:

1. There is no link between compensation and work output.
2. General wage increases are given across the board.
3. Benefits are allocated in the same amount to all employees.
4. Time is the basis for increasing compensation.
5. Compensation is dispensed from power moves, threats, or legal acts.
6. Paternalism is practiced.
7. Compensation is automatically allocated from "escalators."
8. Appraisal systems are highly subjective.

The new demand for accountability is raising many kinds of questions about performance. What was accomplished? Who accomplished it? What resources were consumed in the process? Could it be accomplished with fewer resources? This new demand for accountability requires more than explaining and reporting. It requires an agreement on expected performance and a clear and measurable way of evaluating performance. Several guidelines for accountability are established.

1. Nebulous and elusive goals must be replaced with specific and measurable objectives.
2. Loosely assigned responsibilities must give way to individual commitments.
3. Opinionated judgment must give way to measurable achievements.
4. Looking to others to be accountable must give way to holding oneself accountable.
5. Nebulous incentives must be replaced with motivators for accountability.

Accountability requires an appraisal process that evaluates productivity. Several appraisal methods have been developed because of the varying uses and purposes appraisals are intended to accomplish: to justify pay increases, to evaluate results, to account for productivity, to set up conditions for achievement motivation, to provide feedback for organizational change, to develop personnel for positional changes, and to identify employees with hidden potential. The eight appraisal methods described in this chapter—trait appraisals, essay appraisals, process appraisals, critical-incident appraisals, standards of performance appraisals, ranking appraisals, forced-choice appraisals, and managing by objectives—do not adequately evaluate productivity.

Managing Productivity By Objectives (MPBO) is a multipurpose performance appraisal process. A variety of objectives is expected to be accomplished in its use. The evaluation of productivity provides meaningful data to reach these objectives. The practice of MPBO has several advantages:

1. Gives focus on productivity.
2. Institutes controls for resource allocation.
3. Forces evaluative measures into plans.
4. Provides accountability for resources consumed.
5. Increases productivity mindedness.
6. Heightens motivation for productivity.
7. Encourages preventive rather than corrective management work.
8. Forms a natural vehicle for progress and evaluation reviews.

The disadvantages of MPBO (competent skills are required for its use; more time is required in the planning and commitment phase; and personal traits and behavior are given a low emphasis) can be minimized and controlled. (A complete guide of a performance appraisal for productivity planning, measuring, and evaluating is included on pp. 237–245.)

The issue of time contracting versus performance contracting was discussed in this chapter. Time contracting pays employees for their time; performance contracting pays employees for the assignment or project completed. Each has advantages and disadvantages. Nonetheless, a productivity-based compensation system of performance contracting is emerging as the most likely successor to the old time contracting system. MPBO as a management system is a natural process for this innovation.

QUESTIONS TO THINK ABOUT

1. List the effects of inflation on your organization.
2. How has your organization attempted to moderate the rise of inflation? Discuss the approaches.
3. Is the concept "fair day's pay for fair day's work" working in your organization?
4. Is your organization practicing the "compensation iceberg" effect?
5. List at least five practices in organization that lead to overpayment of employees.
6. If the concept of accountability is practiced in your organization, describe how it works.
7. If you had to redesign your appraisal process, what changes would you make? How could you make it an appraisal for productivity?
8. How might you justify pay increases while holding and controlling inflation in your organization?

REFERENCES

1. Irving S. Friedman, *Inflation: A Growing World-Wide Disaster.* Anchor Press/Doubleday, New York, 1975. pp. 19.
2. John Sheahan, *The Wage-Price Guideposts,* The Brookings Institute, Washington, 1967, pp. 15.
3. *A Study of Potential Changes in Employee Benefits,* Middletown, Connecticut, Institute for the Future, 1969.

4. Niels H. Nielsen, "Running Benefits Like a Business," *National Industrial Conference Board,* August 1970, pp. 20–25.

5. W. D. Conley and F. W. Miller, "MBO, Pay and Productivity", *Management Review,* American Management Association, New York, January–February 1973. pp. 21–25.

6. Peter A. Pyhrr, *Zero-Base, Budgeting,* Wiley-Interscience, New York 1973, p. 5.

7. Donald Andreson, "Zero-base Budgeting: How to Get Rid of Corporate Crabgrass," *Management Review*, American Management Association, October 1976, pp. 12–14.

8. N. B. Winstanley, "Performance Appraisal Another Pollution Problem?" *National Industrial Conference Board.* New York, September 1972, pp. 59–63.

9. Paul Mali, *Managing By Objectives,* Wiley-Interscience, New York, 1972, pp. 237–243.

10. Report of a Special Task Force, *Work in America,* W. E. Upjohn Institute for Employment Research. MIT Press, Cambridge, 1972, pp. 106.

11. Antom K. Kekom, "The Internal Consultant," *American Management Association Special Report, New York, 1969, pp. 41–73.*

A MANAGER'S
and
SUPERVISOR'S
GUIDE

PRODUCTIVITY PLANNING, MEASURING, AND EVALUATING

Foreword to Supervisors

This guide provides a way to assist supervisors and managers at various levels when appraising the performance of employees. It is similar to performance appraisals that have been used in the past except it gives a specific focus on productivity. This does not mean all other important performance expectancies are ignored. It means a supervisor must give careful attention to the requirements of productivity when work is planned, delegated, implemented, controlled, and evaluated. Every time work is planned and assigned, the supervisor must think of the most productive way it can be accomplished! *Productivity is defined as reaching the highest level of performance with the least expenditure of resources.*

This guide consists of: (1) policy statement; (2) steps in the appraisal process; (3) planning for results and productivity; (4) evaluation of results and productivity.

1. *Policy Statement.* Every manager and supervisor is responsible and held accountable for ensuring that every employee understands the specific criteria that will be used to evaluate his or her effectiveness of performance and his or her efficiency of resource utilization. Every manager and supervisor will conduct:

   (a) Planning sessions annually with employees to agree on objectives for the year.

   (b) Verbal appraisals quarterly to evaluate progress toward objectives and performance on the job.

   (c) Written formal appraisals annually to evaluate achievements of objectives and performance on the job.

2. *The Appraisal Process in Steps* (Figure 8.4)

Step 1. Look for Ways to Improve Productivity. Examine ongoing day-to-day work that needs to be improved. Review large-scale projects that need to be accomplished. Analyze what needs to be done to accomplish the organization's annual plan.

Step 2. Meet with Individual Employees. Review with employees future work projects and work procedures. Collect suggestions, get participation in the areas of responsibilities, and agree on commitments to be pursued in the coming year.

Step 3. Write Formal Statements of Objectives. Write clear, concise targets to be reached as formal commitments by individuals and the group. The number of these commitments should be kept to a minimum, but they must be significant.

Step 4. Specify Evaluative Measures within Objectives. Include in objective statements evaluative measures for appraising progress toward or achieving the objective. Productivity measures should include ratios that connect performance to resources. Establish how progress will be monitored.

Step 5. Develop Action Plans. Each statement of objective should have an action plan or a set of activities that, when completed, will achieve the objective. Action plans should be developed when objectives are being formulated. They validate the statements of commitments.

Step 6. Meet with Individual Employees Quarterly. Quarterly appraisals should be made to evaluate the progress toward targets. These quarterly appraisals can be discussions with the responsible individuals.

Step 7. Conduct Formal Annual Appraisals. An annual appraisal should be made to evaluate total accomplishments. A written summary is made of the results. A complete review is made of the areas of agreement, differences, interests, and conflicts. Future plans are formulated.

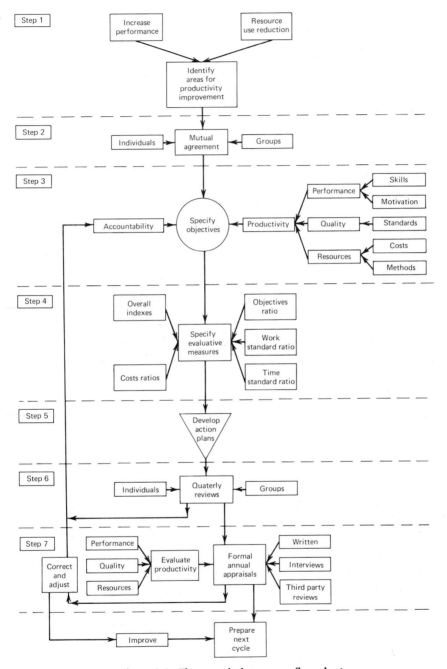

Figure 8.4 The appraisal process—flow chart.

Name _____John Smith_____ Date _Jan. 15_ Appraisal Period Beginning _____Jan._ Ending _Dec._

Position _Foreman of Electrical Distribution_

Productivity Expected—Objectives and Evaluative measures. List the major
results expected for the section, group, or department. Include evaluative
measures and relative priority of each item. This plan should be revised
to reflect changes as they occur during the year.

Priority	Objectives To Be Achieved (Performance Expected with Resources to Be Used)	Evaluative Measures (Indicators)	Target Date
1	Complete 1400 commercial electrical installations with no more than two personnel	$PI = \dfrac{1400\ installations}{2\ workers}$	Oct. 30
2	Install 150,000 feet of three #4 wire for less than $2500 per foot	$PI = \dfrac{150,000\ feet\ of\ wire}{\$2500}$	Feb. 10
3	Total rework is less than 10% of total installations	No more than 10%	Dec. 30
6	Supervise transportation system to keep incidents to five or fewer	Checklist of incidents: (a) Complaints by customers (b) Unable to start work by schedule (c) Vehicle breakdown (d) Vehicle accidents	Dec. 30
5	Assist superintendent in certifying 300 installations with no more than 5% recertifications	$PI = \dfrac{285\ certifications}{300\ total}$	25 per month
4	Complete four departmental budget checklist items within required planning time	Budget checklist: (a) Estimates of all costs (b) Completion of all forms (c) Validation in the field (d) All approvals	July 1

4. Evaluation and Summary of Performance Appraisal

Name _____ *John Smith* _____ Date _____ *Jan. 15* _____

Department _____ *Electrical Distribution* _____ Location _____ *Field Engineering*

Position Title _____ *Foreman* _____ Supervisor _____

Time in Position _____ *17 years* _____ Last Appraisal Date _____ *Jan. 22*

Performance Results   List objectives expected and the actual results
achieved for each of the major commitments agreed upon on the
planning phase. Include comments on the quality of attainment and
circumstances affecting results.

1. Objective expected	Target Date	Priority
Complete 1400 commercial installations with no more than two personnel	*Oct 30*	*1*

Results Achieved		
Completed 1200 installations with no more than two personnel	$PI = \dfrac{Actual}{Planned} = \dfrac{1200}{1400} = 86\%$	

2. Objective expected	Target Date	Priority
Install 150,000 feet of three #4 wire for less than $2500 per foot	*Feb. 10*	*2*

Results Achieved		
Installed 160,000 feet for $2200 per foot	$PI = \dfrac{Actual\ PI}{Planned\ PI} = 120\%$	

3. Objective expected	Target Date	Priority
Total rework is less than 10% of total installations	*Dec. 30*	*3*

Results Achieved		
1200 installations completed, 60 reworked installations	$PI = \dfrac{1200\ completed}{1400\ planned} = 86\%$	

4. Objective expected	Target Date	Priority
Complete budget within expected time	*July 1*	*4*

Results achieved		
Budget preparations completed	$PI = \dfrac{4\ checklist\ items}{4\ expected\ items} = 100\%$	

5. Objective expected	Target Date	Priority
Assist certify 300 installations	*July 1*	*5*

Results Achieved		
250 certifications were completed	$PI = \dfrac{250\ certifications}{300\ expected} = 83\%$	

<u>Job Performance Factors</u>   Check the appropriate block to indicate the employee's degree of effectiveness in looking for and actually contributing to performance improvement. Cite examples of observed performance improvement where applicable.

		Strong	Satis— factory	Needs Improve— ment	Comments
1.	Problem analysis — finds critical factors and arrives at sound solutions.	☐	☑	☐	————
2.	Organizer — plans and completes own work by target dates.	☐	☐	☑	*Suggest he learn scheduling techniques*
3	Quality — work quality meets expected standards of job and profession.	☐	☑	☐	————
4.	Amount of work — produces volume of work on a day— to—day basis.	☐	☑	☐	————
5.	Controls—understands standards, measures results, and corrects.	☑	☐	☐	*Sets up standards even where they do not exist.*
6.	Motivation — motivated to complete work to a successful end.	☐	☑	☐	————
7.	————	☐	☐	☐	————
8.	————	☐	☐	☐	————

<u>Resources Use Factors</u>   Check the appropriate block to indicate the employee's degree of efficiency in following methods and responsibilities for best utilization of resources. Cite examples of observed efficiency in resource use.

	Strong	Satis—factory	Needs Improve—ment	Comments
1. Cost—mindedness — does work with best cost judgment.	☐	☐	☑	*Needs to make cost benefit analysis before proceeding*
2. Budget use — completes work within prescribed limits.	☐	☑	☐	
3. Time use — utilizes time efficiently and eliminates unnecessary activities.	☐	☐	☑	*Personal activities excessive*
4. Space — makes best use of space allocated for completing work.	☐	☑	☐	
5. Supplies — uses only supplies needed to accomplish work.	☐	☑	☐	
6. Fellow workers — does not waste efforts and time of colleagues	☐	☑	☐	
7. _____	☐	☐	☐	
8. _____	☐	☐	☐	

243

Personal Factors   Check the appropriate block to indicate the employee's degree of acceptable behavior in interpersonal relations and personal conduct in job responsibilities. Cite examples of observed personal qualities.

		Strong	Satis—factory	Needs Improve—ment	Comments
1.	Learning — learns quickly and effectively applies skills to job.	☐	☑	☐	
2.	Self—development — aware of strengths and weaknesses and plans development.	☐	☐	☑	Needs to be reminded continuously
3.	Communication — selects proper media and effectively writes, listens, and speaks.	☐	☑	☐	
4.	Team relations — works well as a member of a team.	☐	☑	☐	
5.	Adaptability — ability to react to changes in job requirements or expectancies.	☐	☑	☐	
6.	Self—starter — does not have to be told to start and works with limited supervision.	☐	☐	☑	Tends to forget
7.	_____	☐	☐	☐	

<u>Development Plans</u>   Indicate plan for further development of employee in the next appraisal period. Relate plans to the strengths and improvements cited earlier.

1. Should enroll in course on scheduling techniques
2. Would like him to visit another department to see cost control practices
3. Suggest the development of a personal planner and time log for recording deadlines

<u>Summary and Recommendations</u>   Record any additional comments and make whatever recommendation deemed necessary to other individuals in the organization such as merit increase, promotion, transfer, development, or termination.

No significant change is presently recommended

Employee's acknowledgment and Agreement	*John Smith*	Date *Jan 12*
Employee's Acknowledgment and Disagreement		Date
Appraised by	*Bob Doe*	Date *Jan. 12*
Reviewed by		Date *Jan. 30*

9
MANAGING THE
NEW MOTIVATION
OF EMPLOYEES

IN THIS CHAPTER

Erosion of traditional view of authority.
Educational levels changing worker expectations.
Legalized participative management.
Unions growing in effectiveness.
Value conflicts.
Affluence shifting priorities and attitudes.
Three approaches to motivation.
Needs coincidence: a theory of generating motivators.
How to motivate with the costliest motivator: money.
The developing new work ethic.

The search is intense for the foolproof formula that could be followed—cookbook style—to get every employee to work at the highest possible productivity level. With the wave of a "magic-wand" formula, masses of employees would act energetically, quickly, and efficiently. Since no such formula has been found, the search continues. At best we have discovered factors of the individual, the environment, and the work that both positively and negatively affect the processes that generate and sustain motivation. We have gained insight into how these factors can be used to create the motivational process. But human nature is too complex to turn motivation on and off when we please. Managers, however, cannot wait for a crystal-clear set of attitudes, processes, and practices to guide them down the path to motivational excellence. The problems of motivation are here and now. Getting employees to face and meet the productivity challenge must be achieved immediately. A primary reason why workers do not step up their output or the pace of their work whether they are union members or not is the fear that they will work themselves out of a job. This may be union's single most skeptical attitude toward cooperative efforts for productivity. History does verify the reason for this feeling of insecurity which has been nurtured by the fluctuating economic cycles.

The purposes of this chapter are (1) to describe why motivating employees is different and more difficult than in the past; to identify and describe trends that have an impact on managing motivation; (2) to describe three approaches to motivation—economic, behavioral, and managerial—that have developed over the years; and (3) to describe the expectancy alignment process, which managers may use in a practical way to motivate employees toward greater productivity. Several special motivational questions are also answered in this chapter. Does money motivate? Are certain motivators effective for certain groups such as minorities, older employees, women, the affluent, and managers? Is the work ethic dead? The theory of expectancy alignment introduced in this chapter is the foundation for building ideas for the process for motivating employees and for developing motivators that are unique and specific to an organization.

WHY IS MOTIVATING DIFFICULT?

Motivating employees is difficult today because motives have become more diffused and complex. Motives are sometimes defined as needs, wants, drives, or impulses within the individual. Motives are the reasons for behavior. They direct workers toward goals. They may be conscious or subconscious. They affect not only the "ability to do" but also the "will to do." The behavior of a person depends on the strength and intensity of these motives. These motives arouse and maintain human activity in certain directions. Motivation, then, is motive strength, the intensity of the "will to do" to meet or satisfy a need. The sequence for developing the "will to do" is: (1) a want emerges; (2) wants become needs; (3) needs become motives; (4) motives become purposes to act; and (5) purposes to act become the "will to do."

The motives and purpose factors of workers have changed because their needs have changed. Current needs are different in both type and amount from those of the past. These needs are individualistic and insatiable. They have changed the reasons a worker will work, how far he or she will respond to the pressures and demands of an organization. Today's worker is better educated, better informed, more independent, more aware, more secure, and more affluent. Factors operating within an organization are creating this new type of worker. Six of the factors that greatly affect motive strength—the motivational process—are examined briefly to give further insight on why present day motivating is difficult, different from, and not aligned with that of the past.

Changing View of Authority

The traditional view of authority is breaking down. Employees are less responsive to authority than in the past. People do not respond simply because someone in authority commands response. Years ago when a supervisor commanded a subordinate to move, the subordinate would merely ask when. Today, when supervisors command subordinates to move, they ask why. If the answer to the question is unsatisfactory, the subordinate may not move. Supervisors and managers who expect employees to do as they are told, asking a minimum of questions and giving no argument, are experiencing frustrations and reduced performance. Such managers assume that employees are passive and receptive to commands for accomplishing work. The command range of a supervisor and the acceptance zone for employee are not coincident (see Figure 9.1). The supervisor perceives a large range of orders that an employee should and must accept. The employee perceives a smaller range in which he will accept orders from his supervisor. This difference in perception between giving and accepting commands is the cause of the breakdown of the traditional view of authority. Many supervisors are looking toward the motivation processes to help expand the zone of acceptance of subordinates. They will be disappointed. They discover that employees wish to be active and participate in making decisions that affect the activities within their jobs. The traditional perception of authority is being replaced by a new form of authority that relies heavily on the work process—how it is assigned and delegated to the subordinate. A supervisor may see this as an obstacle in getting employees to perform work, but actually both supervisor and subordinate are forced to engage in the requirements of work productivity.

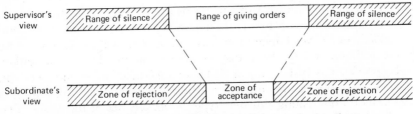

Figure 9.1   Authority as perceived by supervisor and subordinates.

Worker Expectations Increasing because of Rising Educational Levels

Education for all is now moving toward higher education for all. More people are receiving college degrees than ever before. Thirty years ago only 20 percent of high school graduates went to college; today 70 to 90 percent of high school graduates attend college. In fact, in some community colleges, a high school diploma is not necessary to study for advanced degrees. To be an adult is enough. As a result, the average educated worker in our society is moving up in the skills spectrum (see Figure 9.2).

This move on the skills spectrum results in new levels of awareness and new attitudes that have an impact on employee expectations. This awareness generates inquiries that seldom existed before—inquiries into the nature of organizations, the employees role in them, and how much satisfaction can be derived from day-to-day work. This new level of awareness forces an individual's expectations from his job to rise. Individuals want more from their jobs. They want more from the work. They want more from their supervisors. They want more from the organiza-

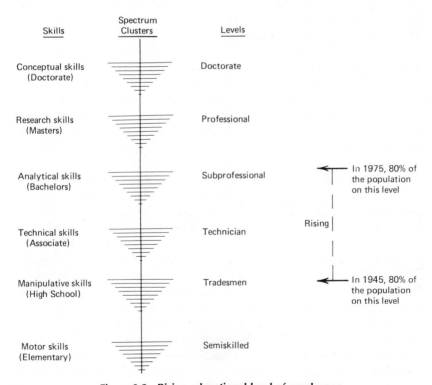

Figure 9.2   Rising educational level of employees.

tion. The expectations are rising too fast for the organizational system to meet them.

The move up the skills spectrum is affecting attitudes. For example, a recent survey found a change in the attitude, "hard work will always pay off."[1] In 1968, 69 percent affirmed this attitude. In 1971, 39 percent affirmed it. As rising levels of education cause levels of awareness to rise, workers are expecting a greater quality in work life. Traditional attitudes are being challenged and often discarded.

"Legalized Participative Management"

Unions and federal, state, and local governments have intruded into organizations making demands related to conditions of employment, freedom of association, government codes, unfair practices, benefits of employment, mediation, security, safety, employee activities, picketing, injunctions, health, welfare, and education. These enactments clarify the rights of workers and introduce new "rights" that were formally prerogatives of management. They introduce a "system of equal prizes" that does not reward those who build better products or provide better services. Although the ingenious, the inventive, and the hard worker should be favored, individual differences are ignored. Legislative enactments have shifted decision-making away from management toward collective bargaining. As legislative enactments increase, the shift of management prerogatives into the collective bargaining agreement also increases. Union and government intrusions are viewed as "legalized" participative management. Figure 9.3 shows enactments that have forced managerial prerogatives into the collective bargaining agreements during the period from 1930 to 1970.

In the past the collective bargaining process, legalized and encouraged by the government, has had a positive effect on organizations. However, government intrusions into the managerial decision-making processes have now reached a point of diminishing returns. Many government decrees are hurting, not helping, organizational productivity. Government grows bigger and potentially more dangerous as a result of the legislative process. In many instances government's impact on organizations is oppressive. A review and analysis of bargaining contracts would show: (a) most contracts emphasize compensation based on time and not productivity; (b) pay scales are based on "putting in" time rather than pay for increased productivity; (c) most contracts tend to be the same, ignoring the uniqueness and differences in organizations; and (d) vacation time and grievance handling are detailed, but little attention is given to "a fair day's work for a fair day's pay." Few firms have been able to get productivity

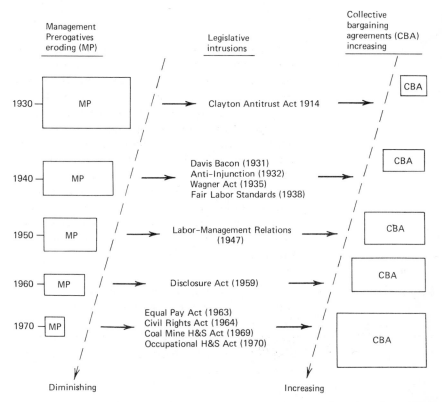

Figure 9.3 Enactments that have shifted management prerogatives into bargaining agreements.

clauses into collective bargaining agreements. In a national survey conducted by the Prentice-Hall Research Staff to which 600 firms responded, only 10 percent, a small minority, reported productivity clauses in bargaining agreements.[2] The following are excerpts from this survey.

	Clauses
Reasonable productivity	An employee shall perform all assigned work at a reasonable productivity rate which is in accordance with sound time study practices.
Maintain high level of productivity	The Union recognized that continued large-scale employment of a fair wage can continue only as long as a high level of productivity is maintained.

The parties agree that this result is dependent upon achieving a high quality of individual employee performance and efficiency and the union undertakes to encourage its members in the attainment of this objective. This can be done by reducing scrap and spoilage, good care of tools and equipment, a minimum amount of time wasted and careful and economical use of supplies, including water, steam and electricity. Efficiency of production requires cooperative effort toward finding easier, better, and faster ways of performing operations and the ready acceptance of higher production bases due to improvement in operations or methods.

Required productivity

The purpose and intent of the parties to this agreement is that the employee will provide a fair day's work for a fair day's pay and that the required productivity and effort of an employee must be consistent with his safety and proper working conditions.

Control over productivity

It is the Company's policy to pay incentive (bonus) wages to hourly paid employees assigned to jobs in which there is opportunity through increased effort and/or attention to turn out additional good production.

Jobs must be such that the employee has control over productivity so that he can increase and sustain production over what is normally expected. This increase in productivity must be such that it can be readily measured.

Individuals should be able to relate increases or decreases in effort and/or attention with proportionate increases or decreases in bonus compensation.

Accepted industrial engineering practices will be used for measuring the employee's productivity and/or contribution to profit in determining bonus payments. If productivity is limited, the crew size may be adjusted commensurate with work requirements so as to provide bonus opportunity wherever possible.

Productivity of a normal employee

The test which shall be used as a basis for disciplining or discharging an employee for productivity not up to standard shall be the productivity of a normal employee reasonably exercising his working capacity.

Increasing productivity

The Company may, in its discretion, establish production standards and apply wage incentives to jobs where, in the opinion of the Company, sound and proper incentives can be applied with the objective of increasing productivity.

Fair day's work for fair day's pay

The Company and the Union recognize the principle of a fair day's work for a fair day's pay. Each and every employee is expected to meet certain requirements of performance, including quality and quantity of production as determined on the basis of time standards based on the principles mentioned above. Employees who repeatedly fail to meet normally expected production requirements shall be advised of such failure by their supervisors. If the employee still fails to meet such requirements, he will be subject to disciplinary action, including discharge.

Reasonable day's work for reasonable day's wages

The Union hereby recognizes that it is the duty of every employee covered by this Agreement to carry out and abide by the provisions thereof, and to promote at all times, the efficient progress of the Company's plant expecially in such matters as safety, economy, quality and quantity of the output of the plant. The Union further agrees that it is the duty of each employee to give a reasonable day's work for a reasonable day's wages. The Company agrees that it will not require any employee to give more than a reasonable day's work for a reasonable day's wages.

The parties recognize and acknowledge that increased wages and other benefits guaranteed to the employees by this Agreement will depend to a great extent upon increased productivity resulting from increased employee efficiency, technological progress, better tools, improved methods, processes and equipment, and a cooperative attitude on the part of the Company and the Union. The parties agree to encourage such progress to the end that costs may be reduced and a higher level of productivity maintained so that competition may be aggressively met and beaten.

Produce at no less than standard levels

It is expected that each employee will attain and produce at no less than the standard production levels. If, in the opinion of the company, an employee fails to attain and produce at said standard production level for reasons other than conditions beyond his control, disciplinary action may be taken by the Company.

High degree of efficiency in workmanship

The Union agrees to cooperate with the Company in all matters pertaining to improving and expanding the Company's business and shall assist in every way possible to promote the sale of company products and shall do everything within reason to promote a high degree of efficiency in the workmanship of its members.

Such clauses are a contractual commitment by both management and labor. The few firms that have them in their collective bargaining agreements are to be commended, but problems of interpretation may arise as to the intended level of productivity.

Worker's Unions Growing in Effectiveness and Strength

Collective bargaining in the United States is working and working well! Union membership exceeds 21 million—an historic all-time high. "Strike power" has made unions formidable, and contracts gains for workers have hit an all-time high. This growth in strength and effectiveness will continue because union strategies for organizing new workers are agressive, and negotiating strategies at the bargaining table are at parity and in many cases above parity with management. Here is a sample list of strategies that indicate the growth toward effectiveness:

1. *Unions have increased their communications* of regular, meaningful, conveyance of management misuses, abuses, and mistakes.
2. *Unions have urged employees to submit grievances* whenever there is any evidence of contract violations. In some cases they have provided financial incentives.
3. *Unions train their stewards for effective contract administration.* They insist union leadership must know the contract better than supervisors.
4. *Unions urge members to communicate all matters*—contract and noncontract—through union channels. Unions want to transfer management prerogatives (silent issues) to the negotiating table.
5. *Unions urge their leadership to practice the "open door" policy.* In this manner leadership focal point is moved from supervision to the union ranks.
6. *Unions are quick to identify rising, strong leaders.* Opportunities are given to rising potential leaders to move into the union ranks.
7. *Unions are quick to take credit for benefits given to employees.* All benefits are derived from the organization, its operations, and performance; but unions are quick to exploit their efforts on behalf of the employees.
8. *Unions use collective bargaining as a "power tool."* Strength and power to management is deliberately displayed by strategies of stubborness, walkouts, crisis bargaining, job acting, and strikes. Unions want to bargain from strength.
9. *Unions take the initiative to win employee allegiance.* Unions seek benefits for employees as a matter of purpose and aim. Management gives benefits to employees as a matter of concession and compromise.
10. *Unions exploit the elusive role of the first-line supervisor.* Unions bypass first-line supervisors in the decision process, creating a "weak" first-line level of management.

Labor unions are continually amassing power. In some organizations management no longer controls the situation. In others its effect is on motivation. The traditional authority breakdown now demands that managers cannot threaten employees into performance. This makes motivation different and more difficult.

Since the number of blue-collar workers is declining and white-collar workers increasing, there's a bright future for white-collar unions. White-collar workers are better educated, more aware, more sensitive to rights, more affluent, and more articulate. These qualities will make white-collar unions even stronger in both numbers and strategies for reaching the goals needed and wanted.

Worker's Goals and Employer Objectives in Conflict

Human cooperation has often been portrayed as a peaceful and tranquil scene. More often, organizational life is a "web of tensions" rather than a "network of togetherness." Some give and others take; a few get their way and most compromise their ways. A moderate level of conflict may have many constructive effects. In fact, a degree of tension and conflict would provide differing viewpoints and additional alternatives most useful in the decision-making process. But when the level of conflict is high and frequent, the consequences are harmful and disruptive.

Competition for rewards or benefits is one cause of conflict. The process of dividing "the pie" inevitably leaves some out or allows a smaller share to each. It may often mean satisfaction for one while producing dissatisfaction for another. The increasing tempo of participative management is a second cause of conflict. If six people were asked to set goals independently, conflict would be at a minimum. However, when the six are asked to collaborate for consensus on goals, conflicts increase. A third cause differs in convictions and values. Worker values are guides to decisions and behavior. They are inner beliefs or convictions that influence "choice" and thus "will." Values affect a worker's motivation either to work hard or not. The following are examples of general and specific values.

CLASSICAL VALUES (ACCEPTED BY MOST)

1. Life has purpose.
2. Man can reason.
3. A human is more important than the state.
4. Do to others what you wish them to do to you.
5. Man does not live by bread alone.

MODERN VALUES (ACCEPTED BY MOST)

1. A company is in business to make a profit.
2. All people should be given equal employment opportunities.
3. The government protects person and property.
4. Rewards should go to those who merit them.
5. All people should have the opportunity to reach their highest possible educational level.

OBSOLETE VALUES (REJECTED BY MOST)

1. The earth is flat.
2. The white race is superior to the black race.
3. Communism is evil.
4. When the poor work hard, they will not be poor.

RECENT VALUES (CONTROVERSIAL)

1. Corporations should assume social responsibilities.
2. Freedom without limits brings anarchy.
3. Competition results in gain for the consumer.
4. Hard work produces great rewards.
5. Conflicts can be resolved at the conference table.

There are many sources of values: family, religion, unions, associations, community, school, place of employment, books, clubs, leaders, friends, and newspapers. They flow from society. They emerge from the crucibles of life's experiences. Since society is changing, values that workers hold are also changing. Values are in a state of transition. They will form a new basis on dealing with workers. Here are some new emerging values:

NEW VALUES (BEING TESTED)

1. The world should have one government.
2. There should be one language throughout the world.
3. Populations should be controlled by government.
4. Every employee should be a manager.
5. A person should be paid for what he does and not for the time he puts in.

As our society becomes more oriented toward goal setting and value fulfillment as a basis of motivation, conflicts with existing or new goals will increase. The need to align goals with compromising rewards becomes apparent. Harmony of goal expectancies between employees and managers can be developed through the process of expectancy alignment and coordination. We discuss this further in the section on how to motivate for greater productivity.

Worker Affluence Shifting Priorities and Attitudes

Economic achievement in the United States ranges from bare subsistence levels to levels of incredible riches. These levels are not easy to identify; they rise in a continuum. Compared to other countries, the United States worker is wealthy indeed. American workers have the highest per capita income and the highest bare subsistence level in the world. Abundance continues to grow in spite of occasional fluctuations due to economic stall or recessions. As workers and families achieve relatively higher incomes and standards of living, they assume lifestyles with attitudes and priorities that are characteristic of affluence. This greatly affects views of work and the remuneration for it.

One view of the continuum from the poor to the super-rich is shown in Figure 9.4, where three groups are identified: underaffluent, affluent, and superaffluent. The largest group is the affluent group—households with a family income in excess of $15,000 a year.[3] In 1955, 6 percent of the families in the United States were affluent. In 1970 23 percent were affluent. In 1975 the number reached 34 percent. It is projected to reach 42 percent by 1980. In the affluent group a larger amount of discretionary income is available for optional spending, and a smaller amount is needed for essentials. The definition of affluence is related to the share of consumer income that is not needed for essentials and is available for discretionary spending. The superaffluent group is high in discretionary income and spending. The ratio changes as a family moves up the affluence continuum. This ratio of prescriptive spending to discretionary spending is shown diagrammatically in Figure 9.4.

Attitudes toward work among affluent workers are of necessity. Those on the lower end of the continuum expect dissatisfying work along with some satisfying work, but they expect financial rewards. As an individual rises on the continuum, satisfying work seems to be the primary expectation because financial rewards are already high.

The problem of motivating the affluent class is difficult and complex. It involves the degree of dissatisfying work people will accept along with the degree of satisfying work they already have as their ratio of prescriptive

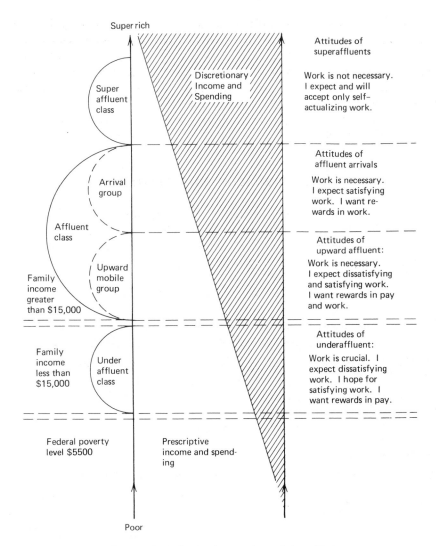

Figure 9.4 Attitude changes from rising affluency.

and discretionary income changes. The motivational problem becomes more complex because the nature of satisfying and dissatisfying work varies with each individual. Affluent workers want both pay and satisfying work, regardless of where they are on the affluency scale, but they want it to differing degrees as they change their positions on the scale. Those who are the affluent arrivals want rewards and satisfaction in the work itself.

Those who are the upward affluent want rewards and satisfaction in both pay and work. Those who are underaffluent want rewards and satisfaction primarily in the one thing they lack most—money. Those who are engaged in work that can never be satisfying will seek more time off with pay or more leisure time. If they cannot find satisfaction in their work, they will find it in the off-job activities that may be started in leisure time or paid time off. For this reason, shorter work weeks, early retirement, and more paid holidays are goals that unions actively seek.

THREE APPROACHES TO MOTIVATION

There are three general approaches to motivating workers toward greater productivity: the economic incentives approach, the behavioral approach, and the management approach. Before describing each approach a distinction among the three should be made.

THE ECONOMIC INCENTIVE APPROACH

1. How to use rewards and work conditions to perform well on the job.
2. How to use incentives to get people to meet job expectancies.
3. How to urge and persuade people to behave in certain ways.
4. How to help people get what they want by showing them how to get what an organization wants.

THE BEHAVIORAL APPROACH

1. How to meet the needs of people on the job.
2. How individual motives will form the basis of the will to work.
3. How organizational behavior can be modified by getting individuals to modify their own behavior.
4. How to improve the quality of organizational life by changing conditions of the job.

THE MANAGERIAL APPROACH

1. How to meet the needs of both people and the organization.
2. How to set incentives so that people and organization profit.
3. How to "fit" people and organization goals into the situation at hand.
4. How to select, from the range of possibilities, the necessary approach that will work for workers and the organization.

Although these three approaches are perhaps oversimplified, they represent three general approaches to motivation. The third approach, a synthesis of the two, is termed the eclectic approach. It selects from the other two, the motivational process that fits the situation at hand. My intention is not to evaluate the weaknesses or limitations of these approaches. They are included to give the reader an overview of the variety of motivational methods available as a basis for recommending the method to be used for greater productivity. Let's examine the contribution in each approach.

Incentive Approaches to Motivation

Incentive approaches to motivating employees are based on the view that workers are eager to maximize their monetary status, power and prestige. Managers who follow this approach usually "dangle the carrot" to get workers to produce.

Financial Incentives Approach (Adam Smith).[4] Adam Smith's book *The Wealth of Nations* published in 1776 had a tremendous influence on economic and political theory. Smith lived in an era in which people struggled for basic material needs. Consequently, Smith insisted that people are oriented toward self-interest. Free people in free markets create the greatest well-being for the greatest number of people. They can be motivated by the carrot-and-stick process. Give them incentives that are strong enough and they will be motivated. Smith said this would work because of the following assumptions:

1. Workers want and need monetary gain, hence will do what achieves for them the greatest gain.
2. Workers are only a small element within an organization. The organization controls the monetary gain and therefore can control motivation.
3. Workers do not understand organizational interests and goals and therefore must be prevented from interfering.
4. Workers' feelings must be controlled by the organizational structure. The organization should even encourage and develop workers' feelings and goals to be the same as those of the organization.

To Smith, monetary rewards should be set in steps with levels and amounts based on the results contributed to the organization. Enormous increases in productivity and output would occur because each person has strong economic self-interests. When operating in a fully free and competitive market, it would result in the greatest gain for the individual.

How to motivate according to Smith:

Give workers financial incentives strong enough to experience monetary gain.

Piece Rate Work Standards Approach (Frederick Taylor).[5] Frederick Taylor started systematic approaches for accomplishing work with time and motion studies. He would divide the work into "chunks," determine the best time to produce these chunks, establish these work chunks as standards, assign pay rates for completing these standards, and give training and development to workers to perform to the standards. Taylor used this approach because his analysis of the worker and the work showed a haphazard and random process for its accomplishment. The inefficient, wasteful movements and energy frustrated and demotivated the worker. Taylor pursued these assumptions:

1. Workers can be driven only to a point, and therefore the work situation must change.
2. Workers would work more if their work were made simpler and easier.
3. Workers get greater results if the work were separated into parts and people were allowed to specialize in these parts.
4. Workers contribute more to the organization when work is defined into chunks and standards of performance are established with pay increases.

Taylor felt people would work to high levels when the job and its processes allowed them to do so. Although Taylor placed great importance on the value of money, he stressed the need for examining the job situation and developing a systematic approach to utilizing workers for accomplishing the work. Work must be divided and assigned to those best fitted to do it. Workers needed to be scientifically selected, trained, and developed in the jobs they are best suited to do.

How To Motivate According To Taylor:

Give workers a job situation in which work is broken up into standards, assign pay to these standards, and give an easy procedure to reach the standards.

Job Analysis and Wage Structure Approach (Hugo Munsterberg).[6] Hugo Munsterberg classified worker traits, skills, and knowledge in an effort to match worker abilities and skills with job requirements. His work analysis was a process of measuring worker traits and assigning weights of importance for making compensation decisions. Munsterberg used this approach to differentiate jobs and to measure successful performance on these jobs. Munsterberg pursued these assumptions:

1. Workers see importance in their reward levels in one organization compared to working for another reward level in another organization.
2. Workers see job satisfaction and wage level as an important measure for deciding on one job from among many.
3. Workers see the money rate structure from low to high as a promotional opportunity to go up the organization. The rate structure is a measure of how well one is succeeding.
4. Workers will contribute more if merit recognition will allow them to jump steps in the rate structure.

Munsterberg felt that once job classes and levels, with their money rates, are established, workers have a scorekeeping way to compare their achievements in their present jobs with other jobs in other organizations.

How To Motivate According To Munsterberg:

Give workers a job structure in steps, assign money rates and provide merit evaluation when it is recognized these jobs have been well achieved.

Behavioral Approaches to Motivation

A survey conducted by the National Conference Board (1970) showed that 241 out of 300 American companies (80 percent) reported some movement from the incentive approaches to the behavioral approaches.

Hierarchy of Needs Approach (Abraham Maslow).[7]   Humans are wanting beings. There is always some need they want to satisfy. Maslow indicates that humans are motivated by these needs as they perceive them. These needs are urging individuals toward fulfillment and satisfaction. They are driving individuals to certain states of behavior. The higher order of needs become potent only after basic needs have been satisfied.

NEEDS HIERARCHY WITH THE LOWEST ASCENDING TO THE HIGHEST

1. *Physiological Needs*—food, water, shelter, sex—are geared to survival.
2. *Safety Needs*—protection, safety, freedom from fear—are concerned with physical and mental well-being.

3. *Love Needs*—belonging, acceptance—are geared to the social well-being.
4. *Esteem Needs*—respect, recognition, status—are geared to self-confidence.
5. *Self-Actualization Needs*—filling one's potential, growth—are geared to one's ideals for fulfillment.

Maslow emphasizes that after a need is satisfied, it is no longer a motivator of behavior for the individual. As the needs at one level are reasonably well met, the worker will strive to satisfy higher ones. These needs overlap and interact. Workers' need for satisfaction is insatiable because needs never end. The lower level needs are more demanding, but those higher on the scale are more lasting and effective as motivators.

How to Motivate According to Maslow:

Give workers opportunities in a work situation in which they can fulfill their needs.

Theory X and Theory Y Approach (Douglas McGregor).[8] McGregor develops two sets of contrasting assumptions about humans and their perceptions about work. These assumptions become determinants of leadership styles and motivation of people.

THEORY X ASSUMPTIONS

1. Workers inherently dislike work and when possible will avoid it.
2. Workers have little ambition, shun responsibility, and prefer direction.
3. Workers want security.
4. Workers have to be coerced, controlled, and threatened to attain organizational objectives.

THEORY Y ASSUMPTIONS

1. Workers will seek responsibility when conditions are favorable.
2. Workers want to direct and control their own commitments.
3. Workers want rewards commensuate with their commitments.
4. Workers want opportunities to make significant contributions to organizations objectives.

According to McGregor, managers have trouble motivating their workers because they hold erroneous assumptions about the nature of people.

Managers need not accept the assumptions of Y, but neither should they abandon the limiting assumptions of X. This would mean opportunities for developing employees for growth and productivity would be motivational. According to McGregor, you cannot motivate people directly. Motivation comes from within. This motivation expresses itself in outcome behavior when conditions allow it.

How to Motivate According to McGregor:

Give managers a new view and set of attitudes about people and their environment for best advancing goals of people and the organization.

Motivation-Hygiene Theory Approach (Frederick Herzberg).[9] Herzberg identifies job elements that generate positive feelings as satisfiers and job elements that generate negative feelings as dissatisfiers. Satisfaction and dissatisfaction are separate factors, not end points on a continuum. Satisfiers are also called motivators because they are effective in motivating employees to greater productivity. Dissatisfiers are called hygiene factors because they prevent dissatisfaction from occurring but do not induce people toward extra effort. Five job conditions that stand out as high determinants of satisfaction are:

1. Achievement.
2. Recognition.
3. Work itself.
4. Responsibility.
5. Advancement.

Herzberg claims these satisfiers can motivate individuals to long-term superior performance and effort. He also identifies job conditions that stand out as high determinants of dissatisfaction. They may produce changes in attitude and productivity, but they are only short-term in nature. The dissatisfier factors are:

1. Organization policies.
2. Administration.
3. Supervision.
4. Salary.
5. Interpersonal relations.
6. Job security.
7. Working conditions.

Herzberg argues that managers tend to create conditions of stressed environmental dissatisfiers while ignoring the potential value of the satisfier factors.

How To Motivate According To Herzberg:

Give workers motivators within the job content that will lead to satisfaction.

Achievement Motivation Theory Approach (David McClelland).[10]
McClelland states that high levels of accomplishment at work are due to the fact that a high level of "achievement needs" exists among people. People who accomplish large undertakings are turned on by the accomplishment. Money, position, status, power are secondary considerations. McClelland notes that patterns of achievement motivation are found with founders (entrepreneurs) of companies or presidents of small organizations. Entrepreneurs are imbued with a sense of accomplishing things. Executives of large corporations have done well enough to relax a little. The high achiever has these characteristics:

1. Assumes responsibility for solving problems.
2. Reaches for goals in spite of high risks.
3. Develops situation that offer frequent feedback of results.

An interesting point with McClelland's achievement motivation is that entrepreneurial behavior can be developed. Once learned, entrepreneurial activity usually results. The outstanding characteristic of entrepreneurial behavior (high achievement) is the desire to approach tasks for which there is reasonable chance for success and to avoid those that are either too easy or too difficult.

How To Motivate According To McClelland:

Give workers entrepreneurial development opportunities to experience high levels of achievement.

Expectancy Theory Approach (Victor Vroom).[11]   Vroom has formulated one of the more popular versions of expectancy theory based on three concepts:

1. *Valence.*   The value or importance that a specific outcome has for a worker.
2. *Instrumentality.*   Worker's view of how high performance will help him get a promotion.

3. *Expectancy.* Worker's feeling of whether his efforts will lead to high levels of performance.

Vroom's expectancy theory models assign mathematical probabilities to predictions about work behavior. In a given situation human behavior is a joint function of the degree to which that behavior is instrumental (effective) in attaining an outcome and the subjective probability (hunch) that the outcome will be forthcoming. Individuals will choose the behavior—and its needed motivation—that they perceive as leading to the things they want.

Expectancy theory suggests that people tend to expend more effort toward reaching goals when both the probability of receiving a reward and the magnitude of that reward are known in advance:

magnitude of reward × probability of receiving reward
= high motivation

magnitude of reward × probability of receiving reward
= low motivation

How To Motivate According To Vroom:

Give workers, in advance, opportunities in which rewards are great and the probability of achieving them is high.

Management Approaches to Motivation

The management approach to motivating workers is based on the view that there is no best way to motivate. Different organizations with different tasks, different competitive environments, and different worker needs require different approaches to motivating. Management approaches are therefore an eclectic synthesis of other approaches that will best fit the factors of a situation. It is difficult to isolate each approach since there is a great deal of overlapping and similarity.

Contingency Approach. There are many contributors to the contingency approach.[12] It recognizes the substantial differences between and among organizations and their constituencies. No one model for motivating will work for all organizations. The appropriate organizational structure, leadership, staffing, planning, motivating, and control are contingent upon the nature of the organizational environment and the task to be performed. Thus the emphasis is on researching the practices and methodology that are appropriate for the situation and adopting the one that works. These are the assumptions of this viewpoint and approach:

1. Worker situations differ. These differences affect how managerial knowledge is applied. Different organizations with different tasks and different competitive environment require different plans. Just as every human personality and every organization is unique, so every managerial position or situation is unique.
2. Differences in working environment, rather than similarities, are the basis of establishing a management practice.
3. Worker motivational practices cannot be applied across the board. They may be true and useful for a particular problem in a particular situation.

The contingency approach is based on the major idea but there is no one best way to handle any of the various management functions and problems. There is no one best way to plan; there is no one best way to control; there is no one best way to motivate. The best way is developed after careful research and analysis of the particular situation faced and applying a planned effective approach to the problem.

How to Motivate According to Contingency Approach:

Analyze the situation and select elements from the vast array of principles and techniques that would form a model for motivating workers in a given situation.

Systems Approach.   In recent years increasing use has been made for a body of systematic relationships within the organization. These system constructs provide key tools for a diagnosis of human interactions of persons, groups, organizations, and communities. These are the assumptions of this approach:

1. A systems model can be developed that has universal applicability to physical, social, and human relationships, whether the organization be small or large.
2. A systems model brings a "unity" or "coherence" for the wide variety of needs, interest, attitudes, and motives of an organization.
3. A systems model captures the way in which the organization works and predicts what would happen if some new motivational factor were introduced.

A systems model is designed to link the critical parameters of the operations and environment situation. The model is then used to simulate the effects of human interactions and motivations when changes are introduced or situational factors are removed.

How to Motivate According to The System Approach:

Develop a system model for the organization to establish its current motivational process and proceed with finding the change-agents for its improvement.

Expectancy Alignment Approach. I recommend the expectancy alignment approach.[13] It recognizes that the complexities of people, situations, goals, and organizational needs are too formidable for simplistic methods. Differences are important, but similarities are important as well! Most important are purposes and expectancies. What do we want? What do we expect? What are we trying to achieve? Literally, this motivational approach requires an assessment of the needs of both the organization and people and a way of creating a situation in which both these needs are accommodated within "states of expectancies." Let's make these assumptions:

1. Worker needs are extremely complex and change with changing values, attitudes, interests, and wants. Similarly, organizational needs are extremely complex and change with changing markets, products, services, environment, legislations, and goals. Both of these "packages" of needs are continually changing. A purpose for both groups must be established to provide something to which complex changing needs can be related or made coincident.

2. Workers' needs are in disparity with organizational needs. Both cannot have their needs fully and completely satisfied. A compromise between two packages of needs is often workable for both.

3. Worker and organizational needs vary not only in number but in the degree of importance assigned to these needs. The degree of importance changes as the situation changes for both worker and organization.

4. Worker needs that are aligned or coincident to organizational needs are more apt to be pursued intensively because workers are reaching to satisfy their own needs and in the process they satisfy organizational needs.

5. The alignment between organizational needs and worker needs is at best an "accommodating fit" among all of the variables in a given situation at a given time.

How to Motivate According to Expectancy Alignment

Plan and obtain the closest possible alignment (needs coincidence) between employee expectancies and organizational objectives.

I describe in greater detail this approach for motivating workers to greater productivity in the next section.

MOTIVATING WITH EXPECTANCY ALIGNMENT

The basic problem in the motivation of employees is neither the lack of a framework for thinking about motivation or the lack of insight for understanding people and their needs. Many good motivational concepts and principles useful for understanding human behavior.[14] The big problem is being able to translate these principles and concepts in a practical manner consistent and useful to the organization for improving productivity. The complexity of motivational problems suggests that managers should acquire a strategy that works well and use it as he or she proceeds to execute the responsibility of delivering results for the organization. This section describes the strategy of expectancy alignment which is an effective managerial approach for motivating toward productivity. But first some preliminary ideas must be described.

Needs Coincidence: A Theory for Generating Motivators

Employees work primarily for themselves and only secondarily for their employer. They work to meet their needs and personal goals. These needs and goals are termed *expectancies*. Worker expectancies do not usually fall within the framework of company expectancies. They may or may not coincide with the set of expectancies the organization has for an employee. A disparity exists between these two expectancies (see Figure 9.5). There is a managerial need to align these two packages of expectancies and to reduce the angle of disparity.

At the time of employment the disparity is diffused because employee and employer both role-play—that is, they behave in roles for trying to gain an advantage for negotiating trading and compromising toward a commitment for employment. During employment the disparity becomes clearer because role playing ceases. Each party pursues a path of action that primarily attempts to meet their own package of expectancies, even at the sacrifice of the other party. Employees struggle to reach their expectancies. Employers, likewise, struggle to reach their packages of

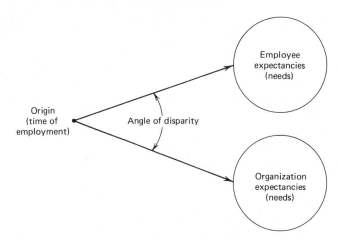

Figure 9.5 Disparity between employee and organizational expectancies.

expectancies. The result of this struggle is a compromise between the two for the situation. This compromise represents the best "coincidence of needs" of a wide array of complex needs by both employee and employer. It is the line of "fit" or "agreement" between two sets of expectancies. This line of needs coincidence between two parties forms the basis of managing motivation. Needs coincidence between employee and employer is the basis of driving both parties to reach their packages of expectancies so that both gain. This concept is illustrated in Figure 9.6.

One can see from this concept that the greater the coincidence of needs of both parties, the greater the intensity of drive toward mutually established results. The less the coincidence of needs, the less the intensity of drive toward results. This was described earlier in Chapter 3 as the *principle of expectancy alignment*. The greater the alignment of employee expectancies with organizational objectives, the greater the motivation to accomplish both. The less the alignment, the more difficult the motivation. Therefore, motivational intensity (MI) in an organizational setting is a function of needs coincidence (NC).

$$MI = f(NC)$$

Perfect alignment between organizational expectancies and employee expectancies is virtually unattainable. If it should be attained at any point, it will last only briefly. The changing nature of both parties makes coincidence of the vectors for a long period of time a highly improbable event. Managers should strive to move both vectors or states of expectancies to a closer alignment in (case I of Figure 9.7). How the manager does

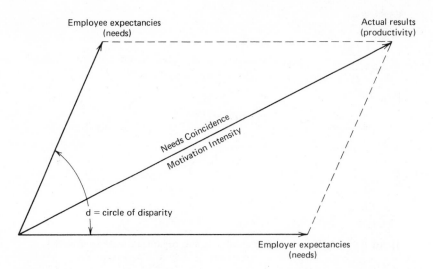

Figure 9.6   Needs coincidence between employer and employee expectancies.

this is with *motivators,* which are described in the next sections. The three cases described in Figure 9.7 indicate different position of the vectors which will yield different motivational intensities. Employers who hire workers whose goals and expectancies can never be met within the confines of the organization are most unfortunate indeed. This type of employee has the most difficult motivational problem to solve. It would be better to leave these employees at the door—on the outside. The manager should strive to move both vectors or states of expectancies to as close an alignment as possible (case I). Motivational intensity becomes stronger as disparity becomes smaller. The employee is accomplishing his own personal goals while at the same time meeting the employers' objectives. Conversely, motivational intensity becomes weaker as disparity increases (case III). The employee is attempting to meet his own expectancies but is in disalignment with his employer. When objectives of both employer and employee are brought into alignment in substance and time phase, greater contributions to the organization are made. Motivational intensity is high when the needs of both the employee and the employer are coincident. Therefore managing motivation toward productivity is managing needs coincidence between workers and the organization.

Motivators: Job Conditions That Produce Needs Coincidence

Motivators are job conditions that satisfy the needs of both employees and the organization. From a management standpoint, a motivator cannot

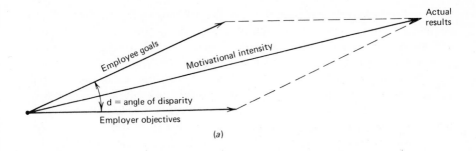

(a)

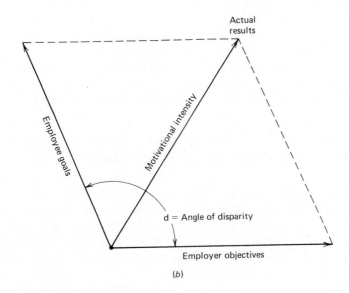

(b)

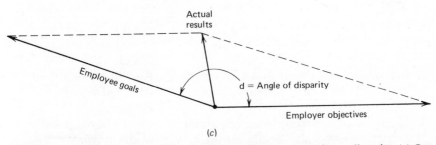

(c)

Figure 9.7 Motivational intensity caused by employer and employee disparity. (*a*) **Case I: close alignment, high results, strong motivation.** (*b*) **Case II: wide alignment, moderate results, moderate motivation.** (*c*) **Case III: very wide alignment, poor results, weak motivation.**

exist if the employee gains at the sacrifice of the employer. Similarly, a motivator cannot exist if the employer gains at the sacrifice of the employee. When job conditions are developed and arranged to allow satisfaction for both parties, a motivator prevails. In other words, when job conditions are arranged to meet the needs of both parties, a motivational intensity will emerge to drive both parties toward objectives.

Job conditions refer to how the work situation is developed, arranged, executed, measured, and controlled. It is structuring and restructuring both process and procedure with tasks and duties—for example, the organizational need to complete a task within a given period of time. If you combine this with employee's need to control time commitments that affect them on the job, a motivator emerges. When a process is developed so that both participate in agreeing on a commitment for time, a motivator is developed. In this case the motivator is participation.

As a motivator, participation implies a process in which both parties can gain. It implies a process in which there is needs coincidence. It implies a process in which two sets of expectancies are brought into alignment.

Motivators are processes for arranging job conditions to enhance needs coincidence and satisfaction for a worker and his organization.

Several nonfinancial motivators that have the capability of setting up this process of needs coincidence have been developed over the years. The following is such a list. It is presented to show how the needs of both parties are met. The list is not intended to be definitive. Additional motivators can be developed if needs coincidence can be identified. Financial motivators can also be developed.

Motivator	Organizational Need	Employee Need
1. Challenge	Need to get greater and improved results	Need to be unique and to do things others cannot
2. Independence	Need to delegate work and responsibilities	Need for freedom to form individual judgment
3. Recognition	Need to do important and significant work	Need to project self-worth to peers and family

Motivator	Organizational Need	Employee Need
4. Participation	Need to get commitments to complete work before work commences	Need to know what is going on and why and an opportunity to exert our influence
5. Achievement	Need to see that extended resources are being used in meaningful milestones of progress toward larger accomplishments	Need to see that efforts and energy lead to progressive steps of advancement toward a long-range goal
6. Innovations	Need new ideas, suggestions, and proposals to improve processes	Need to have ideas, suggestions, and' proposals accepted and used
7. Enlargement	Need to get the maximum use of time as a resource	Need to avoid boredom and fatigue
8. Enrichment	Need to perpetuate organization with management succession	Need to feel job assignments are stepping stones toward advancement in the organization
9. Overview	Need to have individuals optimize to the organization and not to individuals	Need to see where individual contributions fit in the overall operations
10. Learning	Need to have personnel who can handle new and different type of job assignments	Need work that fascinates and generates intense interest

GUIDELINES FOR USING MOTIVATORS

1. *Motivators are individualistic.*   They may work well for one individual but are not so effective for another. If they are effective in mass applications, it's probably due to common conditions affecting many people in a similar way. Each individual may be like other individuals in some ways. But human difference is the rule, not the exception.

2. *Motivators diminish in value over time.* Motivators are set up on the basis of conditions prevailing at a given time. When conditions change, the value of motivators change. For example, note in Figure 9.8 how motivators change through employment tenure.

3. *Motivators in mulitple sequence may be required.* It's naive to think only single motivators are required. More often multiple motivators over a period of time may be required because workers want to satisfy a range of needs rather than only one or two.

4. *Motivators have variable effectiveness with different organizational levels.* Motivators of intense value to top managers are of low value to foremen and vice versa. Each level in the organization will have its effective motivators.

5. *Motivators must be planned for individuals as the level decreases.* Top managers are in the position to plan their own motivators (self-motivation). Lower levels of management are least able to do this (see Figure 9.9). Job designs or organizational changes with appropriate conditions must be instituted or motivation will not take place in the lower levels of the organization.

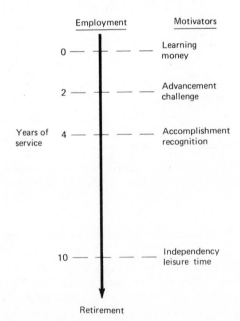

Figure 9.8 Motivators change with years of service.

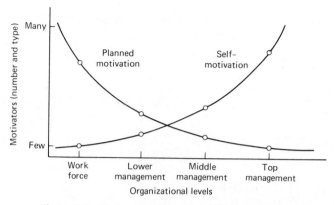

Figure 9.9   Motivators change in effectiveness by levels.

6. *Motivators are highly effective when they project a person's worth.*   Since we live in an affluent society where biological and safety needs are generally provided for, an individual looks to personal worth and fulfillment needs.

7. *Motivators may be identified through careful assessment of individual and organizational needs.*   The need of the individual at a given time is the clue for the development of a motivator. Since needs are driven or pulled by wants, the number of possible motivators are great. When the needs of both organization and individuals are coincident, a motivator is identified.

8. *Motivators can become demotivators.*   Too much or too little of a motivator will turn it into a demotivator. For example, too much or too little challenge causes problems.

9. *Motivators are largely effective in the work processes itself.*   The nature of organizational life prevents us from looking beyond the job where there is little or no control. The manager must be content with managing motivation within the boundaries of the work.

10. *Motivators should be tested.*   Motivators change with changing needs and wants. Managers must use the experimental approach to check the validity of assumed motivators.

11. *Motivators are highly influenced by the style of the boss.*   Motivators will operate effectively only if they fit the style of the leader. There must be harmony or compatibility between the leadership style of the boss and the type of motivators in a work situation. How different

motivators are effective for different leadership styles is illustrated as follows:

Leadership Styles	Effective Motivator
1. Autocratic "I" style	*(a)* Provide challenges
	(b) Schedule training and development
	(c) Set-up "pride" system for work
2. Integrative "we" style	*(a)* Allow participation
	(b) Enlarge job for variety
	(c) Give an overview of the work
3. Permissive "you" style	*(a)* Recognition of contribution
	(b) Job for promotion
	(c) Delegate for independency

12. *Motivators vary in effectiveness with different types of worker.* Different groups of workers have different sets of needs. This suggests that different motivators will be highly effective for one group but not so effective with another. This is illustrated as follows:

Type of Worker	Effective Motivator
1. Older worker	Sense of independence
2. Contented employee	Challenging job assignments
3. Minority employee	Learning and training
4. Young affluent employee	Job enrichment
5. First-line supervisor	Recognition
6. Middle manager	Participation in policy making
7. Top executive	Opportunity for large scale accomplishment

How to Motivate with Expectancy Alignment

The challenge for managing motivation for greater productivity is not in understanding why people work or in developing models of human behavior or in conceptualizing a list of motivators for satisfying both organization and employees. The challenge lies in implementing motivators in a practical way that results in greater productivity. Four steps are described.

1. *Establish the productivity objectives you wish to achieve.* Motivation does not begin with people. It does not begin with the job. It starts with purpose, expectations, and objectives the organization is trying to

reach. Defining expectations is the first step in bringing about the conditions for its fulfillment. Previous chapters described in detail how to find and write good statements of objectives. These objectives define the targets and set the entire motivational process that follows.

2. *Identify organizational needs from productivity objectives.* This is an analysis of the statement of objective into the human requirements that would be needed for its completion. There may also be nonhuman requirements such as technical, financial, procedural. The manager will find this step difficult without an understanding of organizations and why they are formulated.

3. *Acquire insights into employee needs.* These needs represent employee expectations. They are the "whys" of employee behavior. They are the purpose factors for employees seeking and obtaining employment in the organizations. They are motives for which a person's "will to work" is established.

4. *Decide on the motivator to be used.* The list of motivators suggested in the previous section is not intended to be definitive. It is suggestive only. There is no magic laundry list of motivators. Nor can one expect a motivator to have mass applications. Once a manager acquires insight into what motivators are and how they are used, he or she should proceed to identify additional ones, such as early time off, flexitime, discretionary decision making, pride system, and personal interest.

5. *Establish an alignment between organizational needs and employee expectancy with motivators.* The manager aligns the needs of subordinates with the productivity goals with the use of motivators so that both needs are accomplished within an expected period of time. When subordinates see that their work performance for the organization also meets their personal needs, drive becomes intense.

The entire process of motivating with expectancy alignment is illustrated in Figure 9.10.

Here are some examples of how the process works. Each example is described from an actual practice in an organization.

COMPUTER FIELD ENGINEERING COMPANY

1. *Productivity Objective.* Complete five preventive maintenance procedures per month within the region.

2. *Organizational Need.* Engineering company needs to keep equipment from failing since its shutdown has a serious disruptive effect on the total operation of the customer's organization.

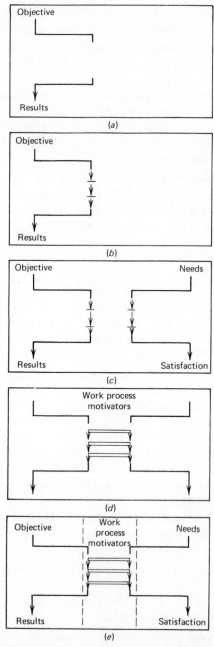

Figure 9.10 How to motivate with expectancy alignment. (*a*) Establish productivity objective of the organization. (*b*) Identify organizational need. (*c*) Acquire insights into employee needs. (*d*) Decide on motivators. (*e*) Align two sets of expectancies.

3. *Employee Need.*   Employee needs to feel his work is important and fulfilling.
4. *Motivators.*   Participation and overview.
5. *Alignment.*   Give employee preventive maintenance responsibility while allowing him to study and participate in the customers' overall operations and how the computer "fits in."

TOWN GOVERNMENT

1. *Productivity Objective.*   Complete management information systems for 10 departments by January 1979.
2. *Organization Need.*   Town government needs to give accurate accountability to town council on the expenditure of city-allocated funds.
3. *Employee Need.*   Employee needs accurate and equitable information base to establish the basis of performance appraisals and his rewards.
4. *Motivators.*   Participation and sense of accomplishment.
5. *Alignment.*   Allow employee to participate in the development of a management information system that measures the allocation and expenditure of resources by program achievements and individuals.

COSMETIC MANUFACTURING COMPANY

1. *Productivity Objective.*   Reduce cost of turnover 30 percent within 12 months.
2. *Organization Need.*   Cosmetic company needs workers to operate a process that requires specialized job stations even though the work is boring and routine.
3. *Employee Need.*   Employees need interesting work with variety and challenge.
4. *Motivators.*   Job enlargement, learning, and overview.
5. *Alignment.*   Redesign work process to enlarge individual responsibilities and train workers to rotate to different positions at different intervals. Let workers see the end product of their jobs.

INSURANCE COMPANY

1. *Productivity Objective.*   Reduce time lag in total work process 50 percent within next budgetary year.
2. *Organization Need.*   Insurance company needs to process new subscribers, claims, and accounts receivables faster since cash flow is hurting organization. Time requirements must be increased.

3. *Employee Need.* Employees want more independence and freedom from work since work routine is boring.

4. *Motivators.* Flexitime.

5. *Alignment.* Set up standards of time productivity for each station and allow employees to set their own hours on a sliding scale as long as standards are met and work is completed.

HEALTH-CARE CENTER

1. *Productivity Objective.* Complete 15 treatment plans with no more than two regressions by start of next budgetary year.

2. *Organization Need.* Health-care center needs to implement therapeutic programs for effective care of resident patients.

3. *Employee Need.* Employee needs opportunity to exercise and contribute professional competence in the care of resident patients.

4. *Motivators.* Achievement and recognition.

5. *Alignment.* Treatment plans under schedule are developed and administrative support is given to professional staff for their implementation.

DOES MONEY MOTIVATE?

There are probably many viewpoints on money as a motivator. Two are examined here—behavioral and management.

The Behavioral Viewpoint

Behaviorists are interested in the motives of people since motives are the basis of motivation. They are interested in how these motives develop through wants and needs and how these wants and needs drive people and cause behavior. According to behaviorists, these wants and needs are what really cause changes in behavior since they are internal—they cannot be directed or manipulated from the outside. What a person really wants to do is satisfy internal needs. Money, therefore, to the behaviorist symbolizes a purchasing power for meeting present needs and future needs that are yet to emerge. Money is worthless in itself, but it derives its unique power as a "symbolic motivator" for whatever the individual can acquire that he considers to be most important in life. The individual can "keep score" with money. The more one has, the more present and future needs can be bought. The less one has, the fewer present and future needs can be bought. Efforts to accumulate money reflect a person's attitude about present and future levels of needs. Money as a motive actually becomes an instrument of purchasing power. The compulsive accumulation of money is probably due to the fact that money has become the universal common denominator for meeting the needs of people everywhere. An assessment of the amount of money accumulated tells an individual how much progress has been made in this direction. If the assessment is low, new drives emerge. *Therefore, to the behaviorist money does not motivate, but satisfying individual needs does. Money is the "score" of how well an individual will meet these needs.*

The Management Viewpoint

The manager's view is somewhat different, although not contradictory. The manager must deal with the realities of the situation. People are only one component. The organization is the other. The manager must act and react in such a way that both needs are taken care of, if not simultaneously, then in a complementary way. Managers are very much aware of the fact that people come to work to meet their personal needs. But these needs continually change, are very complex and often beyond his control. He does not have the time to function as a behaviorist. He is concerned with behavior on the first level—how to get a person to do a job that also meets the needs of the organization. Money and the way it is dispersed has a high influence on behavior. A lower salary relative to others tends to demotivate; a higher salary relative to others will motivate. Employees see salary reviews as an important feedback regarding appraisal of their performance. He cannot however raise or lower salaries whenever he wants to! At best, he tries to find the compromise between organization and the individual. The manager makes every attempt to find where "needs coincidence" can occur. It is difficult to find in nonfinancial areas, but in the financial areas it becomes easy because money is both the universal common denominator of meeting the needs of people and a common area to form "needs coincidence" between people and the organization . The more money an organization has or can make, the more of its needs it can meet and the more of its employee's needs it can meet. *Therefore, to the manager, money does motivate because it is the means by which a host of present and future needs can be made coincident between organizations and employees.* Money is a source of pride, security, and satisfaction for both organizations and individuals. The profit a company desperately wants is a way of meeting present and future needs. The chief problem a manager has with money as a motivator is that in many situations *it's the most expensive of all motivators!* To reduce costs in motivating employees is one reason why nonfinancial motivators are sought by managers. Here is a list of financial motivators that are practiced by managers in many organizations. They motivate—and motivate well. The biggest problem of these motivators is that they are expensive.

1. Give large increments of money.
2. Set up profit sharing programs.
3. Give opportunity for ownership.
4. Provide better than average fringe benefits.
5. Give a chance for early retirement.
6. Give tuition rebate for educational courses.
7. Give extra holidays, vacations, and time off.
8. Set up flexitime (leisure or independent time).
9. Provide medical-expense reimbursement.
10. Set up use of company-owned equipment, such as cars.

In short, managers view nonfinancial motivators as adjunct with financial motivators. Intangible rewards are as important as tangible rewards. Both will cause behavior.

IS THE WORK ETHIC DEAD?

Work ethic is the value that people place on work in their lives. To answer the question, "Is the work ethic dead?" is to answer the question, "Is the value of work dead?" The answer is no! But certainly the work ethic and the meaning it has for people has been changing because work values have been changing. The power previously held by organizations over workers existed because it exploited how employees valued work in their lives. Since the meaning and value of work for individuals has been changing, the power to exploit workers is changing. This is measurably and dramatically seen with increasing clashes between authority and self-expression, between how supervisors want to supervise and how employees want to be supervised, between what organizations will give and what unions will take. Several forces in society are feeding trends toward changing the value and meaning of work. Let me cite them briefly. They have been covered in more detail previously.

1. *Increasing Educational Level.* The rising level of educational background of employees brings with it both higher skills to offer employers and a higher level of awareness and expectations.

2. *Travel and Mobility.*   Employees travel more than any of their predecessors in history. This traveling leverage offers employees more alternatives and options in different labor markets and organizations than at any time in history. These broader options allow them to select alternatives for the meaning of work in their lives.

3. *Growing Affluence.*   In spite of recessions and inflation, economic affluence continues to grow, greatly reducing the emphasis on the necessities of life. More often than not, pay and security are taken for granted. This allows employees to seek gratification on higher levels of needs. An identifiable self-concept, self-fulfillment, and self-esteem are sought by affluent workers.

4. *Erosion of Traditional Authority.*   Values from schools, the family, churches, and self-responsibilities and self-conceived forms of fulfillment conflict drastically with the traditional boss–subordinate structure in organization. Employees are looking for individual fulfillment in the context of the meaning of work.

5. *Social Commitment.*   The growing appreciation of the role and effects of an organization in a community stresses the need for interdependence and connection with community needs and concerns. Employees are concerned with how their work output affects the community and how work contribution gives them identity, self-concept, and self-esteem.

These forces are shaping a new meaning of work for people everywhere. It has evolved over many years. This history of man's view of what work means has shaped the new work ethic. A view of this history can be briefly outlined as follows:[15]

THE EGYPTIANS.   *Work was a way of accomplishing great projects and programs.*   Since many people were the only way to achieve these programs, people were indentured into slavery. There was no way to build, construct, and develop without huge masses to labor. Slavery, the whip, and taskmasters were the way to complete great works. Work was important to complete the many projects needed.

THE HEBREWS.   *Work was a way to get ahead.*   Work was to be pursued intensely to gather the harvest for lean times. "He that tilleth his land shall have plenty of bread" (Prov. 28:19). Hard work was demanded (Ecc. 9:10) for in all labor there is profit (Prov. 14:4), but rest was commanded—one day in seven (Ex. 23:12). To the Hebrews, work was necessary not only to meet daily and future needs and thereby avoid poverty and starvation, but the way to increase (Prov. 10:4).

THE GREEKS. *Work was to be avoided.* The Greeks relied on slaves to do their work because work was demeaning. The Greek word *ponos* for work means "suffering" and was to be avoided. The Greeks sought leisure and contemplation. Work was a necessary evil to be delegated to slaves. As long as slaves did the work, the Greeks conducted dialogs and pursued intellectual activities.

THE ROMANS. *Work was needed to build the empire.* Leisure was no longer the ultimate goal of life. Leisure was only a relief from work. Everyone had to work to build and maintain the good of the empire which provided the good for all.

THE CHRISTIANS. *Work was to be done and done well.* Work was the means to earn leisure time to meditate on God. Individuals must do their own work to provide for their own necessities and families. Economic pursuit and gain was a means of helping families and others. "If anyone will not work, let him not eat" (II Thess. 3:10, I Tim. 5:8).

THE CATHOLICS. *Work was a means of glorifying God.* To work was to fill the mission of life. To work was to pray. The ultimate goal of work was an opportunity for contemplation with God.

THE PROTESTANTS. *Work was a moral activity that fulfilled a predestined grace.* Hard-earned material success was a sign of heavenly approval of a good and moral life. Idleness was a serious misdemeanor. The ultimate goal of life was to make full use of God's gifts during one's lifetime. Hence a person guilty of idleness or leisure pursuits, poverty or wastefulness was thought to be committing acts against God. Work was a way of pleasing God.

THE AMERICANS. *Work is a means of fulfilling personal needs.* Work provides a self-sufficiency and supports society in its many functions and pursuits. It gives man the means to pursue other activities. Work gives man employment, keeps the economy moving, and provides the process for human power to be used to meet organizational objectives. Full employment is necessary for individuals and for making society work.

The work ethic is alive and well, though it has changed considerably. It is being changed and reshaped by the new desires and demands of workers. People still live to work, but many are now acquiring the new attitude of working to live. Here is my analysis of how the new work ethic is emerging:

THE NEW WORK ETHIC

Work means shaping an identity and individuality.
Work means doing something important and meaningful.
Work means reaching for self-fulfillment.
Work means giving to those who are less fortunate.
Work means creating leisure time and play.
Work means developing and subduing the environment for high quality of human living.

SUMMARY

The search for motivating employees toward greater productivity is intense because the problems of motivation are here and now.

This chapter described how motivating employees is different and difficult these days. Six factors were cited and examined briefly.

1. Workers' view of authority is changing.
2. Worker expectations are increasing due to rising educational levels.
3. Worker rights are changing due to legislative intrusions.
4. Worker unions are growing in effectiveness and strength.
5. Workers' goals and employer objectives are conflicting.
6. Worker affluence is shifting priorities and attitudes.

Three general approaches to motivating workers toward greater productivity were described. The incentive approach is based on the view that workers are eager to maximize their monetary status, power, and prestige. This is the "dangling the carrot" approach. Three contributors to this approach are:

1. *Adam Smith.* Motivate by giving workers financial incentives strong enough to experience monetary gain.
2. *Frederick Taylor.* Motivate by giving workers a job situation in which work is broken up into standards assigned pay and a procedure is developed to reach the standard.
3. *Hugo Munsterberg.* Motivate by giving workers a job structure in steps, assign money rates, and provide a merit evaluation when these jobs have been well achieved.

The behavioral approach is based on the view that workers work to meet their needs. They come to the organization to see how many of these needs can be met. Five contributors to this approach are:

1. *Abraham Maslow.* Motivate by giving workers opportunities in a work situation in which they can fulfill their needs.
2. *Douglas McGregor.* Motivate by giving managers a view and set of attitudes about their environment for best achieving goals of people and the organization.
3. *Frederick Herzberg.* Motivate by giving workers motivators within the job content that will lead to satisfaction.
4. *David McClelland.* Motivate by giving workers entrepreneurial development opportunities to experience high levels of achievement.
5. *Victor Vroom.* Motivate by giving workers opportunities in which rewards are great and the probability of achieving them is high.

The managerial approach is based on the view that there is no one best way to motivate. Different organizations with different tasks and different competitive environments with different worker needs require different approaches. Managerial approaches are, therefore, eclectic approaches. Three techniques in this general approach are:

1. *Contingency Approach.* Motivate by analyzing the situation and selecting elements from a vast array of possibilities and form a model that will work for a given situation.
2. *Systems Approach.* Motivate by developing a systems model for an organization in which the current motivational process is identified and proceed to find the change agents for its improvements.
3. *Expectancy Alignment Approach.* Motivate by planning and obtaining

the closest alignment (needs coincidence) possible between employee expectancies and organizational objectives.

Motivating with expectancy alignment is the approach I recommend. It is based on the theory of expectancy alignment—the greater the alignment of employee expectancies with organizational objectives, the greater the motivation to accomplish both. The less the alignment, the more difficult the motivation. Motivated intensity is therefore how well a manager can align or bring needs coincidence between these two parties.

$$MI = f(NC)$$

Motivators are job conditions that satisfy the needs of both employees and the organization. Where job conditions can be arranged to meet the needs of both parties, a motivator emerges. Several motivators with a wide appeal have been suggested: challenge, independence, recognition, participation, achievement, innovations, enlargement, enrichment, overview, and learning. Several guidelines were described in using these motivators, but five steps represent a process for motivating employees with expectancy alignment.

1. Establish the productivity objectives to be achieved.
2. Identify organizational needs from objectives.
3. Acquire insights into employee needs.
4. Decide on motivator to be used.
5. Establish an alignment between organizational needs and employee expectancy with motivator.

Finally, two important questions covered with motivation were answered: "Does money motivate?" and "Is the work ethic dead?" Various viewpoints were presented to both questions. I favor the management viewpoint of both questions. Money does motivate because it is the universal common denominator for meeting the present and future needs of people and organizations everywhere. It is the quickest way of getting needs coincidence, but it is the most expensive way. The work ethic is not dead, although it has changed considerably and continues to change. Various views of the meaning of work through history were presented. I presented my perception of the new work ethic.

Work means shaping an identity and individuality.
Work means doing something important and meaningful.
Work means reaching for self-fulfillment.

Work means giving to those who are less fortunate.

Work means creating leisure time and play.

Work means developing an environment for high quality of living.

QUESTIONS TO THINK ABOUT

1. Has the motivation challenge in your organization changed within recent years? In what way?
2. Identify the management prerogatives that have been shifting more toward employers' decisions or participative employee decisions.
3. What are the attitudes that are characteristic of your affluent employees?
4. What is your process for motivating employees? Has it worked well? What changes could make it more effective?
5. Would the theory of expectancy alignment described in this chapter work for you in developing motivators that are unique to your situation and organization?
6. Define motivators and conceptualize three new ones that would fit your work situation.
7. List and describe guidelines in the use of motivators.
8. Contrast your own perception of the new work ethic with that of the author.

REFERENCES AND NOTES

1. Report of Special Task Force, *Work In America*, MIT Press, Cambridge, 1971, p. 44.
2. Prentice-Hall Research Staff, *Productivity: The Personnel Challenge*, Englewood Cliffs, N.J., 1973, pp. 28–29.
3. *Guide to Consumer Markets*, National Industrial Conference Board, New York, 1973, p. 251.
4. Hodgetts, Richard M., *Management: Theory, Process and Practice*, W. B. Saunders & Company, Philadelphia, 1975, pp. 28–33.
5. Taylor, Frederick W., *Scientific Management*, Harper and Brothers Publishers, New York, 1911, p. 71.
6. Munsterberg, Hugo, *Psychology and Industrial Efficiency*, Houghton Mifflin Co., Boston, 1913.
7. Maslow, Abraham, "A Theory of Human Motivation" *Psychological Review*, July 1943, pp. 388–389.
8. McGregor, Douglas, *The Human Side of Enterprise*, McGraw-Hill Book Company, New York, 1960, pp. 33–38.

9. Herzberg, F., Mausner, B., and Snyderman, D. B., *The Motivation To Work,* John Wiley and Sons, New York, 1959.

10. McClelland, D. C., *The Achieving Society,* Van Nostrand, Princeton, N.J., 1961.

11. Vroom, Victor H., *Work and Motivation,* John Wiley & Sons, New York, 1964.

12. No one individual can be cited as a sole proponent to this approach. Many have made contributions. The reader is urged to read the following for more insight into the management approaches: D. Meister and G. Rabidean, *Human Factors Evaluation in System Development,* John Wiley & Sons, New York, 1965; Howard Carlisle, *Situational Management,* American Management Association, New York, 1973. Gary Dessler, *Organization and Management,* Prentice-Hall, Englewood Cliffs, N.J., 1976.

13. Mali, P., *Managing By Objectives.* John Wiley & Sons, New York, 1972, pp. 55–60.

14. Many perceptions of the motivational processes are available in the literature. The reader interested in pursuing these ideas will find the following useful: S. W. Gullerman, *Management by Motivation,* American Management Association, New York, 1968; F. Herzberg, B. Mausner, and B. B. Snyderman, *The Motivation To Work,* John Wiley & Sons, New York, 1965; D. McGregor, *Human Side of Enterprise,* McGraw-Hill Book Company, New York, 1960; V. H. Vroom, *Work and Motivation,* John Wiley & Sons, New York, 1964.

15. Morrison, Donald M., "Is the Work Ethic Going Out of Style?" *Time,* October 30, 1972, p. 96.

PART FOUR

TOOLS AND TECHNIQUES FOR ACHIEVING GREATER PRODUCTIVITY

The time-tested principles of organization, specialization, supervision, communications, and work procedures are still largely valid. The missing ingredient has been the will and know-how of managers to implement them in a coordinated way. Implementation has and always will be the mark of the professional manager. Part IV presents, in two chapters, tools and techniques of analysis and implementation for bringing about productivity improvement in an organization. Management is becoming less a matter of issuing directives and more a skill of communicating the processes for getting things done.

10

MANAGING COMPLEXITIES TO DRIVE PRODUCTIVITY UP

IN THIS CHAPTER

Three causes of organizational complexities.
Work focus productivity generator.
Work flow productivity increaser.
Resource-accountability clarifier.
Time-scheduling productivity multiplier.
Productivity tracker.
Cost-productivity allocator.
Productivity-effectiveness planner.

Costs soar as organizations become more complex! These costs result from diffused and inefficient work procedures; growing management levels; loosely related functions; empire building that enhances individuals, not the organization; government legislative intrusions that add red tape, paperwork, and more indirect workers; uncoordinated mergers and acquisitions; expanding product information and equipment technology of the firm; and a growing union effectiveness. While organizations are becoming ever more complex, they are becoming less manageable, which in turn affects productivity. The name of the "productivity game" is managing complexity. Organizations become more complicated which leads to further complexity, which is unwanted.

This drift toward unwanted complexity is seen in businesses, corporations, private firms, government agencies (federal, state, and local), hospitals, schools, universities, professional associations, trade associations, labor unions, and many community groups. Organizational complexity means performance complexity, decision-making complexity, time-delivery complexity, work-organization complexity, planning-evaluating complexity, resource-utilization complexity and unpredictable-change complexity.

This chapter describes the effects of complexity on productivity in an organization. Three causes of complexity are cited and briefly described, and seven techniques are introduced as managerial practices for handling complexity in an organization.

1. Work-focus productivity generator.
2. Work-flow productivity increaser.
3. Resource-accountability clarifier.
4. Time-scheduling productivity multiplier.
5. Productivity tracker.
6. Cost-productivity allocator.
7. Productivity-effectiveness planner.

COMPLEXITY IS HERE TO STAY!

The future of complexity for organizations is assured. There are many reasons for this. Only three are discussed here.

Government Intrusions into Organizations Are Causing Legislative "red tape."   The expanding role of government in nearly all functions of an organization is perhaps one of the most significant forces causing the growth of complexity in the organization. The impact of laws on business has had a significant influence on the development of new and innovative methods to improve effectiveness and efficiency in organizations. Government has always been active in regulations, but government is now moving into new regulatory areas. A series of excellent articles has appeared in the Associated Press by Brooks Jackson and Evans Witt describing the growth of these regulatory agencies.[1] These newsmen note that the number of major regulatory agencies in 1965 was 58 and has now risen to 455, employing 105,000 persons. The survey conducted by the Associated Press reveals that more than 9800 forms are generated by the government and sent out to the public. An estimated 586 million responses are sent back every year requiring hundreds of millions of hours to gather data and complete the forms. The cost of this process to the American taxpayer has more than doubled since 1965. No end is in sight. Obviously, there is controversy about the value to be gained by these regulatory intrusions. In many cases there have been advantages such as saving lives and improving the quality of life, but in some cases there are disadvantages of "petty tyranny" and "inciting" potential causes of organizational failure. *In either event, the legislative intrusions introduce new regulators which require a great deal of paperwork, tons of "red tape," and additional indirect staff to assure compliance and process to the regulations.* The government

itself has discovered that these regulations demand surveillance and
controls that in many cases generate a complex bureaucracy of red tape
within government to support the complexity they have generated in
organizations. The following legislative enactments are samples of increasing government influence and actions that bear down on private and
public organizations. My purpose here is not to discuss the "pros" and
"cons" of these acts; it is to point out that the acts add to the complexities
of organizational life.

1. *Civil Rights Act of 1964* prohibits discrimination in employment on the
   basis of race, religion, sex, nationality, and age. Heavy fines are enacted
   for violations. The act is enforceable through several executive orders.
2. *Noise Control Act of 1972* regards noise as a pollutant that is hazardous
   to the health and safety of the individual. Protective measures and new
   work procedures are mandatory to keep the noise level within limits.
3. *Occupational Safety and Health Act of 1970* allows the government the
   right to inspect virtually every organization in the country for possible
   violations of the new OSHA standards and to impose heavy fines
   whenever violations are not corrected within a stated period of time.
4. *Wheeler-Lea Act of 1938* gives the Federal Trade Commission power to
   prohibit unfair or deceptive practices in advertising and broadcasting.
   The FTC has established rigorous rules and principles for organizations to follow.
5. *Foreign Trade and Investment Act of 1972* places a high tax burden on
   U.S. companies on their overseas operations and empowers a new
   federal agency to scrutinize foreign investment plans and to set quotas
   on imported goods.

A Library of Congress study found that during 1974 Congress passed
404 laws, while the federal bureaucracy churned out 7496 new or
amended regulations. That's 18 regulations for every law. That means the
cost of regulation has jumped from $4.43 to $10.36 per American. Its
effect on productivity is very obvious. Violations of legislative regulations
have stepped up the pace of litigation. There was a time when the legal
function in an organization was a relatively low-pressure effort. But today
the pace is overwhelming. In her article on the "legal explosion," Eleanor
Carruth terms it the "litigious new era of shell-shocking organizations."[2]
Apparently, anyone can sue an organization for just about anything. The
number of lawsuits for violations of legislative regulations filed in federal
district court is shown in Figure 10.1.
Organizational management is having trouble escaping legal matters.

Litigation Issues	1961	1964	1968	1970	1972
Environmental	N.A.	N.A.	42	140	268
Fair-employment practices	N.A.	N.A.	N.A.	N.A.	1015
Antitrust	421	480	707	929	1379
Securities regulations	267	419	689	1211	1919
Patents, copyrights, and trademarks	1585	1832	1829	2150	2194
Labor law	2484	3336	3518	3999	4987
Total	4757	6067	6785	8429	11762

Figure 10.1   Growth in lawsuits affecting organizations in the United States.

The new legal and regulatory constraints not only threaten the survival of organizations, but have introduced complexity to management that seriously affects productivity. These statements are not intended to mean that laws should be repealed or amended. They do mean that the purpose and the impact of such laws on organizational effectiveness and efficiency should be reviewed in the light of our current national, state, and local priorities and needs for productivity. If a law renders marginal benefits but inhibits tremendous productivity gains, a serious analysis should be made of its continuance or its modification. In any case, the impact legislative intrusions make on productivity should be readily perceived.

Union Effectiveness Now a Formidable Complexity.   Collective bargaining is working and working well! This is another cause of increased complexity. Pressures, group actions, and strikes have hit an all-time high. The Department of Labor reports the number of walkouts rose almost 18 percent from 1969 to 1970, and the number of workers participating in those strikes increased by more than 77 percent.[3] Furthermore, strikes in the public sector are also on the upswing. In 1965 there were 42 strikes by public employees. In 1968 the number of strikes by public employees rose to 254—a sixfold increase. But more alarming than these statistics is the loss in man-days. In 1965 the loss was 46,000 man-days. In 1968 it rose to 2,540,000—a figure 55 times greater. The impact of this loss in man-hour activity on productivity is well recognized. Unions continue to be hard at work organizing groups into collective bargaining units and calling walkouts where and when desired. Ever since the merger of the AFL and CIO in 1956, a big impetus has been generated for organizing all nonorganized groups. An all-time high of 21 million members of unions in the United States continue to grow.

The strike, which is the unions' ultimate "economic weapon" for gaining its ends, is an antiproductivity force. The loss in man-hours alone affects productivity radically. In 1971 strikes in this country involved 3.3 million workers and a total loss of 47.6 million man-days.[4] This is equivalent of one full year of employment by 183,000 people, or the startling loss in income of about $1.3 billions. As unions become more established, they also become more effective. The results of strikes are visible and measurable; the results of union effectiveness are not so visible and are difficult to measure. Nonetheless, they have an impact on complexity and productivity.

1. *Labor Costs Go Up!* Disputing, processing, grieving, and bickering merely wastes man-hours, which raises labor costs. Hostilities and harsh words eventually affect morale and costs.

2. *Operations Improvement Resisted.* New procedures to improve the operation are resisted. Redesigning jobs for greater efficiency is blocked because it may cause job reclassification. Reorganization of sections to improve work flow is halted. In most cases, these moves are regarded as a direct threat to individual security. In most cases it's job insecurity. A great deal of time in meetings is required to resolve these conflicts and gain agreements.

3. *Hiring and Promotion Policies Disrupted.* Contract agreements are moving more and more into policies for advancement, transfers, and promotion in addition to layoffs, recalls, and termination. "Due process" has become a sticky and complex procedure.

4. *"Industrial War" Breaks Out.* Few contract negotiations result in both sides winning or both sides losing. Most contracts result in either one side winning more or losing more. This sets up a recrimination ripple for the next round of negotiations. If this continues cycle after cycle, "industrial war" prevails.

5. *Management Prerogatives Erode!* Many rights have now been established. The rights of minorities, the poor, women, the elderly, the sick, and possibly others. Management must deal with these rights while preventing erosion of their own rights.

Organization Growth Means Size and Complexity. Organizations themselves have contributed substantially to the increasing complexity they face. They have pursued mergers, acquisitions, conglomerates, divisionalization, branching, and expansion which have resulted in superorganizations, corporation giants, or huge empires. Adding to the complexity is the fact that these giant organizations frequently institute changes with respect to products and services. "Empire building" significantly reduces productivity in four ways: overstaffing, increased number of levels, imbalance among the functions, and "title inflation." Managing for productivity under these conditions becomes a challenge! A comparison of selected factors of 500 of the largest corporations in the United States shows this growth in one decade (Figure 10.2). The growth by these organizations has meant a complexity of products, services, work processes, environment, situations, technology, skills, and even the organizational structure itself.

The traditional organization chart has evolved to reflect this growth. Historically and traditionally, the organization has been basically a line-staff or functional form. However, new forms have emerged such as matrix and ball organizations. These organizational forms are illustrated in Figure 10.3. Matrix organization, sometimes called systems management, involves two groups: project managers and functional managers. Under this scheme the unity of command concept is abandoned and replaced with a situation wherein an individual may report to several supervisors. Project managers are responsible for the completion of their projects, and they draw on the functional or specialized groups for resources and assistance to complete their responsibilities. Functional managers are responsible for managing their resources and draw on project managers to determine how best to use resources.

Ball organization goes still further and abandons completely the functional managers and operates on a project or program basis. Unity of

Factors	1961	1970	Percent Change
1. Gross sales (billions)	209.2	463.9	122
2. Assets (billions)	186.8	432.1	131
3. Net profit (billions)	11.6	21.7	87
4. Invested capital (billions)	121.1	227.0	87
5. Employees (millions)	9.3	14.6	57
6. Average number of employees	18,500	29,200	58
7. Average return on sales (%)	4.2	3.9	−7
8. Return on investment	8.3	6.5	−22
9. Companies with sales over $1 billion	41	120	193

Figure 10.2   Percent change of 500 largest corporations in the United States.[5]

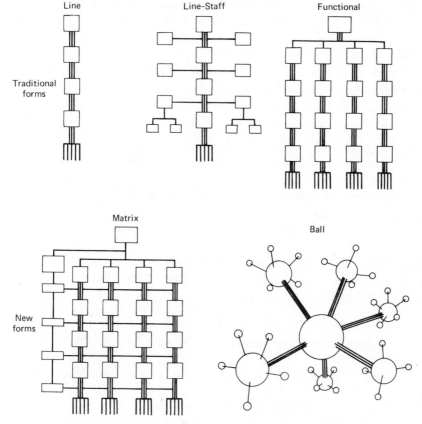

Figure 10.3   Development of organizational forms.

command is reestablished within the projects. The ball organization is a collection of major projects or programs operating from a small central-ized center. The key question asked about these evolving organizational forms is if they can handle the complex requirements emerging in the organization. While a structure may have worked well in the past, does it work well as the organizations grow? Jerald Hage found evidence that complex organizations usually have low centralization and formality (rules or guidelines established by the organization). The superorganizations acquire flexibility by having fewer rules and regulations. In *Future Executive* Harlan Cleveland points out that organizations that get things done will no longer be hierarchical pyramids with most of the real control at the top. They will be systems—interlaced webs of loose control, diffused power, and several decision centers.[7]

The changes in organization size, form, and structure reflect increases in complexity. This is seen in the type of problems related to

1. Coordinating human relationships.
2. Identifying the degree of independence that's needed.
3. Arranging of tasks and levels of authority.
4. Keeping open communication channels to the political, economic, and social aspects of the community.
5. Minimizing the gaps between planning and achieving.
6. Allowing the interchange and interaction of ideas between and among different parts of the organization.
7. Collecting sufficient information in time for control.
8. Minimizing conflicts.
9. Assuring that a management system exists for producing results.

Examining areas in which organizations are drifting toward complexities is itself a complex task. A safe conclusion is that complexity is here to stay and will no doubt increase!

MANAGING COMPLEXITY FOR GREATER PRODUCTIVITY

A slogan that has circulated in management circles for years is

Work smarter, not harder!

There's no question that the slogan offers good advice. But the fact still remains that despite the best, well-laid, innovative plans, hard work is required to get the job done. The greatest achievements that one can identify—putting a man on the moon, controlling a spiralling inflation, or eliminating cancer—will require both smart work and hard work. The slogan should be rephrased

Work smarter while working harder!

Hiring "brains" was formerly the one way for a manager or supervisor to get things done. With the challenge of complexity, we now see that intelligence is only a first quality. Other qualities are needed—energy, perseverance, ability, calm, collaboration, agreeableness, and others! Managers and supervisors must even enjoy, to some degree, complexity and constant change or they won't survive in this age of drift toward complexity. Still more, they must have skills or strategies for dealing with day-to-day complexities that affect productivity. They must be able to sense the emergence of problems, to "cut through" and identify the causes, and then be able to muster enough resources and energy to solve problems.

Seven productivity techniques to aid in managing complexity for greater productivity are suggested: (1) work-focus productivity generator, (2) work-flow productivity increaser, (3) resource-accountability clarifier, (4) time-scheduling productivity multiplier, (5) productivity tracker, (6) cost productivity allocator, and (7) productivity-effectiveness planner. They are described briefly and illustrated. The names assigned to them, despite their apparent jargon, are intended to convey the end results and the process of achieving the results as a managerial strategy.

Work-Focus Productivity Generator. Changes in organizations, in departments and in individual jobs are uncertain and, hence, unpredictable. A single change triggers several changes, creating a "domino effect" in the level and type of work demand that must be met. Supervisors and managers attempt to keep pace with by stretching wider and wider the scope of activities to cover both old and new demands. They must give time and attention to many more responsibilities over a wider area of requirements. They literally "spread themselves thin." Consequently, they end up doing many things but doing few of them well. Managers who give equal time, energy, and resources to each demand find that their productivity drops because dilution of effort has occurred. As organizations continue to grow in complexity, more dilution of effort appears to be the prospect for the future.

Some years ago an Italian economist, Vilfredo Pareto, observed this dilution of effort process and expounded his law. He said, "In any set or collection of objects, ideas, people and events, a few within this set or collection are more significant than the remaining majority. To achieve results you must concentrate on these vital few significant elements." The ratio of the vital few with the trivial many is 20 to 80 percent.[8] Several organizations have shown this law to be true. Twenty percent of a bank's customers account for 80 percent of the dollars invested; 20 percent of the hospital's patients have 80 percent of the medical need; 20 percent of the inventory accounts for 80 percent of the sales; 20 percent of the budget dominates 80 percent of the organization's results.

The *work-focus productivity generator* is a management technique based on Pareto's Law for achieving great gains in productivity. It finds the core of vital problems in a haystack of trivia. Managers who face too many demands are forced to sort, select, and concentrate on the critical few.

These tasks should receive the most skillful treatment because concentrating on them results in the greatest productivity for the organization. The technique is described as follows:

(a)   *List All the Demands and Responsibilities Faced by a Manager.*   These demands might be: position requirements, work and service requirements of customers, task commitments stated in plans or budget, and general responsibilities of managing a section or department within the organization.

(b)   *Arrange the List in Order of Importance.*   Develop a priority order for the demands that yield greatest results in productivity. Other criteria may be used, but the productivity criteria should be primary.

(c)   *Select the Top 20 Percent as the Critical Few.*   The 20:80 percent rule for focus has been verified. On the average, 80 percent of the results from a situation can be attributed to 20 percent of the possible causes.

(d)   *Write Demands as Productivity Targets.*   Assess the amount and level of results to be achieved and the resources to be used. Quantify the targets as stretches in productivity. Formalize the targets with others through involvement, participation, and commitment.

(e)   *Stretch productivity Targets 5 to 15 Percent.*   Build a 5 to 15 percent productivity stretch within each objective. Make each productivity stretch realistic and attainable.

The entire process of the work-focus productivity generator is illustrated in Figure 10.4.

PSYCHOTHERAPIST: A CASE EXAMPLE

(a)   *List the Demands.*
   (1)   Perform administrative duties.
   (2)   Participate in agency planning session on agency's psychological services.
   (3)   Conduct individual and group psychotherapy.
   (4)   Perform routine tests.
   (5)   Provide surveillance of child-care workers' activities.
   (6)   Assist in developing agency programs relative to child care.
   (7)   Evaluate test results and complete treatment plans for clients.
   (8)   Write progress reports on clients.
   (9)   Make referrals and keep contact with social agencies.
   (10) Recommend routine expenditures within budgetary limitations.

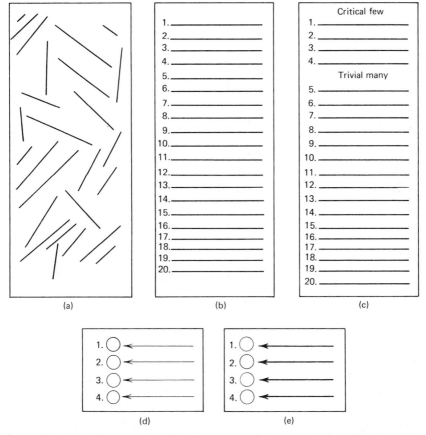

Figure 10.4 Work-focus productivity generator technique. (a) Make a list of random demands. (b) Rearrange list in priority. (c) Separate on the list the critical few from the trivial many. (d) Write critical few as objectives. (e) Stretch targets 5 to 15%.

(b)   Arrange List in Order of Importance.

(1)   Evaluate test results and complete treatment plans for clients.

(2)   Conduct individual and group psychotherapy. Write progress reports on clients.

(3)   Provide surveillance of child-care workers' activities.

(4)   Assist in developing agency programs relative to child care.

(5)   Perform routine tests.

(6)   Make referrals and keep contact with social agencies.

    (7)   Recommend routine expenditures within budgetary limitations.

    (8)   Participate in agency's planning session on psychological services.

    (9)   Perform administrative duties.

(c)   *Select the Critical Few (20%).*

    (1)   Evaluate test results and complete treatment plans for clients.

    (2)   Conduct individual and group psychotherapy.

(d)   *Write Demands as Productivity Targets.*

    (1)   Complete 10 treatment plans for an admission rate of five clients per month. (Productivity index = 10/5 = 2.)

    (2)   Complete eight therapeutic individual and group sessions per week. (Productivity index = 8/5 = 1.6.)

(e)   *Stretch Productivity Targets (5 to 15%).*

    (1)   Complete 12 treatment plans for an admission rate of five clients per month. (Productivity index = 12/5 = 2.4.)

    (2)   Complete 10 therapeutic individual and group sessions per week. (Productivity index = 10/5 = 2.0.)

Work-flow Productivity Increaser. Complexity can be seen in many aspects of organizational life. It causes "lagging reaction time," which drives costs up. Lagging reaction time refers to the situation in which a work-flow process is not effective in response to a particular decision. The work flow in the process slows down and in some cases is held up because there are too many problems to be solved or obstacles to circumvent. Examples of problems or obstacles that contribute to lagging reaction time are excessive handling, unnecessary activities, rework, duplication of effort, bottlenecks, red tape, delay procedures, too many people in the act, idle time, and plurality of decision makers. Complexity in organizations seems to increase the capacity to generate more of these kinds of problems. Complexity introduces some loss of control in reaction time which slows down the work flow and ultimately affects productivity.

    The work-flow productivity increaser is an organized view of a work process to force a series of questions that may lead to improvement. For example:

1. *Better Service.*   Can you deliver better and more effective results?

2. *Less Expensive.*   Can you deliver existing results at less cost?

3. *Faster.*   Can you deliver existing results at the same cost faster?

4. *Fewer Errors.* Can you deliver existing results at the same cost with fewer errors?

5. *Less Paper and Fewer Records.* Can you deliver existing results with less paper and fewer records?

6. *Fewer Processing Operating Points.* Can you deliver existing results with fewer processing operating points?

7. *Use Less Space.* Can you deliver existing results in less space?

8. *Fewer Hours.* Can you deliver existing results with fewer hours?

9. *Less Complex.* Can you deliver existing results while making it easier?

10. *Less Equipment or Energy.* Can you deliver existing results with less equipment and energy?

The work-flow productivity increase describes in detail the work elements that must be performed from an inception decision to a concluding evaluation. Through this process, work is observed for its distribution, defined for its sequence, and measured for its volume and quality. This organized approach analyzes each work element in the context of the overall work flow to see if improvement can be achieved through manipulating work elements to find a smaller number of simple motions to complete a task. Doing things the same old way is challenged and questioned. The work-flow productivity increaser is based on the principle that there is always a better method of doing a job regardless of who developed the present method. Every detail of a job is challenged for the purpose of spotting wasted energy or motions. The chief value of the work-flow productivity increaser is to examine how the work-flow process can be changed for increasing productivity. Development of new ideas is not an easy process. There is no easy way to teach or show a person how to get an idea that he has never had before. Raising questions is most helpful. Deliberately adjusting a situation is also useful, but probably the most effective way is to think differently about the old ways or problems.

The work-flow productivity increaser is described as follows:

(a) *Describe a Work-Flow Process from Start to Finish.* Use a systems approach (input-output); describe in detail how work is completed from a beginning point to its conclusion. Describe the work-flow process with line diagrams and the following symbols:

—— work-flow	☐ inspection
——► directed work-flow	▽ delay
◯ work operation	◇ decision
⇨ movement	▽ storage or wait

(b) *Analyze for Work-Flow Improvements.* Analyze the entire work-flow procedure to determine if improvement can be made in the following ways:

    (1)   Reduce the cost of the operation.

    (2)   Eliminate nonessential activities that waste effort.

    (3)   Increase effectiveness of each necessary activity.

    (4)   Eliminate duplication of effort.

    (5)   Make work safer and less fatiguing.

    (6)   Remove bottlenecks or delays.

    (7)   Improve customer service.

    (8)   Reduce complex motions and procedures.

    (9)   Remove "red tape" procedures.

  (10)   Eliminate idle time.

  (11)   Minimize rework.

  (12)   Keep labor trouble to a minimum.

  (13)   Avoid backtracking in work flow.

  (14)   Reduce excessive handling.

The analysis starts with a series of deliberate questions that lead to information on how to simplify the work flow. The complacent individual with a closed mind is a major obstacle to the use of this procedure. The following checklist is useful for this analysis.

Questioning Checklist

Problem analysis

(a) What directives, policies, positions, and organizational conditions are impeding performance growth or efficient resource utilization?

(b) What productivity problems can be expected within three months? Six months? Twelve months?

(c) What changes can be made in job requirements to enlarge responsibilities and effectiveness?

(d) What are the barriers that have prevented the organization from reducing cost and being more efficient?

Opportunity analysis

(a) Where is the most attractive opportunity for making a change for the better?

(b) Where are the possible technological breakthroughs, and what are the effects on present facilities and equipment?

(c) Where can the organization's services and abilities be more closely aligned with customer or taxpayer needs?

(d) Where are the unique advantages of organization's products that could be expanded?

Personnel analysis

(a) Who are the marginal or submarginal personnel who are draining the resources of the firm? What can be done about it?

(b) Who are those impeding improvement and what can be done to help them better their performance?

(c) Who are the individuals who have ideas but have not been able to implement them?

(d) Who are the individuals who would double their performance if they were shifted to a new set of challenges?

(e) Who are the individuals who are too big for their small jobs or too small for their big jobs?

Schedule analysis

(a) When can existing commitments be moved up for completion?

(b) When can a new schedule be adopted for implementing a new idea?

(c) When can additional manpower be added to complete commitments earlier?

(d) When can cost targets be given to personnel to meet commitments?

(e) When can changes be included to reduce rejects and defects?

Methods analysis

(a) How can we regroup or alter the sequence of work assignments to reduce costs and improve schedules?

(b) How can we revise our layout for improved coordination and shorter distances?

(c) How can a rearrangement improve morale, satisfaction and results?

(d) How can a suboperation be modified, changed, or redesigned to incorporate the functions of other suboperations?

(e) How can a major operation be improved to eliminate or modify a suboperation?

(c) *Develop an Improved Network-Flow Process.*   Once improvements and positive changes have been identified, redescribe the work-flow process in detail from the beginning point to its conclusions. Incorporate the changes into the new process.

(d) *Make a Comparative Analysis.*   Make a comparative analysis to discover possible savings from the new work-flow process. Savings can be recorded in terms of dollars, operations, time, space, morale, and other organizational measures. The analysis could be organized as shown in Figure 10.5.

(e) *Validate the Estimated Savings.*   Estimated savings proposed from the new process must be validated. There must be high confidence that the savings proposed are real and probable. Several methods of validation can be used: short-period trials, simulation, third-party reviews, and sampling.

(f) *Set Productivity Objectives and Implement New Work-Flow Process.*   Tell all concerned parties that the new work-flow process will result in productivity increases. Set productivity objectives and implement MPBO is a helpful strategy to use for this implementation.

The procedure for the entire technique is illustrated in Figures 10.6 and 10.7.

Resource-Accountability Clarifier.   When responsibility assignments are diffused, accountability is nebulous. When matching work load with work

		Old Process	New Process	Difference	Cost Savings
Operations	○	30	28	2	$12,000
Movement	⇨	135	121	14	$2,000
Inspection	□	20	15	5	$500
Delays	D	40	32	8	$1500
Decisions	◇	12	8	11	$200
Storage	▽	10	10	0	——
				Total	$16,200

Figure 10.5   Old and new process analysis.

force is fuzzy, effectiveness and efficiency are uncertain. As organizations continue to become more complex, accountability effectiveness and efficiency of actions are strained. How resources are allocated becomes difficult to trace. The *work-flow productivity generator* and the *work-flow productivity increaser* give a graphic picture of the steps in the work process. However, it is often desirable to have a breakdown of how resources are allocated in relation to expectancies.

The resource-accountability clarifier is of special value for analyzing the total work situation at a glance. It examines the relation between the profit

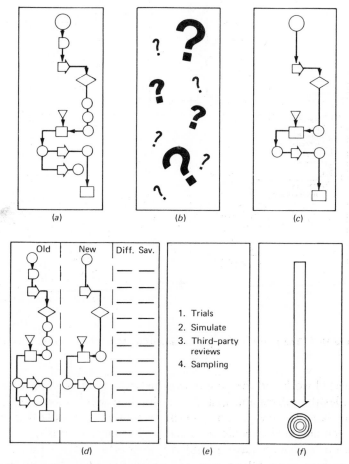

Figure 10.6   Work-flow productivity increaser technique. (a) Describe work flow. (b) Analyze for improvements. (c) Improve work flow. (d) Make comparison. (e) Validate the savings. (f) Set productivity objectives.

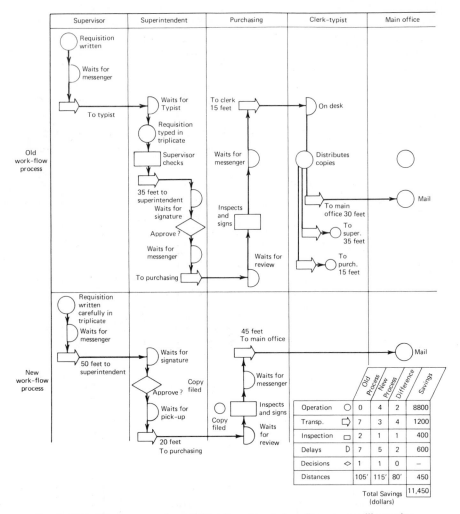

Figure 10.7   The process of requisitioning of tools in a firm: a case illustration.

of expected work and the people who are expected to complete the work. It clarifies the effects anticipated in a situation when a job is assigned. It provides an overview of how specific resources, particularly personnel, have been allocated to achieve certain performance objectives. In times of expansion, managers have a tendency to overhire. The optimal staffing level appears to be 90 percent of apparent needs. The matrix format encourages the shifting, reducing, increasing, and staffing of personnel to critical areas. It provides a view of using the most capable people for the most critical jobs. But more than that, the resources-accountability clarifier provides an overview of who is consuming which resources and for what purpose. It helps with over- or understaffing. Duplication of effort and other evidences of wasted time can often be spotted on the clarifier better than by simply observing the sequences of work steps in a process. It helps avoid bogging down creative people in routine tasks. It helps in spotting simultaneous assignments. The clarifier aids in matching capable people with critical functions and helps identify capable people in job assignments that lead nowhere or at best produce marginal benefits. It aids in allocating resources to workers to facilitate work effectiveness and reduce frustration at not having the resources at their disposal when needed to get the job done. The technique is described as follows:

1. *Establish a Matrix of Performance Objectives Versus Resource Allocations.* Performance expectations or objectives are plotted on one side of the matrix opposite resources to be used in the process. Examples of performance objectives are: increase sales revenues 15 percent, expand territorial coverage to 60 percent, reduce customer complaints from 50 to 20, hold travel expense to 6 percent of billing. Examples of resources are: time, employees, space, budget, machines, supplies, equipment, and facilities.

2. *Identify Activities Needed to Reach Performance Objectives.* The cells of the matrix are filled with the actions or activities that are needed to complete the objectives. These activities are specific and highly related to the job.

3. *Analyze to Clarify How Resources Are Assigned to Objectives.* With an overview of the entire matrix, an analysis is made to clarify how resources are assigned to performance objectives. Changes can be introduced for shifting or reducing resources where needed.

The entire process of the resource-accountability clarifier is illustrated in Figures 10.8 and 10.9.

Time-Scheduling Productivity Multiplier.   Time is crucial in organizational life. Liveliness of pace has an effect on volume output, in-process work, schedule delivery, and the personnel who are parts of the process. Few things are more demoralizing than a slow, sloppy, lackadaisical pace. Employees who are absorbed, enthusiastic, and skillful with an established lively pace tend to spread their enthusiasm to others. The great output of organizations is paced by the individuals whose skills and abilities are pitted against time and performance. Managers and supervisors are well

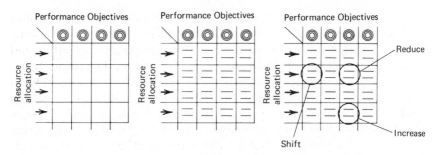

Figure 10.8   Resource-accountability clarifier technique. (a) Establish matrix of expectancy. (b) Identify necessary activities. (c) Clarify resources to be used.

aware that getting results is only half the battle. The other half is getting the results within a period of time. The manager "plays the clock." Increased complexity in organizations puts managers in a race against time. This is often due to the elasticity of work. That is, personnel have a tendency to stretch their work commitments to their own goods rather than organizational commitments. Many will recognize this as Parkinson's Law.[9] If a scheduling deadline is extended for a task to be completed, the individual responsible for completing the task will pace himself to the deadline. If the deadline is moved up, the individual will step up the pace to complete the same work within a shorter time. The pace of work is directly related to reaching and meeting a deadline. When deadlines are changed by shortening the amount of time available for work, efforts are increased. This acts against Parkinson's Law. Increased complexity due to delays in deadlines stretches work, causing the characteristic problem of a superorganization—"lagging reaction time."

The *time-scheduling productivity multiplier* is a technique for "playing the clock." Deadlines are changed to increase productivity. The basic principle of the process is

When performance is held at a given level, productivity increases as an inverse function of time.

The manager of productivity uses shorter periods of time to achieve the same amount of work. This forces productivity up (see Figure 10.10). The productivity index (PI) in Figure 10.10 changes from 50 to 200 by advancing deadlines and working against the elasticity of work.

The procedure for using the time-scheduling productivity multiplier

Resource-Accountability Clarifier
Performance Objectives (Annual)

Weekly Resource Allocation	Increase Sales Revenues 15%	Expand Territorial Coverage to 60%	Reduce Customer Complaints from 50 to 20	Hold Travel Expense to 6% of Billing	Total
Frank Thomas Sales Manager *too much time!*	Sales planning −4 Customer conferences 8 Sales proposals −2 Sales reports −4 *(circled)*	Sales planning −4 Customer conferences −14 Sales proposals −4	Interviewing clients −3 Follow-up −1 *(circled)* *sufficient attention?*	Dept. meetings −3 Expense reports −1 *(circled)*	
Hours	18	22	4	4	48
Joseph Sully Sales Representative	Telephone calls −3 Customer contacts −12 Correspondence −1 Travel −7 Sales reports −1	Telephone calls −2 Customer contacts −9 Correspondence −1 Travel −2 Sales reports −2	Quality checks −3 *too little time!*	Department meetings −3 Expense reports −2 *(circled)* *Isn't there a system for handling?*	
Hours	24	16	3	5	48
Harry Bane Sales Representative	Telephone calls −2 Customer contacts −10 Correspondence −2 Travel −9 Sales reports −1	Telephone *(circled)* calls −1 Customer contacts −9 Correspondence −2 Travel −2 Sales reports −2	Quality checks −3	Dept. meetings −3 Expense reports −2 *(circled)*	
Hours	24	16	3	5	48
Mary Clark Administrative	Processing orders −7 Preparing reports −3	Assembling proposals −6 Handling calls −4 Correspondence −6 Take dictation −2 *(circled)* *her job?*	Interviewing clients −5 Checking −2	Checking office expenses −5	
Hours	10	18	7	5 *(circled)*	40
Helen Case Steno Pool	Take dictation −2 Typing −12 Handling calls −3 Filing −1	Take dictation −2 Typing −5 Handling calls −1 Filing −2		Errands −10 Filing −2	
Hours	18	10		12	40
Total hours	94	82	17	31	224

Figure 10.9   Field sales office analysis: a case illustration.

Time allocation profile (125, 100, 75, 50, 25, 0) — *Expected*, *Actual*

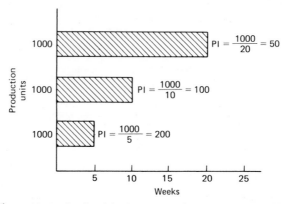

Figure 10.10   Productivity increases with shortening deadlines.

technique is described as follows:

1. *Set up a Schedule of the Work to be Completed.*   Using a standard type schedule such as bar chart, Gantt or PERT, plot work activities or tasks as events on a linear time scale. The work activities or tasks are indicated vertically, and future time is spread horizontally. Indicate start and finish of work.

2. *Analyze Schedule and Set Productivity Objectives.*   Once a schedule has been established, identify specific productivity objectives. MPBO process steps would be useful to set up evaluative measures.

3. *Use Backward Planning Advance Expected Deadlines.*   Starting with the completion time, advance the deadlines for work to be completed earlier. The amount of the advance should be an attainable challenge. Measure the productivity index.

4. *Rearrange Schedule to Assure Completion with New Deadline.*   Rearrange the work activities or tasks to assure the work planned will be completed according to the new deadline. Compare the productivity gains in the new schedule.

The entire process of the time-scheduling productivity multiplier is illustrated in Figures 10.11, 10.12 and 10.13.

Productivity Tracker.   One of the significant characteristics of complex organizations is that no two accomplishments or performance outputs are ever exactly alike, even with the same people, processes, or materials. Resources are never consumed in exactly the same manner and amounts, although the variations may be small. When variations in accomplish-

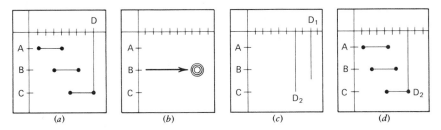

Figure 10.11   Time-scheduling productivity multiplier technique. (a) Set up a schedule. (b) Set productivity objectives. (c) Use backward planning advance deadlines. (d) Rearrange process elements as required.

ments, performance, or resources consumed are small, changes in productivity can often be ignored; but when they are great, productivity is critically affected. Wide fluctuations in productivity cannot be ignored.

Many factors contribute to variations in complex organizations—for example, employees who do not complete a work process in exactly the same manner, miscommunications among departments and people, situations that change the conditions in which a process is carried out, materials that are not the same because of different ingredients, and fatiguing equipment. But the primary cause of variations is the growth or decline of the organization itself. Changes, up or down, from employee turnover, sales growth, budget cuts, expansion, competitive strategies, and different policies create fluctuating cycles in organizations. Organizations have long recognized the inevitability of these variations, and great effort is expended to control them.

The productivity tracker is a graphical time comparison of the actual productivity measured and evaluated in a work process compared to the desired or targeted productivity. This comparison is observed, tracked, and controlled under limits. When the limits are judged as necessary and vital for the organization, the productivity tracker aids in keeping the variations of productivity under surveillance. The tracker recognizes the fundamental tendency of most processes to drift in undesirable directions or fluctuate beyond desirable limits. It is an information reporting system for revealing productivity variances in time to allow for correction and adjustment. A continuous feedback is collected from the chart to indicate the corrective action needed to stay in control. The productivity tracker provides these benefits to the manager of productivity in organizations:

1. *Predicts* when actual productivity will drift beyond desired limits.
2. *Evaluates* on a time basis of actual versus planned productivity.

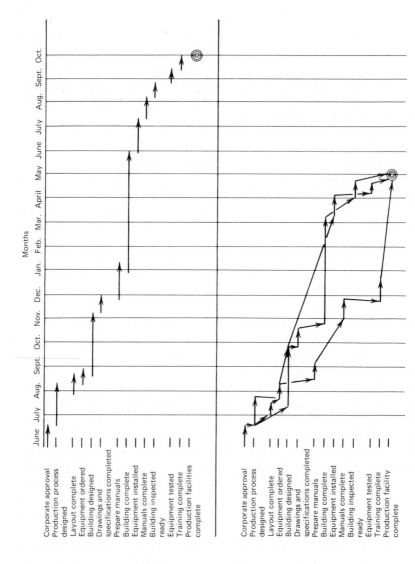

Figure 10.12 Scheduling process for pencil tab manufacturing facility: a case illustration.

3. *Corrective action* is signaled when actual productivity falls below a limit.

4. *Control points* are pinpointed for formal reviews.

5. *Progress overview* is seen at a glance toward objectives.

The productivity-tracker technique is described as follows:

(a) *Plot Productivity (PI) on a Time Matrix Toward an Objective.* Establish the objective to be achieved. Measure the productivity index to be followed for reaching the objective. Plot over a period of time to be controlled. Set down time control points.

(b) *Set the Control Limits.* Establish the control limits that allow variations to take place within acceptable tolerances. Those limits also define unacceptable variations in which corrective action is indicated. An alert line and action warning line are established to signal actions to be taken for "real-time" corrections.

(c) *Plot Actual Productivity.* Compute actual productivity with the productivity index and plot values over the time period to be controlled. The difference between actual and planned productivity is the variance that will be tracked for control.

(d) *Evaluate for Corrective Actions.* Evaluate the degree of variance between actual and planned productivity. If the variation falls within limits, no actions are indicated. If the variations fall beyond limits, corrective actions should be instituted. If variations fall within limits but the trend or drift is heading out of limits, the manager or supervisor is signalled to take preventive corrective action.

The entire process of the productivity tracker is illustrated in Figures 10.14 and 10.15.

Cost-Productivity Allocator.   Every move a complex organization makes has an effect on costs! Most moves force costs to go up; sometimes moves force costs down. But either way, productivity is affected. The inescapable fact is that cost moves always have an impact on productivity. Practically all resources can be considered as costs with money as the common measure. Most organizations pay close attention only to costs! They track them, control them, and keep them at rock-bottom levels. This could be a mistake for two reasons. *First,* costs should not be detached or disconnected from performance. Costs and performance go hand in hand. Driving costs down for the sake of costs alone inevitably drives performance down. This eventually causes productivity to drop. Cost-cutting and last-ditch slashing by panicked managers are desperate moves that may

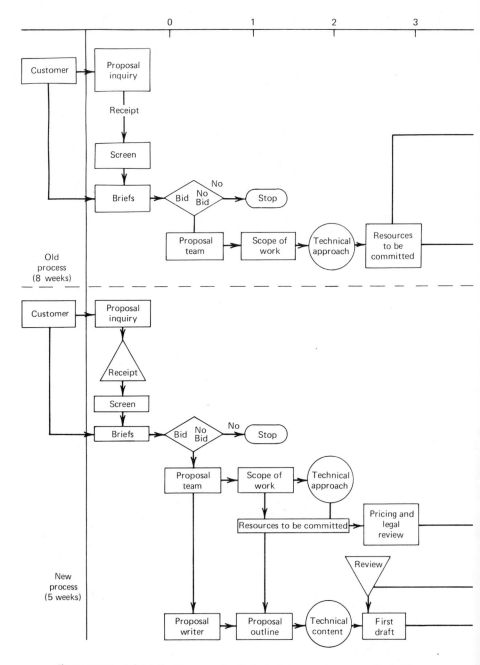

Figure 10.13   Scheduling process for technical proposals: a case illustration.

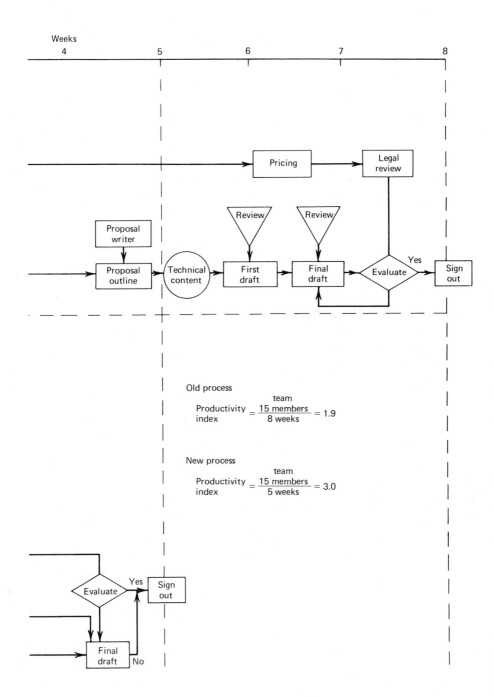

Weeks

Old process

$$\text{Productivity index} = \frac{15 \text{ members (team)}}{8 \text{ weeks}} = 1.9$$

New process

$$\text{Productivity index} = \frac{15 \text{ members (team)}}{5 \text{ weeks}} = 3.0$$

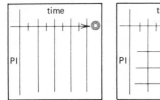 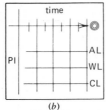 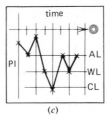 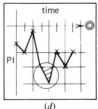

(a)   (b)   (c)   (d)

Figure 10.14 Productivity tracker technique. (*a*) **Plot productivity on a time matrix.** (*b*) **Set the control limits; CL—control line, WL—warning line; AL—alert line.** (*c*) **Plot actual productivity.** (*d*) **Evaluate for corrective action.**

reduce costs in the short-run but ultimately affect productivity in the long-run. Cost-cutting patterns should be made with its affects on performance and productivity. *Second,* there are many times when costs must be allowed to go up if this accomplishes an important performance target. That is, the manager of productivity cannot afford to overlook the prospect of getting more productivity through a greater outlay of costs. The key question is where the outlay of money will come from if budgets are tight and money is not available.

The cost-productivity allocator is a technique for the reallocation of money to improve productivity. It works against the traditional, across-the-board percentage cuts. These costs cuts remove the good with the bad. For example, an organization may set a cost reduction objective and cut the budget in every department. Some departments tend to collect less fat than others because of the nature of the work or because of superior managers. The result of an across-the-board cut is that the departments that were the fattest are now nearer to required size. However, the originally lean departments are now seriously under budget, which leads to a serious drop in performance and eventually productivity is lowered. Such budget cuts ignore the importance of some items over others.

The cost-productivity allocator is a technique to identify cost items that are critical and find the small outlay of money that is needed to improve productivity. Before this technique is described, some definitions are in order.

1. *Cost Avoidance.*   Removing or eliminating a cost item that is anticipated and budgeted but not expended.
2. *Cost Reduction.*   Reducing or decreasing the amount of a cost item that has been budgeted for and is in a process of expenditure.
3. *Cost Control.*   Spending but holding the amount of a cost item according to a budget standard.

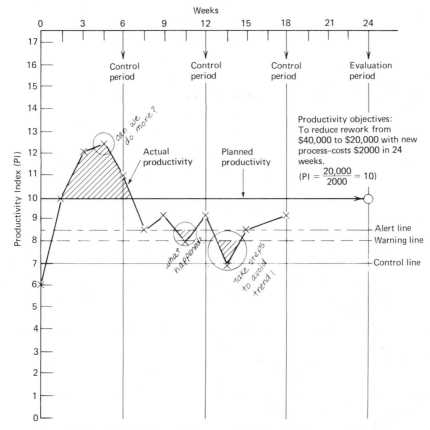

Figure 10.15   Control of rework in manufacturing plant: a case illustration.

4. *Cost Effectiveness.*   Increasing the spending allocated in a budget because it will affect performance improvement or reduce costs in the long run.

In any array of cost items, these four cost concepts are roughly related in a percentage distribution shown in Figure 10.16.[10]

The cost-productivity allocator technique is described as follows:

(a)   *List the Cost Demands in a Budget or Cost Array.*   This listing may be past, present, or future demands on an individual or a department.

(b)   *Arrange the List in Order of Greatest Benefit to Least Benefit.*   The term *benefit* is intended to mean great return for the amount of cost invested.

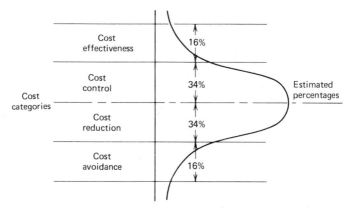

Figure 10.16 Cost-productivity curve.

(c) Separate List According to the Cost-Productivity Curve. Starting from the least payoff or benefit, identify in the cost array the percentages of each category—cost avoidance, 16%, cost reduction, 34%, cost control, 34%, cost effectiveness, 16%.

(d) Redistribute Savings to Cost Effectiveness Items. Money saved from the cost avoidance and cost reduction categories are reallocated to the effectiveness category.

The entire process of the cost-productivity allocator is illustrated in Figures 10.17 and 10.18.

Productivity-Effectiveness Planner. A novel approach to evaluating an organization, a function, a program, or a budget is through the use of the productivity-effectiveness planner, also called the productivity-benefit planner. This method evaluates, during the planning period, the benefits that might be expected from a decision to go ahead with a program, project, function, or the organization itself. It is a systematic analysis of approximating the major costs and benefits involved in various patterns of resource allocation. The method is especially useful during the period of budget formation. This implies that a budget when formed but not yet approved should undergo an analysis to assure maximum benefit is obtained for the planned expenditure. The productivity-benefit analysis requires options or alternatives that might be selected to give other beneficial effects. If the organization has been structured into cost centers where budgets are allocated to these centers and performance measures are also aggregated, a productivity-benefit analysis can be made between and among cost centers. Through this process productivity, trade-offs can be made. Such a trade-off analysis can begin with a series of questions.

1. Do programs contain objectives indicating the results wanted?
2. Are they accomplishing their intended objectives? Can the benefits be articulated and measured?
3. Do program objectives contain priorities that suggest different degrees of value and worth?
4. Do program objectives solve problems that gave rise to the formation of the program? What are these problems?
5. Do program objectives reach for results on a level that is significant and important for everyone concerned?
6. Have program objectives been formed from a reasonable number of attractive options or alternatives?
7. Are program objectives supported with a sufficient number of well-specified activities?
8. Are program objectives connected with a complete description of program resources and costs needed to attain objectives?
9. Do program costs measure significantly less than the benefits for which the program exists?

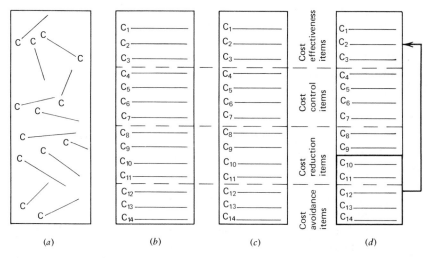

Figure 10.17   Cost-productivity allocator. (a) List the cost demands. (b) Arrange in order of benefit. (c) Categorize according to curve. (d) Redistribute savings to cost effectiveness.

(a) *List the cost demands.*
1. Travel expense
2. Office decor and posters
3. New telephone contact program
4. Rental
5. Salaries
6. Utilities
7. Supplies and materials
8. Advertising promotion
9. Client luncheons
10. Janitorial expense
11. New sales proposal process
12. Promotional giveaways
13. Information and subscription service
14. Printing expense

(b) *Arrange in order of benefit.*
1. New telephone contact program
2. New sales proposal process
3. Advertising promotion
4. Salaries
5. Travel expense
6. Special taxes
7. Rental
8. Utilities
9. Janitorial expense
10. Supplies and materials
11. Printing expense
12. Office decor and posters
13. Information and subscription service
14. Client luncheons

(c) *Categorize according to cost-productivity curve.*

(d) *Redistribute savings* (R)

1. New telephone contact program	Cost	
2. New sales proposal process	effectiveness	
3. Advertising promotion		
4. Salaries		
5. Travel expense	Cost	
6. Special taxes	control	
7. Rental		
8. Utilities		
9. Janitorial expense	Cost	
R→10. Supplies and materials	reduction	
R→11. Printing expense		
R→12. Office decor and posters		
R→13. Information and subscription service	Cost	
R→14. Client luncheons	avoidance	

Figure 10.18   Cost allocation of fields sales office: a case illustration.

10. How well are programs operating for which no final output can be readily defined?

11. Do program activities planned for attaining objectives introduce new problems with costs that will reduce the benefits of the program?

12. When program objectives are complete, can the results be measurable, accountable, and reputable?

13. Are the people who decided on the program, know the program objectives, and have implemented the program, also evaluating the program?

Productivity-effectiveness planning fundamentally examines the options or alternative ventures of action that might be taken to achieve a specified program objective in some future period of time. In many ways it is priority setting. Decisions to adopt any one option are based on several reviews of the options that are available. The analysis requires a systematic search to all possible attractive options. The user is constantly changing. Many things that were important two months ago may not be so important as a new problem. This causes a change in priorities which has an impact on the original decision. Often the program objective itself must be modified or changed in order for a highly beneficial option to be selected. The examination of options typically involves assessment of resource costs and gains in costs, time, or productivity. The general approach to productivity-effectiveness planning is illustrated in the following table.

| | | Benefit Analysis | | | |
Ventures	Costs (C)	Poten- tial Bene- fits	Proba- bility of Occur- rence	Expected Benefits (B)	Produc- tivity P = B/C
Option A	$4000	$6000	.80	$4800	1.20
Option B	1000	4000	.95	3800	3.80
Option C	2000	4000	.95	3800	1.90
Option D	3000	4500	.75	3375	1.13

Where dollars and cents may not be available but quality items are, an alternate approach is to use a checklist of items. Resources are items of commitment. Benefits are items of gain. Probability of occurrence are risk factors. This is illustrated in the following table. For purposes of the illustration the items are assumed to be at parity. In actual cases a weighting method should be used if they are not at parity.

		Benefits Analysis			
Ventures	Re- sources (R)	Poten- tial Bene- fits	Proba- bility of Occur- rence	Expected Benefits (B)	Produc- tivity P = B/R
Option A	30 (items)	20 ×	.70	14.0	0.47
Option B	24	22 ×	.85	18.7	0.78
Option C	14	20 ×	.90	18.0	1.28
Option D	32	26 ×	.80	20.8	0.65

The cost-effectiveness planner technique is now described as follows:

(a) *Clearly Define the Program Objective.* Any benefit analysis is made toward a well-defined objective to be reached. A program can be effective only if it achieves the objectives that gave definition to the program.

(b) *Identify and List Program Objective Options.* These are the several possibilities that exist for the achievement of the objective.

(c) *Estimate the Cost of Resources.* Each option is analyzed to the total estimated costs that would be needed to adopt and implement the option.

(d) *Estimate the Benefits.* Each option is analyzed for the benefits each would deliver if the option were adopted. Benefits should be defined in the same terms as its' costs—that is, dollars with dollars, time with time, people with people, space with space, and so on. Occasionally a benefit may be expressed in general items that are different from the costs needed to deliver it. The probability of occurrence of each benefit is determined to translate potential benefits to expected benefits (see Chapter 3, Principle 5.)

(e) *Calculate the Productivity Index and Evaluate.* The productivity index is calculated for each option to be considered. The productivity index ratio will reveal the greatest performance possible with the least expenditure feasible. Evaluation is made from the greatest estimated productivity. The entire process of the productivity-effectiveness planner is illustrated in Figure 10.19.

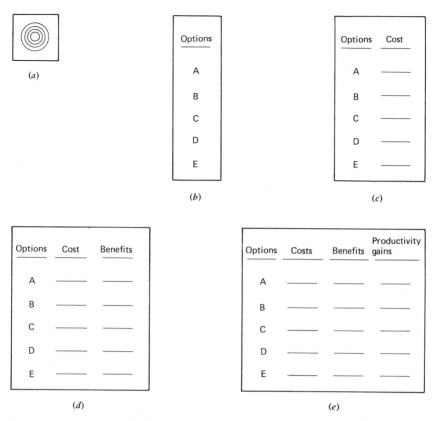

Figure 10.19 Productivity-effectiveness planner. (a) Define objective. (b) Identify options. (c) Estimate option costs. (d) Estimate options expected benefits. (e) Evaluate and calculate productivity gains.

CASE ILLUSTRATION: PRODUCTIVITY EFFECTIVENESS FOR A FIRE
PROTECTION PROGRAM

A fire protection program is being planned for a community of three towns in New England which experiences an average annual fire damage of $1,500,000. In general, the objective is to reduce the average annual damage that occurs from fire losses throughout the three-town area. Five major approaches have been identified as possible options. The comparative estimates for option costs and option benefits with estimated productivity gains are in the following table.

Venture Plans	Annual Cost of Project	Annual Expected Benefit (Reduction of Damage)	Productivity Gains
1. No protection	0	0	0
2. Three-unit system	$150,000	$300,000	2.22
3. Three-unit system with preventive program	200,000	475,000	2.38
4. Six-unit system	275,000	500,000	1.82
5. Six-unit system with preventive program	375,000	575,000	1.53

From the point of view of the analysis, the three-unit system with an active preventive fire protection program yields the greatest benefits from the expenditures to be made in the program. One might argue that a "political decision" might be crucial here in exploring the greatest possible reduction of fire loss. The analysis would merely continue to explore two three-unit systems, three three-unit systems, two four-unit systems, three five-unit systems, and so on. If the checklist approach were used instead of the dollars and cents approach, the analysis would be as follows:

Venture Plans	Resources (Items of Commitments)	Annual Expected Benefits (Items of Gain)	Productivity Gain
1. No protection	0	0	0
2. Three-unit system	14	22	1.57
3. Three-unit system with preventive program	9	20	2.22
4. Six-unit system	18	22	1.22
5. Six-unit system with preventive program	16	24	1.50

The reader should have observed at this point that combining dollars and cents with checklists could be the most viable way to conduct a productivity-effectiveness analysis.

SUMMARY

There's a natural drift toward unwanted complexity in private firms, government agencies, hospitals, schools, universities, labor unions, and trade associations. These complexities drive costs up and productivity down! Many factors are causing this complexity. Three were cited and described in this chapter. *First*, government is moving into organizations causing legislative "red tape." Legislative enactments are regulatory intrusions requiring paperwork, indirect staff, and time-consuming procedures. *Second*, union effectiveness is now a formidable challenge in organizations. Collective bargaining is not only working, and working well, but in some cases, has overwhelmed the management of the organization. *Third*, complexities increase when organizations grow in size. Superorganizations, giant corporations, and huge empires have resulted in complexity in decision making, planning and evaluating, resource utilization, work-flow organization, time delivery and unpredictable predictions.

Managing complexity for great productivity will require attitudes and strategies for dealing with these complexities. The attitude that complexity is here to stay and one must look at it in a positive way is a must for the manager of productivity. This manager should have several strategies that could be used to deal with problems caused by complexity. Seven productivity strategies were introduced in this chapter to deal with seven specific problems of the complex organization.

1. *Work-focus productivity generator* to counteract the domino-effect of trivia in an organization. This technique requires concentration and focus in the high payoff areas.
2. *Work-flow productivity increaser* to define the work elements in a work process. This technique requires identifying overlays, duplications, omissions, and antiproductivity barriers.
3. *Resource-accountability clarifier* to clarify the allocation of resources toward objectives and personnel. This technique requires an overview of how resources are utilized toward results.
4. *Time-scheduling productivity multiplier* to counteract the elasticity of work found in complex organization. This technique requires arranging work in process toward advancing deadlines.
5. *Productivity tracker* to control the wide fluctuations that often occur in the performance of work. This technique requires plotting actual productivity with expected productivity and suggests the corrective action that must be taken to reduce the gap.

6. *Cost-productivity allocator* to prevent the traditional practice of cutting costs across the board, which greatly affects productivity. This technique requires a series of deliberate cost managing steps to separate the nonessentials from the essentials.

7. *Productivity-effectiveness planner* to assist in decision making for the greatest benefits possible with the least expenditure of costs. This technique requires the identification of options to reach an objective and the estimated costs of these options with their associated benefits.

Managing complexities to drive productivity up requires a "style" for cutting through the issues caused by complexities. The style becomes effective when it is developed for this purpose.

QUESTIONS TO THINK ABOUT

1. Describe the complexities that exist in your organization. In what ways have they disrupted productivity?
2. List the demands made upon you in the course of one week and apply the work-focus productivity generator.
3. Use the resource-accountability clarifier for the department you are in and make an analysis for better allocation of resources.
4. Use the time-scheduling productivity multiplier for three planned objectives that result from the resource-accountability clarifier.
5. Using the productivity-tracker, set up a tracking system for productivity for the past 6 months. With the same system, set up the control of productivity for the next 6 months.
6. Use the cost-productivity allocator for the cost demands made in your department.
7. Consider a situation in which there are five options open to you. Using the productivity-effectiveness planner, decide on the option that gives the greatest gain.
8. Use the work-flow productivity increaser for the work flow that presently exists in your department. Analyze for improvements, make a comparison, and set productivity objectives.

REFERENCES AND NOTES

1. Brooks Jackson and Evans Witt, Associated Press newsmen in a series of articles, "Regulatory Agencies Growth Called Explosive." Series appeared in the *New London Day*, March 16, 1976, New London, Conn.

2. Eleanor Carruth, "The Legal Explosion Has Left Business Shell-Shocked," *Fortune,* April 1973, pp. 65–71.

3. Walter E. Baer, *Strikes: A Study of Conflict and How to Resolve It.* American Management Association, New York, 1975, pp. 1–23.

4. *Op. cit.* p. 7.

5. Editors of Fortune, *Fortune Directory,* New York, 1962 and 1971.

6. Jerald Hage, *Social Change in Complex Organizations.* Random House, New York, 1970, pp. 38–45.

7. Harlan Cleveland, *The Future Executive.* Harper and Row, New York, 1972, pp. 13.

8. Alan D. Scharf, "More Pareto's Law," *Industrial Business Management,* Saskatchewan Research Council, Saskatoon, Saskatchewan, January 1974.

9. C. Northcote Parkinson, *op. cit.* pp. 2–8.

10. The normal probability distribution curve needs no justification here since it is a reasonable estimate of how cost items are distributed in a total array. The normal curve has been a useful device for estimating, according to the laws of probability, the percentages within each cost category. For a thorough discussion of the normal curve, see R. M. Barnes, *Motion and Time Study,* John Wiley & Sons, 1968, pp. 380–387.

11
MANAGING TIME FOR IMPROVING PRODUCTIVITY

IN THIS CHAPTER

Time is decreasing in availability and increasing in cost.
The productivity calendar.
Systems overview for time control.
Biological rhythms for greater output.
Behavioral aids for getting things done.
Coordinating productivity with time schedules.
Gantt productivity schedules.
PERT schedules for time control of complex programs.
PERT productivity networks.
Critical ratio scheduling.
Overtime deterioration.
How to manage overtime.
Four-day workweek.

The only way to distinguish between the "activity person" and the "productive person" is to see the results they deliver. Both put in approximately equal amounts of time and energy, but the productive person works intelligently toward objectives and therefore achieves more results. The productive person makes best use of time which he knows is an eroding resource. The activity person tries to deliver more results by putting in a lot more time. Eventually he finds he does not have enough time. But let's face the fact of these times! There are never enough hours in a day to accomplish all the things all of us want to do. There may never be enough hours in a day, in a week, or in a month. Most managers work long hours. They probably put in more hours than any other occupational group. According to the Bureau of Labor Statistics, the statistical average of hours per week of various occupational groups is as follows: managers, 47; craftsmen and foremen, 41; operators, 40; professional and technical workers, 40; sales workers, 36; laborers, 34; and private household workers, 22. These figures may not take into consideration the time taken to do work and reading at home. This too would probably put managers at the top. Bringing work home or working after hours is an occupational expectancy for those in decision jobs who give leadership and direction.

Time has always been a limited resource. It still is. It is becoming more limited. Managers must pack into days what was formally done in weeks. They must budget and schedule this scarce resource or experience the waste of valuable opportunities or the slippage of important accomplishments for the organization. Managers must know how to connect planning and results with time schedules to utilize effectively all allocated resources.

This chapter intends to give managers who are searching for more hours, searching for more time tools, or searching for time effectiveness, several strategies for managing time. The chapter consists of three parts: (1) four time tools for finding time, (2) four time schedules to connect planning to controlling effectively, (3) overtime as an organizational practice and how it affects productivity, and (4) how to use overtime hours and still maintain productivity.

FOUR TIME TOOLS FOR MANAGING PERSONAL TIME

Getting more done in less time, or at least getting the job done within expected time, is a great measure of managerial performance in complex organizations. As organizations continue to grow in complexity, time, like other resources, becomes limited. Managers who can deliver, through effective use of time, establish themselves as managers of productivity. Organizational complexities cause routine work processes and commitments to become stressful to both organizations and individuals alike. Stresses emerge as moving deadlines, unavailable personnel at a given time, shifting priorities, lack of resources when needed, decision crises, product and service stockouts, and the relentless rise in costs as time ticks on. They cause a series of time management failures:

1. Failure to plan needed action by specific dates.
2. Failure to be concise, thus consuming much time.
3. Failure to connect just enough resources toward achievements within a time frame.
4. Failure to decide in time, thus losing much time.
5. Failure to signal starts and stops of other efforts in time coordination.
6. Failure to do now what has to be done, thus saving money, people, and efforts later.

Administrators and supervisors alike are well aware of time management failures. This sensitivity prompts them to react by working longer hours to assure that time commitments are met. This reaction is normal. Instead, managers should develop practical methods for saving time and managing it more efficaciously. There are four suggested time strategies.

The Productivity Calendar: Monthly Strategy for Getting Results. Productive people who get things done organize and effectively control allocation of their time. They pry loose more time by identifying their time wastes. They meet deadlines and turn out work in spite of conflicting pressures, interruptions, or limited resources. They have an operating style in which they "play the clock" and never "play it by ear." They adhere to deadlines as an important part of their style for achieving. They may even advance their deadlines to drive productivity up. They make a time layout on a daily, weekly, or monthly calandar.

The productivity calendar requires managing priorities as well as managing activities. The manager allows a secretary, department personnel, or others to schedule appointments and conferences only after he or she has set down as a priority of important work. The strategy is described as follows:

1. *Using the Productivity Calendar, Block Out Committed Time.* Committed time might be activities or appointments over which you have no control. This might include department meetings, customer conferences, or necessary travel.
2. *Write Monthly Targets With Deadlines.* Write productivity objectives that are to be achieved within the month. On the calendar spot the deadlines that must be met with these targets. Assign priorities to these activities. Allow a secretary and other department personnel to schedule appointments in between.
3. *Evaluate Monthly Results.* At the end of the month, evaluate the results accomplished.

Fill in the monthly summary. Decide on future action. The entire process of the productivity calendar is illustrated in Figures 11.1 and 11.2.

Systems Overview for Time Control.   Managerial offices are centers of complex processes. Paperwork, telephone calls, visitors, mail conferences, correspondence, inter- and intradepartment traffic, and decision making converge in a situation that produces difficult transactions. A clearly defined office system can be of great help in conserving time so that those

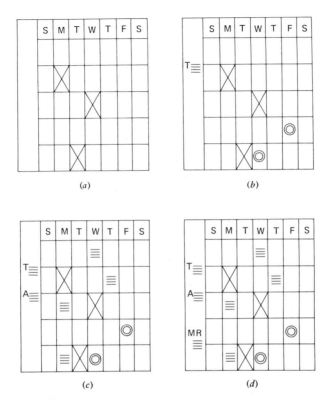

Figure 11.1 The productivity calendar technique. (a) Block out commitments. (b) Write targets and spot deadlines. (c) Describe activities and assign priorities. (d) Evaluate monthly results.

transactions take the least amount of time possible. A systems overview of the entire situation encourages the identification and correlation of the many inputs that come into the office and the many outputs that must be delivered within a necessary time framework. The system view encourages thinking in terms of how resources are organized to handle the myriad of demands that must be processed. Tracing and retracing, working and reworking, communicating and recommunicating are viewed to see if reasons for duplication can be avoided. The existing system for processing the office transactions should be captured on paper, and a critical analysis should be made to eliminate unnecessary or nonessential activities, duplication of effort, excessive operations, or excessive time to complete activities. The main criteria for reorganizing the office process into a system are simplicity, economy, accuracy, and speed. The systems ap-

June 1978	Sunday	Monday	Tuesday	Wednesday	Thursday	Friday	Saturday
Achievement Targets: 1. Reduce idle time from 200 to 100 hours 2. Cut down overtime from 4 to 2%	"You'll never get accountability until you get commitment."		1 HP-2 Accelerate work in Dept. K to get work in early.	2 HP-1 Do preventive maintenance on 3 lathes, section D	3	4	5
Activities and priorities: HP- High priority AP- Average priority LP- Low priority	6	7 Commitment	8 AP-2 closer coaching	9	10	11	12
	13	14 LP-1 Conduct Retraining	15	16	17 Commitment	18	19
	20	21	22 Commitment	23	24	25	26
Monthly results: 1. Idle time reduced from 200 to 150 hours 2. Overtime reduced from 4 to 1%	27	28	29	30			

① ② "Chunk your work – so that you can start it, measure it, manipulate it, and evaluate it."

Figure 11.2 The productivity calendar for a machine shop: a case illustration.

proach as a tool for controlling and managing time is described as follows:

1. *Analyze and Record the Existing Situation.* Make observations, record facts, identify transactions as they come into the office and are processed and serviced. In particular, reports that show a great deal being used should be noted.
2. *Diagram the Existing Situation into a System.* When a situation is diagrammed into a systems flow chart, the whole picture is visible at a glance. This provides the view that's needed to institute corrective action. It puts the manager in control of the situation.
3. *Revise Situation Toward Improvements.* The questioning technique could be used to make improvements. Is all paperwork necessary? Are employees doing the job for which they are best suited? Is the physical layout conducive for efficient transaction flow? Are time aids used wherever possible?
4. *Work the New System.* Once a new systems flow chart has been developed for the situation, institute it and get everyone to follow the new procedures.

The systems approach for managing time should not stop once a new system has been developed. Evaluation should be continuous. Conditions change and another review must begin again. Incidentally, employees are a good source of ideas. Allowing them to participate in the reviews of office transactions is a sound approach. They will come up with sensible ideas and work toward making these ideas work. The entire process is illustrated in Figures 11.3 and 11.4.

Biological Clocks: Finding Your Best Time. Your biological clock is different from your mechanical clock. The mechanical clock is geared to the rotations of the earth on its axis and the revolutions of the earth around the sun. The biological clock is geared to cycles within your body, which are called biorhythms. A great deal of interest in these cycles exists because these rhythms can be charted and used to predict human feelings and behavior. According to Vincent Mallardi, there are three biorhythms to each individual: physical, emotional, and intellectual.[2] The three combined rhythms begin at the moment of or shortly after birth (see Figure 11.5).

The three cycles gradually move out of phase from each other because of their different frequency lengths. The physical cycle is 23 days; the emotional cycle is 28 days; and the intellectual cycle is 33 days. Although no one knows exactly how these biorhythmic cycles are controlled,

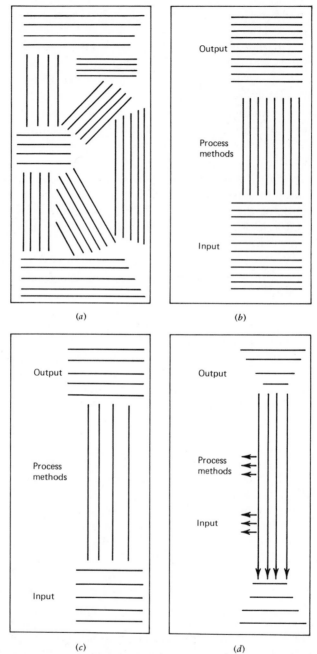

Figure 11.3 Systems approach for managing time in an office. (*a*) **Analyze and record facts.** (*b*) **Flow diagram the situation.** (*c*) **Improve the situation.** (*d*) **Work the new system.**

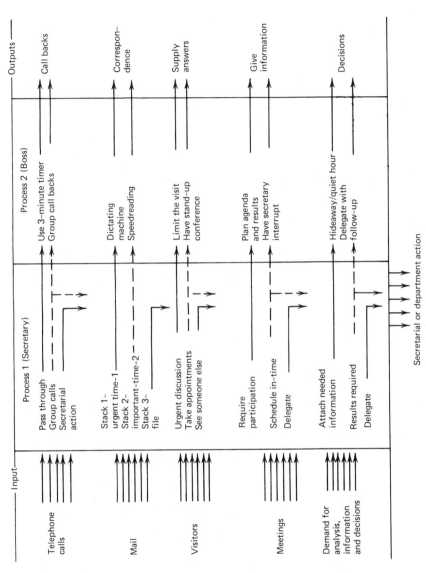

Figure 11.4 The office as a system: a case illustration.

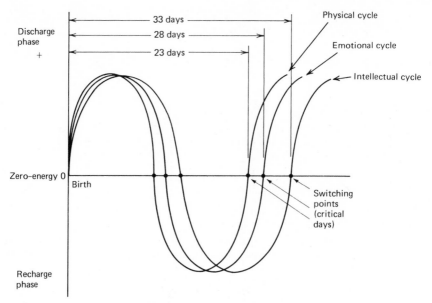

Figure 11.5   Biorhythmic cycles.

theorists say they are influenced greatly by glandular activity. In any event, biorhythms signal the highs and lows of your ability to perform. They function as follows:

1. *The Physical Biorhythm.*   When the cycle is at a high peak, a great deal of energy is available and can be deployed for long periods of time. When the cycle is in a low dip, energy availability is low. This is the time when error and fatigue are most likely. Athletes are well aware of their highs and lows of energy and endurance. Accident-prone people are also aware of cyclical weaknesses.

2. *The Emotional Biorhythms.*   When the cycle is at a high peak, feelings and enthusiasm are high and working with others is positive. When the cycle is in a low dip, feelings and enthusiasm are low, and working with people causes annoyance and irritability. People generally are well aware of the changes in moods, temperment, sensibilities, and optimism, often for no reason at all.

3. *The Intellectual Biorhythm.*   When the cycle is at a high peak, the brain processes are alert, and thinking is sharp, quick, and logical. When the cycle is in a low dip, judgments and alertness slow down, and problem solving is a difficult and tiring procedure. Many people have experi-

enced how responsiveness and mental agility leave and come back cyclically.

The best possible period for performing and accomplishing is when the three biorhythmic cycles are high or near high. The time is worst when the cycles are switching. These are considered "critical days" or "bad days."

The reader is urged to study the planning program suggested by Mallardi to determine the planning and selection of best days for best results. As an application of this concept, I have developed my bio-rhythmic cycles (see Figure 11.6).

The value in examining biorhythmic cycles is to spot the highs and lows of energy levels in the immediate future. It also shows the "switching points" or "bad days" of energy availability. If an informal study is preferred, the reader should just note the best time of day for thinking, feeling, and moving. When is it best during the week? Is there a time in which all three coincide? A biological clock could be set up to identify these peak periods and to schedule work accordingly. Conversely, when is the worse time for thinking, feeling and moving? Is there a time in which all these three coincide? This should be noted on your biological clock and kept in mind when work is scheduled.

The study of cycles, long known to scientists and layman, will be pursued increasingly by individuals and groups as a new insight into time, matching energy, feelings, and thinking with the task and objectives to be accomplished.

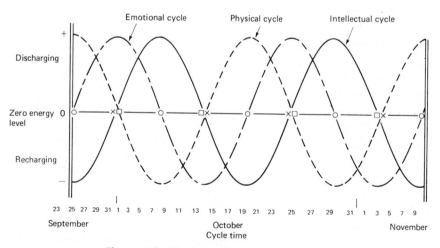

Figure 11.6 Biorhythmic cycles of the author.

Behavioral Aids in Getting Things Done. Productive managers who acquire a reputation for getting things done are people who have work styles that are governed by deeply instilled behavioral practices. That is, effective time performers naturally act and react, play and interplay, thrust and rethrust in such a way that they work on the right things, work well with other people, and have ample work energy. Those who are "natural" in this way have no time problem. Those who are not must attempt to develop a time work style for arriving at this style of getting things done. The following list, briefly stated, represents behavioral aids extracted from experiences of the reputable "productive person" who gets things done. Readers who are interested in pursuing these aids in greater depth are urged to examine other books by writers such as Alec MacKenzie and Joseph Cooper.[4]

Behavior	Behavioral Aid
1. Saying "yes" when you want to say "no"	Develop a polite apologetic statement that shows the desire to be cooperative, but urgencies prevent saying yes. Once a statement is developed, use it when appropriate
2. Disinterested in getting dull but important work out	Organize work in a sequence from dull to interesting. Interesting and pleasant work becomes a self-imposed dangling motivator
3. Fluency in writing is very slow and time consuming, but fast in speaking	Writing behavior and speaking behavior are two distinct roles. Write like you speak. Use a dictating machine
4. Projects scheduled early slip and conflict with projects scheduled later	Don't overschedule. Expect some slippage. Build slack time into early projects
5. Work peaks are heavy and continuous	Manage by exception. Do comprehensive planning and practice total delegation of the entire project, expecting to be informed only when something goes wrong. Failure to delegate responsibilities and their attendant decisions will keep work loads heavy and peaked
6. Frequent interruptions cause poor concentration	Institute quiet hours in an organization for individual work. Also, block out large segments of hideaway time

7. Enjoy socializing	Schedule socializing at coffee breaks, lunch, and dinner times or weekends
8. Conferences about secondary or side issues consume a great deal of time	Set up an item agenda for each conference. Limit the time for each conference and stick to the agenda
9. Terminating visit when visitor wants to stay	Practice going to visitor's office with pre-set time limit. Have secretary interrupt with drop-in visitors
10. Difficulty in restarting a task after leaving it because of other pressing demands	When you put away an incompleted task, leave it in a condition that enables you to retrace your last steps easily
11. Personal energy runs out when important work must be completed	High-energy periods are in the morning and for a short period mid-day. Schedule important work at this time and routine and passive work at other times
12. Delegated work does not seem to get done	Delegate the task and the procedure for accomplishing the task. Give sufficient authority to complete the task
13. Retrieving information from a loaded file system takes excessive time	Develop a file retrieval system in which all paper generated has a label to show where it is to go. "File" most in the trash basket
14. Telephone conversation is difficult to terminate	Indicate to your listener that you must relay the information discussed to someone. Use a small telephone timer
15. Old time habits prevent using new time aids	Write down a model of behavioral expectancies as a checklist and read it at the start of each day

These behavioral aids and others add up to an important managerial guideline. Working intelligently and efficiently is far superior to working long hours. The smart racehorse, not the workhorse wins the race.

TIME SCHEDULES: THE WAY TO COORDINATE PRODUCTIVITY

Productivity begins with planning and setting objectives and ends with controlling and evaluating. The schedule is the coordination between the two. The purpose of any schedule is to keep activities, jobs, or work packages on a prescribed course that will lead to a set of results. The schedule requires four dimensions to ensure that what is intended to be accomplished is accomplished. These dimensions are quantity (how much), quality (how well), cost (what expense), time (when accomplished). Jobs, tasks, and activities are kept in perspective within these dimensions.

What a Schedule Is and Its Development

Scheduling is a common time management practice found in almost every organization. Simply and briefly, *a schedule is a timetable for signaling when things should get done.* We see and are a part of many types of schedules— train schedules, airline schedules, workweek schedules, compensation schedules, production schedules, material usage schedules, and others. A more formal definition is: *a schedule is a time-negotiated agreement on how allocated resources will be committed to achieving an objective.*

Organizations that use schedules effectively experience the following advantages:

1. Delegating and spreading responsibilities to many groups.
2. A time baseline for coordinating starts and stops of various projects and programs.
3. Surveillance of work progress toward completion.
4. Signaling to a variety of groups when they are to start coordinating their actions toward a coordinated completion.
5. Forming the basis of a negotiated agreement on how resources will be deployed to organizationed programs.
6. Less dependence on personal relationship and "politics" and more on formal organizational links to gain commitments.
7. Reduced costs because time-cost functions are made formal.
8. Enhanced managerial worth, since the greatest measure of management is achieving a project within cost and on time.

To achievement-oriented managers, time presents an opportunity to achieve their programs or objectives, but it also provides limitations that contrain them. Time flows at a uniform, constant speed, every minute like any other, yet to managers time seems uneven, fast, slow, depending on how a program is progressing. No question about it—a measure of effectiveness of managers is their ability to manage time to get the job done within the limited time committed to the program.

Scheduling may sound scientific, but much of it is an art. The strongest element in its discipline is common sense. However, certain skills can lead to efficient scheduling.

1. Ability to sense, predict, and forecast an accomplishment at a point in time.
2. Ability to perceive ends from beginnings, even with cold orientation.
3. Ability to see, relate, and pace constituent parts into a sequenced whole.
4. Ability to focus on the critical and separate the trivial.
5. Ability to analyze a mass of complexity into numbers and quantification.
6. Ability to measure deviation, variance, and drift from prescribed directions.
7. Ability to measure indicators of progress on a time spectrum.
8. Ability to feed back corrective actions to effective variables.
9. Ability to stimulate control within prescribed limits.
10. Ability to align, dovetail, and correlate two or more directions.
11. Ability to move ahead despite risk, uncertainty, and unknowns.

A great deal of judgment is required for good scheduling. The following guidelines may serve to develop a personal approach to scheduling.

1. *A Schedule Must Start with Well-Defined Objectives.*   A schedule is a plan-ahead process with a series of deliberate phases, events, and work processes from start to finish. The objectives provide the perspective for setting and structuring the schedule. All the details in the schedule are timed for start and finish in order to coordinate the interrelationship of these details with the clock and calendar to accomplishing the objective. Therefore, objectives must be formally stated in terms of results, quantified for measurement purposes, given the time requirements intended to cover a single-ended result, clearly stated to indicate the resources and facilities needed for completion.

2. *A Schedule Must Be a Combination of Backward and Forward Planning.*   Backward scheduling starts with a deadline and calculates the events necessary to reach the deadline. Forward scheduling starts with present time and calculates the events necessary to complete the project as soon as possible. Both have delivery dates. In the backward method the "customer" dictates delivery. In the forward method the events, resource allocations, or work processes dictate delivery. Good schedul-

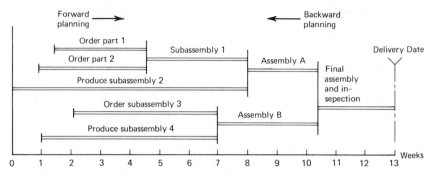

Figure 11.7   Good scheduling requires backward and forward planning.

ing requires a combination of the two (see Figure 11.7). Although the "customer" may not dictate, he should always be kept in mind.

3. *A Schedule Must Provide Readouts for Real-Time Reporting.*   After-the-fact information helps only in future actions. It cannot control present activities. Real-time reporting means that progress variances must be identified and given to the manager in sufficient time to make a useful correction before the target deadline. It may require day-to-day, week-to-week, or month-to-month surveillance. Real-time reporting puts the manager in position to make changes in the work processes or resource allocation in order to meet deadlines. Real-time reporting is infused into the schedule with the inclusion of the "now" time-baseline (see Figure 11.8).

4. *A Schedule Must "Play The Clock" with All Critical Items.*   A schedule has "pace" as a theme. This means that work elements are arranged in a sequential process under a time tension. It is not practical to include all items in a schedule. However, all critical items, especially those with short lead times, must be included to signal the start and finish of less

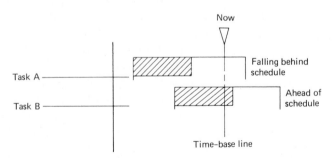

Figure 11.8   Good scheduling requires "now" time-baseline.

significant items in the program. A schedule may include work phases, work centers, work packages, cost centers, machines, departments, workers, orders, operations, and assemblies. Efficient managers know their entire performance is pitted against time. They have no choice but to "run the race." They can only assure that critical results are accomplished as they "run" along.

5. *A Schedule Must Give Overview of Progress at a Glance.* An overview of the entire program, graphically displayed, gives a manager the whole picture of progress at a glance. But more than this, variances between progress expected and progress experienced can flag the manager to give special attention. Thus, status reporting on a schedule that has benchmarks where start and finish commitments are related to milestones of progress puts the manager "in control" of the program. These benchmarks can be performance standards or expected productivity levels as measured by the productivity index (see Figure 11.9). Setting these benchmarks for milestones of progress gives the manager a guide for spotting "on-schedule," "off-schedule," "falling down on productivity," or "ahead of expected productivity." Progress on the overall program as it works toward an objective can be noted at a glance.

6. *A Schedule Must Follow "Progressive" Planning.* In the past fixed time schedules were undisturbed until the work was completed. Today flexible time schedules are the only workable kind. Conditions that may have a major impact on the completion of a program or project are changing continuously. The scheduler should be prepared and willing to take a "progressive" attitude and revise schedules when a change is indicated. Progressive planning as a technique for flexible schedules requires short-range results in the context of long-range expectancies. Suppose the short-range was one year and the long range five years. In progressive planning this means that at the end of the first year, when short-range results are evaluated, long-range expectancies are revised

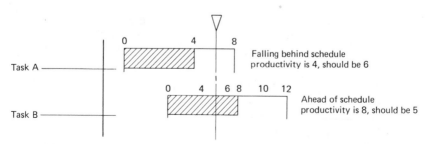

Figure 11.9 Productivity performance as benchmarks in a schedule.

in terms of this evaluation. At the end of the second year, short-range results are evaluated, and long range expectancies are revised accordingly. This process continues each year.

7. *A Schedule Must Be Analyzed For "Potential Failure" Points.* Many indicators are "potential failure" points for rendering a schedule useless. The scheduler should be alert to these indicators:

(a) Confused work allocations or fuzzing loading.

(b) Incorrect and unreliable information for developing a schedule.

(c) Loading a schedule without coordinating with other schedules and consulting with those who will implement the schedule.

(d) Contingencies not built in for flexibility.

(e) Results expected by the scheduler not measurable.

(f) Control points not set in for its implementation.

(g) Analysis of what could go wrong not made.

(h) Too high risk and impossible dates.

(i) Oversimplified schedule that ignores complexity.

Gantt Productivity Schedules: What they are; How They're Constructed.[5]

A Gantt productivity schedule is a visual graph of the work activities plotted as bars on a linear time line that is scaled with productivity measures. Usually the work activities or programs are indicated vertically, and future time is shown horizontally. Work activities are the variables— that is, the scheduler can increase or decrease them in terms of the project needs. Time is the constant—that is, work is pitted against an even, uniform flow of time increments that does not change. Time divisions can be hours, days, months, weeks, or years. Productivity measures are plotted along the time line to give standards that must be met in a completed work package. The productivity index is used as this measure. Typical symbols and descriptions used in developing Gantt schedules are shown in Figure 11.10.

The Gantt productivity schedule is easy to construct and understand. The graphical display presents, at a glance, the total project on a time grid with time and productivity standards.

It shows the estimated time each phase will take for completion and the work that has been accomplished thus far. The Gantt productivity

Term	Symbol	Comments
Gantt		Henry L Gantt, originator of the scheduling technique in 1916
Inverted L left-hand	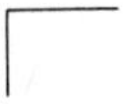 ⌐	Start of a planned work activity
Inverted L right-hand	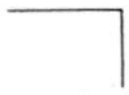 ⌐	End of a planned work activity
Bar	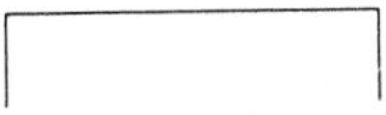 ⌐_____⌐	Line connecting two inverted L's-estimated time for a complete work activity
Carot	 ▽	Indicates present date on time scale
Bar with half crosshatching	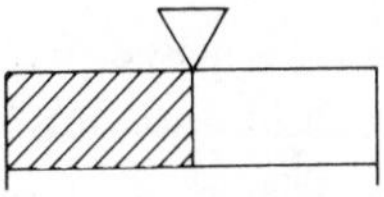 ▽ ▨	Work activity half completed at the present date
Bar with full crosshatching	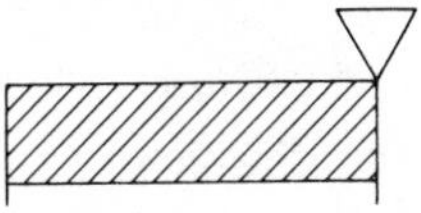 ▽ ▨	Work activity fully completed at the present date
Bar with a productivity index scale, partially crosshatched	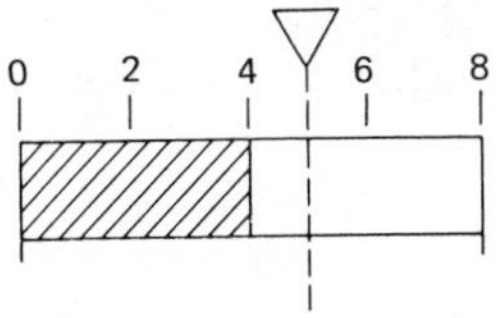 ▽ 0 2 4 6 8 ▨	Work activity falling behind-productivity index is 4. It should be 5 at present time
Circle with letters	Ⓜ	Explanatory notes: In this case delay due to material (M) shortage
Long flat "X"	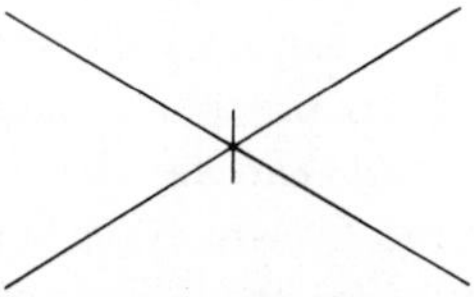 ✕	Reserved time for anticipated delays (contingency)

Figure 11.10   Gantt productivity definition of terms.

schedule is a moving picture of the work planned and the work completed. That is, work progress is seen from the time grid by noting the variances of the work from the "now" time line. There isn't a great deal of detail in the Gantt productivity schedule because it is intended as an overview of how the project or program is planned, the sequences of its activity, and the work progress to date. From this standpoint, the schedule facilitates communications and coordination among many groups in the programs and projects. To develop a Gantt productivity schedule the following steps are suggested:

1. List the work packages or work phases needed to complete the entire project.
2. Arrange the list in a sequence of how the work packages will actually be completed from start to finish.
3. Estimate the amount of time for each work package.
4. Estimate the productivity expected for each work package. Use the productivity index.
5. Using forward scheduling, plot each work package on a time grid as a bar indicating when each are started and finished.
6. Project on the time grid any special requirement such as overtime or contingency for delays.
7. Indicate with a carot the date in which work progress is to be reported.
8. Identify in each work package the degree of work completion—that is, the variance with the now time line. Draw a progress line or crosshatch. This line shows actual progress to date.
9. Project on the schedule a note when a work package is falling behind and corrective action is to be taken.

The steps for developing a Gantt productivity schedule are illustrated in Figure 11.11.

The Gantt productivity schedule can be quantified to give a percentage completion approach for controlled targeting. "How much" is just as essential as "when accomplished." This requires calculating a ratio of work packages to be completed which gives the percentage of the project or program completed. A table or curve can be developed to serve as a reference to the amount of lead time by which each work package must precede final completion. A cumulative frequency distribution is developed that gives a measure of rise or fall in relation to a total. The productivity scheduler will find an effective visual display of reporting progress of actual work and productivity relative to expected work and expected productivity. These scheduling ideas are illustrated in the following example (also see Figure 11.12).

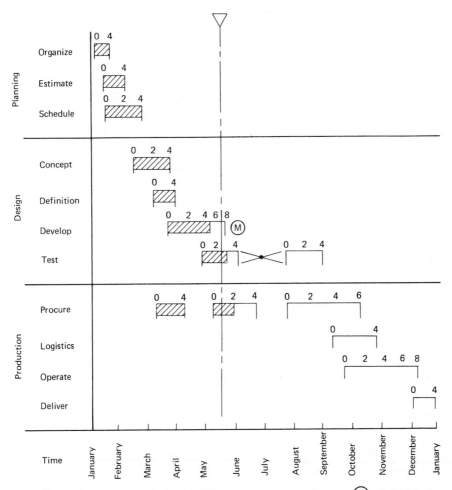

Figure 11.11 Gantt productivity schedule. *Note*: **Manpower shortage (M). Completed in one week. Productivity is 5.2, should be 7.**

EXAMPLE

A program contains 90 work packages to be completed by five staff members within 7 months. Halfway through the program, 30 work packages were completed. Determine the percentage completion and percentage productivity at the halfway mark. Show actual progress relative to scheduled progress in a cummulating productivity progress chart (see Figure 11.13).

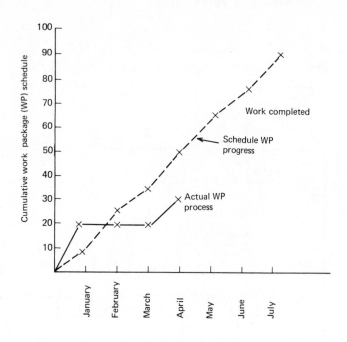

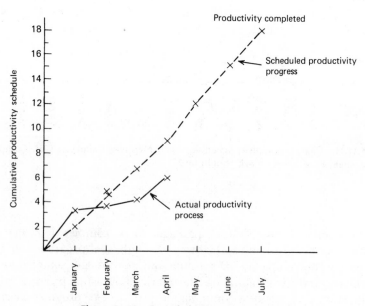

Figure 11.12 Cumulative progress charting.

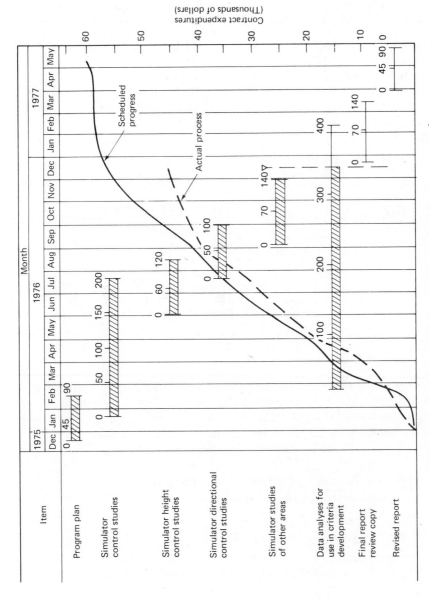

Figure 11.13 Cost accomplishment progress schedule: a case example.

The Planned Schedule

Time	Work Package Schedule	Cumulative Work Package Schedule	Percent Cumulative Work Package Schedule	Productivity Schedule	Cumulative Productivity Schedule
January	10	10	11.1	2.0	2.0
February	12	22	24.1	2.4	4.4
March	14	36	40.0	2.8	7.2
Midway April	13	49	54.4	2.6	9.8
May	14	63	70.0	2.8	12.6
June	12	75	83.3	2.4	15.0
July	15	90	100.0	3.0	18.0
Total	90			18.0	

$$\text{Percent work completed} = \frac{\text{work package completed}}{\text{total work packages}} \times 100$$

$$= \frac{30}{90} \times 100 = 33.3$$

$$\text{Percent work completed} = \frac{\text{productivity completed}}{\text{productivity expected}} \times 100$$

$$= \frac{30/5}{9.8} \times 100 = 61.2$$

Schedules are inevitably affected by changes. In addition, information at the time of scheduling is usually partial and imperfect, so schedules must be changed when this information is complete and precise. There should be no hesitancy to change schedules if it is to be a realistic control tool. Advantages to Gantt productivity schedules are as follows:

1. Easy to understand for people outside the program.
2. Gives an overview of the entire program.
3. Easy to construct. Takes little time.
4. Status readouts give sense of work progress and productivity achievements.
5. Requires very little space compared to amount of information given.

6. Changes in the form of corrections or improvements can be acted upon with ease and dispatch.

PERT Schedules for Time Control of Complex Programs

A time-control technique that has gained wide acceptability as a network scheduling device and a network for scheduling nonrecurring projects or programs is called PERT (Program Evaluation Review Technique). Like Gantt, PERT is a visual graph of the work activities and events spread out in a network to show clearly the interrelations between and among the work packages. The concept deals with a range of planning and control problems of a nonrepetitive nature. Unlike Gantt, there are no linear time scales. Time is assigned and controlled within the work package itself. Overall time is computed to provide a sense of accomplishment through all work packages in a network. By definition:

> *PERT is a visual network that time-controls the individual work events and activities to give progress toward a deadline of completion.*

The purpose of PERT scheduling is to put a complex and uncertain plan on a structure and to analyze what is to be done, when is it to be done, and what is the probability of getting there. It permits a program manager to "play the clock" in such a way that a job is accomplished in the shortest period of time with well-organized resources and activities. Special definitions and symbols are described in Figure 11.14.

The Advantages in Using A PERT Schedule. PERT as a scheduling technique has several distinguishing characteristics which make it valuable for certain applications.

1. *Develops Planning and Controlling Skills for Program Management.* PERT skills provide a development of a logical discipline in the defining, planning, scheduling, and control of projects. Seventy-five percent of the value of PERT for a program managers is that it gives them a sense of mission, direction, start, finish, scope, interconnections, coordination, progress, and overview. It contributes greatly toward what is to be accomplished but not how it is to be accomplished. It helps to define and develop the program.

2. *Efficient For "One-Shot" Programs.* A PERT schedule gives a high degree of controlled targeting for one-of-a-kind programs that must meet deadlines. Repetitive programs usually have developed standards

Term	Symbol	Comments
PERT		Abbreviation for Program Evaluation and Review Technique.
Event	◯ ▢ ⬭	Events are shown as squares or circles and indicate what has gone before. Therefore, events are phrased in the past tense. Events are "checkpoints" and show that work has been accomplished up to this point.
Activity	5 →	Activity lines represent the work needed to accomplish an event. An event is completed when the activity is accomplished. No work can start on the next activity until the preceding event is completed. The activity lines are not scaled, but the numbers over the line indicate time required.
Network (sequential flow diagram)	⬦	A web of events and activities with one starting event and one objective event.
Time estimates		Discussed more fully in text.
Optimistic time	t_o	There is very little chance that the activity can be done in less time than t_o.
Most likely time	t_m	The best guess of the time required. If only one time were available, this would be it. This is the "mode" of the distribution.
Pessimistic time	t_p	There is little chance that the task would take longer than t_p.
Expected time	t_e	There is a 50% probability that the activity completed will take less time—and 50% probability, of course, that it will take more time. $$t_e = \left[\frac{t_o + 4t_m + t_p}{6}\right]$$

Earliest expected time	T_e	The summation of all times, t_e, up to an event, staying with a single path from start to finish. When two paths lead to an event, use the one with the greatest time. For example:

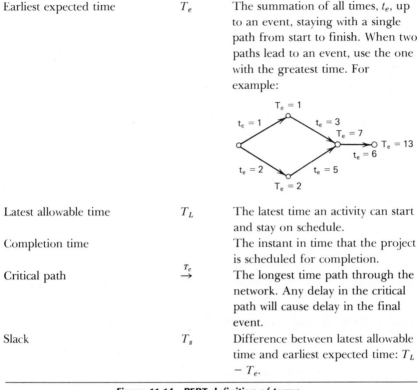

Latest allowable time	T_L	The latest time an activity can start and stay on schedule.
Completion time		The instant in time that the project is scheduled for completion.
Critical path	$\xrightarrow{T_c}$	The longest time path through the network. Any delay in the critical path will cause delay in the final event.
Slack	T_s	Difference between latest allowable time and earliest expected time: $T_L - T_e$.

Figure 11.14 PERT definition of terms.

for which case Gantt schedules are more efficient. PERT is superior to Gantt when standards are not available and only estimates are available.

3. *Program or Project "At a Glance" Communicates Interrelations.* The network approach for connecting and interconnecting events and activities not only gives the overview of the project but the relationships in terms of input and output of all participating groups. In addition, the network services do monitor or control the work program as it proceeds to its destination. The overview shows the best possible use of resources to achieve a goal within overall time and cost. It provides a means of documenting and communicating to all groups the commitments of time and cost performance.

4. *Schedule Can Be Structured in Spite of Uncertainties.* A schedule is no better than the information used for its development. When information is uncertain, schedules are weak. PERT allows for dealing with

uncertainties so that risk factors are identified and carefully watched. Each PERT schedule has a probability factor for reaching a deadline.

5. *PERT Schedule Provides Control Where It Is Critical.* In each PERT schedule the work package that is significant to the project is identified as the critical path. This identification allows special surveillance and control for the scheduler and program manager. The critical element of the plan, usually 20 to 30 percent of the project, is brought into focus as it constrains the whole project. Potential trouble spots can be also identified through simulation and network manipulation. Debugging is made easier because program errors are visible.

6. *Innumerable Complex Number of Parts are Planned on an Orderly Basis.* PERT is efficient for handling large numbers of detailed events that must be brought together at the right time to produce an extremely complex project or product. Concept, development, design, procurement test and assembly of projects where work-time execution is critical are handled in an orderly and consistent basis by PERT. PERT allows preplanning of involved work packages that can "signal" early a special action that should be taken by the manager.

How to PERT a Project or Program. PERTing a project or plan consists of five steps: (1) Define the work to be done for the entire project; (2) use backward planning and sequence the work definition from finish to start; (3) sequence into a network on a flow chart; (4) assign time estimates for each major activity or milestone of progress in the network: (5) calculate the risk factor for meeting the deadlines.

Step 1. Define the Work To Be Done for the Entire Project. Work should be thought of as a "package" that is made up of an event with its associated activity. This could also mean an objective, with its action plan, or an end item, with its tasks, or a phase, with its processes. All events are paths leading to the terminating event. Defining the work is the first step in a PERT network. The most important analytical tool for definition of work is "work breakdown structure." It is a planning tool for linking objectives with resources in a framework in which other planning activities can be correlated. The work breakdown concept is a logical separation into related units of the total work required to do a job or reach an objective. It breaks the work down into logical divisions and subdivisions. Work breakdown structure is in principle an expanded definition of work into logical subunits. The concept of work breakdown into levels with logical divisions and subdivisions is not new to the average person. It is part and parcel of our whole way of life. Many examples come to mind that illustrate this grouping into logical functions, departments, and branches. The organization chart is a graphic display of the division of labor, showing how work is grouped by specialties and hierarchy levels. A book such as this one, or a dictionary, or the Bible, is divided into smaller and smaller sections: chapters, sections, paragraphs, sentences, and words. These subordinate parts are tied logically into a framework to give meaning to the whole. Geographical location has the following breakdown structure: country, state, town, street, and number. The finished automobile is another illustration of work breakdown; we can trace engine level, carburetor level in the engine, float level in the carburetor, and aluminum material level of the float, each level depicting, respectively, an assembly, a subassembly, a component, a part, and a new material. The manufacturing process offers another example of grouping by levels and functions: (1) concept feasibility and design level create the product; (2) development, test, and feasibility checkout assure the product concept; (3) process planning, material ordering, and production control set the stage for hardware; (4) implementing and operating produce the hardware; (5) packaging, shipping, and distributing get the product into the hands of the consumer. From initial concept to consumer utilization, work breakdown provides a logical framework of divisions from system to subsystem, through task, subtask, level 1, level 2, level 3, and so on.

The following chart structures in Figures 11.15–11.18 are examples of

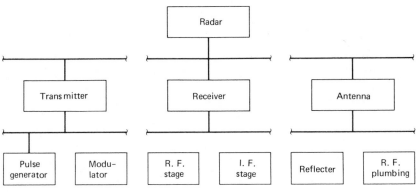

Figure 11.15 Hardware breakdown structure.

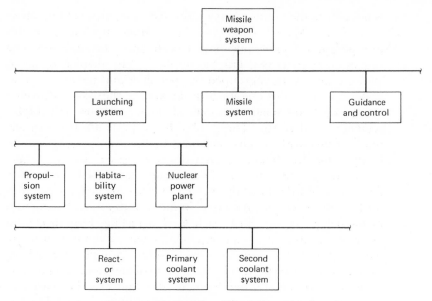

Figure 11.16 Functional breakdown structure.

four general types of work breakdown structures: Hardware breakdown structure, functional breakdown structure, process breakdown structure, and questioning breakdown structure, give a number of important uses to a project or a program manager. These uses are:

1. Overview of the work is provided for the work team.
2. Structure of the work shows how the work packages are logically divided into work units and how they are different from one another.

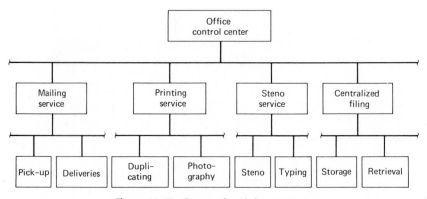

Figure 11.17 Process breakdown structure.

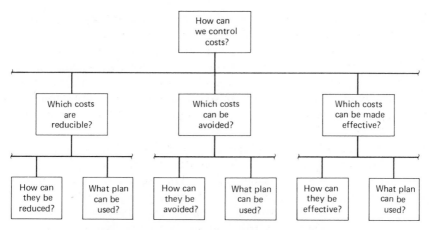

Figure 11.18 Questioning breakdown structure.

3. Definition of the work reveals omissions and overlapping.
4. Focus of the work is make in pyramid fashion toward an objective.
5. The number of work packages gives clarity, definition, and scope of the work of the total project.
6. Levels of the work provide the basis for a time schedule.
7. Each work package contains a clear indication of the objective to be achieved; its measurability, starting point, and ending time; and estimated cost and accountability.

The use of the concept of work breakdown as a scheduling procedure starts with the objective to be reached. The practitioner relates all elements of the breakdown structure to this objective. He begins the breakdown by identifying the total effort required at the top level to support the objectives. The second level contains work that must be completed to support the first level. The third level contains more detail and a finer division of the work necessary to support the second level. This work breakdown continues until the last level of work that can be delegated is identified. The subdivisions of the work at each level are verified by examining the whole to be sure that the whole equals the sum of its parts. The subdivisions under a particular item must define completely all considerations making up that item.

Alternate to Step 1. Sequencing input/output modules. An alternate to work breakdown structure for work definition is using the concept of input/output modules in a tandem flow. A module is a complete work package but conveys the idea that the completion of the package feeds into an overall plan of work. When connected, the supply of individual modules "flows" or "adds" to form a total contribution. But more than this, a view of work packages for measuring productivity emerges since productivity is the ratio of output to input. When total work can be seen as a series of connected work packages, a clarity of work definition and productivity emerges. Using the missile weapon system application cited earlier, the total work flow using input/output modules is illustrated in Figure 11.19.

Step 2. Sequence the Work Packages on a Time Grid.   Each unit of a work breakdown structure can be considered as making up one or more events with an associated activity. The event is the end item to be accomplished at a recognizable point in time. If each subunit of a work breakdown structure can be regarded as an event, the structure contains starting events, terminating events, interface events, and feeder events. All events are milestones connected along paths leading to a terminating event which is the ultimate completion of the work. Events and activities are symbolically shown in the table of symbols. Circles are events, and arrows are their supporting activities. Figure 11.20 shows how events are connected on a start-finish grid. Since events are end items, they take up no time, money, or resources in themselves. Activities, however, require time, money, and resources. Sequencing event activities on a time grid sets the stage for flow charting.

Suppose a market research program is to be the first step in the development of a new product. Event 1 would be described as marketing research begun; event 2 would be described as finished

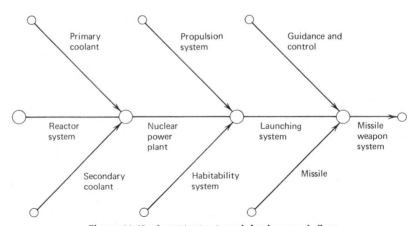

Figure 11.19   Input/output modules in a work flow.

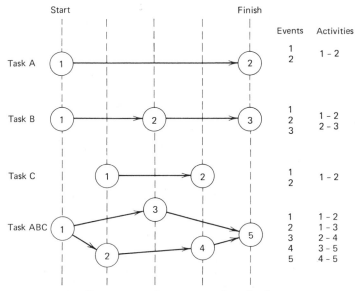

Figure 11.20   PERT sequencing of tasks.

market research. The arrow between these two events is described as the activity necessary to conduct market research. Task A is seen as two events and one activity; task B is seen as three events and two activities; task C is seen as two events and one activity, but shifted in time phase; task ABC integrates all events with their time phases. Task ABC ties together all items that must reach the terminal event 5. Event sequences and priorities of the original tasks have been changed and shifted when integrated in the task ABC network. As described earlier, development of a new product in the network may now require in addition to market research, a production status analysis, an engineering feasibility study, and a state-of-the-art technological forecast.

The work breakdown structure can be a useful tool for sequencing and interrelating the work packages. By rotating the structure 90 degrees clockwise, placing it on a time grid, and shift the events forward or backward, the stage is set for flow charting into a network. This is illustrated in Figure 11.21.

Step 3. Flow Chart Sequence into a PERT Network. The term *network* indicates that several events and activities are combined in such a way that input-output relationships lead to an ultimate end. There are no formulas that provide a precise and logical series of steps

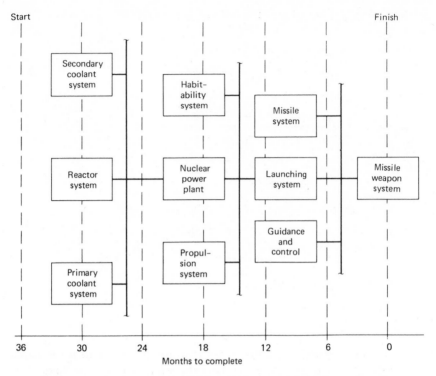

Figure 11.21   Setting work breakdown structure rotated 90° to a time grid.

leading to an excellent and foolproof network. There is an art and skill to developing meaningful networks. The following are some suggested guidelines:

1. The network should be developed by the individuals familiar with and committed to the objectives and requirements of the program.
2. The work breakdown structure, which includes the logical sequence of end items and activities, must be agreed upon by those developing the network.
3. The development of the network should start with the ultimate targeted objective and move backward to the beginning event. The end objective is constantly and clearly in view, and the network is developed in direct relation to it.
4. As the network is developed, the question is asked about each end item. What activities must be completed before this event is completed?

5. An activity cannot begin until an event or end item preceding it has been completed.

6. Wherever possible, two or more end items and associated activities that can be accomplished concurrently should be set up in parallel paths. This allows a high degree of delegation because of the related parallel efforts.

7. A critical path should be identified to discover the longest time it will take to accomplish end items and their associated activities. It's critical because there is little time to do many things. Increased paralleling will decrease critical path time. Increased sequencing will increase critical path time.

8. A slack path should be identified to discover the shortest time it will take to accomplish end items and their associated activities. It's slack because there is a great deal of time to do the few things. Decreased paralleling will increase slack path time. Decreased sequencing will decrease slack path time.

9. When an event or an end item keeps two or more activities from starting, there is an even constraint. This event should be broken down into smaller end items.

10. When two or more activities hold back the completion of an end item, there is an activity constraint. The activities should be combined to lead to the end item.

An illustration of the development of a network is shown in Figure 11.22.

Step 4. Assign Time-Estimates for Each Activity in the Network. Once the tasks to be performed have been developed into a PERT network, it is necessary to establish some definite schedule of when each end item will be completed and the approximate date each activity will be started. By including a schedule as a part of the program for

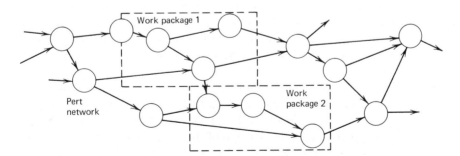

Figure 11.22 Work packages in a PERT network.

implementation, the PERT plan not only helps keep actions in the proper phase, but it also sets target dates for those who are assigned the responsibility for completion. These target dates will go a long way toward ensuring that committed individuals execute their work before others commence theirs. This automatically forces coordination in starting and completing activities among several committed individuals. Time is clearly the basic variable in the PERT network since it measures how long parts of the project will take. PERT time is expressed in days or weeks and is estimated on a probability projection of most likely time (t_m), most optimistic time (t_o), and most pessimistic time (t_p). Most likely time is an estimate of the normal time an activity would take if the same activity were repeated an independent number of times under identical conditions. It coincides with the central interval of a probability distribution curve encompassing 68 percent of the area on each side of the arithmetic mean. This is illustrated in Figure 11.23. The most likely time is the time estimate at the mean. The most optimistic time indicates work completed under better than normal conditions. It is an estimate of the minimum time an activity will take if unusually good circumstances and favorable conditions are experienced. It coincides with the interval segment of the probability distribution curve encompassing approximately 16 percent of the area to the left of the first standard deviation. The most pessimistic time concerns work completed under conditions that are less favorable than normal. It is an estimate of the maximum time an activity will take if unusually bad circumstances and unfavorable conditions are experienced. It coincides with the interval segment of the probability distribution curve encompassing approximately 16 percent of the area to the right of the first standard deviation. An estimate of expected time, considering the effects of favorable and unfavorable conditions, can be calculated with the formula for expected time (t_e), as shown in Figure 11.23. Time estimates in a PERT network can now be assigned in terms of most likely time (t_m), most pessimistic time (t_p), most optimistic time (t_o), expected time (t_e), and the variance (t_e) measured in the calculation of expected time.

Step 5. Calculate the Risk Factor for Meeting Schedules. An opportunity to determine the probability of completing a project by a certain time is a unique feature of PERT. This probability is called the risk factor. It requires a knowledge of the mean time and variance for each activity. The accuracy of t_o, t_p, t_m will largely determine the shapes of the distribution curves (see Figure 11.24).

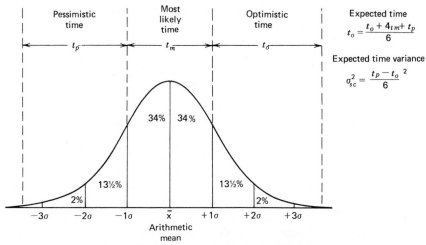

Figure 11.23 Estimating time for PERT activities.

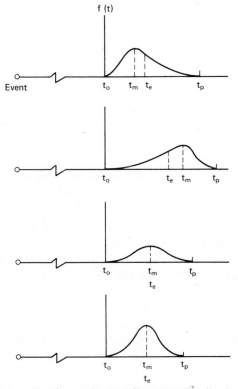

Figure 11.24 Time estimates effect PERT distributions.

In calculating the risk factor of a PERT network, the distribution is assumed to be unimodal, and the peak at t_m is substantially normal.

Once the three time estimates are obtained and assigned to activities of the PERT network, an analysis can be made of the total time requirement for the entire network to reach the terminal event. Each activity time of a specific event is cumulated along the paths of the network so that cumulated expected time and cumulated variance of expected time can be estimated for the objective to be reached. A PERT network that has several paths will obviously have different cumulated time estimates. Paths that have the longest cumulated time are called critical paths because the entire project or program will be held up because of them. Paths that have the shortest cumulated time are called slack paths because a great deal of slack time occurs in completing their chain of events. To estimate the probability of meeting the schedule of events or work packages in the completion of an objective, the critical path must be calculated. Time estimates from this path are used as a basis for entering the normal probability distribution tables. The following will illustrate this calculation.

EXAMPLE: DEVELOPING A PERT TIME NETWORK

A research lab has tentatively decided to construct a new lab facility in Florida. An objective—to complete this facility in 18 months—has been tentatively set. The management of the lab would like an estimate of the probability of completing the facility within the estimated period.

Step 1. Define the work packages with work breakdown structure (Figure 11.25).

Step 2. Sequence work packages on a time grid (rotate work breakdown structure 90° clockwise) (Figure 11.26).

Step 3. Flow chart sequence into a PERT network (Figure 11.27).

Step 4. Assign time estimates for each activity and calculate expected time (t_e), expected time variance (t_e^2) total earliest expected time (T_E), and latest total allowable time (T_L). Determine the slack ($t_L - T_E$).

A step-by-step calculation procedure is as follows:

Step 1. Estimate, on the basis of past data, the time required to complete each of the events and enter these estimates in three columns: t_o, t_m, t_p.

Step 2. Calculate, using the formula from Figure 11.23, expected time,

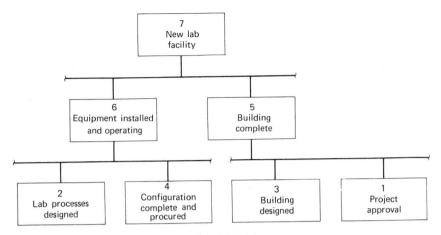

Figure 11.25

and expected time variance, and enter those values in two columns: t_e, $O_{t_e}^2$.

Step 3. Calculate for each branch total earliest expected time, which is the cumulation of t_e along a path, and enter those values in the column T_e. It should be noted that this results in three paths: 1-2-4-6-7; 1-2-4-5-7; 1-3-5-7. Since the path 1-2-4-5-7 has the longest expected time for completion, it is termed the critical path. Completion of the events in the longest time can hold up the entire program. It is the path of least slack time.

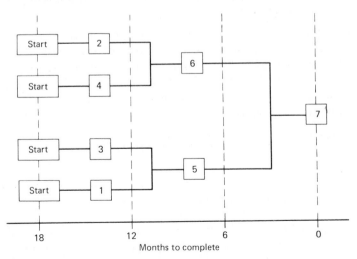

Figure 11.26

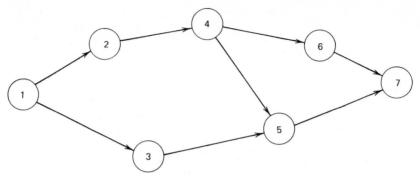

Figure 11.27

Step 4. Calculate, using the 18-month constraint, latest allowable time (T_1) by working backward through the paths. Tabulate this under column T_L. Latest allowable time (T_L), which represents the scheduled constraint of 18 months, is the maximum allowable time in which an event can be completed without affecting the completion of the network.

Step 5. Calculate slack time (S_L) by getting the difference between the latest allowable time (T_L) and the earliest expected time (T_E). The slack of each event and the branches are illustrated in the following flow chart. Critical path 1-2-4-5-7 has the least slack time because the cumulated slack time of events is at a minimum. Enter the values calculated in this procedure in the following table and flow chart (Figure 11.28).

Step 6. Calculate the Risk Factor for meeting schedule. A probability estimate of meeting the scheduled time of 18 months should be of major concern in the completion of the production facility. Low values of probability indicate the schedule is not feasible. High values indicate the schedule is feasible. The calculation of this probability is as follows:

$$\text{probability factor} \quad \text{PF} = \frac{T_L - T_E}{\sigma_{T_E}} = \frac{18 - 16}{1.48} \; 1.35 \; (\tfrac{1}{2} \text{ normal curve})$$

For PF = 1.35, estimated probability to meet schedule is .4115. For full normal distribution curve, .5000 + .9115 or 91.2 percent.

The standard deviation of the time activities (T_E) of the critical path is 1.48. This is determined by adding the variances $\sigma_{t_e}^2$ of critical path 1-2-4-5-6 and extracting the square root. The probability factor (PF) 1.35 is calculated. The area of the normal distribution curve is identified from

Event Number	PERT Events	Suc-cessor Events	Past Estimates				Calculations			Slack Time (S_L) $(T_L - T_E)$
			t_o	t_m	t_p	t_e	$\sigma_{t_e}^2$	T_E	T_L	
1	Project approval	2	1	2	9	3	1.28	3	5	2
		3	3	4	5	4	.112	4	8	4
2	Laboratory process designed	4	2	4	6	4	.448	7	9	2
3	Building designed	5	3	5	13	6	2.78	10	14	4
4	Configuration complete and procured	5	4	45	8	5	.448	12	14	4
		6	1	2	3	2	.112	9	15	6
5	Building completed	7	4	4	4	4	.0	14	18	2
6	Equipment installed and operable	7	2.5	3.0	3.5	3	.278	12	18	6
7	Laboratory facilities completed	—	—	—	—	—	—	—	—	—

Figure 11.28 Calculating the critical path in a schedule.

373

the figures of the table. This is .9115, interpreted as 91.2 percent. This means the probability of meeting the 18-months schedule for the completion of the new lab facility is 91.2 percent.

Probability of Meeting Schedules

PF	.00	.01	.02	.03	.04	.05	.06	.07	.08	.09
0.0	.0000	.0040	.0080	.0120	.0160	.0199	.0239	.0279	.0319	.0359
0.1	.0398	.0438	.0478	.0517	.0557	.0596	.0636	.0675	.0714	.0753
0.2	.0793	.0832	.0871	.0910	.0948	.0987	.1026	.1064	.1103	.1141
0.3	.1179	.1217	.1255	.1293	.1331	.1368	.1406	.1443	.1480	.1517
0.4	.1554	.1591	.1628	.1664	.1700	.1736	.1772	.1808	.1844	.1879
0.5	.1915	.1950	.1985	.2019	.2054	.2088	.2123	.2157	.2190	.2224
0.6	.2257	.2291	.2324	.2357	.2389	.2422	.2454	.2486	.2518	.2549
0.7	.2580	.2612	.2642	.2673	.2704	.2734	.2764	.2794	.2823	.2852
0.8	.2881	.2910	.2939	.2967	.2995	.3023	.3051	.3078	.3106	.3133
0.9	.3159	.3186	.3212	.3238	.3264	.3289	.3315	.3340	.3365	.3389
1.0	.3413	.3438	.3461	.3485	.3508	.3531	.3554	.3577	.3599	.3621
1.1	.3643	.3665	.3686	.3708	.3729	.3749	.3770	.3790	.3810	.3830
1.2	.3849	.3869	.3888	.3907	.3925	.3944	.3962	.3980	.3997	.4015
1.3	.4032	.4049	.4066	.4082	.4099	.4115	.4131	.4147	.4162	.4177
1.4	.4192	.4207	.4222	.4236	.4251	.4265	.4279	.4292	.4306	.4319
1.5	.4332	.4345	.4357	.4370	.4382	.4394	.4406	.4418	.4429	.4441
1.6	.4452	.4463	.4474	.4484	.4495	.4505	.4515	.4525	.4535	.4545
1.7	.4554	.4564	.4573	.4582	.4591	.4599	.4608	.4616	.4625	.4633
1.8	.4641	.4649	.4656	.4664	.4671	.4678	.4686	.4693	.4699	.4706
1.9	.4713	.4719	.4726	.4732	.4738	.4744	.4750	.4756	.4761	.4767
2.0	.4772	.4778	.4783	.4788	.4793	.4798	.4803	.4808	.4812	.4817
2.1	.4821	.4826	.4830	.4834	.4838	.4842	.4846	.4850	.4854	.4857
2.2	.4861	.4864	.4868	.4871	.4875	.4878	.4881	.4884	.4887	.4890
2.3	.4893	.4896	.4898	.4901	.4904	.4906	.4909	.4911	.4913	.4916
2.4	.4918	.4920	.4922	.4925	.4927	.4929	.4931	.4932	.4934	.4936
2.5	.4938	.4940	.4941	.4943	.4945	.4946	.4948	.4949	.4951	.4952
2.6	.4953	.4955	.4956	.4957	.4959	.4960	.4961	.4962	.4963	.4964
2.7	.4965	.4966	.4967	.4968	.4969	.4970	.4971	.4972	.4973	.4974
2.8	.4974	.4975	.4976	.4977	.4977	.4978	.4979	.4979	.4980	.4981
2.9	.4981	.4982	.4982	.4983	.4984	.4984	.4985	.4985	.4986	.4986
3.0	.49865	.4987	.4987	.4988	.4988	.4989	.4989	.4989	.4990	.4990
4.0	.4999683									

PERT/Cost Time Schedules. PERT/cost is an extension of PERT/time. PERT network surveils times as PERT/cost network surveils costs. A PERT network becomes the basis of analyzing cost alternatives for deciding the best plan of action. PERT/cost analysis develops time-options to find the best mix of time and cost for the project or program. The traditional approach follows a single line cost estimate for each work package, but this prevents a study of noting the amount of time that could be saved if more money were spent or, conversely, the amount of money that might be saved by extending completion deadlines. Research and experience has verified the inverse relationship between costs and time as shown in Figure 11.29.

The implementation of PERT/cost networks follows three general approaches.

1. *Single-Point Cost Estimates of Expected Actual Cost.* Estimates are made for the total direct costs of each work package. Indirect costs are added either to each work package or added to the total cost of the project.
2. *Three-Cost-Estimate of Expected Actual Cost.* Three estimates are made: C_p pessimistic cost estimate, C_o optimistic cost estimate, and C_L most likely cost estimate. The expected cost estimate formula combines the three.

$$C_e = \frac{C_p + 4\,C_L + C_o}{6}$$

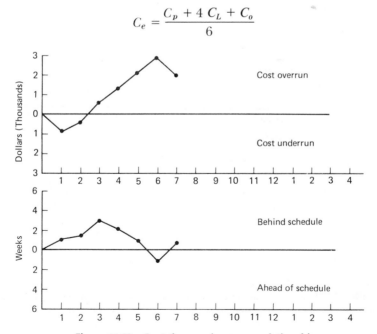

Figure 11.29   Cost-time performance relationship.

3. *Variable Estimates Based on a Known Cost Function.* Estimates are made from a time-cost curve. Differential costing with time is the variable. This approach assumes a direct relationship between time and cost.

An example of time-cost trade-offs is shown in Figure 11.30. Time-cost tradeoffs give the cost priority for reducing the project time. Several patterns suggest how much flexibility is possible in a tradeoff (see Figure 11.31). The program manager must determine which function may apply to his project.

PERT Productivity Time Schedules. PERT productivity is an extension of PERT time. PERT networks controls time; PERT cost networks control

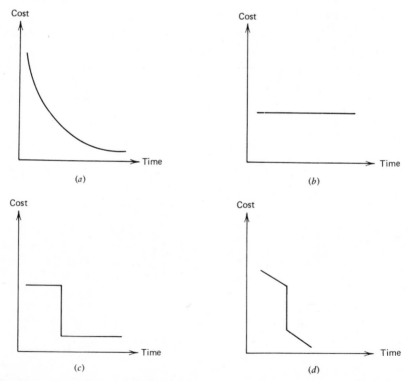

Figure 11.30   Cost-function trade-offs. (a) Marginal cost function. (b) Constant cost function. (c) Step-increase constant cost function. (d) Step-increase increasing cost function.

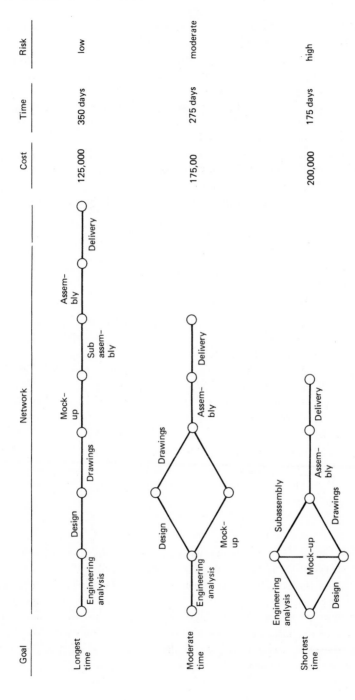

Goal	Network	Cost	Time	Risk
Longest time		125,000	350 days	low
Moderate time		175,00	275 days	moderate
Shortest time		200,000	175 days	high

Figure 11.31 Cost-time trade-offs.

costs with time and PERT productivity networks control productivity with time. A PERT productivity network becomes the basis of analyzing productivity alternatives for deciding the best plan of action. The analysis develops time options in order to find the best mix of time and productivity for a project or program. A PERT productivity network is developed to estimate the probable productivity within a probable delivery date. With that figure, decisions can be made to accept or trade off productivity with time or trade off time with productivity.

The previous example will be used to illustrate how PERT productivity schedules are developed. The latest allowable productivity for the program is 6.5. The expected productivity formula combines the three productivity estimates made of each work package. This formula is:

$$P_e = \frac{P_o + 4P_m + P_p}{6}$$

$$\sigma_{P_e}{}^2 = \left(\frac{P_p - P_o}{6}\right)^2$$

where P = productivity as estimated from the productivity index (PI)

P_e = expected productivity in the network

P_o = productivity when work package (wp) conditions are optimistic (PI = wp/t_o)

P_p = productivity when work package (wp) conditions are pessimistic (PI = wp/t_p)

P_m = most likely productivity (PI = wp/t_m)

$\sigma_{P_c}{}^2$ = expected productivity variance

P_E = total expected productivity

P_L = latest allowable productivity (6.5 for the entire program)

$P_L = P_E$ = slack productivity

Productivity figures for the previous example are now calculated. The results are showed in the followed table (Figure 11.32).

The critical path 1-2-4-6-7, where estimated slack is minimal, is the path that should be of major concern in the completion of the laboratory facilities design and construction. An option is always available to the manager who is to make the decision to trade off productivity with cost or time. Alternatives in this option would necessitate recalculations of alternate time and cost estimates.

Critical Ratio Scheduling for Developing Priorities

Program managers who are responsible for the completion and delivery of many programs that often conflict will find critical ratio scheduling a useful technique of resolving these time conflicts.[7] The scheduling technique attempts to organize, surveil, and control the priorities of the many programs that need to be completed.

What Critical Ratio Scheduling Is. Critical ratio relates the time relationship between service needs and the organization's capacity to supply these needs. The ratio is as follows:

$$\text{critical ratio (CR)} = \frac{\text{service demand time (DT)}}{\text{organization's supply time (ST)}}$$

$$\text{CR} = \frac{15 \text{ weeks}}{20 \text{ weeks}} = .75$$

The critical ratio indicates how fast or how slow a program should be completed in relation to normal time. In the above example the program should be accelerated and completed in three quarters of the normal time. When this program and its critical ratio is compared to other programs and their critical ratios, a sense of priorities is established. Priorities are determined primarily by the customer. Critical ratio is useful for the following reasons:

1. *Gives Overview of Relative Priorities of Several Programs.* A matrix can be set up that provides the relative priorities of the respective programs at a given date. At that date all programs are directly comparable regardless of when they are needed or why they will be completed.

	Reporting Dates			
Programs	January	February	March	April
A	1.26	1.25	1.25	1.25
B	1.00	1.00	0.75	0.50
C	1.50	1.50	1.50	1.50
D	2.00	2.00	2.00	2.00
E	0.50	0.75	1.00	1.00

In complex organizations these relative priorities signal places where special attention is needed and where resources are critically required.

Event Number	PERT Events	Successor Events	Work Packages	Productivity Estimates			Calculations				Slack Productivity
				P_o	P_M	P_p	P_e	σ_{Pe}^2	P_E	P_L	$(P_L - P_E)$
1	Specs and approval	2	8	8	4	.88	4.2	1.44	4.2	2.2	2.0
2	Lab processes designed	3	5	1.6	1.3	1	1.3	.01	1.3	.5	0.8
		4	4	2	1	.67	1.1	.05	5.3	3.3	2.0
3	Building designed	5	10	3.3	5	.77	4.0	.187	5.3	4.5	0.8
4	Configuration complete and processed	5	6	1.5	1.3	.75	1.2	.02	6.5	4.5	2.0
5	Building complete	6	2	2	1	.65	1.1	.05	6.4	5.8	0.6
		7	8	2	2	2	2	0	7.1	6.5	0.6
6	Equipment installed and operating	7	2	.8	.67	.57	.7	.001	7.3	6.5	0.8
7	Lab facilities completed	—	—	—	—	—	—	—	—	—	—

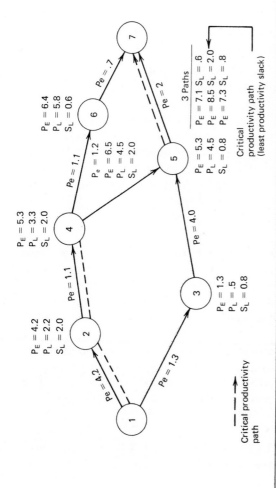

Figure 11.32 Calculating the Critical Productivity Path

2. *Senses Trends in Which a Delivery May Be Faulted.*   To trace through the reporting periods on a program matrix gives the drifts that may prevail for each program. Action may be required to change the drift:

> when CR = 1.00—program on time and delivery will be
> as expected

> when CR > 1.00—program ahead of schedule and delivery will be
> in advance

> when CR < 1.00—program behind schedule and delivery may be
> faulted (critical)

Note program B will be in trouble in March and April. Program E will improve by March and April. Spare capacity in other programs can be shifted to help Program B.

3. *Relates Service Demands with Capacity System.*   A procedure is created that relates the capacity to provide customer services with the time demands of the system. This procedure utilizes frequent feedback information of the demand and supply placed on the capacity system. Programs whose delivery demands are low are "set aside" for the critical programs to move faster. In this way a master schedule can be set up and made dynamic for the organization.

4. *How to Set up a Critical Ratio Schedule*

> *Step 1. Establish a centralized cost, or productivity center.*   This center records programs that arrived first and last. It identifies the oldest job based on start date and finish dates. It records and centralizes all information for program expediting. In most cases the productivity center is not a place, but the program manager.

> *Step 2. Formulize the capacity system.*   In complex organizations the functional groups are the operating resources that provide the capacity system. A master schedule should be set up to know, in general, *the total capacity available, and the capacity being utilized.* When the system is placed on a time grid, supply time readouts are readily available.

> *Step 3. Establish the critical ratio for the program.* Use the generalized formula for the supply-demand time relationship.

$$\text{critical ratio (CR)} = \frac{\text{date required} - \text{present date}}{\text{time required to complete job}} = \frac{\text{demand}}{\text{supply}}$$

> *Step 4. Establish program queues in tabular form.*   After calculating all critical ratios for the programs within a work center, sort and

display them in a tabular sequence as shown as follows. Arrange the sequence in a priority queue.

Program Productivity

Programs	Man-hours	Cumulative	Critical Ratio	Critical Programs
C	300	—	.55	*
A	250	550	.75	*
D	570	1120	1.00	
E	1300	2420	1.21	
B	450	2870	1.35	

Advantages in using the critical ratio scheduling approach for time management are as follows:

1. Gives status of a specific job relative to the capacity system.
2. Shows where the program manager should focus his or her attention.
3. Provides a basis for adjusting priorities.
4. Permits tracking program progress to completions.

Master Scheduling for Tracking Total Capacity

Most organizations are faced with scheduling many programs and projects that must utilize the same resources. Rarely are resources developed and used solely for one program or project. Management of several programs in the same time sequence with the same resources is the order of the day. No change in this practice seems likely in the near future.

What Master Scheduling Is. Master scheduling is a centralized scheduling concept that tracks the total capacity of the system and how the system is being utilized. It is especially useful when many items must be sequenced for accomplishment, and the capacity system is limited. Program work loads are apportioned so that individual work requirements are subordinated to a master scheduling program. Due dates for customer orders and completion times for delivery are critical in master scheduling formats.

Master scheduling procedures are developed within the conditions prevailing for a capacity system. There is no one "model" that fits the master scheduling needs of all organizations. Each organization must develop its own model. The following are some of the essentials that each model should contain:

1. *Sales or Service Demand Forecast.* This is a projection of the future work to be placed on the capacity system. The projection should be both short and long range over a variety of customers or those requiring service.
2. *Customer Completion or Delivery Service Requirements.* Customer demands or specific delivery service requirements must be made specific to a time baseline in a context of all programs and projects of the organization.
3. *Total Capacity of the System.* Total capacity in quantitative terms such as man-hours per month or productivity per month should be displayed on a time grid. This is illustrated in Figure 11.33. Spaces that are not used represent open capacity still available.
4. *Operating Department Capacities and Loads.* The effectiveness of a master schedule is directly related to how well surveillance can be conducted of the utilization of resource departments, how well "spare" capacity can be identified during different periods of time. An example of surveillance of total forecasted work in relation to available capacity is shown in the following table. One can see the value of master schedules when several departments are under surveillance.

			Forecasted Work					
Month	Week	Total Ca-pacity	Pro-gram A	Pro-gram B	Pro-gram C	Mis-cellan-eous Pro-grams	Total Fore-casted Work	Avail-able Capa-city
January	1	9600	1200	1000	500	200	2,900	6700
	2	9600	6500	3000	1000	500	11,000	(1400)
	3	9600	4600	3800	2500	1000	11,900	(2300)
	4	9600	5000	2500	1800	200	9,500	100
		38,400					35,300	3100

5. *Project Status Details That Indicate Action Needed.* A need develops from time to time in master scheduling practices to collect the status of several projects or programs. A project or program status board should be developed that lists the projects and programs on a time matrix. The status of each project or program is indicated on this same matrix for an overview. Action required to correct the status may also be

indicated on the status board. An example of this is shown in Figure 11.34.

MANAGING OVERTIME FOR PRODUCTIVITY

The much debated and often criticized organization practice of scheduling overtime is far from dead. It is so firmly entrenched into organizational scheduling practices that its critics have had no headway in dislodging it. One reason for this entrenchment is that overtime offers additional capacity to an organization without additional staff. There is, however, some serious question of the usefulness of overtime relative to productivity. There seems to be general agreement that the length and profile of the workweek influences productivity. There does not seem to be the same general agreement that extended hours of work give a proportionate increase in output.

Effects of Prolonged Overtime

I contend that overtime practices have a significant impact on productivity. After 40 hours, you may get as little as one hour real output for three work hours—at time and one-half or double time. In the process production may go up, but productivity drops significantly. Some production is gained, but at high cost. Here are some reasons why an organization may not be getting one hour's real output for the equivalent premium pay.

Adding Staff Causes Productivity to Decline. Parkinson, a notable economist, made a discovery that *work expands to fill the time available for its completion.*[8] He made considerable studies to show how staff (or man-hours) grows at the rate of 5.75 percent per year (5.17 to 6.56%) when no controls are instituted. This he discovered in cases where the final output actually decreased. According to him an organization will multiply in subordinates or expand in man-hours at a predetermined annual rate *regardless of the amount of work the staff actually turns out.* This is another way of viewing that an organization will cope with maintaining its production or output by adding staff. This process inevitably leads to reduced productivity. This important point was made in an earlier chapter. *Production is not productivity.* Unless there is careful control of resources, increased production could reduce productivity in the same proportion. Parkinson's law was developed while observing the increases in staff in numerous cases and revealed the finding that *irrespective of any*

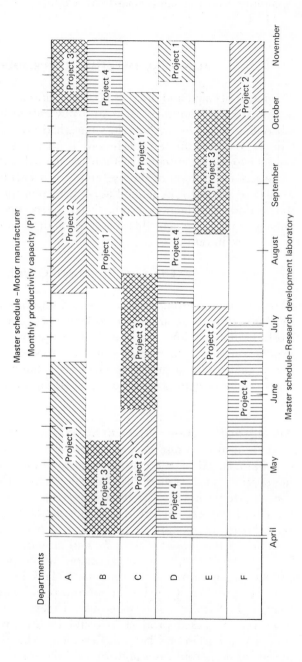

Master schedule –Motor manufacturer
Monthly productivity capacity (PI)

Master schedule– Research development laboratory

Master Schedule—Motor Manufacturer

	January	February	March	April	May	June	July	August	September	October	November	December
AC Model												
Units scheduled	500	400	500	400	400	400	500	400	500	400	400	400
Actual units	500	900	1,400	1,800	2,200	2,600	3,100	3,500	4,000	4,400	4,000	5,200
Monthly hours	6,000	5,000	6,000	5,000	5,000	5,000	6,000	5,000	6,000	5,000	5,000	5,000
Actual hours	6,000	11,000	17,000	22,000	27,000	22,000	38,000	43,000	49,000	54,000	59,000	64,000
DC Model												
Units scheduled	1,000	1,000	1,000	1,000	1,000	1,000	1,000	1,000	1,000	1,000	1,000	1,000
Actual units	1,000	2,000	3,000	4,000	5,000	6,000	7,000	8,000	9,000	10,000	11,000	12,000
Monthly hours	10,000	10,000	10,000	10,000	10,000	10,000	10,000	10,000	10,000	10,000	10,000	10,000
Actual hours	10,000	20,000	30,000	40,000	50,000	60,000	70,000	80,000	90,000	100,000	110,000	120,000
AC/DC Model												
Units scheduled	30	20	20	30	30	20	20	30	30	20	20	20
Actual units	30	50	70	100	130	150	170	200	230	250	270	290
Monthly hours	5,000	3,000	3,000	5,000	5,000	3,000	3,000	5,000	5,000	3,000	3,000	3,000
Actual hours	5,000	9,000	11,000	16,000	21,000	24,000	27,000	32,000	31,000	40,000	43,000	46,000
Total units	1,530	1,420	1,520	1,430	1,430	1,420	1,520	1,430	1,530	1,420	1,420	1,420
Total hours	21,000	18,000	19,000	20,000	20,000	18,000	19,000	20,000	21,000	18,000	18,000	18,000

Figure 11.33 Examples of master schedules.

Figure 11.34 Programs status board.

Programs		1976 J	F	M	A	M	J	J	A	S	O	N	D	1977 J	F	M	A	M	J	J	A	S
A	A		○																			
	T			○	○	○	○	○	○	○	○	○	○	○	○	○	○					
	S			○	○	○	○	●	●	●	†	†	*	*	●	●	○					
	Q			●	●	●	●	○	○	○	○	○	○	○	○	○	○					
	C			†	†	†	†	†	†	●	●	○	○	○	○	○	○					
	F			*	*	†	†	●	●	○	○	○	○	○	○	○	○					
B	A						○															
	T							○	○	○	○	○										
	S							○	●	●	○	○										
	Q							○	●	†	*	†										
	C							○	○	○	○	○										
	F							○	○	○	○	○										
C	A										†	●	●	○								
	T											○	†	†	●							
	S											●	●	○	○							
	Q											○	○	○	○							
	C											○	○	○	○							
	F											○	○	○	○							
D	A			†																		
	T			●	●																	
	S			*	*																	
	Q			○	○																	
	C			†	†																	
	F			†	†																	
E	A					○																
	T							○	○	○	○	●	●	●	●	○	○					
	S							†	†	*	*	*	*	*	†	†	●					
	Q							●	●	●	●	●	○	○	○	○	○					
	C							○	○	○	○	○	○	○	○	○	○					
	F							○	○	○	○	○	○	○	○	○	○					

A = Program plan approved
T = Technical status
S = Schedule status
Q = Quality status
C = Cost status
F = Funding status

○ = Work OK
● = Work OK but be alert
     to conditions that
     could cause trouble.
† = Warning, action needed
     to avert trouble.
* = In trouble-out of
     control.

variation of work (if any) to be done, staff or man-hours will increase approximately 5.75 percent per year unless controls are instituted. This implies that productivity declines in the same proportion. *The task to be done swells and expands in importance and complexity in a direct ratio to the time spent in much the same* way as a long-range runner after long practice who maintains a speed rate gauged to the distance he has to run and the amount of time available to do it. The validity of Parkinson's proof rests mainly on statistical data based on two axiomatic statements:

1. Supervisors prefer to increase subordinates rather than rivals (seeking promotion and advancement through appointment of subordinates).

2. Supervisors make work for others.

Parkinson's law is $NS = \dfrac{2K^m + L}{N}$

where NS = number of new staff required each year (number of subordinates or additional manhours)

     K = number of supervisors seeking promotion and advancement

     M = number of man-hours devoted to each subordinate for answering question within the department

     L = difference between ages of appointment and retirement

     N = number of groups being supervised

An example will show how productivity decreases with the addition of staff. The reader should bear in mind that Parkinson's law is valid when no controls are imposed to work against it. Obviously, the law will not apply when controls are instituted.

EXAMPLE:STAFF GROWTH WHEN NO CONTROLS EXIST

Three departments, each with a supervisor who has on the average 10 years to retire, give to their subordinates 20 minutes per day personal time. Each supervisor is expected to complete his assigned 30 work packages within the week with only 12 people. Estimate the number of subordinates who will be added annually if no controls are instituted. What will be the productivity index (PI) at the end of two years if the staff is added with no change in assigned work packages?

SOLUTION

$$NS = \frac{2K^m + L}{N} = \frac{2(3)^{1/3} + 10}{3} = \frac{2(1.4) + 10}{3} = 4.3$$

$$\text{PI (first year)} = \frac{\text{work packages}}{\text{staff}} = \frac{90}{36} = 2.50$$

$$\text{PI (second year)} = \frac{\text{work packages}}{\text{new staff}} = \frac{90}{44.3} = 2.03$$

Human Efficiency Drops With Longer Workhours. M. D. Kossoris, Regional Director of the United States Department of Labor, Bureau of Labor Statistics, made a comprehensive study of the effects of working overtime on productivity efficiency.[9] His studies have consistently verified those of the British on the effects of overtime on productivity. He attempted to answer questions such as: Where do you get the maximum rate of output for the number of hours worked? Is there a change in efficiency when the work is increased from 40 to 48 hours? How are absenteeism and labor turnout affected by longer daily and weekly hours? His findings can be summarized as follows:

1. There is *no ideal workweek* that would fit every organization. It depends on degree of mechanization, physical effort needed, and worker control over speed of operation.

2. You don't lose much efficiency in the short run when you go from 40 hours per week to 48. With a 20% increase in the workweek, you will raise output 18% to 19% on the average.

3. After 48 hours, *look out!* True, you may get more production. But at what cost? You may get as little as one hour's output for 3½ hours of pay (at time-and-a-half).

4. Beyond 58 hours, *efficiency slumps sharply.* Over the long pull, you'll get as much total production in 48 hours as in 66.

5. If you're thinking about a 7-day workweek, *forget it!* Even supermen go stale without some time off. Upshot: You'll pay double time for the seventh day, and the *workers will be put out on straight-time days.* In one plant, a cutback to 6 days actually increased total production 12%.

6. As the manpower bottleneck closes in, *absenteeism will jump,* especially on the sixth day of the workweek. That's a big problem, but there's plenty you can do to control it.

7. *Injuries* will go up, too, because longer hours mean greater *fatigue.* So watch the injury curve.

8. That soft-drink slogan, "The pause that refreshes," isn't an advertising man's hallucination. Organized rest periods, with proper snacks and soft drinks for a quick pick-up, conserve energy.

Burtt has conducted extensive experiments in measuring industrial fatigue by collecting figures on amount of output, errors, steadiness of reduction over long periods of time, accidents during work, illness, complaints, and turnover.[10] The data that has been collected in these studies were compiled into a work curve as indicated in Figure 11.35.

Chiselli and Brown have investigated and shown quantitively the drop in productivity as the work day was lengthened (see Figure 11.36).[11]

These show relative productions during various hours of the day for light and heavy work. Notice in Figure 11.36 that *fatigue* is more pronounced with heavy handwork than with light beyond the 8-hour normal day.

Workweek Patterns Affect Optimum Performance.   Fuller conducted a 2-year study to establish general patterns of deterioration when overtime is prolonged.[12] He attempted to answer this question: *"Can we expect from overtime the same performance hour to hour that we get from straight time?"* He answered the question by establishing standards of performance based on his experience in measuring actual working performance with these standards. As a result, he has identified weekly patterns and a number of working days where optimum performance (OP) and point of no return (PNR) occur for these patterns (see Figure 11.37).

In Figure 11.37 vectors *a-b* are regular standard 40-hour workweek. Vectors *b-c* are the amounts of overtime added to the regular workweek.

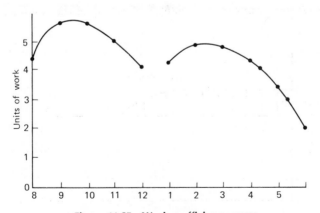

Figure 11.35   Worker efficiency curve.

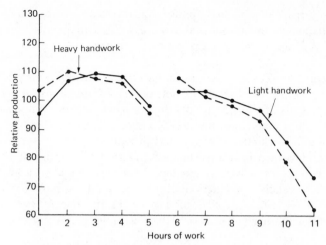

Figure 11.36   Worker efficiency curve as day is extended.

These overtime vectors tend to change in magnitude up to the point of no return (PNR). The optimum (OP) overtime is the point beyond which some production may be expensive but with great cost. It is the point beyond which productivity falls off rapidly. According to Fuller, the optimum point occurs at two-thirds of the point of no return. The relative effects of different lengths of weekly patterns are shown in Figure 11.38.

Is the 4-Day Workweek the Road to Productivity?   The four-day work week, in which overtime is not considered, is an arrangement of workdays and hours scheduled by an organization where one or more groups of employees fill their work commitments in fewer than the standard five full

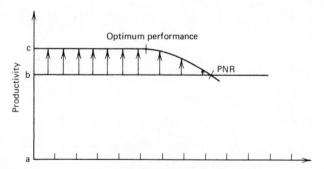

Figure 11.37   Concept of optimum performance and point of no return.

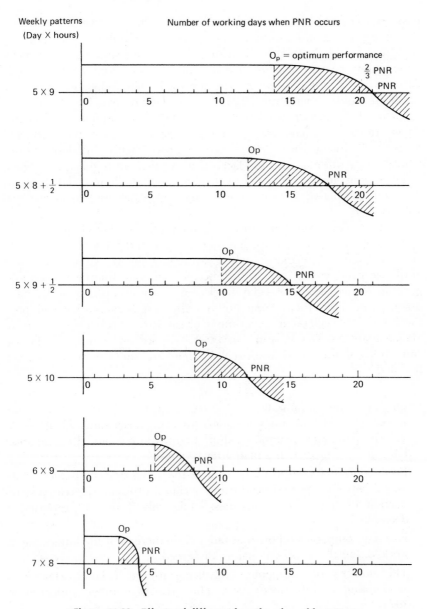

Figure 11.38 Effects of different lengths of weekly patterns.

days. Considerable interest has emerged in this workweek pattern as shown by the growing number of companies adopting it, number of conferences and seminars discussing it, and the number of articles appearing in nearly every business and management publication of worth. At this writing, unions are now pressing for it. The 5-day, 40-hour week has been standard since the 1930s. Unions have returned to the issue of reducing this standard workweek. The UAW is a leader in this regard. Their efforts so far have not been too successful because of the productivity issue. Reducing the workweek could prove highly inflationary since management will make up the lack of productivity in higher prices. As a result, unions are trying to get in through another door—paid days off. The union's motive for this is to spread the work and to ensure job security.

In either event, paid days off or shortening the workweek, productivity is the issue. You can't pay people not to work and have a growing and viable economy. Any move toward shortening the workweek without a justifiable productivity increase will become an issue for the economy in general. Nonetheless, the 4-day workweek is the eventual goal for most unions, if not all of them. Some nonunionized organizations have adopted the 4-day workweek on an experimental basis. A comprehensive American Management Association study surveyed 1056 organizations about the use and effect of the 4-day workweek.[13] Here are some items the survey revealed:

1. Of the 1056 organizations, 143 companies are now on a 4-day workweek, 663 companies are not considering a rearranged workweek, 237 companies are planning a shortened workweek, and 13 companies have discontinued such a plan after trying it.

2. Production increased in 62 percent of the 143 4-day companies, while only 3 percent reported production declines. Efficiency increased in 66 percent of the 4-day companies, while only 3 percent reported a decrease.

3. Five-day companies report that fatigue will increase if the longer day is worked, but the 4-day companies disagreed.

4. The number of companies converting to the 4-day workweek is accelerating rapidly since 1969. The greatest number appeared in 1971.

In another survey, reported in the article "Can Unemployment Be Fought with Shorter Hours?" Levitan and Belous estimated that approximately 10,000 firms with about one million employees are currently on a

4-day, 40-hour workweek.[14] This requires a daily shift of 10 hours. In the majority of cases creating blocks of leisure time and giving workers more choice over when they will work have been motivating for those workers. This study also revealed that companies that used flexitime found a majority of workers like the choice. For example, the Control Data Corporation found 77 percent of its 25,000 employees took advantage of flexitime work hours. But there are dissenters who would not prefer the flexitime opportunity. A big factor uncovered in this study is the many companies who turned to the 4-day workweek and reverted back to five days per week because they found it impractical to operate a 4-day workweek in a 5-day workweek world.

In all fairness, the 4-day workweek is still an innovative movement and the benefits accrued from its usage must still be termed modest. Studies still must be conducted of the effects on productivity. It is my observation, however, that where the 4-day workweek is working well, it's due to its role as a motivator. A flexible work schedule or a longer weekend appeals motivationally to the emerging new leisure class. These are primarily people who do not find high satisfaction in their work lives, consequently they seek more leisure time in order to pursue the activities that will give them satisfaction off the job. For this reason, these people drive for more leisure time, early retirement, or paid time off. Those who find this longer weekend important to their needs will "work harder" or deliver "more productivity" to make it work. Consequently, the 4-day workweek or flexitime may succeed more as a motivator than as a scheduling tool in time management.

How To Handle Overtime For Productivity

The studies cited earlier seem to indicate that a causative relationship exists between increased work hours and lessened productivity. The exception to this is when the increased work hours are used as a motivator for the kind of individual employed in the organization . These individuals will respond to make up the lessened productivity. But generally, the effects of prolonged weariness and fatigue are measurable and pronounced. This fatigue and weariness does not necessarily mean a gross falling off in performance, extensive errors, long batches of bad work, but rather an occasional slip or a momentary confusion of two similar events, or greater variability of performance or bad timing in required responses. High-level complex performance and critical allocation of resources that require deliberate and delicate decision making, as found in white-collar workers, will probably suffer from this fatigue and weariness.

Another implication from the studies is that there is no ideal workweek for all organizations. The optimum production depends upon many variables such as type of work force, age composition, individual differences, nature of the work performed, routinized operations, repetitive tasks, and the type of incentives. Except for short periods, extended hours of work do not give a proportionate increase in output. Some productivity is gained, but at a high cost. High production that follows the inception of overtime is generally not maintained for a long period because the worker's efficiency keeps dropping until it stabilizes at some sort of plateau. As Parkinson puts it, work expands to fill the time available for its completion. You may get as much production in 66 hours as you do in 44 hours. The longer the workday, the worse the efficiency. The point of no return (PNR) occurs when overtime is the number of days at which the return is no greater than that of a regular 40-hour workweek (5 × 8). As indicated earlier, optimum overtime productivity is obtained by confining overtime to two-thirds—the PNR. An example will clarify this.

EXAMPLE

If 30 days of overtime are scheduled and the PNR is estimated at 21 days, what is the optimum productivity time?

SOLUTION

$$OP = \tfrac{2}{3}PNR = \tfrac{2}{3}(21) = 14 \text{ days.}$$

Here are some guidelines in scheduling overtime:

1. *Schedule Overtime for Short Periods.* If overtime is absolutely necessary for production and service demands or when manpower availability is tight or when a state of emergency exists, overtime should be scheduled, but for short periods. If long periods of overtime are needed, interrupt the schedule to establish the difference between overtime workweek and normal workweek. A minimum period of two weeks without overtime provides a recovery for employees so that overtime does not become a form of conditioning. Overtime can be rescheduled after the interruption.

2. *Schedule Overtime for Certain Days.* Best results for scheduling overtime can be achieved with the following:

Number of Days to Be Scheduled	Best Time of the Week
1	Wednesday
2	Wednesday and Thursday
3	Tuesday, Wednesday, and Thursday

Mondays and Fridays are poor days for scheduling overtime. When they are, productivity is most likely to decline.

3. *Schedule Overtime Only When It Doesn't Start "Conditioning."* Scheduling of overtime carries an inherent problem of the effects on employees' pay when overtime is removed. The human tendency of resisting a reduction in pay will cause employees to drag out their work to maintain the 20 to 30 percent pay increase that they are receiving from overtime pay. This develops a form of conditioning that causes employees to press for wage increases in labor contract negotiations if the overtime is curtailed.

4. *Schedule Overtime Only When Task Targets Are Assigned.* Give employees *task targets* within time limits when overtime is scheduled. *Press* for the accomplishment of these tasks within allowable time. This managerial practice alone could very well be the most effective way to get the productivity level required by the higher cost of premium pay. Task target assignments should also be varied to avoid boredom and fatigue.

5. *Schedule Overtime Only When It's Worth It.* Remember overtime is expensive—with premium pay it is 34 percent more. Is it worth the cost? This question should be answered in accepting probable lowered efficiency and lowered productivity to meet schedule. Also, increases in working hours could lead to increases in loss time, absenteeism, and sickness.

SUMMARY

Managers probably put in more hours than any other occupational group. But this does not mean they know how to manage time better than any other group. Since time is and will always be a limited resource, the manager of productivity must be an effective time manager. The productivity manager must know how to budget and schedule this scarce resource or experience the waste of valuable opportunities for important accomplishments in the organization.

This chapter provided managers searching for effective ways to manage time with four tools to give time effectiveness. These are:

1. The productivity calendar—a monthly strategy for getting results.
2. Time system overview of the total situation.
3. Biological clocks—finding the best time.
4. Behavioral aids for getting things done.

These four time tools are strategies on how to allocate time as a resource toward greater results.

Time schedules were also described in this chapter as the way to coordinate productivity. What a schedule is and its development was described along with six guidelines for good scheduling. They are:

1. A schedule must start with well-defined objectives.
2. A schedule must provide readouts for real-time reporting.
3. A schedule must "play the clock" with all critical items.
4. A schedule must give overview of progress at a glance.
5. A schedule must follow progressive planning.
6. A schedule must be analyzed for potential failure points.

Several types of schedules were described in considerable detail—what they are and how they are constructed. Examples are included in each type of schedule. These schedules are:

1. *Gantt Productivity Schedule.*   A visual graph of work activities plotted as bars on a linear time scale which shows at a glance the total projects to be done and the progress made in each project.
2. *PERT Schedules for Time Control of Complex Networks.* A visual network of individual work events and activities with estimated time as required to complete deadlines. PERT/cost schedules and PERT/ productivity schedules were also included as methods to bring cost and productivity under time control.
3. *Critical Ratio Scheduling for Developing Priorities.*   The time relationship between service needs and the organization's capacity to supply these needs. The ratio is:

$$\text{critical ratio (CR)} = \frac{\text{service demand time (DT)}}{\text{organization's supply time (ST)}}$$

4. *Master Scheduling for Tracking Total Capacity.*   A centralized scheduling concept for tracking the total capacity of the system and how the system is utilized. Program work loads are apportioned so that individual work requirements are subordinated to a master scheduling program.

The much debated and often criticized organizational practice of scheduling overtime was also discussed in this chapter. Serious questions have been raised on the use of overtime and its effects on productivity.

The discussion of why an organization may not be getting an hour's real output for the equivalent premium pay included these topics:

1. Adding staff causes productivity to decline.
2. Human efficiency drops with longer workhours.
3. Workweek patterns affect optimum performance.
4. The 4-day workweek affects productivity.

Several guidelines have been suggested for handling overtime for productivity. They are:

1. Schedule overtime for short periods.
2. Schedule overtime for certain days.
3. Schedule overtime only when it won't start "conditioning."
4. Schedule overtime only when task targets are assigned.
5. Schedule overtime only when it's worth the cost.

QUESTIONS TO THINK ABOUT

1. What is it about time management that disrupts management in your organization?
2. How could a productivity calendar be made useful for your work?
3. What time management systems are being used in your organization? How can they be improved?
4. Do you think the biorhythm phenomena explains the highs and lows that you experience?
5. To what extent is scheduling employed in your organization?
6. What do you employ to get coordination in your department?
7. What changes could you suggest to improve the practice of scheduling?
8. Select your most important objective to be accomplished this coming year. Develop the following:

   (a) Work breakdown structure.
   (b) PERT network.
   (c) Productivity index values.
   (d) PERT productivity network.
   (e) Validate for completeness, attainability, and risk.

9. Is overtime being practiced in your organization? What changes could you recommend in the practice of overtime to experience highest productivity?

10. Have you considered the 4-day workweek for your organization? Compare the advantages with the disadvantages.

REFERENCES AND NOTES

1. *Employment and Earnings,* Volume 17, No. 11, Washington, D.C., Bureau of Labor Statistics, May, 1971.

2. Vincent Mallardi, *Biorhythms and Your Behavior,* Media America, Inc., Philadelphia, 1976, pp. 7–14.

3. Biorhythmic theory is new, and information on it is fragmentary. More experiments and validation are needed. Obviously, as a theory to explain the cyclic phenomena in humans, it is controversial. For additional reading, see Daniel Cohen, *Biorhythms in Your Life,* Fawcett Publishing Co., New York, 1976.

4. Several good books are available in time management. Two are especially recommended: R. Alec MacKensie, *New Time Management Methods For Your Staff,* Chicago, Dartnell Corporation, 1975; Joseph D. Cooper, *How To Get More Done In Less Time,* Garden City, N.Y., Doubleday & Co., 1971.

5. Gantt productivity schedules are basically Gantt schedules but modified for productivity progress. Readers who are interested in greater details on Gantt schedules may find the following references useful: Wallace Clark, *The Gantt Chart, A Working Tool of Management,* 3rd ed., New York, Pitman Publishing Co., 1953; Lewis L. Goslin, *The Product Planning System,* Homewood, Ill., Richard S. Irwin, 1967.

6. Robert W. Miller, *Schedule, Cost and Profit Control with PERT,* New York, McGraw-Hill Book Co., 1963; J. Moder, *Project Management with CPM and PERT,* New York, Reinhold Publishing Co., 1964.

7. Several good books on scheduling are available. Two are especially recommended: J. J. O'Brien, *Scheduling Handbook,* McGraw-Hill Book Co., New York, 1969; and J. H. Green, *Production and Inventory Control Handbook,* McGraw-Hill Book Co., New York, 1960.

8. C. Parkinson, *op. cit.,* pp. 15–27.

9. M. D. Kossoris, "The Facts About Hours of Work Versus Output," *Factory Management Maintenance,* Vol. 109, No. 2, February 1951.

10. H. E. Burtt, *Psychology in Industrial Efficiency,* D. Appleton & Company, New York, 1929.

11. E. E. Chiselli and C. W. Brown, *Personnel and Industrial Psychology,* McGraw-Hill Book Co., New York, 1948.

12. D. Fuller, *Organizing, Planning and Scheduling for Engineering Operations,* Industrial Educational Institute, Boston, 1962.

13. Kenneth E. Wheeler and Dale Tarnowieski, *The Four-Day Week,* an AMA Research Report, American Management Association, New York, 1972, pp. 4–5.

14. Sam Levitan and Richard Belous, "Thank God It's Thursday", *Across the Board,* Vol. 14, No. 3, March 1977, p. 28.

WHERE DO WE GO FROM HERE

Managers will agree that better planning, more effective performance, and greater resource utilization are essential if productivity is to be improved. Parts I through IV have been written to that end. This Epilogue deals with where we go from here. Actions to get a formal productivity program started in an organization are suggested.

EPILOGUE
WHERE DO WE GO FROM HERE?

The growing complexity of today's technological society in the context of shrinking resources, high energy costs, and the mushrooming population makes the case for managing productivity stronger and more urgent than ever in the past. Pressures, from most segments of our society are growing so that breakthroughs in productivity are necessary if the standard of living and the quality of work life are to continue to improve. Historians will view this period of time as one of the emergence of the awareness that a single change in one organization produces reverberations throughout the community of organizations, causing changes to other parameters that affect the first parameter that started the original change. This is the cyclical history of inflation. The interrelationships among the components of productivity in and among organizations are sensitive enough that "parts can hurt the whole."

This book probed for the issues and concerns for managing productivity. But more than that, it provided the view, the approach, the tools, the techniques to bring about its improvement. Managing productivity in organizations was not presented as a panacea to solve all managerial problems. It was presented mainly as an attitude about the importance of productivity that must be acquired followed by suggestions for how to bring about its development. In this epilogue several actions are presented that a manager can take in getting it off to a good start. The newcomer to productivity often wonders where to push in the shovel first to cover the entire area that must be spaded. These actions may be decisive. It may be the difference between raising productivity or hastening its erosion.

ACQUIRE PRODUCTIVITY KNOW-HOW

A manager should acquire as much knowledge and skill as is available on the nature and practice of productivity. This does not preclude the

403

opportunity to innovate, but a good starting point is to "catch up" with others who have penetrated further into this discipline. It must be prudent to get some practical advice and guidance by visiting organizations in which a formal program is already in operation. The objective would be to review successes, failures, obstacles, hurdles, achievements, disappointments, and so on. Attending courses, meetings, seminars would help.

GET OTHERS INVOLVED

The productivity effort is not a solo effort. Eventually the entire organization will need to get on board. But until then, having colleagues who see and understand the productivity mission can be useful collaboration in the early stages of a formal program. The support, involvement, and motivation of a small, hard-core group of productivity-minded managers is far more likely to help the program ahead than to do it alone. A presidential decree will not work! A hard-working group, acting as points of influence, can effect enthusiasm for what needs to be done and why better than any number of presidential decrees.

SET UP A TASK FORCE

The responsibility of productivity improvement does not rest with top management nor with all of management nor with only employees; it rests with all members of the organization. I realize that such a pervasive statement of responsibility is going against specified criteria of accountability, but too often the "buck is passed" to one person or group and then things continue as usual. A task force from representatives of all segments of the organization—management, union, employees, and supervisors— can be a healthy way to stir up attitudes that productivity will be a total organizational approach. The task force will collaborate on several important actions:

1. Institute an evaluation procedure to diagnose the strengths and weaknesses in relation to productivity and the quality of working life.
2. Train and set up the development and collaboration of the entire organization to make productivity improvement work.
3. Identify the specific elements of productivity that are critical and unique to the organization. Careful attention must be made to the factors that influence productivity and how they do so.

4. Design a total formal program with productivity objectives and evaluation within a time schedule. The task force should recognize that this effort will not be completed within 1 year. In fact, some organizations may take as much as 4 to 5 years for the full operation of a formal productivity effort.
5. Propose policy changes to top management for getting the program moving. These policy changes must be accompanied with why and how it will affect the organization.
6. Communicate with local, state, or federal agencies that are related in any way to operation of the program. Legislative policy changes may be needed to keep the program moving.

USE CONSULTANTS

Individuals or firms with the know-how and experience can often work wonders in getting a program under way. They can speed the time needed for the "diagnosis phase" and make suggestions for the "prescriptive phase." They can bring to the organization skills and techniques that might not be available within the organization. The outsiders might provide objective views that may be valuable for generating alternative ways in opportunities. They could stimulate the speed and vigor the program may need to keep progressing.

PROPOSE AND GET TOP MANAGEMENT INVOLVEMENT AND SUPPORT

Any kind of organizational thrust, such as a formal program of productivity improvement, must involve the top management personnel in the organization. This could be a problem or an opportunity. Top management people are receiving proposals on how to improve the organization almost daily. Unless the proposal for productivity improvement is persuasive and worth the effort, organizations will continue as they have in past years.

No one needs to be told that our period of time is fraught with many perils as well as many opportunities. This fast-moving world requires managers to make decisions like never before. The central issue facing the manager with respect to productivity is to keep it where it is or to move it to where it can be.

INDEX

3

32